Management Control in Nonprofit Organizations

THE WILLARD J. GRAHAM SERIES IN ACCOUNTING

Consulting Editor   ROBERT N. ANTHONY

Harvard University

Management Control in Nonprofit Organizations

ROBERT N. ANTHONY
Ross Graham Walker Professor of Management Control

REGINA E. HERZLINGER
Assistant Professor of Business Administration

Both of
Graduate School of Business Administration
Harvard University

 1975

RICHARD D. IRWIN, INC. Homewood, Illinois 60430
Irwin-Dorsey International London, England WC2H 9NJ
Irwin-Dorsey Limited Georgetown, Ontario L7G 4B3

First Printing, June 1975

ISBN 0-256-01748-4
Library of Congress Catalog Card No. 74–31595
Printed in the United States of America

Preface

So far as we know, this is the first book of its type. There are many books on accounting in nonprofit organizations and many books on organization theory and organization behavior. The territory staked out for this book is in between: It is much broader than books on accounting, but it is focused on only one aspect of organization behavior. As such, it runs two principal risks.

First, it attempts generalizations about topics for which no generalizations have existed. As is the case with all management subjects, there is an inadequate basis, either deductively or inductively, for such generalizations, but there is the additional hazard in a new field that the current authors do not have the generalizations of earlier authors as a starting point. (The obverse of this is that they are not tempted to perpetuate generalizations that in other fields have been passed along from one author to another, even though they are not based on adequate evidence.)

Secondly, there are great problems in organizing the material in a way that is useful, and in deciding on what topics should be included and the amount of space to be given to each.

Nevertheless, a beginning has to be made. We would much appreciate comments on improvements that can be made on either of the above matters.

USE OF THE BOOK

This book is intended for two principal audiences.

First, it is intended as a text in advanced undergraduate or graduate courses or in continuing education courses. Such a course might deal with management control in nonprofit organizations in general, or it might focus on a particular type of nonprofit organization. Continuing education courses are likely to be of the latter type.

The text alone is inadequate as course material; it should be augmented by cases and readings as a basis for classroom discussion. We have examined some 500 cases that might be considered for use in such a course, and we have selected over 300 of these for mention in a separate Instructor's Guide that is obtainable from the publisher. This instructor's guide contains course outlines and suggested cases; it contains order forms in which packets of cases for various types of courses or individual cases may be obtained from the Intercollegiate Case Clearing House; it contains summaries of all the cases and teaching notes for many; and it contains suggested readings. The outlines cover courses in management control in nonprofit organizations in general and also courses focused on specific types of organizations: federal, state and local government organizations, health care organizations, and education organizations.

The second audience consists of persons who are interested in the management of nonprofit organizations, either because they are themselves involved in management or because as an interested outside party they seek ideas on how management of such organizations can become more effective.

ACKNOWLEDGMENTS

Persons with whom the senior author worked in various assignments for nonprofit organizations have of course influenced his thinking. In particular, colleagues at the Department of Defense have given stimulating and useful ideas; they include Robert S. McNamara, Cyrus S. Vance, Clark Clifford, Paul Nitze, Alain Enthoven, Robert S. Moot, Leonard Marks, Jr., Charles Bowsher, Brewster Copp, George Berquist, Melvin Baker, Meyer Tartasky, Thomas S. Johnson, A. Ernest Fitzgerald, and Don Brazier.

Versions of this book have been used in manuscript form since 1969 in a course with the same title at the Graduate School of Business Administration of Harvard University. Each new version has benefited greatly from these class discussions. Students pointed out weaknesses in the logic, ambiguities, and inconsistencies; and they contributed new insights and new examples based on their own experiences. Some or all of the manuscript has also been used at other schools, and we have had useful comments from the instructors. Those by William Rotch at the University of Virginia and Lt. Col. James D. Suver of the U.S. Air Force Academy, and Col. Bernard L. Beatty, Air University, were particularly helpful.

Dennis Mulvehill of Touche, Ross & Co., participated in developing and teaching the course at Harvard. His contributions reflect his broad and deep experience in this area. Gerard G. Johnson also participated in the course work and gave many extremely helpful suggestions.

At the risk of overlooking some important contributions, we want to mention some students whose ideas and work are directly contained in this book: Elizabeth Allison, Robert J. Lord, Joseph P. Mullinix, James R. Roche, Peter J. Siris, John Moore, and Stephen Sadove.

From practioners, we acknowledge with respect ideas from Charles A. Anderson, president of Stanford Research Institute; Norman Waks, Mitre Corporation; Edward Shapiro, president, New Hampshire College; John Connelly, Bunker Hill Health Center; Elsa A. Porter, Department of Health, Education and Welfare.

Many people in other government agencies have been helpful, among whom are Elmer Staats, Frank Weitzel, Ellsworth Morse, and Daniel Borth of the General Accounting Office; Senator William Proxmire; Charles Schultze as Director of the Budget and subsequently at the Brookings Institution; Gen. Edwin W. Rawlings of the USAF; C. Jackson Grayson, Jr., chairman of the Price Commission; and William McLean, Naval Ordnance Test Center.

We, of course, do not hold any of these persons responsible for the contents of this book.

May 1975   ROBERT N. ANTHONY
                                                    REGINA E. HERZLINGER

Contents

xi

Basis for Prices: *Full-Cost Pricing. Tuition. Pricing at Other than Full Cost. Market-Based Prices. Subsidy and Penalty Prices.* Measurement of Cost: *Depreciation. Capital Employed and Fees. Gifts and Endowment Income. Opportunity and Imputed Costs.* The Pricing Unit: *Qualifications. Hospital Pricing as an Example.* Prospective Pricing.

chapter one

Nonprofit and Profit-Oriented Organizations

In all organizations, except possibly the tiniest, there is a process called management control. It has been defined as the process by which managers assure that resources are obtained and used effectively and efficiently in the accomplishment of an organization's objectives. The process has existed as long as organizations have been in existence, but it has not been the subject of much systematic study and analysis until fairly recently. A landmark book, Barnard's *Functions of the Executive*,[1] which dealt with this as well as other management processes was originally published in 1938.

From this book and from a number of other studies published in recent years, there have evolved principles which are helpful in designing management control systems and in carrying on the management control activities. As is the case with all principles of management, these control principles are tentative, incomplete, inconclusive, vague, sometimes contradictory, and inadequately supported by experimental or other evidence. Some of them will probably turn out to be wrong. Nevertheless, they seem to have sufficient validity so that it is better for managers to take them into account than to ignore them. They seem to work in a considerable number of actual organizations.

Most studies of the management control process have been done in business organizations, and most of the new control techniques were developed in these organizations. Most descriptions of the management control process therefore tend to assume, usually implicitly but some-

---

[1] Chester I. Barnard, *Functions of the Executive*, 30th anniv. ed. (Cambridge, Mass., Harvard University Press, 1968.)

1

times explicitly, that the process being described is taking place in a business enterprise.

This book, by contrast, is a study of management control in nonprofit organizations. Its thesis is that the basic control concepts are the same in both profit-oriented and nonprofit organizations, but that because of the special characteristics of nonprofit organizations, the application of these concepts differs in some important respects. Some, but not all, of the control techniques developed in profit-oriented organizations are applicable to nonprofit organizations. Certain other techniques are appropriate for nonprofit organizations, but not for profit-oriented organizations.

NONPROFIT ORGANIZATIONS

For the purposes of this book, we must frame a dichotomy, so that any organization can be classified as either "profit-oriented" or "nonprofit." These labels do not suggest the precise distinction that we intend to make between the two types of organizations, however.

The Basic Distinction: Purpose

The idea that comes closest to explaining the intended distinction is that of organizational purpose. The dominant purpose, or at least one of the major purposes, of some organizations is earning profits. Decisions made by their managements are intended to increase (or at least maintain) profits, and success is measured, to a significant degree, by the amount of profits that these organizations earn. This is not to say that profit is their only objective, or that their success can be measured entirely in terms of profitability; that would be, of course, an overly simplistic view of most businesses.

By contrast, other organizations exist primarily to render a service. Decisions made by their managements are intended to result in the best possible service with the available resources, and their success is measured primarily by how much service they render and by how well they render it. More basically (but unfortunately also more vaguely), their success should be measured by how much they contribute to the public welfare. This type of organization is here labelled "nonprofit."[2]

Some nonprofit organizations do not recognize this distinction in purpose; they act as if their purpose is to earn a profit rather than to provide the services for which they supposedly exist. For example, an

---

[2] Some people prefer "not-for-profit" to "nonprofit." They point out that a profit-oriented company that operates at a loss can be labelled logically as a "nonprofit" company. We doubt that anyone actually is misled, and we prefer "nonprofit" because (1) it is shorter, and (2) it is used in the Internal Revenue Code and Regulations and in the statutes of many states and hence is familiar.

important objective of the New York Port Authority is to improve the transportation system in the New York metropolitan area. Consistent with this purpose, the Port Authority has built bridges, tunnels, and airports, and has improved surface transportation. But the Port Authority has also constructed the World Trade Center in lower Manhattan—two gigantic skyscrapers housing thousands of people in an area where the facilities to move people to and from work are already at the saturation point. This project, therefore, worsens the transportation problem; it is exactly contradictory to the objectives of the Authority. Why, then, was the project undertaken? Because it promised to add profits to the Port Authority. It can be argued that the Trustees of the Port Authority lost sight of the intended purpose.[3]

The converse situation also exists; that is, some organizations that technically are ordinary business corporations do not have profitability as their primary objective. Usually, these organizations are dominated by a single individual and reflect personal desire to render a service of some type. In such a company, profits are of secondary importance, and many of the control principles appropriate to profit-oriented organizations do not apply. Some companies that operate professional football or baseball teams are of this type; other sports organizations are profit-oriented companies in the usual meaning of the term.

Different Message of the Income Statement

This difference in purpose is not easily discernible in all cases. Many nonprofit organizations publish income statements which resemble those of business corporations in that they show amounts for revenues, for expenses, and for the difference between them, which is "profit." The essential distinction is that the management of a business corporation makes decisions that hopefully increase the net profit, and its success is judged by the size of that number—the bottom line—whereas the management of a nonprofit organization has a quite different purpose.

A nonprofit organization may indeed report an excess of revenue over expense—which is profit[4]—in a given year, but it should not do so consistently year after year. If a nonprofit organization regularly shows a profit, it is not accomplishing its objective of providing as much service as possible with available resources. Either it should provide more service, and hence increase its costs, or it should reduce its prices. A nonprofit organization's financial policy should be to break even. This attitude toward the "bottom line" is quite different from that of a profit-oriented company.

---

[3] See Theodore Kheel, "How the Port Authority is Strangling New York City," *New York Magazine*, vol. 2, no. 46 (November 17, 1969).

[4] Some nonprofit organizations are so skittish of the word "profit" that they label this amount in a way that avoids the term, such as "Difference Between Income and Outgo."

Also, a nonprofit organization may consistently earn a profit on some part of its operations without being profit oriented. The U.S. Forest Service, for example, earns a "profit" on some of the recreational facilities which it operates, but the Forest Service is not a profit-oriented organization. Its objective is not to make the profit number as high as it can.

Our distinction is not black and white. A profit-oriented company must render services that its customers find adequate if it is to earn a profit, whereas a nonprofit organization must receive funds from revenues or other sources that are at least equal to its costs if it is to continue to render a service. The distinction is based on the predominant attitude towards purpose.

Alternative Terms

The profit-oriented/nonprofit dichotomy seems better than other familiar terms, such as "business," "private sector," or "economic" organizations on the one hand and "service," "public sector," or "sociopolitical" organizations on the other hand. Many nonprofit organizations are properly called service organizations, but "service" is not a good label for the whole class of such organizations because profit-oriented hotels, restaurants, barber shops, auto repair shops, and so on are properly labelled as service organizations in the Standard Industrial Classification. Many nonprofit organizations are "public sector" organizations, in the sense that they are Federal, state or local agencies,[5] but "public sector" is not a good label for the whole class because trade associations, other membership organizations, many colleges and universities, and many health care organizations are nonprofit organizations, although they are not in the public sector. The labels "economic" and "sociopolitical" are indeed practically synonymous with "profit" and "nonprofit" as used here, but "sociopolitical" is a term that is not in common usage, and seems a little fancy. Educational and health care organizations probably would not recognize themselves under the label "sociopolitical."

Special Cases

Some organizations that literally do not seek profits are excluded from our class of nonprofit organizations. A mutual insurance company, for example, does not make a profit in the literal sense, but it returns an equivalent amount to its policyholders labelled "dividend." Its management control problems are similar to those of stock insurance companies, which do seek profits. Mutual investment funds, mutual savings banks, cooperative banks, and similar types of financial institutions are excluded on the same grounds. As mentioned above, a profit-oriented

---

[5] This definition of "public sector," is from the *McGraw-Hill Dictionary of Modern Economics*, 1965.

business that reports a loss is also excluded; it is not "nonprofit" as the term is used here.

Conversely, some government organizations are in fact businesses and are therefore excluded from this study even though they do not literally seek to earn a profit. Municipally owned power plants are an example.

Authorities and government corporations are borderline cases. These include port authorities, airport authorities, highway and bridge authorities, parking authorities, industrial development authorities, and the like at the municipal and state level; and Tennessee Valley Authority, Communications Satellite Corporation, Amtrak, and the U.S. Postal Service at the Federal level. Tennessee Valley Authority, for example, operates a number of power generation and transmission facilities. Its decisions about these facilities are economic decisions, and its management control problems and practices with respect to them are essentially the same as those in an investor-owned utility. TVA also is involved, however, in the development and preservation of natural resources. Its purposes with respect to these functions are service purposes, not profit-oriented purposes. The management of these activities therefore comes within our purview. Moreover, authorities and government corporations tend to be responsible to political bodies, and this affects their management control problems in the same way as is the case with other public sector organizations.

Some hospitals, medical clinics, schools, and even religious organizations are set up explicitly as profit-oriented organizations. These are borderline situations. Many of the problems to be discussed here do arise in these organizations. Some of the generalizations that apply to nonprofit organizations apply equally well to these organizations; others do not.

An even more complicated situation exists with the tendency labelled by the jawbreaker, "privatization" (conversion of a nonprofit organization into a profit-oriented company) or the even worse "reprivatization" (return to the private sector of an organization that previously had been taken over by the government). For example, in health care, profit-oriented companies have been set up to acquire nonprofit hospitals, especially in the West and South. The first such company, and currently one of the largest, was organized in 1956. In 1971 it operated 19 facilities with 2,150 beds. American Medicorp, which began in 1968, operated 40 hospitals with 6,637 beds in 1973.[6] These organizations are probably best viewed as profit oriented, although in most respects their management control problems are similar to those of nonprofit hospitals. In any event, nonprofit hospitals can probably learn much from studying privatized health-care facilities.

Regulated investor-owned companies such as public utilities, railroads,

---

[6] Source: American Medicorp, *Annual Report,* 1973.

and other transportation companies also are borderline cases. To the extent that their profitability depends on their allowed rates, profitability is not a good measure of their performance, at least from the standpoint of society as a whole. Nevertheless, in other respects they are similar to industrial companies, and therefore are not considered in this book.

Research/development organizations are also borderline. Although some of them are profit oriented and others are not, this is not what makes them borderline because management control problems of both types are essentially similar. They are borderline because they provide services whose quality and quantity are quite difficult to measure. As will be discussed at length in Chapter 3, much of the difficulty in exercising good management control in a nonprofit organization arises because of the difficulty in measuring the quantity and quality of services provided by the organization, and to this extent research and development organizations come within our purview.

Staff Departments

Several of the staff departments in profit-oriented companies have the essential characteristics of nonprofit organizations; that is, they exist to render services to other components of the company and it is difficult to measure the amount and quality of service rendered. For reasons suggested above, the research/development department is in this category. So is the legal department, and in some companies the personnel department, the treasurer's department, the secretary's department, and production and marketing staffs. Since this book focuses on the organization as a whole, it does not deal specifically with these components in profit-oriented companies. Nevertheless, the analysis here is relevant to management problems in these components.

Legal Distinctions

Nonprofit organizations are distinguished from profit-oriented corporations in law. In general, although both are chartered by the State, individual owners benefit from the activities of business corporations (in the form of dividends), and individual owners share in the residual value of the business corporation in the event of dissolution; whereas no benefit can accrue to individual persons in nonprofit organizations, and in the event of dissolution, residual assets belong to the State.

Summary

Although there are borderline cases which can lead to nitpicking about the precision of the distinction made here, most organizations can be classified into one of two groups without much difficulty: (1)

those whose objective is to earn profits and whose success is measured primarily by the amount of profits earned; and (2) those whose objective is to render a service and whose success is measured primarily by the amount and quality of the services they render. We are interested in the latter group.

SIZE OF NONPROFIT SECTOR

Exhibit 1–1 gives some idea of the magnitude of the class of organizations on which this book focuses. The figures are not exact because the Census categories do not quite conform to the definition of "nonprofit" that is used here and because National Income data do not measure the real magnitude of the resources controlled by these organizations. They are, however, satisfactory as a basis of some general

EXHIBIT 1–1
Income of Nonprofit Organizations and Industries, 1971*

SIC Code	Industry		Income (in $ millions)
80	Medical and other health services		$ 30,299
801–4	Offices of physicians, surgeons, and dentists	$ 5,812	
806	Hospitals	19,335	
807	Medical and dental laboratories	713	
809	Health and allied services, N.E.C. (includes sanatorium and rest homes)	4,442	
82	Educational services		7,356
821	Elementary and secondary schools	1,896	
822	Colleges and universities	4,614	
823	Libraries and information centers.	95	
824	Correspondence and vocational schools	437	
829	Schools and educational services, N.E.C.	279	
86	Nonprofit membership organizations.		8,449
861	Business associations	953	
862	Professional organizations	269	
863	Labor organizations	1,128	
864	Civic and social organizations	1,562	
865	Political organizations	43	
866	Religious organizations	1,725	
867	Charitable organizations	1,213	
869	Nonprofit member organizations, N.E.C.	1,600	
892	Nonprofit research agencies		1,612
	Federal government		53,114
	State and local government		73,406
	Total National Income.		$795,887†

* Statistics compiled from *Survey of Current Business,* National Income Issue, vol. 51, no. 7, July 1971, and *County Business Patterns,* Bureau of the Census, 1970, and with the much appreciated assistance of Dr. Ernest C. Harvey of Stanford Research Institute. Because these are National Income data, they exclude certain transactions between industries and, therefore, understate the amount of money spent by each industry.
† Equals 100 percent.

impressions. The nonprofit organizations listed in the Exhibit generate over 20 percent of the national income. Government is by far the largest category. Contrary to what many people think, state and local governments combined are larger than the Federal government. The next largest category is health care. Technically, the largest category after that is nonprofit membership organizations, but this category consists of so many diverse elements, ranging from business associations to religious organizations, that for most purposes it is not useful to think of this as a single category. Next comes education, which is a relatively homogeneous category. For many purposes, it is useful to think of the most important categories as (1) government, (2) health care, and (3) education.

Exhibit 1–2 shows what has happened to nonprofit organizations over

EXHIBIT 1–2
Growth of Nonprofit Organizations from 1950–1973*

	Income 1950 (in $ millions)	Income 1973 (in $ millions)	Percent Growth
Medical and other health services	4,412	41,127	832
Education services	1,109	9,154	725
Nonprofit membership organizations	1,803	10,780	498
Federal government	12,699	63,056	497
State and local government	10,903	101,031	827
Total National Income	241,074	1,065,590	342

* Based on statistics from the U.S. Department of Commerce Office of Business Economics, *The National Income and Product Accounts of the United States 1929–1965* and *Survey of Current Business,* vol. 54, no. 7, July 1974.

the past two decades. All categories have grown much more rapidly than the growth in National Income, with most growing at about twice the rate of National Income growth.

The *Federal Government* consists of three coordinate branches, Executive, Legislative, and Judicial. Although the Legislative and Judicial branches do have management control problems, they are relatively small organizations, and we shall focus primarily on the Executive branch. In the Executive branch there are 11 cabinet departments and several score agencies, boards, and commissions. Although most agencies are relatively small, collectively they spend more than $15 billion a year. The largest department in terms of employees is the Department of Defense which in 1974 spent $79.5 billion and had 3.2 million employees. The Department of Health, Education and Welfare spent more money ($96.8 billion), primarily because of the sizable amounts it disbursed for transfer payments, such as those for welfare, social security, education and research grants, but it has far fewer employees, 125,000.

There are about 80,000 government units in the United States below the federal level. This number has decreased by about half in the last 25 years. The greatest decrease is in the number of school districts.

As for *education,* in 1973 there were 17,000 school districts, enrolling some 46 million students. Expenditures to support these schools amounted to $56.2 billion. About 8 million students attend colleges, universities, and other schools above the secondary level. Collectively, these institutions constitute "higher education." About 75 percent of these students are in 1,000 public institutions (i.e., schools supported by state and local governments), about 25 percent are in 1,500 private colleges and universities. It is estimated that by the late 1970s, 80 percent of students will be enrolled in public institutions.

In 1974 outlays for *health services* exceeded $100 billion, almost double the 1967 expenditures of $51 billion. About 40 percent of the 1974 expenditures were to pay for the services of over 7,000 hospitals, while the remainder was for physicians' and dentists' services, drugs, appliances, nursing home care, health care research, and medical facilities construction. These expenditures are financed 60 percent by private sources and 40 percent by public sources. Much of the public funds comes from the Medicare legislation while a large proportion of private expenditures on personal health care is financed by third parties, such as Blue Cross/Blue Shield and insurance companies.

CATEGORIES OF NONPROFIT ORGANIZATIONS

Although this study will usually discuss the nonprofit organization as a class, for some purposes it is useful to distinguish among two types, which we call (1) client-oriented and (2) public-oriented.

Client-Oriented Organizations

Client-oriented organizations are those that exist to render service to individual clients. In most cases, the amount of service rendered is measured by a fee that is charged to the client or to some third party. Included in this group are hospitals and other health care organizations (except for their research functions); colleges and universities (except for research and public service activities); municipal services such as refuse collection, subway and bus transportation, and utilities; the U.S. Postal Service, the Communications Satellite Corporation (COMSAT), and similar government corporations; theatres, symphony orchestras, and other fine arts organizations. Fire departments are not in this category; although the person whose house is on fire is a "client" in one sense, the main purpose of the fire department is to protect the whole community. Police departments are also excluded for the same reason. Welfare organizations are borderline cases; they do serve individual clients, but their relationship to their clients is quite different from that of, say, a hospital to its patients. The hospital expects to receive revenue from its individual clients; the welfare department does not.

In client-oriented organizations, the technical problems of management control are in many respects similar to those in profit-oriented companies. This is because the measurement of output, which is essential in a management control system, is facilitated by the fact that the number of clients can at least be counted, and in many cases the amount of service can be measured by the revenue that is collected from them.

Public-Oriented Organizations

Public-oriented organizations exist to provide service to, or in the interests of, the public at large or some large segment thereof and they do not directly collect revenues. Included are: the legislative and judiciary branches of government; public primary and secondary education; government policy making and regulatory agencies; the Departments of Agriculture; Defense; Health, Education and Welfare; Housing and Urban Development, and State; the Atomic Energy Commission (except for its production activities); and police and fire departments.

Most of the services provided by these organizations are what the welfare economists call "public goods," of which the classic case is the lighthouse. There is no way of charging a fee for the service that a lighthouse renders since there is no way of withholding the service from those who refuse to pay the fee. Management control in public-oriented organizations is difficult, and one of the primary reasons is the difficulty of measuring the amount of services that they render. In many cases service itself is difficult to state in operational terms; "diplomacy" in the State Department, and "readiness to defend" in the Department of Defense are fuzzy concepts, not readily subject to measurement. In public-oriented organizations also, decisions tend to be influenced by social and political considerations, and therefore are not easily susceptible to economic analysis.

Another distinction between a public-oriented organization and a client-oriented organization is that many public-oriented organizations are unique. There is only one State Department and one Department of Defense, whereas there are many hospitals and many schools. A client-oriented organization therefore can compare its costs or other data with similar organizations, and such comparisons provide extremely useful information for management control purposes.

Borderline Cases

As is the case with most aspects of this study, the above distinctions are by no means clearcut. Some organizations are partly client-oriented and partly public-oriented. To the extent that the Postal Service exists to deliver mail for those who are willing to pay for it, it is a client-oriented organization—but the Postal Service also exists to ensure that good communication is available to the public at large (and it therefore maintains Post Offices in small towns that do not generate enough revenue to equal their expenses), and to this extent it is public-oriented.

Also, it can happen that a public-oriented organization is converted to a client-oriented organization. The public school system is generally public-oriented since it is willing to provide service to all children in the community; but some school systems are experimenting with a "voucher system," in which each student is given a voucher that can be used at any school—public or private—selected by the student. In such a system, the schools can be thought of as being client-oriented. In general, as will be seen, if it is feasible to convert a public-oriented organization, or some part thereof, to a client-oriented organization, it is desirable to do so because management control is facilitated.

Member-Oriented Organizations

For some purposes, it is useful to consider a third category of organizations, member-oriented organizations. These organizations exist to serve their members, but unlike client-oriented organizations, they tend to render the service to the members as a class; ordinarily, they do not render identifiable amounts of service to individual members. Included in this category are unions, trade associations, professional organizations, religious organizations (except for missionary activities), stock exchanges, and clubs.

With respect to ease of management control, member-oriented organizations are in the middle, between client-oriented and public-oriented organizations. Some idea of how highly members regard the output of the organization can be derived from the amount of dues that they are willing to pay, but in general this is a far from accurate representation of output. The best church in town is not necessarily the wealthiest church, for example.

Spectrum of Organizations

Although it is often useful to classify nonprofit organizations into the categories described above, it is also useful to think of them as lying along a continuum with respect to the difficulty of management control. The principal distinguishing features of this continuum seem to be:

1. The extent to which the organization charges its clients prices for services rendered that are approximately equal to cost. At one extreme are general government activities, and at the other extreme are hospitals.

2. The importance of program decisions. At one extreme is the

Executive Office of the President, and at the other extreme are those colleges which plan to continue their current size and curriculum.

3. The relative importance of social and political criteria as contrasted with economic criteria in making program decisions. At one extreme is, again, the Executive Office of the President, and at the other extreme are certain government corporations and authorities.

4. The extent to which several organizations perform comparable functions so that comparative data are available. At one extreme is the Department of State, and at the other extreme are public primary and secondary schools.

FOCUS OF THE STUDY

Management control is an important function of management, but it is by no means the whole of management. Although the definition given above may not convey the distinction clearly, the intention is to exclude a number of activities. Among the activities excluded are those related to the selection of personnel and building an organization. Moreover, most people in management positions spend part of their time on nonmanagement activities, such as talking to the press or listening to personal problems of their colleagues, and such activities are excluded.

Management control is a process that occurs when the organization is engaged in work that is undertaken to reach its objectives; it does not have anything to do directly with the formulation of these objectives. Decisions on what the objectives should be and on the major policies that are to be followed in reaching them are made during another process, the strategic planning process. This book takes the objectives as given. The control process is facilitated when the objectives of the organization are clearly stated, but in most organizations the objectives are by no means clear, and even in organizations whose objectives are reasonably well understood by all concerned, it may not be feasible to state them in an operational way. In many liberal arts colleges, for example, faculty and administration have a common understanding of objectives, that is, of the "character" of the institution. Although committees sometimes devote much effort to finding words that define these objectives, the results are often not useful.

Implicit in the above is the assumption that the organization already exists. We are not concerned with whether or not there should be an organization, or whether it should have the mission that it does have. Neither are we concerned with whether the objectives are good or bad; the management control process occurs both in UNICEF and in the Mafia. Also, our focus prohibits us from criticizing the objectives themselves, on moral grounds or on any other grounds. We do not, for example, debate the question of whether the Department of Defense should have waged war in Vietnam. This is a crucially important question, of course, but it is not appropriately discussed in our context. For the purpose of this analysis, we accept the fact that there is a Department of Defense and that at certain times it is responsible for carrying on combat operations.

Systems Approach

This deliberate focus on management control in an existing organization means that some exciting topics are not given the attention here that their importance warrants. Of these, perhaps the most important is the systems approach. Health care, for example, should be viewed as a system, comprising all the individuals, organizations and policies that are intended to provide an optimum level of health care. When viewed in this way, it is apparent that the health care system in the United States is deficient. Our morbidity rates, infant mortality rates, and other indicators of health rank nowhere near the top of the list of developed countries, despite the fact that we spend more on health care per capita than do most other nations. Health care facilities are poorly distributed. Many ill people whose ailment is one that could be treated inexpensively in a clinic are sent unnecessarily to expensive hospitals. Many people cannot afford adequate health care. All these facts are indications that the health care system needs a drastic overhaul, and that it should be possible to provide better health care at substantially lower cost by emphasizing new organizational arrangements, such as more ambulatory care facilities; a new mix of personnel, such as more paramedics; more emphasis on preventive medicine, and so on. In short, a focus on a study of health care as a system is fascinating, and an analysis of this system can lead to major improvements.

This book, however, takes a narrower focus. It focuses on an individual organization within the health care system, such as a hospital, a clinic, or a nursing home. It accepts the role of that organization essentially as a given, and concentrates on how improvements in the management control process can help the organization to perform its function, whatever it may be, more efficiently and effectively.

Such a focus tends to be less than satisfying to many people because it rules out a discussion of certain glamorous, high pay-off topics. These topics should of course be discussed, but they should be discussed in another context. It is important that there be a proper balance between an analysis of health care as a system and an analysis of the problems of one organization within that system. It is tempting to focus on the global systems problems and to neglect the problems of individual organizations, but that temptation is resisted here.

THE CENTRAL PROBLEM

A nonprofit organization exists to render a service rather than to earn a profit. The central management control problem arises because of this difference in objectives. "Service" is a more vague, less measurable concept than "profit." It follows then that it is more difficult to measure performance in a nonprofit organization. It is also more difficult to make rational choices among alternative courses of action in such an organization. In a profit-oriented organization, there is a well-developed approach to such choice problems: estimated costs are compared with estimated benefits. In a nonprofit organization the relationship between costs and benefits, and even the amount of benefits, are difficult to measure.

Despite these difficulties, an organization must be controlled. Its management must do what it can to assure that resources are used efficiently and effectively. Thus, the central problem is to find out what control policies and practices are useful, despite the limitations.

APPROACH

Any system can be viewed as both a structure and a process. The distinction is similar to that between anatomy and physiology. Anatomy deals with structure—what the body consists of; whereas physiology deals with process—how the body functions. In order to understand the human body, one must understand both structure and process. The two subjects are so closely related that it is not always possible to describe one without considering the other, but the description of the whole system is more orderly if the distinction is maintained to the extent feasible. Such a distinction underlies the arrangement of topics in this book.

Chapter 2 describes the management control structure and process as they exist in well managed profit-oriented companies.

Chapter 3 describes characteristics of nonprofit organizations that affect the management control process. Chapter 4 discusses certain organizational relationships within nonprofit organizations that have a significant bearing on management control. Some of these relationships and some attitudes growing out of these relationships impede the management control process. These are identified, and some ways of improving the situation are suggested.

In the remaining chapters, we discuss the management control structure and process in nonprofit organizations. Some attention is given to describing what this structure and this process *are*, but the main emphasis is on what they *should be* in a well-managed organization. Thus, these chapters are essentially normative, rather than descriptive. As already pointed out, the evidence that supports the normative statements is inadequate. Many of the statements are based largely on personal opinion. Some of them are derived from a conceptual framework that has been tested in many situations.[7]

Chapters 5 and 6 deal with the control structure. Although the data in this structure are by no means entirely monetary, it is convenient to describe the structure in monetary (i.e., accounting) terms since accounting provides a unifying thread for the information. In these terms, the structure consists principally of two interrelated sets of accounts, one constructed in terms of programs, and the other constructed in terms of responsibility centers. In many organizations, a third set of accounts is necessary to meet the specialized needs of the organizations, and in some organizations a fourth set is necessary to meet requirements imposed by outside agencies. These accounts should be used consistently throughout the organization and in each step of the control process. As will be seen, such consistency does not exist in many organizations, and this lack of consistency creates serious control problems. Chapter 5 describes the account structure in some detail. Chapter 6 focuses on the nature of the information that is collected in these accounts. Such information consists of (a) inputs and (b) outputs. Inputs are costs. Since the nature of cost information in a nonprofit organization is essentially the same as that in a profit-oriented organization, relatively little attention is given to inputs in this book. Considerably more emphasis is given to output information. It is significant that a book on management control in profit-oriented companies would contain only brief mention of output information, whereas in nonprofit organizations this is one of the most important and most difficult subjects to be discussed.

Chapter 7 discusses principles and practices for setting prices for the services rendered by nonprofit organizations.

Chapters 8 through 12 discuss the management control process. Chapters are devoted to each of the main steps in this process: programming; budgeting; operating and accounting; and analysis and acting on performance.

Chapter 13 discusses problems of developing and installing a management control system in a nonprofit organization.

Chapter 14 is a summary, and as a summary device we have listed practices that seem to us to account for the excellent management control that exists in some nonprofit organizations.

---

[7] Robert N. Anthony, *Planning and Control Systems: A Framework for Analysis,* (Boston, Graduate School of Business Administration, Harvard University, 1965.)

chapter two

Management Control
in General

This chapter describes concepts and techniques that have been found useful in management control. Most of the generalizations have been developed with a profit-oriented organization implicitly in mind. They nevertheless should be relevant in an organization of any type.

NATURE OF A MANAGEMENT CONTROL SYSTEM

Management control is one of several management functions. Since our focus is on this function, it is easy to lose sight of the fact that other functions are equally or more important. The selection and organization of personnel, for example, is an important function, as indicated in the following comment by Walter Wriston:

> I believe that the only game in town is the personnel game. If you have the right person in the right place, you don't have to do anything else. If you have the wrong person in the job, there's no management system known to man that can save you. . . . Basically, if the fellow you have running London is a highly intelligent and charged up person, with brains and judgment, he will do a fantastic job. If he is dumb and lazy, you can write him all the memos you want and nothing will happen.[1]

Management control is the process by which managers assure that resources are obtained and used effectively and efficiently in the accom-

---

[1] Walter Wriston, Chairman of the Board and Chief Executive Officer of Citicorp, the holding company for First National City Bank, the second largest bank in the world, in an interview reported in *The Harbus News* (April 4, 1974).

plishment of an organization's objectives. The diagram in Exhibit 2–1 will be used to explain this definition.

Any organization, except the smallest, is divided into units which are called *responsibility centers*. A responsibility center is a group of people headed by a manager who is responsible for what it does. In large organizations, there is a complicated hierarchy of responsibility centers—units, sections, departments, branches, and divisions. Except for those at the bottom of the organization, these responsibility centers consist of aggregations of smaller responsibility centers. The entire organization is itself a responsibility center. One function of top management is to plan, coordinate, and control the work of all these responsibility centers; this is the management control function.

EXHIBIT 2–1
Nature of a Responsibility Center

A. Analogy to an Engine

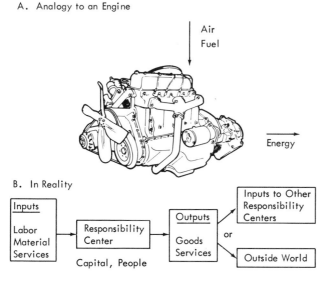

B. In Reality

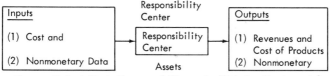

C. As Depicted by Information

Source: Robert N. Anthony and Glenn A. Welsch, *Fundamentals of Management Accounting* (Homewood, Ill.: Richard D. Irwin, Inc., 1974), p. 410.

Exhibit 2–1 shows the essence of what any responsibility center does, using an engine as an analogy. An engine uses air and fuel; these are its *inputs*. With its mechanical and electrical configuration, it does *work* with these inputs. It produces energy, which is its *output*.

A responsibility center exists to accomplish one or more purposes; these purposes are its *objectives*. Presumably, the objectives of an individual responsibility center are intended to help achieve the overall objectives of the whole organization. These overall objectives are decided upon in the strategic planning process, and are assumed to have been established prior to the beginning of the management control process.

A responsibility center has inputs of labor, material, and services. It does work with these inputs, and as a consequence it produces outputs of goods or services. Presumably, these outputs are related to the responsibility center's objectives, but this is not necessarily so. In any event, whatever the responsibility center does constitutes its outputs.

The goods and services produced by a responsibility center may be furnished either to another responsibility center or to the outside world. In the former case, they are inputs to the other responsibility center; in the latter case, they are outputs of the whole organization.

Measurement of Inputs and Outputs

The amount of labor, material, and services used in a responsibility center can be physical quantities: hours of labor, quarts of oil, reams of paper, kilowatt hours of electricity, and so on. In a control system it is convenient to translate these amounts into monetary terms. Money provides a common denominator which permits the amounts of individual resources to be combined. The monetary amount is ordinarily obtained by multiplying the physical quantity by a price per unit of quantity (e.g., hours of labor times a rate per hour). This amount is called cost. Thus the inputs of a responsibility center are ordinarily expressed as costs. Cost is a measure of resources used by a responsibility center.

Note that inputs are resources *used* by the responsibility center. The patients in a hospital or the students in a school are *not* inputs. Rather, it is the resources that are used in accomplishing the objectives of *treating* the patients or *educating* the students that are the inputs.

Although inputs almost always can be measured in terms of cost, outputs are much more difficult to measure. In many responsibility centers, outputs cannot be measured at all. In a profit-oriented organization, revenue is often an important measure of output, but such a measure is rarely a complete expression of outputs; it does not encompass everything that the organization does. In many nonprofit organizations, no good quantitative measure of output exists. A school can easily measure the number of students graduated, but it cannot measure how much education each of them acquired. Although outputs may not be measured, or may not even be measurable, it is a fact that every organization unit *has* outputs; that is, it does something.

Efficiency and Effectiveness

The concepts stated above can be used to explain the meaning of efficiency and effectiveness, which are the two criteria for judging the performance of a responsibility center. The terms efficiency and effectiveness are almost always used in a comparative, rather than in an absolute, sense; that is, we do not ordinarily say that Organization Unit A is 80 percent efficient, but rather that it is more (or less) efficient than Organization Unit B, or more (or less) efficient currently than it was in the past.

Efficiency is the ratio of outputs to inputs, or the amount of output per unit of input. Unit A is more efficient than Unit B either (1) if it uses less resources than Unit B, but has the same output, or (2) if it uses the same resources as Unit B and has a greater output than Unit B. Note that the first type of measure does not require that output be quantified; it is only necessary to judge that the outputs of the two units are approximately the same. If management is satisfied that Units A and B are both doing a satisfactory job and if it is a job of comparable magnitude, then the unit with the lower inputs, i.e., the lower costs, is the more efficient. For example, if two elementary schools are judged to furnish adequate education, the one with the lower costs is the more efficient. The second type of measure does require some quantitative measure of output; it is therefore a more difficult type of measurement in many situations. If two primary schools have the same costs, one can be said to be more efficient than the other only if it provides more education, and this is difficult to measure.

In many responsibility centers, a measure of efficiency can be developed that relates actual costs to some standard—that is, to a number that expresses what costs should be incurred for the amount of measured output. Such a measure can be a useful indication of efficiency, but it is never a perfect measure for at least two reasons: (1) recorded costs are not a precisely accurate measure of resources consumed, and (2) standards are, at best, only approximate measures of what resource consumption ideally should have been in the circumstances prevailing.

Effectiveness is the relationship between a responsibility center's outputs and its objectives. The more these outputs contribute to the objectives, the more effective the unit is. Since both objectives and outputs are often difficult to quantify, measures of effectiveness are difficult to come by. Effectiveness, therefore, is often expressed in nonquantitative, judgmental terms, such as "College A is doing a first-rate job"; "College B has slipped somewhat in recent years."

An organization unit should be *both* efficient and also effective; it is not a matter of one or the other. Efficient managers are those who do whatever they do with the lowest consumption of resources; but if what they do (i.e., their output) is an inadequate contribution to the accomplishment of the organization's goals, they are ineffective. If in a welfare office the employees are invariably busy and if they process claims and applications with little wasted motion, the office is efficient; but if the personnel have the attitude that their function is to ensure that every form is made out perfectly rather than that their function is to help clients get the services to which they are entitled, the office is ineffective. Drucker states that "there is a sharp clash today between stress on the efficiency of administration (as represented, above all, by the governmental administrator and the accountant) and stress on effectiveness (which emphasizes results)."[2] There should not in fact be a "sharp clash" between efficiency and effectiveness, nor is there substantial evidence that such a clash exists. Management's emphasis should be on both these criteria.

The Role of Profits.   One important objective in a profit-oriented organization is to earn profits, and the amount of profits is therefore an important measure of effectiveness. Since profit is the difference between revenue, which is a measure of output, and expense, which is a measure of input, profit is also a measure of efficiency. Thus, profit measures both effectiveness and efficiency. When such an overall measure exists, it is unnecessary to determine the relative importance of effectiveness versus efficiency. When such an overall measure does not exist, it is feasible and useful to classify performance measures as relating either to effectiveness or to efficiency. In these situations, there is the problem of balancing the two types of measurements. For example, how do we compare the profligate perfectionist with the frugal manager who obtains less than the optimum output?

Although profit is an important overall measure of effectiveness and efficiency, it is a less than perfect measure for several reasons: (1) monetary measures do not exactly measure either all aspects of output or all inputs; (2) standards against which profits are judged are not accurate; and (3) at best, profit is a measure of what has happened in the short run, whereas we are presumably also interested in the long-run consequences of management actions.

Source Disciplines

In part, a management control system helps management decide on the optimum allocation of resources, and to this extent it is governed by the principles of *economics*. In part also, the system influences the behavior of people, and to this extent it is governed by the principles of *social psychology*. Both disciplines must be considered jointly in designing and using a management control system.

---

[2] Peter F. Drucker, *The Age of Discontinuity,* (New York, Harper & Row, 1969), p. 197.

Structure and Process

As is the case with any system, a management control system can be described in terms of (*a*) its structure, and (*b*) its process; that is, what it is, and what it does. In studying the human body, for example, one needs to understand both its anatomy and its physiology. The description here is therefore organized according to these two main categories.

We shall divide the discussion of structure into two main parts. One describes the arrangement of accounts, that is, the categories by which information is collected and classified. The other describes the content of these accounts.

THE ACCOUNT STRUCTURE

An account is a device for collecting homogeneous data about some phenomenon, as indicated by its title and as specified in the definition of what is to be collected therein. Accounts collect data on either inputs or outputs. They can collect data on either what has happened (i.e., historical data) or what is planned to happen (i.e., future data). A management control system contains two principal, interrelated account structures, namely, a program structure and a responsibility structure.

The Program Structure

The program structure contains information on the programs that the organization undertakes or plans to undertake. In a profit-oriented company, the principal programs are the company's products or product lines because program decisions are made in terms of products or product lines. The program structure is arranged so that data collected in the program accounts are useful for three principal purposes:

1. To make decisions about the programs that are to be undertaken and the amount and kind of resources that should be devoted to each program.

2. To permit comparisons to be made among programs carried on by several organizations. For example, hospitals typically have a food service program and, thus, food service costs in one hospital can be compared with those in another hospital.

3. To provide a basis for setting fees charged to clients or for reimbursement of costs incurred.

The Responsibility Structure

The second principal way of classifying information is by responsibility centers. Information classified in this way is used for (1) planning the activities of responsibility centers, (2) coordinating the work of the several responsibility centers in an organization, and (3) controlling the responsibility center manager. There are three types of responsibility centers: (1) expense centers, (2) revenue centers, and (3) investment centers.

Expense Centers. If the control system measures the expenses incurred by a responsibility center, but does not measure the monetary value of the unit's output, the unit is an expense center. Although every responsibility center *has* outputs (i.e., it does something), in many cases it is neither feasible nor necessary to measure these outputs in monetary terms. It would be extremely difficult to measure the monetary value that the accounting department contributes to the whole business, for example. Although it would be relatively easy to measure the monetary value of the outputs of an individual production department, there may be no good reason for doing so if the responsibility of the factory supervisor is simply to produce a stated *quantity* of output at the lowest feasible cost.

Thus, most individual production departments and most staff units are expense centers. For these, the accounting system records expenses incurred, but not revenue earned.

Revenue Centers. Revenue is a monetary measure of output, and expense[3] is a monetary measure of input, or resources consumed. Profit is the difference between revenue and expense. Thus, in a profit-oriented business, if performance in a responsibility center is measured in terms of both the revenue it earns and the expense it incurs, the unit is called a *profit center.* Since the term "profit center" seems inappropriate in a nonprofit organization, we shall use the term *revenue center,* instead of profit center.

Investment Centers. In an investment center, the structure measures not only profit but also the capital employed in generating that profit. Thus, the account structure in an investment center encompasses more aspects of the manager's job than is the case with the revenue center, just as the revenue center encompasses more aspects than does the expense center. The investment center concept is rarely used in nonprofit organizations, however.

Mission Centers and Service Centers. It is also useful to classify responsibility centers as either mission centers or service centers. The output of a *mission center* contributes directly to the objectives of the organization. The output of a *service center* contributes to the work of other responsibility centers, which may be either mission centers or

---

[3] The term "expense" is not synonymous with "cost." Cost is a measure of resources consumed for any specified purpose, whereas expense always refers to resources that are matched against revenue *in a specified time period.* Outlays to manufacture products are costs in the period in which the products are manufactured, but they become expenses only in the period in which the products are sold.

other service centers; its output is thus one of the inputs of these responsibility centers.

A service center can be either an expense center or a revenue center. If the latter, it "sells" its services to the units that it services, and its output is measured by the revenue generated by such sales. Its objective usually is not to make a profit—that is, an excess of revenue over expenses—but rather to break even. The extension of the revenue center idea to service centers is relatively new, especially in nonprofit organizations. When properly set up, it can provide a powerful instrument for management control.

Some writers identify a third category of responsibility center, called an *administrative center*. It differs from a service center in that it does not render an identifiable service to other responsibility centers but rather performs administrative functions that benefit the organization as a whole. In most important respects, however, the control problems of an administrative center are similar to those of a service center, so this separate category is usually not needed in the description of a management control system. It will not be used in this book.

Relation of the Program and Responsibility Structures

A responsibility center may work solely on one program, and it may be the only responsibility center working on that program. If so, the program structure corresponds to the responsibility structure. This is so, for example, when a team is created to work on a single program, as is often the case in the aerospace industry when one organization unit is made responsible for developing and producing a single model of aircraft or missile. More commonly, this correspondence does not exist between programs and responsibility centers. For example, there may be a manufacturing organization which manufactures all the products, and a marketing organization which sells the same products; each product line constitutes a program, and the manufacturing and marketing responsibility centers work on several programs.

Even when there is a correspondence between the program structure and the responsibility structure, the way in which costs are constructed for the two structures differs in important respects as will be described in the next section.

Other Information

In addition to the two main account structures described above, a management control system contains other information that is used for special purposes. Information may be required by agencies outside the organization, and these agencies may specify information in a different form than that used by management. Regulated companies, for example, must collect information in accordance with specifications laid down by the regulatory agency even though the information is of little use to management, as is the case with the system for railroads prescribed by the Interstate Commerce Commission. Similarly, agencies of the Federal government must conform to the appropriation structure specified by the Congress, even though such a structure may not be well adapted to the needs of management.

The system also collects information needed for special purposes, such as in connection with litigation, and for any of a number of special studies. Much, perhaps most, output information in nonprofit organizations is in nonmonetary terms: number of patient days in a hospital, number of course enrollments in a school, and so on.

The accounting system provides historical information; that is, information on what has happened, what the costs were. In addition, the management control system provides two other types of information: (1) estimates of what *will* happen in the future, and (2) estimates of what *should* happen. The latter are called standards or budgets, and the former are called forecasts.

Summary of the Account Structure

The essence of the preceding description can be restated by listing four questions for which a management control system is designed to communicate relevant information. Two of these arise before operations take place, and the other two arise after operations have taken place. They are:

Before the event:
1. What activities should the organization undertake? (i.e., its planned outputs)
2. What resources should it use? (i.e., its planned inputs)

After the event:
3. How effectively did the organization do its job? (i.e., its actual outputs related to its objective)
4. How efficiently did the organization use resources? (i.e., its actual inputs related to outputs)

All four questions should be answered both in terms of programs and in terms of responsibility centers.

ACCOUNT CONTENT

Information that is collected in the program structure and also in the responsibility structure can be classified as either input information or output information. Each type of information will be discussed separately.

Basic Types of Cost

Input information essentially consists of costs. There are three basic types of cost construction: program costs, differential costs, and responsibility costs. Each is used for a different purpose, and considerable misunderstanding and misuse arises when the cost construction that is used for a certain purpose is inappropriate for that purpose. Program costs and responsibility costs are ordinarily collected in the accounts; differential costs are not collected as such in the accounts, but are estimated using, in part, information obtained from the accounts.

Program Costs. Program costs measure the full cost of a cost objective, and in profit-oriented companies, this cost construction is therefore usually called *full cost accounting.* In nonprofit organizations, the term *program costs* is more commonly used for the same concept.

A program is a cost objective, and its full cost is the total amount of resources that are inputs to that program. These inputs are the sum of direct costs plus an equitable share of indirect costs. Items of direct cost are those that are directly traceable to a single cost objective, such as the salaries of persons who work directly for a given program.

Items of indirect cost are those that are common to several programs. Each of these programs is assigned an equitable share of the total indirect costs, the amount being determined on some reasonable basis. If feasible the amount assigned to each program is measured either in accordance with the relative benefits received by that program, or in accordance with the relative amount of cost caused by the program. If neither a beneficial or causal relationship exists, the item of cost is allocated in accordance with the overall size of the respective programs. Some nonprofit organizations do not include all elements of full cost in their program costs. They may, for example, exclude certain items of general and administrative costs.

In recording program costs, items of direct cost are identified separately from items of indirect cost. In some management control systems, there is not enough need for full costs to warrant the expense of collecting indirect costs and allocating them to programs. In these *direct cost systems,* no provision is made for such an allocation. Such systems are ordinarily found only in organizations in which the management control process is not highly developed, although this includes some large organizations, such as the Department of Defense.

Differential Costs. Differential costs are costs that are different under one set of conditions from what they would be under another set of conditions. They are used in many problems involving a choice among alternative courses of action, particularly short-run problems, because the analysis of such a problem involves an estimate of how the costs would be different if the proposed alternative were adopted. Because the costs that are relevant for a given problem depend on the nature of that problem, there is no general way of labelling items of cost as differential or not differential, and therefore no way of recording differential costs as such in the formal accounts. The analyst uses information from the program structure or the responsibility structure as raw material for estimating the differential costs for a particular proposed alternative.

In many alternative choice problems, an important classification of costs is whether they are variable or fixed. Variable costs are those that change proportionally with changes in volume; that is, the level of activity. Since twice as much leather is required to manufacture two pairs of shoes as one pair of shoes, the cost of leather used in shoes is a variable cost. The amount of depreciation expense for shoemaking equipment does not change with the number of shoes manufactured on that equipment, so the depreciation is a fixed cost.

Responsibility Costs. Responsibility costs are those incurred by or in behalf of a responsibility center. The focus is on the responsibility center as an organization unit, rather than on the program or programs with which the responsibility center is involved. The total resources consumed by a responsibility center for a period of time, when measured in monetary terms, are the expenses of that responsibility center. Total recorded expenses are at best an approximation of the true inputs. Some inputs are not included as expenses, either because the effort required to translate them into monetary terms is not worthwhile (e.g., minor supplies and services, small amounts of borrowed labor) or because measurement is not possible (e.g., certain types of executive or staff assistance, training).

Responsibility costs are classified as either controllable or noncontrollable. An item of cost is *controllable* if the amount of cost incurred in or assigned to a responsibility center is significantly influenced by the actions of the manager of that responsibility center. Note that "controllable" always refers to a specific responsibility center; all items of cost are controllable by someone in the organization. Note also that the definition refers to a *significant* amount of influence, rather than a *complete* influence; few managers have complete influence over any item of cost.

Responsibility costs are also classified as engineered, discretionary, or committed. *Engineered costs* are those for which the right or proper amount of costs that should be incurred can be estimated with a reasonable degree of accuracy. Most variable costs are in this category. *Discretionary costs* are costs for which there is no rational way of estimating what the "right" amount of costs should be, or at least there is no rational basis that the management is willing to rely on. In the absence of an engineered standard, the amount to be spent must be a matter of judgment. Usually this judgment is arrived at by joint agreement between the supervisor concerned and the manager of the responsibility center during the budgeting process. Most general and administrative costs and many other items of fixed costs are discretionary. *Committed costs* are those that are the inevitable consequences of commitments previously made. They include many items of fixed cost. In the short run, commited costs are noncontrollable. They can be changed only by changing the commitment; for example, by disposing of the building or equipment whose depreciation is a commited cost.

Output Data

The degree to which outputs can be measured quantitatively varies greatly with circumstances. In a department making tangible homogeneous goods (e.g., cement), the *quantity* of output often can be measured precisely; but when the goods are heterogeneous (e.g., different styles and grades of shoes, or different parts produced by a machine shop), problems arise in summarizing the separate outputs into a meaningful measure of the total. Converting the disparate physical goods to a monetary equivalent is one way of solving this problem. The *quality* of the goods produced also involves measurement problems, which often are solved by a "go, no-go" procedure: either the product is of satisfactory quality, or it is not.

When the outputs are services or other intangibles, the problem of measuring them becomes formidable. It is always difficult, and often not feasible, to measure, even approximately, the outputs of such staff units as the legal department or the research department of a company, or the outputs of hospitals, schools, government agencies, or churches.

In addition to the products and services usually thought of as outputs, responsibility centers produce other intangible effects, some intentional and others unintentional. They may prepare employees for advancement; they may instill attitudes of loyalty and pride of accomplishment (or, alternatively, attitudes of disloyalty and indolence); and they may affect the image of the whole organization as perceived by the outside world. Some of these outputs, such as better trained employees, are created in order to benefit operations in future periods; that is, they will become inputs at some future time. Such outputs are therefore *investments,* since a business investment is a commitment of current resources in the expectation of deriving future benefits; however, such investments in intangibles are rarely recorded in the formal system.

Key Variables

Although the control stucture tends to be built around a formal set of accounts, one important aspect of the structure is often not part of this account structure. This is the concept of *key variables*. A key variable is one which can change unexpectedly and in which a change can have a significant effect on the success of the organization. For example, in many profit-oriented organizations, the amount of orders booked is a key variable because the level of incoming orders usually cannot be predicted accurately, and a change in the level can have important consequences. Similarly, in a college, the number of applicants is a key variable.

A management control system is designed to bring to management's attention quickly information about the behavior of key variables. The number of such key variables is small, usually half a dozen or so, but they are extremely important.

THE MANAGEMENT CONTROL PROCESS

As already noted, the management control process takes place in an organization that already exists, that has objectives, and that has decided on broad policies for achieving these objectives. Decisions on these objectives and policies are made in another process, the *strategic planning process*. The strategic planning process is largely unsystematic and informal. The management control system collects information that is useful in strategic planning. Since strategic decisions are made only occasionally, and since each strategic issue requires information that is tailormade to the requirements of that issue, this information cannot ordinarily be collected in any routine, recurring fashion, but must rather be put together when the need arises and in the form required for the specific issue.

There are two systematic aspects to strategic planning information, however. First, a procedure called "scanning the environment" can be used routinely to identify problems and opportunities on which strategic decisions may be needed.[4] Second, the formal *program*, which is described below, serves as a benchmark that is useful in judging strategic proposals. It should be emphasized again that this book deals with management control, not with strategic planning.

Much of the management control process is informal; it occurs by means of memoranda, meetings, conversations, and even by such signals as facial expressions. Such control devices are not amenable to a systematic description. Many organizations also have a formal system. As noted above, the information in this system consists of (1) planned (or estimated) and (2) actual data on (a) outputs and (b) inputs. Prior to actual operations, decisions and estimates are made as to what outputs and inputs are to be; during actual operations, records are maintained as to what outputs and inputs actually are; and subsequent to operations, reports are prepared that compare actual outputs and inputs to planned

---

[4] See Francis J. Aguilar, *Scanning the Business Environment* (New York: Macmillan, Inc., 1967).

outputs and inputs, and action is taken on the basis of these reports. The principal steps in the formal process are:

1. Programming.
2. Budgeting.
3. Operating (and accounting).
4. Reporting and analysis.

Each of these steps leads to the next. They recur in a regular cycle, and together they constitute a "closed loop," as indicated in Exhibit 2–2.

EXHIBIT 2–2
Sequence of Management Control Processes

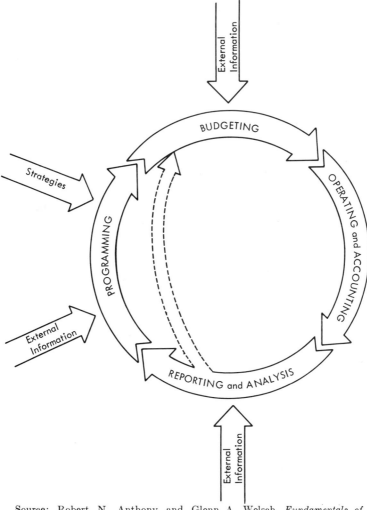

Source: Robert N. Anthony and Glenn A. Welsch, *Fundamentals of Management Accounting* (Homewood, Ill.: Richard D. Irwin, Inc., 1974), p. 303.

Programming

In the programming phase, decisions are made with respect to the major programs in which the organization is to engage during the coming period. These decisions either are made within the context of the objectives and strategies that have previously been decided upon, or they represent changes in strategy. If the latter, they are part of the strategic planning process, rather than the management control process; the two processes merge into one another in the programming phase.

Some organizations state their programs in the form of a "long-range plan" which shows planned outputs and inputs for a number of years ahead—usually five years, but possibly as few as three or (in the case of certain public utilities) as many as twenty. The majority of organizations do not have such a formal mechanism for recording their overall future programs; they rely instead on reports or understandings as to specific, important facets of the program, particularly the amounts to be invested in capital assets and the means of financing these assets.

In an industrial company, the "programs" are usually products or product lines, plus activities (such as research) that are not relatable to specific products. The plans state the amount and character of resources (i.e., inputs) that are to be devoted to each program, and the ways in which these resources are to be used. The accounting information used as a basis for such plans therefore tends to be program data, rather than responsibility data.

To the extent feasible, program decisions are based on an economic analysis, that is, the revenues or other benefits estimated from the proposed program are compared with the estimated costs. For many programs in profit-oriented companies, however, and for an even larger number in nonprofit organizations, reliable estimates of benefits and costs cannot be made. For these programs, decisions are based on judgment and are influenced by the persuasive abilities of program advocates, and by political and other considerations.

Budgeting

A budget is a plan expressed in quantitative, usually monetary, terms and covering a specified period of time. The time period is usually a year, but in a few organizations it may be six months or three months. In the budgeting process the program is translated into terms that correspond to the sphere of responsibility of those who are charged with executing it. Thus, although the plans are originally made in program terms, in the budgeting process they are converted into responsibility terms. The process of arriving at the budget is essentially one of negotiation between the managers of responsibility centers and their superiors. The end product of these negotiations is a statement of the outputs that are expected during the budget year and the resources that are to be used in achieving these outputs.

The agreed upon budget is a *bilateral commitment.* Responsibility center managers commit themselves to produce the planned output with the agreed amount of resources, and their superiors commit themselves to agreeing that such performance is satisfactory. Both commitments are subject to the qualification "unless circumstances change significantly."

Operating and Accounting

During the period of actual operations, records are kept of resources actually consumed and outputs actually achieved. The records of resources consumed, (i.e., costs) are structured so that costs are collected both by programs and by responsibility centers. Costs in the former classification are used as a basis for future programming, and those in the latter are used to measure the performance of the heads of responsibility centers.

Related to the collection of information is the process of *internal auditing.* It consists of the procedures that are intended to insure that the information is accurate and that the opportunities for an undetected departure from plans and policies, and for theft or defalcation, are kept to a minimum. In organizations of any substantial size, a separate internal auditing organization exists to insure adherence to these procedures. In many nonprofit organizations, the internal auditing function is not well developed. In such organizations, the data tend to be unreliable, and this greatly impedes the smooth functioning of the management control process.

Reporting and Analysis

Accounting information, along with a variety of other information, is summarized, analyzed, and reported to those who are responsible for knowing what is happening in the company and for improving performance. As indicated above, these reports essentially compare planned outputs and inputs with actual outputs and inputs.

On the basis of these reports, and of information obtained informally, possible situations requiring action are identified, these situations are investigated, and action is taken when appropriate. This action may involve praise for good performance or corrective steps for unsatisfactory performance, or it may involve a revision of the plan.

GENERAL SYSTEM CHARACTERISTICS

Ordinarily, a formal management control system is a *total* system in the sense that it embraces all aspects of the organization's operation.

It needs to be a total system because an important management function is to assure that all parts of the operation are in balance with one another; and in order to examine balance, management needs information about each of the parts. By contrast, the information used in the strategic planning process is usually collected specifically for the plans under consideration, and these rarely embrace the whole organization. Also, information used in the control of operating activities (e.g., production control, inventory control) is usually tailormade to the requirements of each such activity.

It is reasonable to expect that persons will act according to what they perceive their own best interests to be. A management control system should be designed so that actions it leads managers to take in accordance with their perceived self-interest are actions that are also in the best interest of the organization. In the language of social psychology, the system should encourage *goal congruence*. It should be structured so that the goals of people in the organization are, so far as feasible, consistent with the goals of the organization. as a whole. Perfect congruence between individual goals and organizational goals does not exist, but as a minimum the system should not encourage the individual to act *against* the best interests of the organization. For example, if the system signals that the emphasis should be only on reducing costs, and if the individual responds by reducing costs and at the same time sacrificing quality or providing inadequate service, or by reducing costs by measures that cause a more than offsetting increase in some other department, the person has been motivated, but in the wrong direction.

With rare exceptions a management control system is *built around a financial structure;* that is, resources are expressed in monetary units. Money is the only common denominator by means of which the heterogeneous elements of resources (e.g., hours of labor, type of labor, quantity and quality of material) can be combined and compared. This does not mean that accounting information is the sole, or even the most important, part of the system; it means only that the accounting system provides a unifying core to which other types of information can be related. Although the financial structure is usually the central focus, nonmonetary measures such as minutes per operation, number of persons, and reject and spoilage rates, are also important parts of the system.

The system contains information about both inputs and outputs. In nonprofit organizations, however, output information is often difficult to express in monetary terms, in contrast with input information which can usually be expressed in terms of costs.

The management control process tends to be rhythmic; it follows a definite pattern and timetable, month after month, and year after year. In budgeting, certain steps are taken in a prescribed sequence and at certain dates each year: dissemination of guidelines, preparation of original estimates, transmission of these estimates up through the several echelons in the organization, review of these estimates, final approval by top management, dissemination back through the organization, operating and accounting, reporting, and the analysis of performance. The procedure to be followed at each step in this process, the dates when the steps are to be completed, and even the forms to be used can be, and often are, set forth in a manual.

A management control system is, or should be, a *coordinated, integrated system;* that is, although data collected for one purpose may differ from those collected for another purpose, these data should be reconcilable with one another. In a sense, the management control system is a single system, but it is perhaps more useful to think of it as two interlocking subsystems, one focusing on programs and the other on responsibility centers.

Line managers are the focal points in management control. They are persons whose judgments are incorporated in the approved plans, and they are the persons who must influence others and whose performance is measured. Staff people collect, summarize, and present information that is useful in the process, and they make calculations that translate management judgments into the format of the system. Such a staff may be large in numbers; indeed, the control department is often the largest staff department in a company. However, the significant decisions are made by the line managers, not by the staff.

chapter three

Characteristics of Nonprofit Organizations

This chapter discusses certain characteristics of nonprofit organizations that affect the management control process in those organizations. These characteristics are arranged under the following headings:

1. The absence of the *profit measure*.
2. Their tendency to be *service organizations*.
3. The lesser role of the *marketplace*.
4. The dominance of *professionals*.
5. Differences in *ownership*.
6. Their tendency to be *political* organizations.
7. A *tradition* of inadequate management controls.

Of these, the first characteristic is the most important, and it will be discussed at some length. It affects all nonprofit organizations; each of the others affects many, but not all, nonprofit organizations, and the effects are to varying degrees. They therefore are tendencies, rather than pervasive characteristics. Furthermore, again with the exception of the first, these characteristics are not peculiar to nonprofit organizations. Each of them exists in many profit-oriented organizations; however, these characteristics are important in the *typical* nonprofit organization, but only in the *exceptional* profit-oriented organization.

In Chapter 1, three types of nonprofit organizations were described: client-oriented, member-oriented, and public-oriented. In our discussion

34

here, we shall relate the characteristics to each of these types when such a relationship is relevant.

THE PROFIT MEASURE

All organizations use inputs to produce outputs. An organization's effectiveness is measured by the extent to which outputs accomplish its objectives, and its efficiency is measured by the relationship between inputs and outputs. In a profit-oriented organization the amount of profit provides an overall measure of both effectiveness and efficiency. In many nonprofit organizations, however, outputs cannot be measured to quantitative terms. Furthermore, even when outputs can be measured, many nonprofit organizations have multiple objectives, and there is no feasible way of combining the several outputs, each of which is intended to accomplish one of these objectives, into a single number that measures the overall effectiveness of the organization.

The absence of a satisfactory, single, overall measure of performance that is comparable to the profit measure is the most serious management control problem in a nonprofit organization. (It is incorrect to say that the absence of the profit *motive* is the central problem; rather, it is the absence of the profit *measure*.) In order to appreciate the significance of this statement, we need to consider precisely what the usefulness and the limitations of the profit measure are in profit-oriented organizations.

Usefulness of the Profit Measure

The profit measure has the following advantages: (1) It provides a single criterion that can be used in evaluating proposed courses of action; (2) it permits a quantitative analysis of those proposals in which benefits can be directly compared with costs; (3) it provides a single, broad measure of performance; and (4) it permits comparisons of performance to be made among responsibility centers that are performing dissimilar functions. Each of these points is discussed below.

Single Criterion. In a profit-oriented business, a dominant objective is to earn a satisfactory profit. Profit therefore provides a way of focusing the considerations involved in choosing among proposed alternative courses of action. The analyst and the decision maker can address such questions as: Is the proposal likely to produce a satisfactory level of profits, or is it not? Is Alternative A likely to add more to profits than Alternative B?

The decision maker's analysis is not so simple and straightforward as the above might imply. Objectives other than profit usually must be taken into account, and many proposals cannot be analyzed in terms of their effect on profits; however, these qualifications do not invalidate the general point: profit provides a focus for decision making. In most operations research techniques, a single objective function must be specified, and in a profit-oriented situation, this objective function is profit. Differences of opinion among decision makers in a profit-oriented firm are likely to reflect differing judgments as to the best means of achieving the profit objective; they are unlikely to reflect differing judgments as to the relative importance of several different objectives.

Quantitative Analysis. The easiest type of proposal to analyze is one in which the estimated costs can be compared directly with the estimated benefits. Such an analysis is possible when the objective is profitability, for profit is the difference between cost and revenue, and revenue is equated to benefits. By contrast, when the "benefit" is something other than revenue, the analysis is necessarily much more subjective. When the objective is profit, those elements of the analysis which can be stated in monetary terms can be weighed and balanced against one another in terms of the common criterion, their effect on profits. For example, a proposal to introduce a new product involves such considerations as the estimated revenue, the marketing effort required, the physical facilities, the additional inventory, and the additional production requirements. If reliable estimates of the dollar amount of each of these elements can be made, they can be easily summarized in a single number, the estimated net profit.

Broad Performance Measure. Profitability provides a measure that incorporates a great many separate aspects of performance within it. The best manager is not the one who generates the most sales volume, considered by itself; or the one who uses labor most efficiently; or the one who uses material most efficiently; or the one who has the best control of overhead; or the one who makes the best use of capital. Rather, the best manager is the one who does best, on balance, on the combination of all these separate activities. Profitability incorporates all these separate elements. The key consideration is not the details of the income statement, but, rather, the "bottom line." This measure is valuable both to the managers themselves and to those who judge their performance. It provides managers with a current, frequent, easily understood signal as to how well they are doing, and it provides others with an objective basis for judging the managers' performance.

Comparison of Unlike Units. Finally, the profit measure permits a comparison of the performance of heterogeneous operations that is not possible with any other measure. Assuming that the accounting rules used to measure profits are similar, and that the amount of assets employed is properly taken into account in measuring profitability, then the performance of a department store can be compared with the performance of a paper mill in terms of the single criterion: which was the more profitable? Profitability therefore not only provides a way of combining heterogeneous elements of performance within a company; it also provides a way of making valid comparisons among organizations that have the same objective, the objective of profitability.

Limitations on the Profit Measure

Although we believe that the above statements about the uses of the profit measure are valid as generalizations, they should not be taken as implying that profit is a perfect measure, or even that it is a very good measure in a great many situations. It is better than any alternative, but its limitations should be appreciated. Some of these limitations are listed below.

1. Multiple Objectives. Although profitability is the primary objective of many companies, it is rarely the sole objective. Above all else, a company wants to survive, and it may forego a risky opportunity if the proposed course of action threatens its survival. Also, most managers want to be good citizens; they want to be respected by their colleagues, their customers, their employees and their suppliers; they want to be able to live comfortably with their own consciences. They therefore may forego profit opportunities that would create a bad image or that conflict with their ethical standards. (But even when a possible conflict exists, the profit measure may permit an analysis of how important the questionable proposal is, in terms of lost profits, and thus provide a way of deciding borderline cases.)

2. Omission of Social Costs and Benefits. At best, profitability measures the success of a company as an economic entity. It does not measure the company's net contribution to society, which is the ultimate test of an organization. The cost to society of pollutants that a company may add to the air or the water does not appear on its income statement nor does the benefit to society of the training programs that it undertakes.

3. Long-Run Implications. The income statement measures current, rather than long-run, performance. Managers can take many actions that make current profits look good, but which are detrimental to future profits. A reduction of spending for research/development, for advertising, or for training programs, would lower costs and hence increase profits in the year in which this reduction was made, but such a reduction might well result in decreased profits in future years. One of the important *caveats* in the operation of a management control system in a profit-oriented company is that undue emphasis must not be placed on measures of current profitability.

4. Inadequate Basis of Comparison. On the basis of the profit measure, it can be said that a company performed better than last year, or better than certain other companies, but these judgments are not as important as a comparison of actual performance against the performance that should have been turned in; that is, against the profit potential of the business. A company that reported a high profit may have in fact missed opportunities to do even better; there is no absolute standard, no way of measuring what profits actually should have been. It can be stated flatly that a person who runs a mile in under four minutes is an excellent miler, but a company that reports a $4 million profit in a certain year quite possibly could have done substantially better. Or conversely, under a given set of circumstances, such as a recession, a profit of $1 million in the same company may have been excellent.

5. *Latitude in Accounting.* A company measures and reports its profits in accordance with generally accepted accounting principles, but these principles permit wide latitude in measuring the profits of a given firm. This decreases the validity of comparisons among firms. The profits of a steel company that uses accelerated depreciation are not directly comparable with the profits of another steel company that uses straight-line depreciation, for example. The flexibility of accounting principles affects comparisons among companies much more than it affects comparisons of current profits with prior profits of the same company, because the doctrine of consistency requires that once having adopted a certain accounting practice a company ordinarily must continue to use that same practice indefinitely.

6. *Inadequacy of Accounting.* Costs are supposed to measure the use of resources, but (for good reasons) the principles of accounting do not permit this measurement to be made in a way that conforms strictly to the economic facts. The most important difference between accounting and economics is that in accounting, resources are carried on the books at their historical cost—that is, what was paid to acquire them—whereas the real value of these resources at the time of consumption is their opportunity cost—their current value in an alternative use. This discrepancy has an important effect on the depreciation charge, and it also affects other elements of cost.

7. *Inability to Measure Certain Segments.* Subject to the limitations listed above, the performance of a whole company can be measured by its profitability. So can the performance of operating divisions or certain other segments within the company. But no measure of profitability is feasible for many other responsibility centers. Profit is the difference between revenue and expense, and although the expenses of most responsibility centers can be measured without great difficulty, it is not feasible to measure the revenue for many of them. These include the research/development organization; legal, personnel, accounting, finance, administration, and other staff departments; and even many marketing or production responsibility centers. These are units in which discretionary costs predominate. In these responsibility centers, profit provides neither a focus for the analysis of proposals nor a measure of performance. The technical control problem in these responsibility centers is the same as that in nonprofit organizations.

Measurement of Performance in Nonprofit Organizations

By the definition given in Chapter 1, the objective of a nonprofit organization is something other than earning profits. Thus, even if the outputs in such an organization could be measured in monetary terms (corresponding to "revenue" in a profit-oriented company), the difference between outputs and inputs would not be a measure of performance in terms of the real objectives of the organization. It is not the objective of these organizations to widen the spread between outputs and inputs. In general, their objective is to render as much service as is possible with a given amount of resources, or to use as few resources as possible to render a given amount of service. In most situations, the ideal *financial* performance in a nonprofit organization is a *breakeven* performance; that is, in general and over the long run, outputs should equal inputs.

Even in client-oriented organizations, whose outputs can be measured in monetary terms (for example, in a hospital, if one accepts the premise that patient charges are a good measure of output), the income statement must be viewed in a fundamentally different way from the income statement of a profit-oriented company. If a hospital's revenues exceed its costs, this is a signal that its prices are too high or that it is not rendering enough service for what it charges. If revenues are less than cost, the hospital will go bankrupt (leaving out short-run fluctuations, of course, in both cases). The ideal hospital income statement is one that shows revenue equal to cost.

Thus, although revenue measurement is important and should be attempted in all situations in which it is feasible, the revenue amount must be viewed differently in a nonprofit organization in comparison to a profit-oriented company. The amount of tuition revenue in a college does not reflect the overall effectiveness of the college, at least in the short run. (In the long run, if a college has not lowered its tuition rate, a decline in tuition revenue indicates that the college is ineffective; at least, it indicates that potential students perceive it to be ineffective and consequently are unwilling to attend it.)

The problem is further complicated by the fact that many nonprofit organizations cannot measure their real outputs in monetary terms. The amount of patient charges in a hospital may not actually be a good approximation of output since at best it measures the quantity, but not the quality, of patient care (although it can be argued that if the quality of care is inadequate, physicians will not send patients to that hospital, and this will be reflected as a decrease in revenue). However serious its inadequacies may be, the revenue in a hospital is a much better measure of output than that available in many other types of nonprofit organizations, particularly public-oriented organizations. The output of the State Department is "diplomacy." The output of the Department of Defense is "readiness to defend the interests of the United

States"—terms that are difficult to define and impossible to quantify. The problems of measuring output are discussed at length in Chapter 6.

In passing, it should be noted that the measurement problem relates to outputs, not to inputs. With minor exceptions, inputs, (i.e. costs) can be measured as readily in a nonprofit organization as in a profit oriented organization. The exceptions—such as the problem of measuring the value of volunteers in a hospital—do not arise in most situations and rarely have a significant impact on the control problem. (Although costs *can be* measured, they in fact *are not* measured in many nonprofit organizations. The failure to measure costs reflects the inadequacy of the control system, rather than any inherent measurement problem.)

In passing also, it should be noted that we have not mentioned *cost controllability* as a factor that accounts for the difference between nonprofit and profit-oriented organizations. Although this factor is sometimes advanced, there is little, if any, reason to believe that costs in a typical nonprofit organization are any less controllable than those in a typical profit-oriented organization. In the Department of Defense, for example, some say that 60 percent of operating costs are costs associated with combat forces, that these are not subject to the usual techniques of cost control, and that Department of Defense costs are therefore largely noncontrollable. Even if it were true that combat force costs are noncontrollable (which is arguable), the 40 percent of costs associated with support functions amounts to $20 billion annually, which is more than the total annual operating cost of the largest profit-oriented organization in the country. More importantly, those who allege that nonprofit costs are noncontrollable overlook the fact that large chunks of cost in most responsibility centers in a profit-oriented company are noncontrollable. An automobile must have four wheels, a body, an engine, and certain other parts, and there is nothing the manager of an assembly department can do to change that fact.

Consequences of Absence of the Profit Measure

The absence of a measure that corresponds to profit makes the management control problem much more difficult in a nonprofit organization than in a profit-oriented company. The difficulties can be described by contrasting the situation in a nonprofit organization with the four uses of the profit measure described above.

1. No Single Criterion. Since a nonprofit organization has multiple objectives and since these objectives usually cannot be expressed in quantitative terms, there often is no clearcut objective function that can be used in analyzing proposed alternative courses of action. The management team of a profit-oriented company may debate vigorously the merits of a proposal, but the debate is carried on within the context of how the proposal will affect profits. The management team of a nonprofit organization often will not agree on the relative importance of various objectives; members will view a proposal in terms of the relative importance that they personally attach to the several objectives of the organization. Thus, in a municipality, all members of the management team may agree that the addition of a new pumper will add to the effectiveness of the fire department, but there will be disagreement on how important an expenditure to increase the effectiveness of the fire department is compared to a comparable expenditure on parks, or streets, or welfare. This greatly complicates the problem of decision making.

2. *No Relation between Costs and Benefits.* For most important decisions in a nonprofit organization, there is no accurate way of estimating the relationship between inputs and outputs; that is, there is no way of judging what effect the expenditure of X dollars will have on the objectives of the organization. Would the addition of another professor increase the value of the education that a college provides by an amount that exceeds the cost of that professor? Would the addition of another Army division or another aircraft carrier increase our defense posture by an amount that exceeds its cost? How much should be spent on a program to retrain unemployed persons? Issues of this type are difficult to analyze in quantitative terms because there is no good way of estimating the consequences of a given increment of spending.

New analytical techniques have been developed in recent years that have greatly facilitated decision making in profit-oriented companies, but these techniques all assume that some causal, measurable relationship between costs and benefits can be found. In the absence of such a relationship, these techniques cannot be used. (This is not to say that analytical techniques are inappropriate in nonprofit organizations. They are valuable in many types of problems, as will be discussed in Chapter 8.)

One consequence of the difficulty of relating costs to benefits is that some nonprofit organizations tend to have more personnel than they need. The greater the number of people there are in a responsibility center, the more service it can render and the more important the supervisor's job is perceived as being. Thus, the supervisor is strongly motivated to add personnel. In the absence of a good way of judging the benefits provided by the additional personnel, it is difficult for higher management to appraise the validity of requests for more people. (In some organizations, however, the reverse of this situation may exist; managers may not be permitted to hire additional staff because they cannot justify the need with a quantitative analysis.) A similar situation exists in discretionary expense centers of profit-oriented companies, but the impact is mitigated because the necessity for earning satisfactory profits in the company as a whole tends to keep discretionary expenses in line.

3. *Difficulty of Measuring Performance.* When both revenues and costs can be measured, one goal of a nonprofit organization should be to break even, as mentioned above. But this is never the principal goal,

nor is it a very important goal except in times of financial crisis. The principal goal should be to render service, and the amount and quality of service rendered is not measured by the numbers in the financial statements. Performance with respect to the important goals is difficult to measure. The success of an educational institution depends more on the ability and diligence of its faculty than on such measurable characteristics as the number of courses offered, or the ratio of faculty to students.

Although financial performance should be, at most, a secondary goal, its importance is sometimes overemphasized. If managers who are accustomed to the primacy of profits from their experiences in a profit-oriented company become involved in a nonprofit organization, they may find it difficult to adjust to their new environment and to relegate the financial statements to the lesser status which they should have.

4. Comparison among Units. In nonprofit organizations, organizational units can be compared with one another only if they have similar functions. One fire department can be compared with other fire departments, one general hospital with other general hospitals, and so on, but there is no way of comparing the effectiveness of a fire department with the effectiveness of a hospital. As already noted, dissimilar profit-oriented companies can be compared with one another in terms of the common measure of profitability.

Performance of Subunits

Although a nonprofit organization cannot use profit as a measure of overall performance, it can use profit, or an analogous number, to judge both effectiveness and efficiency in certain responsibility centers within the organizations whose outputs can be reliably measured. These include manufacturing units of all types, and units that render a measurable service (e.g., maintenance departments, typing pools, bookkeeping departments, food service departments).

SERVICE ORGANIZATIONS

Most nonprofit organizations are service organizations; that is, their output consists of intangible services, rather than tangible goods. A company that manufactures goods has certain advantages, from a control standpoint, that a service organization does not have.

Goods can be stored in inventory, awaiting a customer order. Services cannot be stored; if the facilities and personnel that are available to provide the service today are not used today, the revenue from that capability is lost forever.

Service organizations tend to be labor intensive, requiring relatively little capital per unit of output. It is more difficult to control the work of a labor-intensive organization than that of an operation whose work flow is paced or dominated by machinery. (Some service organizations are becoming capital intensive as computers replace clerks.)

It is easy to keep track of the quantity of tangible goods, both during the production process and when the goods are sold, but it is not so easy to measure the quantity of many services. We can measure the number of patients that a physician treats in a day, for example, and even classify these visits by type of complaint, but this is by no means equivalent to measuring the amount of service that the physician provides to each of these patients. For many services, including most of those furnished by public-oriented organizations, the amount rendered by an organizational unit can be measured only in the crudest terms, if at all: number of welfare cases contacted, but not what happened during the contacts; number of aircraft carrier steaming hours, but not what useful things happened during these hours; number of complaints investigated by the police, but not the actual services rendered during these investigations; and so on.

The quality of tangible goods can be inspected, and in most cases the inspection can be performed before goods are released to the customer. If the goods are defective, there is physical evidence of the nature of the defect. The quality of a service cannot be inspected in advance; at best, it can be inspected during the time that the service is being rendered to the client. Judgments as to the adequacy of the quality of most services are subjective; measuring instruments and objective quality standards do not exist.

The literature on control techniques—standard costs, analysis of variances, statistical quality control, production control, inventory control—tends to emphasize production situations rather than service organizations. For example, in 1972 the Price Commission placed great emphasis on the importance of increasing productivity as a way of offsetting higher wage rates. It was able to establish quantitative annual productivity goals for each manufacturing industry, but no one has been able to devise reliable ways of even measuring productivity in most service organizations, let alone suggest reasonable goals for improvement.

Although the absence of productivity data means that statistical comparisons are not possible, there is a general impression that service industries are less efficient than manufacturing industries. For example:

> The long-term steady growth in this country's industrial productivity has been one of our great success stories. Some might argue against concluding, in the absence of relevant statistical series, that local governments have lagged far behind productivity improvement in industry. *Conceivably* they have not. But the indirect evidence strongly supports the view that there is a lag—one great enough, in fact, to present a potential crisis situation. This evidence includes both the data on

rising costs of urban services and the subjective appraisals of managers and analysts in close touch with the operations of local government.[1]

The foregoing description applies to any service organization, whether it is nonprofit or profit-oriented. Indeed, the differences among service organizations as a class and production organizations as a class are probably greater than the differences between a nonprofit and a profit-oriented service organization. For example, many attempts have been made to generalize about the relative efficiency of six types of research/development organizations: (1) a division of a profit-oriented company (e.g., Bell Telephone Laboratories); (2) an independent profit-oriented company (e.g., Arthur D. Little, Inc.); (3) an independent nonprofit organization (e.g., Stanford Research Institute); (4) a Federal Contract Research Center (e.g., Mitre Corporation); (5) a government laboratory (e.g., Naval Ordnance Laboratory); and (6) a university laboratory (e.g., Draper Laboratory at the Massachusetts Institute of Technology). The first two of these types of organization are profit oriented; the other four are nonprofit. Although persons will agree generally on the ratings of certain individual laboratories, there is no substantial evidence that nonprofit laboratories are less effective or less efficient than profit-oriented laboratories, or that the laboratories in any one of the foregoing categories are in general superior to those in the other categories. There is a fairly widespread belief, however, that research/development laboratories in general are not so well managed as are production operations, although there are notable exceptions.

MARKET FORCES

Most nonprofit organizations are less subject to the forces of the marketplace than are profit-oriented organizations. The market dictates the limits within which the management of a profit-oriented company can operate. A company cannot (or, at least, should not) make a product that the market does not want, and it cannot dispose of its products unless their selling prices are in line with what the market is willing to pay. A company cannot survive for long if it cannot equal the performance of its competitors. By contrast, many nonprofit organizations can decide what services they should render according to the best judgment of their managements, rather than according to what the market wants. And, in many cases, a nonprofit organization need not worry about competition. These differences have important implications for management control.

A profit-oriented company wants more customers. More customers mean more profit. In many nonprofit organizations, particularly public-oriented ones, there is often no such relationship between the number

---

[1] Richard Rosenbloom, "The Productivity Crisis in Government," *Harvard Business Review* (September/October 1973), vol. 51, p. 156.

of clients and the success of the organization. If the amount of its available resources are fixed by appropriations (as in the case of government agencies) or by income from endowment or annual giving (as is the case with many educational, religious and charitable organizations), additional clients may place a strain on resources. In a profit-oriented organization, therefore, the new client is an opportunity to be vigorously sought after; in many nonprofit organizations, the new client is only a burden, to be accepted with misgivings.

This negative attitude toward clients is apparent in many nonprofit organizations, especially public-oriented organizations. It gives rise to complaints about the poor service and surly attitude of "bureaucrats," although, as will be shown in Chapter 4, it is technically incorrect to associate the word bureaucracy with nonprofit organizations. An example of this attitude is this announcement posted for the information of students registering in a university:

No questions will be answered that are answered in the printed instructions.

By contrast, clerks in a well managed, profit-oriented retail store are trained to try to answer any question that a customer asks.

In some organizations, the contrast with the motivations associated with market forces is even stronger. A welfare organization should be motivated to decrease its clientele, rather than add to it; that is, it should seek ways of rehabilitating clients, thus removing them from the welfare roles. The Small Business Administration should work to change high-risk businesses into low-risk businesses, which will no longer need the special services that the SBA provides. The idea that the organization should deliberately set out to reduce its clientele should be important in such situations; this idea is foreign to the thinking of profit-oriented managers.

Competition provides a powerful incentive to use resources wisely. If a firm in a competitive industry permits its costs to get out of control, its product line to become out of fashion, or its quality to decrease, its profits will decline. A nonprofit organization has no such automatic danger signal.

Because the importance of what the organization does is not measured by demand in the marketplace, managers of nonprofit organizations tend to be influenced by their personal convictions of what is important. As a substitute for the market mechanism for allocating resources, managers compete with one another for available resources. The physics department, the English department, the library, all try to get as large a slice as possible of the college budget pie.

There are, however, some forms of competition in client-oriented nonprofit organizations. Universities compete for students, faculty, and endowment. Hospitals compete for patients, using better service and affiliation with a medical school as inducements.

Nonprofit educational and health care institutions tend to look down on proprietary schools and hospitals, but the fact is that proprietary schools and hospitals must meet the needs of the market in order to survive, and this can have a positive influence on their operations. There are an estimated 10,000 proprietary schools in the United States with an enrollment of 9 million students.[2] They generally have no endowment and no income from alumni fund drives, yet they survive. Some nonprofit colleges in financial straits might learn from the practices that proprietary schools have developed.

PROFESSIONALS

In many nonprofit organizations, the important people are professionals (physicians, scientists, combat commanders, teachers, pilots, ministers). Professionals often have motivations that are inconsistent with good resource utilization, and their success as perceived by their professional colleagues reflects these motivations. This is also characteristic of profit-oriented organizations where professionals are dominant, such as law offices and research organizations. It happens that a larger proportion of nonprofit than of profit-oriented organizations are dominated by professionals. Some implications of this fact are:

1.   Professionals are motivated by dual standards: (*a*) those of their organizations, and (*b*) those of their professional colleagues. The former standards are related to organizational objectives; the latter may be inconsistent with organizational objectives. The rewards for achieving organizational objectives may be less potent than those for achieving professional objectives.

2.   Professionals who are departmental managers, tend to work only part time on management activities. They spend a substantial part of their time doing the same work that their subordinates do. The head of the surgical department in a hospital does surgery. The head of the physics department in a university teaches and does research in physics. In organizations not dominated by professionals, management tends to be a fulltime job, and managers do not do the same type of work that their subordinates do.

3.   Many professionals, by nature, prefer to work independently. Examples are academicians, researchers, physicians. Because the essence of management is getting things done through people, professionals with such a temperament are not naturally suited to the role of managers.

4.   In a professional organization, the *professional quality* of the people is of primary importance and other considerations are secondary.

---

[2] Estimated by Harold L. Hodgkinson, *The Chronicle of Higher Education* (January 29, 1973) p. 6.

Therefore, managers of professionals spend much of their time recruiting good people and then seeing to it that they are kept happy. The manager has correspondingly less time available for the aspects of the job that relate to efficiency. In a professional organization, the practice of recruiting many and then weeding out unsatisfactory workers is expensive, so management must concentrate on careful preselection.

5. In a professional organization, promotion is geared to the criteria established by the profession and tends to be a function of time (e.g., four years for assistant professor; eight years for Army major). These criteria may not place much emphasis on efficiency and effectiveness. (There are exceptions; exceptional individuals may shortcut the usual rules, if they earn the esteem and recognition of their *professional* superiors.) In some situations, promotions may be influenced by outside qualifications such as degrees, prizes, and published articles; these are not always an accurate reflection of the individual's worth to the organization.

> *Example:* For military officers, the fitness report is an important motivational device. It serves both as a measure of current performance and also as the basis for promotion. Until recently, military fitness reports did not rate officers on how effectively or efficiently they managed the use of resources. Although current fitness reports are still weighted heavily toward personal characteristics and professional capabilities (shiphandling, airmanship, watch officer capabilities), there is a trend toward evaluating effective use of resources. For example, a recent change to the Navy fitness report format included the following instructions:
>
> "In deciding upon the mark to be assigned, consideration shall be given to observed effectiveness in the utilization of men, money and materials, and the implementation of improved management techniques and procedures. Significant contributions to greater economy and efficiency shall be commented on."

6. Professional education does not usually include education in management and quite naturally stresses the importance of the profession rather than of management. For this and other reasons, professionals tend to look down on managers.

> *Example:* "It (Harvard Business School) is a good school. We should be grateful to it for training people who will shoulder the dull, tedious administrative jobs in organizations."[3]
>
> *Example:* In some hospitals, the administrator's status and pay are below that of all professional people; the chief administrator may not even attend the Board of Trustees meetings in which the professionals and the trustees decide on policies.

7. Financial incentives tend to be less effective with professional people either because they consider their current compensation to be

---

[3] Professor John Kenneth Galbraith, *The Wall Street Journal*, April 1, 1969, p. 1.

adequate or because their primary satisfaction comes from their work. In Thoreau's words, the professional "hears a different drummer."

8. Professional status may be legally institutionalized. For example, laws may require that a certain number of physicians be appointed to boards of health.

9. Although the leadership job in an organization unit in a nonprofit organization may require more management skills than professional skills, tradition often requires that the manager of such a unit be a professional. Many military support units are managed by military officers, even though a civilian might be a better qualified manager. Traditionally, the head of a research organization was a scientist; the president of a university, a professor; the head of a hospital, a physician. This tradition seems to be diminishing, however.

10. Professionals tend to give inadequate weight to the financial implication of their decisions. The physician feels that no limit should be placed on the amount spent to save a human life, although in a world of limited resources such an attitude is unrealistic. The late Senator Richard B. Russell, as Chairman of the Senate Armed Services Committee, observed about military professionals:

> There is something about preparing for destruction that causes men to be careless in spending money.
>
> What that is, I do not know, but I have observed over a period of almost 30 years in the Senate, that there is something about buying arms with which to kill, to destroy, to wipe out cities and to obliterate great transportation systems which cause men not to reckon the dollar cost closely.

OWNERSHIP

Although the statement that shareholders "run" a corporation is an oversimplification, it is unquestionably true that shareholders have the ultimate authority. Although they may exercise this authority only in times of crisis, it is nevertheless there. The movement of stock prices is an immediate and influential indication of what shareholders think of their management. In profit-oriented organizations, policy and management responsibilities are vested in the board of directors, which derives its power from the shareholders. In turn, the board delegates power to the president, who serves at the board's pleasure, acts as the board's agent in the administration of the organization, and who is replaced if there are serious differences of interest or opinion.

In many nonprofit organizations the corresponding line of responsibility is often not clear. In nongovernment organizations, the presumably controlling body does not necessarily represent the source of the organization's power. Instead of being selected formally by those ultimately responsible for the organization, it may be self-perpetuating, selected by outside parties, or selected *de facto* by the top management of the organization. Its members are seldom paid for their services. Instead of a single chain of delegation of power—from shareholder to board to president—there are often three somewhat independent power centers: (1) contributors, who can exercise control by withholding contributions; (2) the *board*, which *de jure* controls the organization, and (3) the *chief executive officers* who may in fact hold much control over the board by deciding who shall be appointed, who shall be given special recognition, and what are the rewards of board membership. (The executives of a corporation may have similar powers, but they must face the ultimate shareholder recourse of a new board or a corporate takeover.)

In government organizations, the diffusion of power is also great, but for different reasons:

1. The bureaucracy is often insulated from top management by virtue of job security and rules, and career civil servants may know that they will outlast the term of office of the elected or appointed chief executive. If a pet project cannot be sold to the current boss, bureaucrats may bide their time and hope to sell it to the next one. Conversely, if they dislike a new policy they may be able to drag their heels long enough so that a new management will take over and hopefully rescind the policy.

2. Agencies, or units within agencies, may have their own special-interest clienteles (e.g., Maritime Administration and shipping interests) with political power which is stronger than that of the chief executive of the agency.

3. Top management authority may be divided, particularly in those states where the expenditure authority is vested in committees of independently elected officials, and in local governments administered by commissions whose members each administer a particular segment of the organization (e.g., streets or health). Elected officials, such as the attorney general, the treasurer, the secretary of state, or the director of education may manage their organizations fairly independently of the top management of their state or municipality. The mayor of Los Angeles has much narrower responsibility than does the mayor of New York because the county organization in California is responsible for many services that are performed by the city organization in New York.

4. In State and Federal governments, there is a division of authority among executive, legislative, and judicial branches. When there are coordinate branches of government, there are often conflicting judgments about objectives and the means of attaining them. In a profit-oriented company, the board of directors and the chief executive officer have similar objectives.

5. There may also be a vertical division of authority among levels of government (federal, state, and local), each responsible for facets

of the same problem. For example, the Federal government finances major and many minor highways, and local governments construct and maintain other highways.

This fragmentation of authority complicates management control. A particularly significant consequence is that the public administrator comes to depend upon "political" power, to influence those who cannot be directly controlled. Consequently, managers must manage their political credit as well as their financial credit; they must measure the political cost and benefit of alternative choices, as well as the financial cost and benefit. On the other hand, there are some strong compensating advantages to divided authority. Particularly in the coordinate government, each branch can serve as check on the activities of the other branches.

In summary, in many nonprofit organizations there is no single outside group to which the management is clearly accountable. Even in those organizations in which such a group exists, there may not be a similarity between the objectives of the management and those of the outside group that is close to the similarity that exists when both groups are essentially interested in profits.

POLITICS

Many nonprofit organizations are political; that is, they are responsible to the electorate or to a legislative body that presumably represents the electorate. Some of the consequences of this status are discussed below.

Necessity for Re-Election. In government organizations, decisions result from multiple, often conflicting, pressures, many of them political. In part, these political pressures are an inevitable—and up to a point desirable—substitutes for the forces of the marketplace. Elected officials cannot function if they are not re-elected. In order to be re-elected, they must—at least up to a point—advocate the perceived needs of their constituency, even though satisfying these needs may not be in the best interests of the larger body which they are supposed to represent. Moreover, in order to gain support for programs that are important to them, the elected officials may support certain of their colleagues' programs, even though they personally do not favor them. This "logrolling" phenomenon is also present in profit-oriented organizations, but to a lesser extent.

Public Visibility. In a democratic society the press and public feel that they have a right to know everything there is to know about a public organization. In the Federal government, this feeling is recognized by "freedom of information" statutes. Channels for distributing this information are not always unbiased. Although some media stories that describe mismanagement are fully justified, others tend to be exaggerated and to give inadequate recognition to the fact that mistakes are inevitable in any organization. By contrast, mismanagement in profit-oriented companies is publicized only when there is substantial fraud, a shareholders' suit, or other highly unusual occurrences. In order to reduce the opportunities for unfavorable media stories, government managers take steps to reduce the amount of sensitive, controversial information that flows through the formal control system. This lessens the usefulness of the system. The number of problems to which formal analytical techniques are applied is reduced because such techniques result in reports that may be open to public inspection.

Multiple External Pressures. The electoral process, with institutionalized public review through news media and opposing political parties, results in a wider variety of pressures on managers of public organizations than on managers of private organizations, whether nonprofit or profit. Elected public officials are more controversial and less secure than business managers. In the absence of profit as a clearcut measure of performance, these pressures may be erratic and illogical, influenced by momentary fads. These pressures tend to induce an emphasis on short-term goals, and on program decisions that are not based on careful analysis.

Inadequate External Pressures. Stockholders demand satisfactory earnings, whereas the public and governing bodies of nonprofit organizations tend to exert less pressure for good resource utilization. In part this is because of the difficulty of measuring performance, and in part it is because of the diffused responsibility and multiple pressures already mentioned.

Legislative Restrictions. Government organizations must operate within statutes enacted by the legislative branch, which are much more restrictive than the charter and by-laws of corporations, and which often prescribe detailed operating practices. It is relatively difficult to change these statutes.

Inadequate Management. When the Number One person in an organization is elected by the voters, the person is often chosen for reasons other than ability as a manager. A cabinet officer or other high ranking appointed official is also likely to be selected for reasons other than managerial ability; the official may be more skilled in the process of formulating broad agency policies than in executing policies. The Number One person in an agency may be expected to spend much time on political or politically related activities. In concept, these management inadequacies of the Number One person could be overcome by selecting a fully qualified manager as the Number Two person (e.g., the undersecretary) and giving that person full responsibility for the operation of the agency, but this is not always done.

Management Turnover. In some public organizations top management tends to change rapidly because of administration changes, political shifts, military orders, and managers who only dabble in government jobs. Each change requires a "learning lead time" and many of them result in changes in priorities. This rapid turnover results in short-run plans and programs which produce quickly visible results, rather than longer-range programs.

Inadequate Compensation. Salaries and other compensation of managers in public organizations tend to be relatively low. Consequently, managers of these organizations, especially those near the top of the organization, may be less capable than their counterparts in profit-oriented organizations. The reasons for this discrepancy in compensation are not entirely clear. It probably reflects a lack of understanding by the public and by those who control funds as to the importance of the management function and the importance of compensation as a motivating device. The problem of inadequate compensation is compounded by the widespread belief that nonprofit organizations should not use bonuses or other forms of incentive compensation. (This comment does not apply to the top people in important organizations. The power, prestige, and opportunity for public service associated with their positions offset the low monetary reward.)

Civil Service. Although there is a widespread belief that Civil Service regulations operate to inhibit good management control, it is by no means clear that Civil Service regulations are essentially different from personnel regulations in some large companies. The best case in support of this view of the inhibiting effects of Civil Service can be made in certain state and municipal governments. In many such organizations, Civil Service laws effectively inhibit the use of both the carrot and the stick. A Civil Service syndrome develops as a result of the tacit *caveat* signaled by the system structure: "You need not produce success; you merely need to avoid making major mistakes." This attitude is a major organizational barrier to change.

On the other hand, Civil Service regulations in many other government organizations may be no more dysfunctional than are union regulations and norms in profit-oriented organizations. When one considers the restrictive and inefficient union rules regarding work assignments, such as the number of engineers and other personnel aboard trains, or the division between electricians and plumbers on a joint repair job, it appears that at least in some situations the Civil Service environment may compare favorably. One difference is that union rules mostly affect those near the bottom of the organization whereas Civil Service rules affect nearly everyone.

TRADITION

In the 19th century, accounting was primarily *fiduciary* accounting; that is, its purpose was to keep track of the funds that were entrusted to an organization to ensure that they were spent honestly. In the 20th century, accounting in business organizations has assumed much broader functions. It furnishes useful information about the business both to interested outside parties and to management. Nonprofit organizations have been slow to adopt 20th century accounting and management control concepts and practices. This section contains a brief review of the development and status of management control in nonprofit organizations. The description relates mainly to the Federal government.

The principal concepts and techniques that distinguish modern management control from fiduciary accounting, arranged approximately in the order in which they became generally accepted by business are: (1) the accrual concept, (2) cost accounting, (3) standard costs and variance analysis, (4) budgeting, (5) variable costing and breakeven analysis, (6) responsibility accounting, and (7) programming.

The Accrual Concept

A simple, but fundamental, idea of modern accounting is the accrual concept. Other new techniques would not be possible without it. Essentially, the accrual idea means that accounting should focus on the cost of resources *consumed,* as contrasted with resources *purchased* (which is the "obligation" concept) or with *liabilities incurred* (which is the "expenditure" concept). The Federal government, however, continues to emphasize the obligation and expenditure concepts, even today. The desirability of shifting to the accrual concept was suggested in the First Hoover Commission report in 1949[4] and was emphasized in the Second Hoover Commission report in 1955.[5] As a result of the 1955 report, legislation requiring that accrual accounting be adopted "as soon as feasible" was enacted (Public Law 84-863), but most agencies still have not done so. Indeed, the whole movement received something of a setback in 1967 when a prestigious committee recommended that the basic concepts should be "accrued expenditures,"[6] which is just enough different from, and inferior to, true accrual accounting to muddy the water. Full value cannot be obtained from any of the other new concepts and techniques until accrual accounting is adopted.

The same situation exists in many states and municipalities. For example, in a 1973 report,[7] the Comptroller of the State of New York pointed

[4] U.S. Commission on Organization of the Executive Branch of the Government (1947–1949) *Budgeting and Accounting* (Washington, D.C.: Government Printing Office, 1949).

[5] U.S. Commission on Organization of the Executive Branch of the Government (1953–1955) *Budgeting and Accounting* (Washington, D.C.: Government Printing Office, 1955).

[6] U.S. President's Commission on Budget Concepts. *Report* (Washington, D.C., Government Printing Office, October 1967).

[7] Arthur Levitt, "Discipline in the Fiscal Process," *New York State Comptroller's Studies on Issues in Public Finance,* Study no. 3 (September 1973).

out that accrual accounting had been recommended by a legislative committee as long ago as 1937 but the recommendation was not adopted. He went on to say that the management control inadequacies that resulted from this are as bad currently as they were then. In this report, he once more strongly recommended the adoption of accrual accounting.

Cost Accounting

Early cost accounting systems were used principally for calculating selling prices, and it is not surprising that these systems were not adopted by the government because pricing is a minor problem in most government agencies (with some notable exceptions, such as the Postal Service). In recent years, businesses have found cost information useful for other purposes, but since government does not have even rudimentary cost systems, except in its business related activities, it has not been able to take advantage of good cost information. The absence of accrual accounting means that such cost accounting systems as do exist are necessarily "statistical" in nature—that is, they are not tied to the basic debit-and-credit accounting records. Without the discipline that debit and credit provides, cost information is likely to be so inaccurate as to be useless.

Standard Costs and Variance Analysis

Standard costs are intended primarily as a control device, but they also permit simplifications in record keeping systems. They are widely used in business, but are used scarcely at all in government. Since standard cost systems are built on a foundation of conventional cost accounting, which is rare in government, and since they were originally used in manufacturing organizations rather than in service organizations, this nonuse is not surprising. The analysis of variances between standard costs and actual cost according to the cause of the variance (e.g., volume, mix, price, efficiency) is a fairly recent development in business practice, although it has been described in textbooks for 30 years or more. Such an analysis provides a powerful control tool, which is not available to organizations that do not have standard costs.

Budgeting

Budgeting in government has been around longer than budgeting in most businesses. It was started by the New York Bureau of Municipal Research in 1906, spread fairly rapidly to municipal and state governments, and was adopted by the Federal government in 1921. In the early government budgets, the fiduciary attitude was dominant. The budget set forth how much an agency was permitted to obligate for personnel, for supplies, for travel, and similar "object classifications," rather than emphasizing the programs that should be undertaken and the amount that should be spent for each program. This "object class" or "line item" approach still dominates most parts of the Federal budget although some agencies, such as the Atomic Energy Commission, have successfully broken away from it. Moreover, many agencies continue to regard the budgetary process solely as a device for obtaining money (which is part of its function), rather than as a management tool to guide and control the work of the agency (which is an equally important part).

Variable Costing and Breakeven Analysis

The classification of cost elements into those which vary with volume and those which do not, has facilitated the analysis of many business problems. Although fluctuations in volume are not as prevalent in government as they are in business, there are many situations in government in which such a separation would be useful. In government agencies, such a separation is rarely made, however.

Responsibility Accounting

Responsibility accounting has come into widespread use in business only within the last 20 years. As described more fully in Chapter 2, it focuses on the inputs and outputs of responsibility centers, and provides a powerful tool for communicating with, motivating, and measuring the performance of the managers of such centers. Related developments of profit centers, investment centers, and transfer pricing, are even more recent. These techniques are used in certain government agencies, such as the Department of Defense, but not by any means in all of them.

Programming

The programming process includes both the formal apparatus for deciding on the overall mix of programs for an agency and the tools that have been developed for analyzing individual proposed programs. Currently, few businesses use a formal programming apparatus, but most of them use the analytical tools, particularly in proposals involving capital investments. In the Federal government, the Department of Defense introduced a formal programming system (called "Planning-Programming-Budgeting System" or "PPBS") in 1962. President Johnson became an enthusiastic supporter of the idea, and in 1965 ordered all agencies to install a PPB system. This order was premature, for the proper groundwork had not been laid in most agencies, and most lacked the knowledgeable leadership that was provided by Secretary Robert S. McNamara in Defense. Consequently, the programming systems in most agencies were solely window dressing, with minimal effect on the way in which the agencies were actually managed. Some agencies, such as the Department of Health, Education and Welfare, have gradually developed viable systems; others continue to go through the motions only, or, as permitted by an Office of Management and Budget memorandum of 1971, they have even stopped going through the motions.

Barriers to Progress

Since the Federal government lacks the semiautomatic control that is provided by the profit mechanism, it needs a good management control system even more than a business does. Why has the government lagged so far behind? There seem to be three principal explanations. First, for many years, there was a prevalent attitude to the effect that the differences between government and business were such that government could not use the management control techniques developed by business. Articles to this effect written by eminent authorities appeared as recently as the 1950s, and this attitude continues to be implicit in some texts on government accounting. Second, the Congress, and particularly the House Committee on Appropriations, having become thoroughly accustomed to a certain budget format, is reluctant to shift to a new format; because of the importance of the budget, this affects the whole management control system. In part, this reluctance is based on simple inertia; in part it reflects a suspicion—an unwarranted suspicion—that the change is an attempt by the Executive Branch to "put something over" on the Legislative Branch. Third, many career officials appreciate the fact that a good management control system is two-edged; it provides new information for management, but it also provides new information for outside agencies—the Office of Management and Budget and the Congress. They are not anxious that outside agencies have access to the new and better information. (It is interesting to note the contrast between the second and third reasons.)

Other Nonprofit Organizations

In general—and there are numerous exceptions to each of the following statements—state and municipal governments have even poorer management control systems than does the Federal government. The two largest classes of other nonprofit organizations—health care and education—until recently had poor management control systems. Hospital systems, under the impetus of Medicare and in response to widespread criticism of skyrocketing prices, have been improving rapidly, although resistance to modern budgeting practices continues in many of them. Colleges and universities, led by certain state universities, also are making rapid improvements, although they have a long way yet to go. Public schools generally use a system developed under the auspices of the U.S. Office of Education; although recently revised, it continues to be an antiquated system. Religious organizations generally have only rudimentary control systems, although there are important exceptions.

DIFFERENCES AMONG ORGANIZATIONS

The description in this chapter is intended to apply to nonprofit organizations in general, but of course it is true that the characteristics enumerated do not fit all such organizations equally well. In this section an attempt is made to relate the description to each of the three main types of organizations defined in Chapter 1: client-oriented, member-oriented, and public-oriented.

Client-Oriented Organizations

Many client-oriented organizations closely resemble profit-oriented organizations. Indeed, were it not for the difference in objectives—service rather than profit—their management control problems would be similar to those of their profit-oriented counterparts. There are few differences between a voluntary hospital and a proprietary hospital, or between a private college and a proprietary college. These organizations do differ from many businesses in that they are service organizations rather than production organizations. They face fewer competitive pressures than the typical business, much of their revenue is received from third parties rather than directly from clients (Blue Cross, insurance companies, and the government for hospitals; and parents for colleges), they are dominated by professionals, and they have no clear-cut line of responsibility to a defined group of owners.

Member-Oriented Organizations

The management control problems of member-oriented organizations, such as labor unions, trade associations, and religious organizations are much more difficult than those of client-oriented organizations because their objectives are more vague ("render service to members") and they have few good measures of output. ("Souls saved per pew-hour preached," although often advocated, is *not* a good output measure.) Some of them, such as religious organizations and certain labor organizations, face strong competitive pressures; others have no effective competition. They tend to be dominated by professionals and to have unclear ownership authority. They also have many of the same problems as political organizations, because the membership has a voice in the selection of management that is similar to the voice of the electorate.

Public-Oriented Organizations

Management control in public-oriented organizations is more difficult than in either member-oriented or client-oriented organizations, for two principal reasons. First, their objectives are numerous and not well defined, and it is difficult to measure output in terms of objectives. Second, they are political organizations, with all the problems described in the preceding section on this topic.

CONCLUSION

The characteristics of nonprofit organizations described in this chapter can be grouped into two classes, one technical and the other behavioral.

The first class consists of matters described under the heading, the profit measure, that is, the difficulty of measuring outputs and the relationships between inputs and outputs. The important observation that can be made about this class is that the problems described therein are inherent in the fact that the organization is nonprofit. Great improvements in output measurement are indeed possible, and the problem is so important that a considerable effort to make such improvements is worthwhile; but it must be recognized at the outset that the resulting system will never provide as good a basis for planning or for measuring performance as exists in profit-oriented organizations.

The second class consists of all the other topics. The significance of these behavioral characteristics is twofold: (1) most of the behavioral factors that impede good management control can be overcome by proper understanding and education; (2) unless these other problems *are* overcome, the improvements in the technical area are likely to have little real impact on the management control process.

chapter four

Organizational Relationships

Although the management control process occurs within organizations, it would be inappropriate to attempt here a discussion, or even a summary, of the literature on organizations and organization theory.[1] To do so, would take us far away from our main theme. Some aspects of the behavior of people in organizations are nevertheless crucial to an understanding of the management control process, and these are discussed in this chapter. Comments are made about the following classes of participants:

1. Governing boards.
2. Top management.
3. Management assistants.
4. The controller.
5. Other staff personnel.
6. Operating managers.

Before discussing the role of each of these participants, it seems desirable to have a brief discussion of the concept of bureaucracy.

BUREAUCRACY

In common parlance, bureaucracy is a derogatory term. Any organization that operates by complicated rules and routines, or that is charac-

---

[1] For a good discussion, see Chester Irving Barnard, *Functions of the Executive* (Cambridge, Mass.: Harvard University Press, 1968); Alfred Dupont Chandler, *Strategy and Structure* (Cambridge, Mass.: M.I.T. Press, 1969); and James Gardner March and Herbert A. Simon, *Organizations* (New York: John Wiley & Sons, Inc., 1958.)

terized by delays and buck passing, or that treats its clients impolitely, or that has operating managers who try to build empires, is called a bureaucracy. In particular, all large government organizations are labeled bureaucracies, usually with the implication that *non*government organizations are *not* bureaucracies. In studies of organization theory, however, "bureaucracy" describes an organization with certain characteristics, and no derogatory value judgment about such an organization is implied by the term; indeed, it is recognized that these characteristics are inherent in large and complex organizations, both government and nongovernment.

Nature of Bureaucracy

The classic analysis of bureaucracy is that of Max Weber in *The Theory of Social and Economic Organization*,[2] written in 1922. A summary of his description of a pure bureaucracy follows:

> The supreme chief of the organization occupies his position of authority by virtue of appropriation, of election, or of having been designated for the succession. . . . The whole administrative staff under the supreme authority then consists, in the purest type, of individual officials who are appointed and function according to the following criteria:

1. They are personally free and subject to authority only with respect to their impersonal official obligations.
2. They are organized in a clearly defined hierarchy of offices.
3. Each office has a clearly defined sphere of competence in the legal sense.
4. The office is filled by a free contractual relationship. Thus, in principle there is free selection.
5. Candidates are selected on the basis of technical qualifications. In the most rational case, this is tested by examination or guaranteed by diplomas certifying technical training, or both. They are appointed, not elected.
6. They are remunerated by fixed salaries in money, for the most part with a right to pensions. Only under certain circumstances does the employing authority, especially in private organizations, have a right to terminate the appointment, but the official is always free to resign. The salary scale is primarily graded according to rank in the hierarchy; but in addition to this criterion, the responsibility of the position and the requirements of the incumbent's social status may be taken into account.
7. The office is treated as the sole, or at least the primary, occupation of the incumbent.

---

[2] Max Weber, *The Theory of Social and Economic Organization*, trans., A. M. Henderson and Talcott Parsons; ed. Talcott Parsons (New York: Oxford University Press, 1947), pp. 329–340.

8. It constitutes a career. There is a system of "promotion" according to seniority or to achievment, or both. Promotion is dependent on the judgment of superiors.

9. The official works entirely separated from ownership of the means of administration.

10. He is subject to strict and systematic discipline and control in the conduct of the office.

Weber did not associate bureaucracy with government or with any particular type of organization. He said:

> This type of bureaucracy is found in private clinics, as well as in endowed hospitals or the hospitals maintained by religious orders. Bureaucratic organization has played a major role in the Catholic Church. . . . The same phenomena are found in the large-scale capitalistic enterprise; and the larger it is, the greater their role.[3]

In addition to the bureaucracy, an organization in which authority is derived from law, Weber identified two other principal types of organizations: (1) those in which authority rests on *tradition*—"the belief in the sacredness of the social order and its prerogatives"—of which the patriarchial family, certain religious organizations, and the manorial system are examples; and (2) those in which authority rests on *charisma*—"the affectual and personal devotion of the follower to the lord and his gifts of grace"—of which other religious organizations and any organization held together by the personality of its leaders are examples. In many organizations, each of these three sources of authority—bureaucratic, traditional, and charismatic—are present in varying degrees. A bureaucratic organization is one in which legal authority predominates. Bureaucracy is therefore a matter of degree, and few if any organizations correspond exactly to the description of the "pure" case quoted above.

In the bureaucratic form of organization, complex problems are solved by segmenting them into a series of simpler ones and delegating authority for solving each of the segments to specialized subunits, consisting of trained specialists or experts who are equipped to solve problems in their area of expertise. Such technical superiority based on increased specialization is supposed to lead to objective and impersonal decision making at the subunit level. Weber noted that an individual who applied personal subjective values to policy or decision making could seriously lessen the effectiveness of the organization, and that a bureaucracy avoided this possibility by replacing the subjective judgment of individuals by routinized work tasks and by a set of rules, values and attitudes, or goals, which are approved by the expert's superior.

The bureaucratic organization, in fact, is a continuous system of "official functions bound by rules" which "follows the principle of

---

[3] Ibid.

hierarchy; that is, each lower office is under the control and supervision of a higher one. . . ." Such a hierarchy, in which rules regulate the conduct of any office which can be occupied by "only a person who has demonstrated an adequate technical training," constitutes *rational legal authority*. And such an organization ". . . is, from a purely technical point of view, capable of attaining the highest degree of efficiency."[4]

Dysfunctional Aspects of Bureaucracy

Weber's ideal-construct bureaucracy has a tendency to "dehumanize" the individual. Behavior is clearly prescribed, and interpersonal relationships are dictated by the structure of authority, status, and rank in the hierarchy. Weber's description is a functional one. Many sociologists question whether the heirarchical principle he formulated can be realistically applied to formal organizations of experts who are professionals.[5]

Robert K. Merton pointed the way towards the "human relations" approach to bureaucracy.[6] Merton felt that, first of all, the discipline required for standardizing behavior required in the bureaucratic organization would cause a displacement of goals. Specialization sometimes leads to "blind spots." These blind spots can cause bureaucrats to adhere rigidly to techniques which have been applied successfully to past situations even after conditions have changed. Routinized efficiency may breed inflexibility. Thus, the methodical performance of routine activities can become an end in itself rather than the means to an end.

Merton's argument runs as follows:

1. An effective bureaucracy demands reliability of response and strict devotion to regulations.

2. Such devotion to the rules leads to their transformation into absolutes; they are no longer conceived as relative to a set of purposes.

3. This interferes with ready adaptation under special conditions not clearly envisaged by those who drew up the general rules.

4. Thus, the very elements which conduce toward efficiency in general produce inefficiency in specific instances. Full realization of the inadequacy is seldom attained by members of the group who have not divorced themselves from the meanings which the rules have for them. Overconcern with means, i.e., regulations, "induces timidity, conservatism, and technicism."

---

[4] Ibid.

[5] For a discussion of this problem, which is particularly relevant to many nonprofit organizations, in a specific situation see Mary E. Goss, "Influence and Authority Among Physicians in an Outpatient Clinic," *A Sociological Reader on Complex Organizations,* ed., Amitai Etzioni, 2d ed. (New York: Holt, Rinehart and Winston, 1961), pp. 275–91.

[6] Robert K. Merton, "The Unanticipated Consequences of Purposive Social Action," *American Sociological Review,* I (December 1936), 894–904, and "Bureaucratic Structure and Personality," *Social Forces,* 18 (May 1940), pp. 560–68.

Merton points out that the bureaucratic structure also produces an informal social organization which can be dysfunctional. Since bureaucrats share the same interests, i.e., the organizational objectives, and since there is theoretically relatively little competition among them because promotion is in terms of seniority, in-group aggression is minimized. In such situations an informal social organization usually develops, and personnel tend to defend their entrenched interests rather than to assist clients and elected higher officials. Bureaucrats may minimize personal relations with clients and instead deal with "categories" of problems, thus ignoring the peculiarities of individual cases. And since the bureaucrat's official life is planned "in terms of a graded career, through the organizational devices of promotion by seniority, pensions, incremental salaries, etc., all of which are designed to provide incentives for disciplined action and conformity to the official regulation," the bureaucrat doesn't have to worry about being fired by an incoming elected official at the top of the hierarchy. Bureaucrats become more and more resistant to any change that would upset their way of life.

Ironically, as bureaucrats become more impervious to change, their behavior can become less rational. Behavior which runs counter to the formalized structure can evoke emotional responses of disapproval or resentment.

Conflict begins in the bureaucratic structure when informal or personalized relationships are substituted for the impersonal, formal relationships that the ideal bureaucratic structure requires. If a member within the hierarchy substitutes personal for impersonal treatment towards a subordinate, others within the structure who have identified themselves with the rules and objectives of the organization may become antagonized and level charges of "favoritism." A subordinate who shows too much attention to a superior may be labelled an "apple-polisher."

Weber's theory did not take account of personal goals, only of organizational roles. But personal goals are important in studying the process of decision making in organizations. Thus, "desires for power and concern for personal advancement represent an intrusion of personal goals upon organization role, as do the social and craft satisfactions and dissatisfactions associated with work."[7]

As Blau points out in his *Bureaucracy in Modern Society*,[8] administrative efficiency cannot be served by ignoring the fact that the performance of individuals is affected by their relations with colleagues, but only by taking cognizance of this fact and attempting to create those conditions in the organization that lead to unofficial practices which further rather than hinder the achievement of its objectives.

---

[7] Herbert A. Simon, "On the Concept of Organizational Goal," *Administrative Science Quarterly* (June 1964, vol 9), pp. 1–22.

[8] Peter M. Blau, *Bureaucracy in Modern Society* (New York: Random House, 1956), pp. 58–71.

Bureaucracy in France

Bureaucratic concepts seem to be especially rigid in France, as indicated by the following quotations:

> . . . Because the French assume that men are hostile, they have protected themselves from *"les autres"* (the others) by a complicated network of legality, quite in keeping with the French tendency to limit and define carefully all aspects of man's existence. The resultant legal straightjacket quite naturally inhibits changes.

> . . . On the other hand, we must note here that in France it is never forgotten that these official rules are only man-made and therefore not worthy of the respect ostensibly given rules in the United States. In France one accomplishes the impossible by relying on personal contacts. On the unofficial level, where personal relations and not regulations guide behavior, the rules which so often strangle business deals and in general inhibit change are minimal and may even be successfully bypassed. The existence of this "system D" (the art of wrangling) favors social change in France by permitting individuals to accomplish things which would have been impossible were the paralyzing formalities of the official world respected.[9]

> Impersonal rules delimit, in great detail, all the functions of every individual within the organizations. They prescribe the behavior to be followed in all possible events. Equally impersonal rules determine who shall be chosen for each job and the career patterns that can be followed. In our two cases, as well as in most sectors of French public administration outside the higher executive class, two basic rules dominate the field. The first rule is that open competitive examinations (*concours*) govern promotion from one main category to another. The second rule is that seniority determines job allocation, transfer, and promotions within each main category.

> . . . As a consequence of the combination of these two sets of rules about job specification and job allocations, nothing seems to be left of the arbitrary whim and individual initiative of an organization member. The daily behavior of everyone, as well of his chances of having to perform a different routine later, can be predicted exactly. . . .

> Every member of the organization, therefore, is protected both from his supervisors and from his subordinates. He is, on the one hand, totally deprived of initiative and completely controlled by rules imposed on him from the outside. On the other hand, he is completely free from personal interference by any other individual—as independent, in a sense, as if he were a nonsalaried worker.[10]

Michel Crozier also stressed that "organizational progress has made it possible to be more tolerant of the personal needs and idiosyncrasies

---

[9] Lawrance Wylie, *In Search of France*, Stanley Hoffman, ed. (Cambridge, Mass.: Harvard University Press, 1963).

[10] Michel Crozier, *The Bureaucratic Phenomenon* (Chicago: University of Chicago Press, 1964), pp. 187–192.

of individual members . . ." and, on the other hand, cultural sophistication "has increased the individual's capacity for accommodation and at
the same time, as a consequence, his possibilities of independence."[11]

Bureaucracy in HEW

The following perceptive description of bureaucracy at work in a
large government agency illustrates the general points made above:[12]

> Each agency in the Department of Health, Education and Welfare
> is a separate and busy world. There is little communication among
> them. Each is made up of an assortment of related programs, and these
> determine the agency's personality, character, size, wealth, power, and
> associates.
>
> There are 1400 separate, definable domestic programs administered
> by the Federal government today, and HEW has 323 of them. Each
> is a separate cell in the corporate body of the Department. Each was
> built and is sustained by a special interest group or a coalition of interest
> groups, usually led by a professional specialty. Each therefore has its
> own particularistic pattern of behavior.
>
> Most programs have ties to the "outside world" that are as strong,
> if not stronger, than the ties to their home agency. The exception is
> the Social Security Administration which is a tightly-knit, highly disci-
> plined, unitary organization which receives political support from a broad
> spectrum of outside interest groups.
>
> The interest group or specialty might be relatively broad, like voca-
> tional education, or relatively narrow, like veterinary medicine, but it
> will be characterized by professionalism. The program administrators
> at the Federal level are usually in the top rank of the profession. In
> some fields, experience at the State level is considered a prerequisite
> for appointment to national office. The ties between local, state, and
> federal officials within a "program" area are generally closer than rela-
> tionships among different program directors within a single agency.
> Intergovernmental programs tend to be vertical and self-contained, like
> separate cylinders thrust through a 3-layer cake of government.
>
> Looking at the HEW organization chart, we assume that the Secretary
> possesses the greatest amount of authority, the Assistant Secretaries
> next, the Agency heads next, and so on down the line. People who
> occupy these positions usually *expect* to have such authority. But in
> practice, they find they do not. Real power lies on the bottom layer,
> within the individual programs.
>
> The upper layers do not usually initiate policy. That is done by
> interest groups operating in collaboration with Congressional subcom-
> mittees and bureaucratic "programs." The upper layers of government

---

[11] Ibid., pp. 296–314.

[12] Elsa A. Porter, "Organizational Renewal: The Untapped Potential of PPBS,"
paper prepared for Economics 2540 (Planning & Program Budgeting, Professor
Arthur Smithies), Harvard University, June 1, 1971, pp. 13–18.

can only moderate the making of policy. They can blunt or sharpen a program, strengthen or weaken it, nourish it or kill it. They have responsibility first, for judging the mix and strength of programs needed for larger, collective social purposes, and second for helping those programs to function most efficiently and effectively. They represent larger communities of interest than the single-minded programs.

The Agency and Bureau heads have a different kind of job. Their task is both to integrate the work of programs within their jurisdiction and to give impetus to their development. They are literally "men-in-the-middle." They may belong to a professional interest group, but their loyalties are tempered by larger political responsibilities.

Their political lines of allegiance run both vertically, up to the President, and horizontally, across to the Congressional committee and sub-committee chairmen who share administrative power with the top executives. The vertical line tends to be more tenuous than the horizontal. Presidents come and go, while committee chairmen stay on. Moreover, heavier support tends to come from the committees, which are already committed to the programs and have no obligation to make difficult choices.

It should be emphasized that the foregoing paragraphs are not intended to be an adequate description of a bureaucracy. Rather, they have two main purposes: (1) to emphasize the fact that "bureaucracy" is not a dirty word; it is a necessary condition in most large and complex organizations, whether they are profit-oriented or nonprofit; and (2) to sketch some of the characteristics of the bureaucratic organization that affect the management control process.

THE GOVERNING BOARD

In most organizations, top management is responsible to a governing board, at least some of whose members are not full-time employees of the organizations. In a corporation, this is the board of directors. In nonprofit organizations, it may be a board of trustees, a board of regents, or a "watchdog" committee of a legislature. Some of the functions of this board relate to the management control process. In particular, the board usually approves the program and the budget proposed by management, and it takes notice of the extent to which actual operations deviate from the approved plans.

Traditional Board Functions

The depth in which governing boards become involved in these matters varies widely. Mace's study, for example, indicates that boards of directors of many corporations take a quite perfunctory view of their responsibilities and essentially rubber stamp the proposals of management.[13] Even so, the board almost certainly would act if it should discover that the corporation was in trouble, and the profit measure usually provides an easily understood warning of such trouble (with certain notable exceptions, such as Penn Central).

The governing board of a nonprofit organization, likewise, as an absolute minimum has the responsibility of acting when the organization is in trouble. Since there is no profit measure to provide an obvious warning, the personal appraisal by board members of the health of the organization is much more important in a nonprofit organization than in a profit-oriented corporation. In order to have a sound basis for such an appraisal, board members need to spend a considerable amount of time learning what is going on in the organization, and they need to have enough expertise to understand the significance of what they learn.

Many governing boards do an inadequate job of this. There is not even a general recognition that this is the board's responsibility. In universities, for example, the following is widely quoted: "The function of a Board is to hire a president and then back him, period."[14] In hospitals, boards tend to be dominated by physicians, who are qualified to oversee the quality of care, but who may neither have the expertise, nor are willing to devote the time to check up on the effectiveness and efficiency of hospital management. In government organizations at all levels, auditors check on compliance with the statutory rules on spending, but very few overseeing agencies pay any attention to how well the management performs its functions. Although legislative committees look for headline-making sins, many committees do not have the staff or the inclination to arrive at an informed judgment on management.

A detailed analysis of 7,000 board actions recorded in the minutes of over 100 meetings by 19 trustee boards of public colleges and universities showed that only 6 percent of the decisions were planning decisions. Most actions were routine decisions on administrative and operational matters, and about 25 percent of these were ratifications of decisions previously made by the administration.[15]

In a profit-oriented corporation, the board represents the interests of the stockholders. In a nonprofit organization, the board presumably

[13] Myles Mace, *Directors: Myth and Reality* (Boston: Harvard University, Graduate School of Business Administration, Division of Research, 1971).

[14] Perhaps because the academic environment nourishes writing, more has been written about college and university trustees than about other types of governing boards. Orley R. Herron's *The Role of the Trustee* (Scranton, Pa.: International Textbook Company, 1969) contains much good material and also a comprehensive bibliography. For the purpose of the present book, the classic is still Beardsley Ruml and Donald H. Morrison, *Memo to a College Trustee* (New York: McGraw Hill, 1959).

[15] This study was conducted by the Center for Research and Development in Higher Education at the University of California, Berkeley, and summarized by the Assistant Director of that organization, James G. Partridge, in *AGB Reports* (Berkeley, Calif.: Association of Governing Boards of Universities and Colleges, March 1974), pp. 20–27.

should represent a broader interest; in general, it should represent the interest of the public at large. When the board represents the interests of specific clients (such as physicians in hospitals), or of large donors (as is the case with some university boards), or bondholders (as is the case with many public authorities), it is unlikely that the public interest is adequately considered.

Emerging Board Functions

In recent years, some change in the "hands-off" attitude of governing boards has become discernible. There is much talk, and some action, about the necessity of board members spending more time on their job; of having regular visits to university campuses; of having meetings of the whole board, or of committees of the board, more often than quarterly; and in general of becoming better informed about what is going on. Boards are beginning to exchange information with other boards, so as to obtain a basis of comparing their own organizations with others. In part, this interest has been stimulated by the fact that an increasing number of Boards have been sued, or threatened with suit, for not discharging their legal duties.

With respect to the management control process, the attitude is growing that the board should be actively involved in four activities:

1. *Formulating programs.* Although the initiation and analysis of proposed new programs is the responsibility of the management, board members should be actively involved in at least the final stages of the process, so that the board can have an effective input before the proposal is placed before it formally for final decision.

2. *Approving budgets.* Most of the budgetary process takes place within the organization. It is desirable that the board set general guidelines that govern the preparation of the budget and that a board committee review carefully the proposed budget before it is presented to the board for decision.

3. *Review of current performance.* The board should receive reports of current performance, including both financial performance and also the quality of services rendered. For the latter purpose, some mechanism that provides for communications from clients directly to the board is desirable. These reports should be analyzed so that danger signals are identified and appropriate questions asked of the administration.

4. *In-depth reviews.* From time to time, the board should initiate and participate in intensive reviews of the organization's activities, as a whole, or of important facets thereof. Some boards have staffs that do this work. Others hire outside consulting firms. One comment along these lines suggests that:

> No management has the capacity for impersonal and objective self-appraisal. It cannot evaluate objectively its own management philosophy,

its own structure, its use of decision-making techniques, or its allocation of resources and people to move the organization toward its goal. I suggest, therefore, that it is a prime responsibility of the board to periodically audit the organization structure and the processes of management to ensure that the corporation is healthy in these respects. Directors readily accept the responsibility of employing accountants to guarantee the fiscal health of the enterprise, but precious few ever carry out a methodical audit of management quality—and this can have even greater effect on the future of the enterprise, especially if there is the right breadth of experience and judgement on the board.[16]

This suggestion must be implemented with great care so as to avoid an infringement on management prerogatives.

Size and Composition of Boards

A board, or indeed any group, with more than about a dozen members cannot discuss many issues thoroughly. A larger board can be effective if most of the work is delegated to committees, including an executive committee that makes decisions that in a small board would be made by the board itself. Such an arrangement will work only if the full board is willing to accept most committee recommendations without lengthy debate.

The general rule for selecting board members used to be that a candidate should have at least one, and preferably two, of three criteria: Work, Wisdom, and Wealth. With the decreasing importance of private, individual giving as a source of support, and the increasing recognition of the board's role in governance, the third W has become less important. Board members are expected to be willing to work, that is, to spend an adequate amount of time on board matters, and to have wisdom. A few boards have been able to find professional trustees; that is, persons who serve on a number of boards and who devote substantially full time to board activities. "Amateur" board members often can rely considerably on the judgment of these professionals, especially in their impressions about how well the organization is performing compared with other organizations.

Some governing boards, such as those for hospitals in Florida, are elected; however, it is unlikely that the characteristics that get a person elected to such a board correspond to the characteristics necessary to render sound judgments about the organization.

Obtaining Client Viewpoints

The board needs to obtain the views of the clients that the organization serves. One device that is useful for this purpose is an advisory

---

[16] E. Everett Smith, as quoted in *The Wall Street Journal* (February 7, 1973), p. 4.

council, consisting of a cross section of the organization's clientele. This can be a relatively large body, and it can meet infrequently, perhaps once or twice a year. Although it may make some concrete recommendations for board action, its main function is to communicate client attitudes about the organization. Many member-oriented organizations have such an advisory group, and such groups have been legislated in connection with certain housing, welfare, and similar government programs.

An alternative approach is to have one or a few client representatives on the board itself. Many colleges and universities experimented with this in the early 1970s by adding one or more students to their boards, but this practice has not become widespread.

Staff Assistance

Few governing boards have staff assistance. The practice has begun, however, in the case of boards that supervise the provision of higher education in certain states. These staffs report to the head of the board. They make possible a more thorough analysis of proposals and reports of current performance than is possible when the board members attempt such analyses themselves.

TOP MANAGEMENT

Most organizations have a Number One person, who is the boss, the chief executive officer. In a very few organizations, authority is divided between two persons, or among a small top-management group, but these are exceptions to the rule and usually are not successful.[17] In most business organizations there is no doubt that the Number One person has responsibility for everything. On that person's desk, as on President Truman's, there is at least figuratively the sign, "The Buck Stops Here."

In some nonprofit organizations, the Number One person does not have such overall responsibility. The Secretary of State typically regards his responsibility as foreign policy, but not what is called the "administration" of the State Department. ("Administration," as used here, seems to mean the operation of the support functions of the Department, rather than a term that is synonymous with management, which is the usual context.) In their study, *Programming Systems and Foreign Affairs Leadership*, Mosher and Harr described this phenomenon:

> . . . Secretaries of State and their Under Secretaries are not chosen or appraised on the basis of their managerial competence. They are

---

[17] According to *Newsweek* (February 26, 1973), the Corcoran Gallery of Art in Washington D.C. for four years was managed by two coequal persons, an "artistic director," and an "administrative director." This arrangement ended in 1972 when the two directors exchanged punches in public and then both resigned.

advisers to Presidents, proponents and defenders of the administration's policies before Congress and the public, negotiators with foreign powers, and fire-fighters, before they are managers. They are unlikely to be selected on the criterion of managerial talent. And if they are, they are unlikely to have the time to exercise it. Those few who have been selected with a view to managerial competence have not left particularly distinguished reputations in the Department of State. Rusk, Ball, and Katzenbach have come close to fulfilling the approved roles in the Department. But none has exhibited much sustained interest in the *management* of the foreign affairs agencies or indeed of the Department itself.[18]

Presidents of universities may say that they are the leaders of a "community of scholars," and that they should not soil their hands by becoming involved in other aspects of university management, particularly the "business" aspects (although this attitude is much less prevalent today than it was a generation ago). The minister of a church may feel that it is inappropriate to become involved in temporal matters. The Number One person in a hospital often has the title of "medical director," which has the implication of lack of involvement in nonmedical matters.

The principal reasons for this narrow view of the responsibility of top management seem to be, in some organizations, the dominance of professionals and, in other organizations, the fact that the Number One person is politically appointed. Since the management control process essentially attempts to insure that the organization carries out the wishes of top management, the process is obviously ineffective if top management has no involvement or interest in certain aspects of the organization's affairs.

The notion that the Number One person is not responsible for everything is, fortunately, much less prevalent than it was a few decades ago. It is becoming recognized that when the top scientist is made head of a research/development organization, the organization may "lose a good scientist and gain a poor manager." The Number One person should be the best manager available, all things considered, and this does not usually mean the person most technically skilled in the work that the organization does.

In some organizations, it is feasible to divide top management responsibility between two persons. The Number One person is "Mr. Outside," responsible for overall policy formulation and for relations with the outside world; the Number Two person is "Mr. Inside," responsible for operations. This is the essential idea of the British parliamentary system; the Number One person is appointed by the party in power, and the Number Two person, the permanent undersecretary, is responsible for carrying out policies for whatever party is in power. Such a

---

[18] Frederick C. Mosher and John E. Harr, *Programming Systems and Foreign Affairs Leadership* (New York: Oxford University Press, 1970), p. 216.

division of responsibility exists to a certain extent in U.S. government agencies, but in general it is not as well accepted or as widespread here as in the United Kingdom. A two-headed organization can be effective if, but only if, there is a close relationship between the two persons, and a clear understanding that Number One will not overrule Number Two in disputes relating to operations.

Management Style

Managers differ as to their style, and the management control system should be consistent with the style of the current chief executive officer.[19] Although this is not the place to discuss such differences in style, the following quotation suggests how one outstanding manager, Robert S. McNamara, viewed the job of Secretary of Defense:[20]

> In many respects the role of a public manager is similar to that of a private manager. In each case he may follow one of two alternative courses. He can act either as a judge or as a leader. As the former he waits until subordinates bring him problems for solution, or alternatives for choice. In the latter case, he immerses himself in his operation, leads and stimulates an examination of the objectives, the problems and the alternatives. In my own case, and specifically with regard to the Department of Defense, the responsible choice seemed clear.
>
> . . . Some critics today worry that our democratic, free societies are becoming overmanaged. I would argue that the opposite is true. As paradoxical as it may sound, the real threat to democracy comes not from overmanagement, but from undermanagement. To undermanage reality is not to keep it free. It is simply to let some force other than reason shape reality. That force may be unbridled emotion; it may be greed; it may be aggressiveness; it may be hatred; it may be ignorance; it may be inertia; it may be anything other than reason. But whatever it is, if it is not reason that rules man, then man falls short of his potential.
>
> Vital decision-making, particularly in policy matters, must remain at the top. This is partly, though not completely, what the top is for. But rational decision-making depends on having a full range of rational options from which to choose, and successful management organizes the enterprise so that process can best take place. It is a mechanism whereby free men can most efficiently exercise their reason, initiative, creativity, and personal responsibility. The adventurous and immensely satisfying task of an efficient organization is to formulate and analyze these options.
>
> It is true enough that not every conceivable complex human situation

---

[19] For an interesting analysis of differences in the management styles of Presidents Roosevelt, Truman, Eisenhower, Kennedy, Johnson, and Nixon, *see* Richard T. Johnson, *Managing the White House* (New York: Harper & Row, 1974).

[20] Robert S. McNamara, *The Essence of Security: Reflections in Office* (New York: Harper & Rowe, 1968).

can be fully reduced to lines on a graph, or to percentage points on
a chart, or to figures on a balance sheet. But all reality can be reasoned
about, and not to quantify what can be quantified is only to be content
with something less than the full range of reason.

Compensation

As indicated in Chapter 3, the compensation for higher level management jobs in nonprofit organizations tends to be inadequate; consequently, the calibre of people filling these jobs tends to be lower than
that of people in corresponding jobs in profit-oriented organizations (except where the inadequate pay is offset by power and prestige). In
recent years, compensation of managers has improved,[21] but many governing boards do not yet appreciate the fact that spending a few tens
of thousands of additional dollars to acquire outstanding management
skill can have a very high payoff in increased effectiveness and efficiency.

MANAGEMENT ASSISTANTS

As indicated in an earlier section, the adherence to formal rules and
procedures that is characteristic of a bureaucracy is necessary to the
efficient functioning of any large organization. The personality traits
that make for success in such an organization are traits of conformance,
rather than of innovation. Thus, although a bureaucracy is essential
for the conduct of ongoing operations, it is not a good mechanism for
evolving new strategies or programs. If the organization is to adapt
to changes in its environment, it needs some different arrangement.

One way of solving this problem is to have staff assistants to key
managers, keep them away from day-to-day operating problems, and
charge them with developing new ideas. In order to create such a staff,
the manager usually must go outside the existing organization because
experienced members of the operating organization are too thoroughly
steeped in the existing procedures and know too many reasons why
these rules should not be changed, and also because they are advocates
of current programs. Possible sources are bright, fairly young and inexperienced people almost fresh out of school; managers with business
experience, perhaps on loan from their business company; academic
people, on loan from their university; recently retired executives; people
from consulting firms; and, of course, people lured from similar jobs
in other agencies. Small organizations might use one such person on
a part time basis.

If these staff assistants are to be effective, the managers must make

---

[21] In discussing this problem in 1952, one of us felt that the top salaries in government research laboratories should be approximately quadrupled (*see* Robert N.
Anthony, *Management Control in Industrial Research Organizations* [Boston: Division of Research, Harvard Business School], Chapter 14.) His feeling currently is
that top salaries should be approximately doubled.

sure that they are readily accessible, that they are able to obtain information from anywhere in the organization, and that they are insulated from the influence of operating personnel. The use of such a staff will be discussed further in Chapter 8.

THE CONTROLLER

The person responsible for the design and operation of the management control system is here called the "controller." In practice, the person may have other titles, such as administrative officer or chief accountant.[22]

The idea that the controller has a broader responsibility than merely "keeping the books" is a fairly recent one in profit-oriented organizations, and it is not yet well accepted in many nonprofit organizations. Not too long ago, controllers, who were then invariably called "chief accountants," were expected to confine their activities to collecting and reporting historical data. With the development of formal management control systems and the emphasis on information needed for planning and decision making, the controller's function has broadened.

Notwithstanding the broadened responsibilities, the controller remains, or should remain, a staff person. Decisions about management control should be made by the line managers, not by the staff. The job of the staff is to provide information that will facilitate making good decisions. In an organization whose Number One person is unwilling to assume overall responsibility, an operating manager with a problem of inadequate resources may be told, "Go see the controller." In making such a statement, the top manager abrogates line responsibility, and the controller is put in the position of acting in a line capacity. The controller then, de facto, becomes a manager, with a corresponding diminution in the responsibility of the person who nominally is charged with management. This usually leads to less than optimum management of the whole organization.

In some government agencies, this tendency for the controller to assume line responsibility became quite strong in the 1940s and 1950s. This was usually a consequence of top management's reluctance to accept overall responsibility. The controller, or more specifically the "budget officer," was permitted to make many decisions regarding the allocation of resources. With the "power of the purse," the budget officer became one of the most powerful persons in the organization. It has been said that in some large military installations, the Commanding Officer was principally in charge of ceremonies, and the real boss was the budget officer. With the current tendency to select a good manager as the Number One person, the role of the budget officer has, fortunately, become more like the staff role that it should be.

---

[22] In some organizations, the word is spelled "comptroller," but this is an erroneous spelling, with no basis in etymology, and is, in any event, pronounced as if it were spelled "controller." (Pronouncing it "*compt . . .*" is incorrect.)

When the controller or budget officer assumed the role of a line manager, the control system was usually designed to facilitate the controller's own work. Such a system slighted the needs of operating managers; that is, it did not provide them the information necessary to do their jobs. Consequently, operating managers created their own informal information systems—called a "desk drawer set of books"—because the data were kept there rather than in the formal accounting records. All in all, this was not a good situation, and the practice is dying out.

The role of the controller in the design and installation of management control systems will be discussed in more detail in Chapter 13.

OTHER STAFF

In organizations in which the Number One person is not in all respects the boss, other staff units tend to assume line functions similar to that described above for the controller. The personnel staff, for example, may make decisions about hiring, assignment, and promotion of personnel, quite independently of the wishes of top management. This can impede effective management control. Top management presumably decides on the programs that the organization should undertake and on the resources that are allocated to each program. Personnel is a resource, and in many organizations personnel constitutes more than half the total resources, as measured in money. If the personnel staff makes independent decisions as to the size and composition of various organization units, decisions made by top management can be effectively annulled. Similarly, the purchasing staff can overrule the judgment of line managers, and forbid the procurement of items that are necessary to get the job done.

This is not to imply that staff agencies have no role in the management control process, for they do have an important role. They recommend to line management policies that are within their area of expertise. When these policies have been approved by line management, the staff is at least partly responsible for seeing to it that they are implemented and thereafter adhered to. For example, without some restraining mechanism, operating managers may tend to hire more personnel than are needed ("empire building") and to promote persons to positions for which they are not quite qualified. It is appropriate, therefore, that there be procedures governing the approval of proposed increases in staff; that there be job descriptions that include, among other things, the proper salary levels for each job; and that there be policies governing promotion. It is also appropriate that the personnel staff play a large role in designing these policies and procedures and maintaining surveillance over the extent to which the operating managers adhere to them. In performing this function, however, the personnel staff is presumably carrying out decisions made by top management; that is, it is acting on behalf of top management. Furthermore, it is subject to being overruled by top management when circumstances warrant. The staff members do not themselves manage the organization.

The Civil Service Commission, for example, presumably is a staff agency acting for the President. The President issues Executive Orders that set forth policies. These rules are implemented through the Civil Service Commission's Regulations. The Commission judges the qualifications of persons to be appointed to positions and determines the fitness of applicants by means of open, competitive examinations. But the Commission does not have the authority to place persons on the payroll of the U.S. government (except on its own staff). Appointments are made by the heads of the various departments and agencies or by nomination by the President and confirmation by the Senate. And although officials of the Commission do influence the issuance of Executive orders and often even draft them, the orders are the President's responsibility, not the Commission's.[23]

Size of Staffs

It is extraordinarily difficult to generalize about the size of staffs in nonprofit organizations, for some organizations have staffs that are far too large, while others have inadequate staffs. At one extreme is the 30,000 people who work in the Pentagon, which is a huge staff, but only a small fraction of the total staff of the Department of Defense. Most observers agree that this staff is too large, but no one seems able to do anything to reduce it substantially. At the other extreme, we were told that in 1970 the State of Texas had a staff consisting of four persons responsible for analyzing the performance of all state agencies; this is inadequate.

How can it be that some managements tolerate proliferation of staff activities, while others function with almost no staff help? This is an important question, for which we have no adequate answer. It may be that the size of staffs is unduly influenced by custom and tradition. In some organizations, especially in the Federal government, "everyone knows" that a manager requires a certain level of staff support; the need for it is not questioned. In other organizations, "everyone knows" that staff people are an unnecessary luxury.

OPERATING MANAGERS

The principal differences between the roles of the operating managers—the persons on the firing line—in a nonprofit organization and

---

[23] For a more thorough discussion of the Civil Service Commission and its relationship to the Executive Branch, see Bernard H. Baum, *Decentralization of Authority in a Bureaucracy* (Englewood Cliffs, N.J.: Prentice-Hall, Inc., 1961).

their counterparts in a profit-oriented organization stem from the absence of a profit measure, as described in Chapter 3. Ideally, an operating manager should be told (after appropriate discussion with the manager) *what* to accomplish, but not how to do the job. In a profit-oriented organization—or at least in those responsibility centers of such an organization in which outputs and inputs can be measured—considerable latitude can safely be given to the operating manager in deciding what resources to use in doing the job. If poor decisions are made, these are soon revealed through the signal of inadequate profits, and corrective action can be taken. Without such a signal, such latitude is dangerous. Thus, however distasteful this may be to operating managers in nonprofit organizations, it is generally desirable that they be permitted somewhat less discretion than their profit-oriented counterparts.

It follows that the budgeting process is extremely important in a nonprofit organization. When resource allocation decisions cannot safely be decentralized, the budget is an essential device for communicating how operating managers are expected to act. Operating managers in nonprofit organizations are justifiably required to adhere more closely to the approved budget than is the case in a profit-oriented company. This is a matter of degree and, as will be discussed in later chapters, some nonprofit organizations restrict the actions of operating managers unduly.

In general, decentralization is a good idea; that is, those who are close to "where the action is" are in the best positions to make operating decisions within policies prescribed by higher authority. One of the objectives of those who are seeking to improve management control systems is to facilitate more decentralization by providing better ways of assuring that top management's intentions are in fact carried out. The tendency toward decentralization is increasing in nonprofit organizations, but it must be recognized that because of the inherent limitations of the management control process in such organizations, it probably cannot be carried as far as in profit-oriented companies which can rely on the profit measure as a control device.

chapter five

The Control Structure:
Account Classification

A control system can be described in terms of (a) its structure, that is, what it looks like; and (b) its process, that is, what it does. In this and in the next chapter we focus on structure.

Three principal elements constitute a control structure: (1) there is a method of classifying information into categories, (2) there are rules governing the content of the information contained in each category, and (3) there are techniques for processing the information. In the present chapter we discuss the problem of classifying information into categories, and in Chapter 6 we discuss principles relating to the content of information. Techniques for processing information are not discussed at all; they are the same in nonprofit organizations as in profit-oriented organizations.

In accounting, the device used for classifying information is called an "account." The number and types of accounts determine the character of the information that is available from the system. Thus, if a company needs an accounting record of the amount of cash it has in total, it uses a single account, "Cash," whereas if it needs a record of the amount of cash in each of two different banks, it sets up an account for "Cash Bank A" and another for "Cash Bank B." The accounts are the smallest units of information. The amounts recorded in each account can be summarized in various ways by combining them with other accounts, but the system cannot provide information in more detail than that contained in the most detailed account. For example, if a company has accounts for Cash Bank A and Cash Bank B, it can obtain a summary of the total amount of cash simply by adding the amounts in these two accounts, but if another company has a single account for Cash, it cannot obtain from its accounts information about the cash in Bank A and the cash in Bank B. Thus, the selection of the proper account structure is crucial in the design of an accounting system.

In this description, we shall use the word "account" in a somewhat broader sense than it is used in accounting. An accounting system is generally restricted to (*a*) historical information and (*b*) monetary information; whereas we are interested also in (*c*) estimates of future amounts and (*d*) nonmonetary information.

OVERVIEW OF THE STRUCTURE

INFORMATION NEEDS

A total system provides information for many purposes. By far the largest quantity of information is associated with certain necessary operating activities, such as the preparation of payrolls, keeping track of inventory, and paying bills. These activities are not part of the management control system as such, however, so we are not directly concerned with them here. They are of interest primarily because they provide raw data that can be used for management control purposes.

In designing a management control system, the needs of the following parties need to be considered:

a. Top managers, who need information as a basis for making policy decisions, particularly decisions regarding the balance among programs and the relation of programs to objectives. Top managers also need information on how the organization is performing.

b. Planners and analysts, who need information that will assist in estimating the benefits and costs of proposed programs.

c. Operating managers, who need information classified by responsibility centers because control is exercised through responsibility centers.

d. Outside agencies, who can require certain information (e.g., the Congress requires information from Executive Agencies). The system must be designed to supply this information, whether or not the organization needs it for its own purposes. Also, an organization may have an obligation to furnish certain information to the public, or it may believe that it is good public relations to furnish such information.

Conflicts Among Needs

The needs of these parties may conflict with one another, and the system must strike a balance among the conflicting needs. The system must also represent a balance between the users' needs for information and the cost of collecting and processing the information.

The two principal parts of the account structure are the program structure and the responsibility structure. The former is designed principally to meet the needs of planners and analysts, and the latter is designed principally to meet the needs of operating managers. The program structure emphasizes the full costs of carrying out programs, while the responsibility structure emphasizes the controllable costs of operating responsibility centers. Top management is interested in summaries drawn from both structures.

It follows that in designing a program structure, the needs of the planners should be given more weight than the needs of the operating managers. For example, a program structure usually cuts across lines of responsibility, even though such a structure is not as useful to operating managers as one that is consistent with lines of responsibility. Nevertheless, the system should reconcile both types of needs to the extent that this is feasible. Some information needed by planners that is inconsistent with that needed by operating managers (e.g., cost estimates that include prorated costs) may possibly be obtained outside the formal account structure.

In designing a responsibility structure, the needs of operating managers are paramount. Such a structure must be consistent with lines of responsibility, and this principle cannot be compromised to meet the needs of the planners.

In order to insure that these conflicts are resolved in the most equitable way, the system design team should not be dominated by people who represent the point of view of either the planners or the operating managers. Ideally, systems designers should be independent of both types of users and should weigh equally the arguments of each, but the optimum balance is difficult to achieve in practice.

TYPES OF ACCOUNTS

This section describes briefly the principal account categories that are included in a management control system, together with the relationship among these categories. A more detailed discussion is given in subsequent sections. The two most important categories are the program accounts and the responsibility accounts. The program structure is organized according to the programs, or activities, that the organization undertakes. The responsibility structure is organized according to responsibility centers. The program category is further divided into capital accounts and operating accounts. The responsibility category ordinarily contains only operating accounts. The significance of the distinction between these two types of accounts is explained in a following section.

Within each responsibility center, there are accounts for important expense elements (also called "object classes"). These show the nature of the resources that are used by the responsibility center: labor, material, and services of various types. There may also be accounts for "functional categories" within a responsibility center; these accounts collect information by functions that are common to many responsibility centers, such as maintenance. In certain responsibility centers, there may be cost accounts to collect detailed information on the cost of performing functions of the responsibility center. The cost accounting system is a subsidiary system, which is tied to the main system through appropriate control accounts.

Relation of Program and Responsibility Accounts. Although the program and responsibility categories are necessarily discussed separately, in the actual system they are closely related to one another. The relationship is indicated in Exhibit 5–1, which is based on the Department of Defense system. Hospital X is a responsibility center and is a part of Base A, which is a larger responsibility center. The illustration shows how the operating costs of Hospital X are a part of both the program

EXHIBIT 5–1
Program and Responsibility Structures
(amounts in $ thousands)

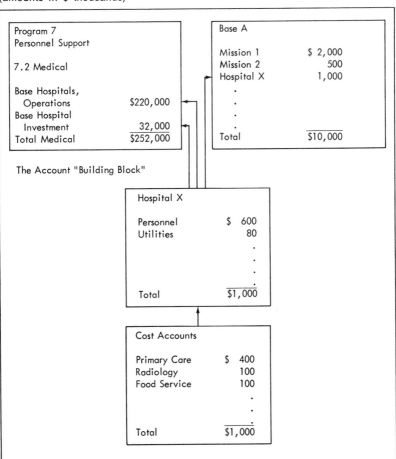

structure and the responsibility structure. In the program structure, the operating costs of Hospital X are part of the program element, Base Hospital Operations, while in the responsibility structure, the costs of Hospital X are a part of the total operating cost of Base A, on which Hospital X is located. The Commanding Officer of Base A is responsible for Hospital X and a number of other responsibility centers. The total cost of Hospital X therefore constitutes a basic "building block" in the sense that Hospital X costs, together with all building blocks having to do with base hospitals, can be aggregated to the Base Hospital Operations element in the program structure; and also Hospital X costs, together with all other building blocks related to Base A, can be aggregated to the Base A item in the responsibility structure.

Hospital X also has a set of expense elements, such as personnel and utilities, and a set of cost accounts, such as primary care and radiology. It could have accounts at a lower level of detail, such as the personnel costs of primary care. Information in these detailed accounts is used primarily by the management of Hospital X.

The important point is that at the lowest level, the level at which information is actually recorded, there are not two separate sets of accounts, one for programs and the other for responsibility centers. Instead, there is one set of accounts, which is aggregated in one way for program purposes and in another way for responsibility purposes.

Relation of Estimated and Historical Costs. The accounts also should be related to one another in the time dimension; that is, the structure that records estimated future costs which are used for planning the program should be consistent with the structure that is used to collect historical costs. In many systems, this relationship unfortunately does not exist. Plans are formulated according to a program structure, but this structure is then put aside, and information on actual spending is not collected in the program accounts; instead, it is collected only in responsibility center accounts. There are two serious defects in such a system. First, since the system does not collect historical costs by programs, it denies the program planners information which is important as a basis for estimating the future costs of programs. Second, management has no adequate way of ascertaining whether its program decisions are actually being implemented. If top management decides that $1 million should be spent on a certain program, it needs to know whether the organization is in fact carrying out this program at the level of effort that $1 million represents. It cannot find this out unless the records classify actual spending in terms of programs.

One may ask why a system with these defects is permitted to exist. The explanation is that the idea of a program structure is relatively new in nonprofit organizations. Many organizations have not yet had the time to make the changes that are necessary to permit the recording of historical costs by program categories. Such changes are complicated and time-consuming and involve the training of a great many people, both accountants and managers. In the Department of Defense, for example, a formal program structure was used for planning purposes beginning in 1962, but the conversion of the accounting system to one which collected costs by program categories did not take place until 1968, six years later.

Cost Accounts. Exhibit 5–1 also shows the relationship of cost accounts to the basic account building blocks. Hospitals need a detailed cost accounting system as an aid to hospital management, but information in this amount of detail is not needed either by those involved in the programming process or by those involved in the overall management of bases. There is therefore a subsidiary cost system designed to meet the special needs of hospital management. It is tied to the general system in the sense that the total costs in the cost accounts must be reconcilable with the total cost of Hospital X. In some systems, no such tie-in between the cost accounts and the general accounts is attempted. Such a cost system is called a "statistical"[1] system, rather than a "tied-in" system. Statistical systems tend to be inaccurate and hence of limited usefulness. Without the discipline that is associated with a tied-in system, there is no way of being certain that the recorded numbers actually are the costs; in particular, certain transactions may have slipped through the cracks and have not been counted at all.

> **Example:** The U.S. Office of Education requires each local education agency that receives Federal funds to submit annually a "Consolidated Program Information Report." This report contains six pages on which cost information is to be reported. Although terms are defined in excellent detail, there is no requirement that the cost data be obtained directly from an accounting system. The data are therefore suspect at best, and in many reports are of little value.

Special Accounts. The foregoing accounts are needed by management. In addition to these accounts, the system may also collect information that is required by outside agencies but which is not obtainable from the structures listed above. In these circumstances, a special set of accounts is required.

Asset and Liability Accounts. A nonprofit organization needs records of the assets that it owns and the liabilities that it owes. With the exception of the treatment of fixed assets, asset and liability accounts in a nonprofit organization are similar to those in a profit-oriented organization; they are not discussed further here. Fixed assets are discussed in the next section, and the related problem of depreciation is discussed in Chapter 6.

---

[1] The word "statistical" may suggest a sample, as contrasted with a complete set of costs. As used here, however, a statistical system means simply a system that is not tied in. Supposedly, it is a complete system, and not a sample.

Fund Accounts. Finally, there is a set of fund accounts. These are peculiar to nonprofit organizations; they have no counterpart in the systems of business firms. They are discussed in a subsequent section.

Number of Accounts. The fact that several categories of accounts are listed above may give the impression that the control structure in a nonprofit organization is unduly complicated, and this impression may be strengthened as additional details are discussed in later sections of this chapter. Actually, the complications are not as great as they may appear. The effort required to record information in a system is not primarily a function of the number of accounts that the system contains; rather, it is a function of the number of transactions that must be recorded. The unit of recording is the individual transaction: the salary cost of one employee, the issuance of the material on one requisition, and so on. It makes little difference whether an individual transaction is recorded in one out of 100 accounts or in one out of 10,000 accounts; it must in any event be recorded in one account. With the advent of computers, the mechanical task of classifying transactions becomes relatively unimportant. Control systems can indeed be unnecessarily complex, but the complexity is likely to arise for reasons other than the sheer number of accounts.

CAPITAL COSTS AND OPERATING COSTS

Throughout the system, a clear distinction should be made between capital costs and operating costs. Costs associated with the acquisition of equipment and real property are capital costs. Such costs give rise to long-lived assets from which benefits will accrue over a long period of time in the future. Operating costs, or *expenses,* measure the resources consumed in operating an activity for a given period of time, such as a month or a year. They include labor costs, materials consumed in use, and services received.

Capital costs and operating costs must be clearly separated from one another because they are managed in fundamentally different ways. Operating costs benefit the current period and must be given appropriate attention in the current period. Capital costs are made for the purpose of benefiting future periods; they require separate attention primarily because of the strategic implications that these expenditures entail.

Although the desirability of separating capital costs and operating costs is generally recognized, in some systems not enough thought has been given as to how to make the separation. An operating manager generally prefers that a given item be classified as a capital cost because capital costs are not associated with current consumption and therefore are not related to current performance in the responsibility center. On the other hand, if too many costs are classified as capital costs, and if the acquisition of capital items is too strictly controlled, operating managers who are forbidden to make needed expenditures for capital items must resort to uneconomical subterfuges. Some examples from student reports:

> When I worked for the National Academy of Sciences as Resident Manager of their summer project facility, we were not allowed to make any investments; we couldn't buy anything that was not expendable. We therefore had to rent office machinery for the summer for about 90 percent of its list price. This went on for at least ten consecutive summers. (Gerald L. Swope)
>
> In the Los Angeles City Planning Department the acquisition of calculators was treated as an operating cost because of the department's failure to make a clear distinction between operating and capital items. The decision to purchase a calculator was based solely on whether the machine was acutely needed at the time of the request. Little thought was given to the potential usage over the life of the machine. Because a purchase could not be justified on the basis of a single year's usage, proposals were turned down year after year and as a result a great deal of personnel time was wasted in calculating manually. (Robin W. Sternbergh)
>
> During 1971, the Department of Corrections of the City of New York was refused permission to buy an ice machine for the facilities at Rikers Island because the $30,000 necessary was not available in the Capital Budget. Instead they were told to arrange an ice supply contract which would be funded from the Expense Budget. This cost the Department about $20,000 for one year. Conversely, adequate monies to properly maintain New York City parks are usually not available in the Expense Budget. As a result, the Parks Department will often provide no maintenance to a neighborhood park and then periodically renovate it with monies from the Capital Budget.

In general, an investment has a relatively long life and a significant unit cost. Each organization should have specific rules that adapt this general concept to its own situation.

A carefully spelled out distinction between capital costs and operating costs is essential in the responsibility structure; indeed, most responsibility structures deal only with operating costs and exclude capital expenditures entirely. The program structure includes both capital costs and operating costs, but they ordinarily should be shown separately. Although in the analysis of a proposed program, it is the total cost—the sum of capital and operating costs—that is relevant, nevertheless, differences in the timing of the expenditures for these two categories require that these costs be separated in the analysis. Capital costs typically are incurred once, at the inception of a program, whereas operating costs are incurred in a stream that extends over the life of the program.

Because planners know that both capital costs and operating costs are equally relevant for programming purposes, they tend to be a little impatient with the system builder's careful effort to draw a line between them. Such impatience indicates that they do not appreciate the crucial importance of this line for the purpose of controlling performance in responsibility centers.

Grants. If an organization makes grants, then these grants should constitute a third category of information, separate from capital costs and operating costs. This will insure that the amount of the grants, which are not part of the costs of operating the organization, will not get mixed up with operating costs and invalidate analyses of costs compared with outputs, or services rendered. Indeed, for some purposes, it is useful to consider grants as a measure of outputs, rather than as a cost item, which is a measure of inputs.

THE PROGRAM STRUCTURE

Uses of Program Information

Information from the program structure is used for one or more of the following purposes: (1) to facilitate decision making about programs, (2) to provide a basis of comparison of the costs and outputs of similar programs, (3) to set selling prices or provide a basis for reimbursement of costs. The structure should be designed to meet these needs. In this chapter, we shall discuss primarily structures designed to meet the first two of these needs, and shall defer to Chapter 7 a discussion of program structures that are useful for pricing purposes.

The information needed for one of these three purposes may differ from that needed by others. In that case, compromises in designing the structure may be required. In most situations, one of these purposes is clearly dominant, however, and the structure can be designed primarily to provide information needed for that purpose. In public-oriented organizations, the use of information as a basis for making decisions on programs tends to be by far the dominant purpose, whereas in many client-oriented organizations, pricing considerations tend to be dominant. If information is to be collected in a way that makes it comparable with information in other organizations, and if such a structure is inconsistent with the best structure for decision making or pricing purposes, then comparable data can be collected by other devices, such as a cost accounting system.

Program Structures for Decision Making

Every nonprofit organization exists to carry out programs. Many organizations are set up in such a way that each program is the responsibility of a distinct responsibility center. There is no problem in formulating a program structure for these organizations; the program structure is the same as the responsibility structure. Devising a sound program structure is a problem only in organizations in which programs cut across lines of responsibility. This problem first became serious in the 1960s when, following the lead of the Department of Defense, many organizations attempted to set up formal program structures.

In the Department of Defense, the need for a program structure was obvious. The lines of organizational responsibility ran to the Secretary of the Army, the Secretary of the Navy, and to the Secretary of the Air Force; whereas Defense programs cut across these lines. For example, the Department of Defense had a strategic program which was essentially related to a nuclear exchange with the Soviets and the Chinese, but part of this strategic mission was the responsibility of the Army (antiballistic missiles), part was the responsibility of the Navy (Polaris submarines), and part was the responsibility of the Air Force (strategic missiles and bombers). A mechanism that facilitated decision making about the strategic mission as a whole was necessary. The Defense Program Structure, in which Program 1 was Strategic Forces, provided such a mechanism.

When other organizations attempted to set up a program structure, however, they found that the selection of the right structure was a difficult task. In fact, several efforts to establish programming systems foundered because the program structure was not arranged in a way that facilitated management decision making. Consequently, managers did not find the new information useful and paid no attention to it. In other organizations the program structure consisted simply of new labels for existing account structures. This was particularly the case when the responsibility structure already provided an adequate basis for decision making. The effort was simply window dressing.

> ***Example:*** An article in the *Journal of Accountancy* (November 1972) extolled the virtues of program budgeting and claimed that it "could evoke greater understanding and support from the citizenry." The sample budget used in the article appears in Exhibit 5–2.
>
> As Jonathon A. Cunitz pointed out in a letter to the editor,[2] the last column of the Exhibit corresponds exactly to the former budget in which costs were divided by departments, and all the new format did was to assign each of these amounts to one of five columns. This was scarcely an innovation that provided significant new information to management, or which warranted an article in a journal.

Nature of the Structure

The program structure consists of three "layers." At the top are a relatively few *program categories* (sometimes called "major programs").

---

[2] *The Journal of Accountancy* (May 1973), p. 35.

EXHIBIT 5–2
How Not to Make a Program Structure

	Public Protection and Adjudication	Health	Community Environment	Social and Economic Improvement	Administration and Support	Total
Mayor's office					21,540	21,54
Controller					22,575	22,57
City clerk					18,821	18,82
City court					13,800	13,80
City council					38,780	38,78
City attorney					8,470	8,47
City engineer			22,675			22,67
Public works and safety			308,037			308,03
Electric department.			18,570			18,57
Fire department.	915,980					915,98
Human relations.				320		32
Police department.	739,800					739,80
Health department		40,792				40,79
Sanitation			188,000			188,00
Total General Fund	1,655,780	40,792	537,282	320	123,986	2,358,16

At the bottom are a great many *program elements;* these are the smallest units in which information is collected in program terms. In between are summaries of related program elements, which are here called *program subcategories.* In a simple system, there may be no need for program subcategories; program elements are aggregated directly into programs. In a complex organization, by contrast, there may be several levels of program subcategories. Some persons call these respective levels "subsubcategories," and so on, but such designations are not usually necessary.

The following from a large School District program structure illustrates these layers:

01 Early Childhood
02 Elementary Education
03 Junior High School Education
   031 Basic Education
      0311 English
      0312 Mathematics

The items numbered 01, 02, and 03 are program categories, or simply, programs. The main subdivision "031 Basic Education" is a program subcategory, and "0311 English" is a program element. The actual accounts are kept by program elements, and the other information is obtained by first aggregating program elements into program subcategories, and then aggregating program subcategories into program categories.

Criteria for Selecting Program Categories[3]

The primary purpose of the classification of major programs is to facilitate top management judgment on the allocation of resources. Similarly, the primary purpose of the classification into program categories is to facilitate middle management judgment on the allocation of resources within programs. The program structure should therefore correspond to the principal objectives of the organization. It should be arranged so as to facilitate making decisions having to do with the relative importance of these objectives. Stated another way, it should focus on the organization's outputs—what it achieves or intends to achieve—rather than on its inputs—what types of resources it uses, or on the *sources of its funds*. A structure that is arranged by types of resources (e.g., personnel, material, services) or by sources of support (e.g., in a university: tuition, legislative appropriations, gifts) is not a program structure.

The designation of major programs helps to communicate what the objectives of the organization are. The development of the management control structure may also clarify organizational purpose, and thus suggest improvements in the structure of the organization. Therefore, the program structure should not necessarily correspond to the *existing* categories on which decisions are based; rather, it should correspond to those categories which can reasonably be expected to be useful for decision making in the future.

The criterion that programs should be related to decision making is, of course, a general one. The following questions may suggest ways of making it more specific:

1. Is the structure output-oriented? Specifically, does it focus on what the agency does and/or the target groups that it exists to serve?

2. Does the structure permit management to decide to enlarge or decrease a program? Are the programs for which this can be done the programs that management actually wants to think about enlarging or decreasing?

3. Within a program, are there opportunities for trade-offs, that is, for different ways of achieving the objectives? Benefit/cost analysis, for example, is often feasible within a program, but rarely between programs.

4. Can management actually influence the scope and nature of the activities that are conducted for a designated program?

5. Is there an identifiable outside pressure group interested in a part of the organization's activities? If so, is there a program category or subcategory that corresponds to the interests of this group?

---

[3] This section is based in part on Office of Management and Budget *Bulletin 68-9*, and on Graeme M. Taylor "Program Structure Design for PPB Systems," in Harley H. Hinrichs and Graeme M. Taylor *Program Budgeting and Benefit-Cost Analysis* (Pacific Palisades, California: Goodyear Publishing Co., 1969).

6. When there are criticisms that not enough effort, or too much effort, is being devoted to a certain activity, can information on the validity of these criticisms be obtained from the program structure?

7. Does the structure identify all important activities, so that none are hidden from management's view? (For example, in a research organization if there is not a separate program for basic research, the pressures to devote resources to more attractive development projects will be strong and basic research may be slighted.)

8. Does the structure require a relatively small amount of cost allocation? If a large fraction of the program cost is an allocated cost, the structure is suspect.

9. Is the structure of some help to operating managers? As a minimum, it should never impede the work of operating managers.

Relation to Output Measures. If it is feasible to do so, it is desirable to structure program subcategories and program elements so that each can be associated with a *quantitative* measure of performance, that is of output. At the broad level of programs, however, no reliable measure of performance can be found in many situations.

Relation to Responsibility. Although there are advantages in relating program categories and subcategories to organizational responsibility, this criterion is less important than that of facilitating top management judgment. Sometimes the system's designers try to change the organization so that it fits the program structure. In general, this should not be done. The system exists to serve the organization, not *vice versa.* Changes in organizational responsibility should be made if, but only if, such changes help the organization get its job done better. Sometimes the system designer does uncover a situation which would be improved by a reorganization. If the system designer can convince management, fine; otherwise, the system should be designed to fit the organization as it exists.

Although the program structure need not, and ordinarily will not, match the organization structure, there should be some person who has identifiable responsibility for each program category or subcategory. In some agencies, each program category has its own program manager. This is the *matrix* type of organization, the matrix consisting of program managers in one dimension and functionally organized responsibility centers in the other dimension. Program managers may have other responsibilities, and they may have to call on other parts of the organization for most of the work that is to be done on their program. The program managers are advocates of their programs and are held accountable for the performance of their programs. In other agencies, there may be managers for subcategories within program categories, even though there is no overall manager for the program. This is the case in the Department of Defense, for example; no one is manager of strategic forces, but there is a manager for the Army subcategory, the Navy subcategory, and the Air Force subcategory.

Number of Programs. The number of major programs in an organization is approximately 10. The rationale for this number is that top management cannot weigh the relative importance of a large number of categories, and the programs should be limited to the number that management can so weigh. There are many exceptions to this generalization, however. The number of program subcategories can vary widely in different situations.

Direct and Support Programs

Programs can be classified as either (*a*) direct or (*b*) support. (The terms "independent" and "dependent" are also used.) *Direct programs* are those directly related to the organization's objectives (in a college, these would be the instruction and research programs). *Support programs* are those that service more than one other program (in a college, the maintenance of grounds is an example). In making decisions about the allocation of resources, management attention will be focused primarily on the direct programs. Within limits, the amount of resources required for the support programs is roughly dependent on the size and character of the direct programs. This does not mean that no attention should be given to support programs, for there is often considerable room for innovation and increased efficiency within support programs.

Administration

Ordinarily, there should be a program category for administration. This support program might well include certain miscellaneous program elements which, although not strictly administrative in character, do not belong logically in other programs and are not important enough to set up as separate program categories. Alternatively, these miscellaneous program elements might be grouped in a separate program category.

The rationale for a separate program for administration is that top management usually wants to give special attention to administrative activities. As a general rule, as large a fraction as possible of the total resources of the organization should be devoted to direct programs and as small a fraction as possible to administration. In the absence of special attention, administrative activities tend to grow, along the lines laid down in Parkinson's first law.

Some Examples

The U.S. Postal Service has a very difficult problem in deciding on its program structure. For some purposes, particularly for decisions on pricing, it needs information on classes of mail. For other purposes, it needs information summarized by functions performed. Thus, it must choose between two essentially different structures:[4]

A. *Classes of Mail*   B. *Functions*

1. First Class Mail.   1. Collection and Delivery of Mail.
2. Second Class Mail.   Collection.
3. Third Class Mail.   Processing.
4. Fourth Class Mail.   Transportation.
5. Support Programs.   Delivery.
                                             Special Services.
                                         2. Non-Mail Services.
                                         3. Supporting Activities.

Neither choice is entirely satisfactory. The classification of functions is perhaps preferable because it seems to match more closely the way in which major decisions are made. If this structure is used, information on the cost of classes of mail must be collected in a separate structure, but this seems to be feasible.

The Peace Corps used the following program categories:

1. Program Direction and Support.
2. Food Supply (the problem of hunger).
3. Education (the problem of ignorance).
4. Health and Sanitation (the problem of sickness and disease).
5. Public and Private Institutions (the problem of nation building).[5]

The implication of this structure was that top management would decide on the amount of resources to be allocated to each of these program categories. In fact, however, top management did not ordinarily make decisions in these terms. Instead, it decided how many volunteers would be assigned to a given country, and it often did not have any idea about what problems the volunteers would tackle when they arrived in that country. A program structure that was essentially geographical would have been more useful in the decision-making process.

The State Department, by contrast, set up its structure by regions and by countries within regions, which corresponded to the way in which decisions are made about the allocation of State Department resources.

Sometimes, programs structured by service provided are useful; for example, in Memphis, Tennessee, the reasoning was that since the purpose of local government is to provide service to its citizens, the program structure should be arranged by "citizen service programs;" i.e., programs that meet the needs of citizens. The recommended programs were:

---

[4] *Program Budgeting*, p. 48.
[5] Ibid., p. 121

Criminal Justice

Transportation

Public Health

Utilities

Public Safety

Education

Welfare and Security

Administration[6]

Culture and Recreation

Similarly, the major programs for the Canadian Government (called by them "functions") are delineated by services and they are:

1. General Government.
2. Foreign Affairs.
3. Defense.
4. Economic Measures.
5. Social Measures.
6. Education, Culture, and Recreation.

In a similar vein, recommended programs for State Governments are:

1. Education.
2. Health.
3. Social and Employment Services.
4. Public Protection.
5. Administration of Justice.
6. Resource Protection and Development.
7. Transportation.
8. General Government.[7]

Conflict Between Program Structures

The development of a sound program structure is an important task. Once it has been implemented, changes in the structure are difficult to make, so much effort is warranted in deciding at the outset on what the most useful structure is. This task can be frustrating, however, because two or more alternative structures may have almost equal merit, and each may have strong advocates in the organization. In these circumstances, it is usually possible to satisfy the needs of each group by structuring program categories according to one concept, subcategories according to an alternative concept, and using program elements or the responsibility structure for other alternatives.

> *Example:* In designing the program structure for a state Division of Special Education, several possibilities were considered. One was by type of disability or target group (e.g., visually handicapped, deaf,

---

[6] Touche Ross and Co., *Management Summary Report to the City Commission* (City of Memphis, October 1967), p. 12. This structure should probably be expanded to meet revenue sharing needs as illustrated below.

[7] Management Analysis Center, Inc., *Report on the State of Alaska,* (Cambridge, Mass.: 1971).

speech handicap, emotionally disturbed, mentally disturbed). Another was by geographic region within the state. Another was by objectives (e.g., improvement of curriculum, improvement of teacher training, improvement of foster homes, improvement of medical services). A solution is to use a target group as the basis for program categories, and to have subcategories for objectives within each of the program categories. Information on regions could be obtained either by program elements or by responsibility centers, depending on whether there were identifiable organization units in each geographic region.[8]

Program Elements

A program element represents some definable activity or related group of activities that the organization carries on, either directly in order to accomplish the organization's objective or indirectly in support of other program elements.

If feasible, a program element should be the responsibility of a single person. In any event, it is essential that program elements be related to the responsibility of a relatively small number of persons, and that the respective sphere of responsibility of each be specified. Items for which responsibility is widely diffused, such as "long-distance telephone calls," are not satisfactory program elements. Such items should appear not as program elements but as functional categories or expense elements in the responsibility structure. Management decisions about program elements cannot be enforced unless they are related to personal responsibility. A congruence between individual responsibility and program elements also leads to an increased sense of personal identification with programs which should result in a greater degree of commitment on the part of responsibility center managers. Management of an organization is difficult when the program structure is at "right angles" with the responsibility structure. The existence of such a situation is a symptom either that the program structure is incorrect or that the organization structure needs to be changed.

Exhibit 5–3 shows a program structure which, at least in elementary schools, probably does not correspond at all to the organization structure and therefore is of doubtful usefulness. Teachers may spend identifiable amounts of time on the subjects listed in the first and the third columns, but the activities listed in the middle column are unlikely to be planned separately or to be identifiable with significant amounts of resources.

Program elements should also be structured so as to facilitate benefit/cost analyses; that is, the activity represented by the program element should, if feasible, be an activity for which there is a plausible relationship between benefits and costs.

To the extent possible, program elements should be defined so that each element has a measurable output. This is much more likely to

---

[8] From Division of Special Education (A), a case distributed by Intercollegiate Case Clearing House, ICH 14C4.

EXHIBIT 5–3
A Dubious Program Structure*

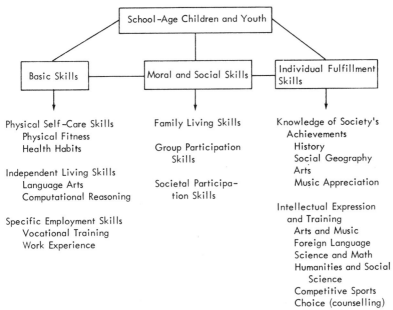

Physical Self–Care Skills	Family Living Skills	Knowledge of Society's
Physical Fitness		Achievements
Health Habits	Group Participation	History
	Skills	Social Geography
Independent Living Skills		Arts
Language Arts	Societal Participa-	Music Appreciation
Computational Reasoning	tion Skills	

Physical Self–Care Skills
Physical Fitness
Health Habits

Independent Living Skills
Language Arts
Computational Reasoning

Specific Employment Skills
Vocational Training
Work Experience

Family Living Skills

Group Participation
Skills

Societal Participa-
tion Skills

Knowledge of Society's
Achievements
History
Social Geography
Arts
Music Appreciation

Intellectual Expression
and Training
Arts and Music
Foreign Language
Science and Math
Humanities and Social
Science
Competitive Sports
Choice (counselling)

* Presented in Selma J. Mushkin and James R. Cleaveland, *Planning for Educational Development in a Planning, Programming, and Budgeting System* (Washington, D.C.: National Education Association, 1968).

be feasible for program elements than for program subcategories or major programs.

As is the case with program categories, program elements can be classified as either direct or support. There can be direct program elements within support program categories; these are direct with respect to the category, even though the category is support with respect to the organization as a whole. In many program subcategories, there will be a separate program element for administration. It includes administrative activities associated with the subcategory (as contrasted with the administration of the organization as a whole), and it may also include miscellaneous "catch all" activities. Catch-all program elements can be used to eliminate the necessity of allocating costs.

The number of program elements depends on the size and complexity of the organization.

Program Element Classification. Each program category is the sum of its program subcategories, and each program subcategory is the sum of its program elements. If an activity relates to more than one program subcategory, there should be a separately numbered program element for each relevant program subcategory.

Example: In the Defense Department, there are the following common program elements in Program 2, General Purpose Forces:

P.E. Number	*Name*
2xxxx86	Base Operations
2xxxx87	Training
2xxxx88	Command
2xxxx89	Military Family Housing

Each subprogram in Program 2 has these program elements. Thus, in Category 2–5, which are Air Force Tactical Forces, these appear as:

2–58–01–86	Base Operations (Tactical Air Forces)
2–58–01–87	Training (Tactical Air Forces)
2–58–01–88	Command (Tactical Air Forces)
2–58–01–89	Military Family Housing (Tactical Air Forces)

Program Structures for Comparisons

If the same program structure is to be used by a number of similar organizations (e.g., schools, colleges, hospitals), then great care needs to be taken to assure that the structure will provide comparable data so that averages and other measures can be compiled and individual organizations can compare their own data with these averages. In such a structure, compromises are necessary because all of the participating organizations will not view their programs in the same way. As a general rule, the program structure that is used for comparisons should be quite short, specifying only the data that actually will be used for this purpose. Each participating organization can then modify this structure (usually by subdividing program elements) so as to collect the more detailed information that is needed by its own management. An example of such a structure, which was designed for public schools, is given in the Appendix.

Although the primary criterion in designing a program structure is its usefulness in decision making, if alternative structures are deemed to be of approximately equal usefulness in decision making, then the structure which is most likely to provide good data for comparisons with other organizations should be selected. For example, all municipalities must report spending under the Revenue Sharing program according to prescribed categories. It seems likely that widespread use will be made of these categories, and that they therefore should be considered as the basis for a municipality's program structure. The categories are:

1. Public safety.
2. Environmental protection.
3. Public transportation.
4. Health.
5. Recreation.
6. Libraries.
7. Social services for aged or poor.
8. Financial administration.
9. Multipurpose and general government.
10. Education.
11. Social development.
12. Housing and community development.
13. Economic development.
14. Other.

Unfortunately, however, only a few structures that provide comparable data of even approximate validity currently exist. A good system does exist for hospitals and another for certain municipal services. In some states there are good systems for primary and secondary education, higher education, municipal activities, and certain other functions. Some religious organizations have systems for their local units, and so do other member-oriented organizations such as college fraternities, professional associations, Chambers of Commerce, and civic organizations. References describing structures for some of these organizations are given at the end of this chapter.

If the structure that has been developed for purposes of comparison does not fit into the program structure that is useful for decision making, then a separate cost accounting system is usually required to develop the comparative data.

The Time Span

The foregoing relates to the program structure in its spacial dimension, that is, how it looks at any one moment in time. Consideration also needs to be given to its time dimension; that is, the number of years for which program information is to be recorded, because the structure will be used to record both historical information and also estimates for future years. The time interval covered by the estimates in the program structure should ideally correspond to the number of years in which significant amounts of cost incurrence are affected by current decisions.

The most distant year for which estimates are included in the structure should be the year whose approximate overall costs and program consequences are needed in order to make current decisions, provided that estimates of key variables can be made for that year with sufficient reliability to be useful in decision making. Thus, the year selected represents a balance between (1) the need and (2) the feasibility of making estimates. Organizations whose future is difficult to estimate because their revenues are uncertain, because technology changes rapidly, or for other reasons, include fewer future years in their program structure than do organizations with a more predictable future. When the degree of uncertainty is high, estimates may extend only two or three years into the future. When the need is great and uncertainty is relatively low, estimates may extend as many as 10 years into the future (e.g., the Apollo Program). If the uncertainty of estimates of key variables is inherently large, the construction of elaborate, and hence expensive, estimates should be avoided.

The time span need not be the same for all parts of the program structure. It may be longer for capital costs than for operating costs, and longer for some programs than for others.

It has become customary in the Federal government and in many other nonprofit organizations for the program to cover five future years. There is no conclusive evidence that this custom is sound, and the custom is being increasingly challenged. Even if a program structure contains estimates for the fifth future year, it need not contain estimates for each of the first four years. An alternative is to include estimates for the first future year (i.e., the budget year), the second year, and the fifth year, omitting the third and fourth years.

Although the formal structure need cover only the time span about which current decisions must be made, the planning *process* should ordinarily extend over a longer period of time in order to identify trends and the need for preliminary studies which may lead to decisions within the next year or so.

All the foregoing comments relate to the time span of the formal program structure, rather than the time horizon that is appropriate in the analysis of individual proposals. In analyzing individual proposals, it is of course essential that costs and consequences be estimated over a period that is long enough to permit valid comparisons of total costs and total benefits.

THE RESPONSIBILITY STRUCTURE

Relation to Organization Structure

The responsibility structure should correspond to the formal organization units; i.e., the responsibility centers that carry out the programs. Although the program structure should also correspond to the responsibility structure to the extent that this is feasible, organizational considerations make it unlikely that there will be an exact correspondence there. The correspondence in the responsibility structure should be exact.

The closer the match of the responsibility structure to the program structure, the easier the implementation of a good control system. When the match is reasonably close, the person who heads a responsibility center can be held accountable for a defined program or some part thereof; this is similar to the responsibility principle in a profit-oriented organization.

> *Example:* When the Navy shifted to a responsibility accounting system in 1968, it changed its organizational responsibility so that it more nearly matched programs. Previously, the Chief of Naval Operations had little authority over the budgets and financial management of the fleets for which he was responsible; the principal authority was vested in Bureaus and other staff agencies that were not under his direct control. Under the new system, the Chief of Naval Operations was given this authority. This led to better decision making, because the new system permitted the Chief of Naval Operations to decide

on resource allocations which were necessary to implement his judgments on fleet activities.

In making the concept of the *responsibility center* a powerful and effective one, considerable emphasis needs to be given to the authority and discretionary power which the manager has. When a new dimension of responsibility is placed on responsibility centers, additional authority must be given to their managers; otherwise, frustration and meaningless effort may result.

> *Example:* The Philadelphia Public Schools developed a structure with individual schools as responsibility centers. School principals were held responsible for extensive budget accounts, but they had little discretionary authority over the ways the money was allocated within their schools. In addition, they prepared lengthy budget documents which were based upon centrally prescribed tables of resource authorization. The result was a feeling of frustration, rather than better decision making by school principals.

Mission Centers and Service Centers

There are two kinds of responsibility centers: mission centers and service centers. A *mission center* receives its spending authority from its next higher echelon, and its expenses therefore appear as such in budgets and programs.

The costs of a *service center* are charged to the responsibility centers to which it renders service; therefore, its costs appear in budgets and programs as part of the cost of mission centers. Monetary amounts for service centers do not appear as such in budgets or programs, except on a memorandum basis. In other words, the sum of the expenses of all mission centers equals the sum of the expenses of all program elements.

Note that a mission center is not synonymous with a direct program element. There are mission centers for all program elements in the program, including direct, support, and administrative. The sole characteristic of a service center is that its costs appear in other responsibility centers, and therefore it does not appear as such in a summary that is arranged either according to programs or according to responsibility centers, except on a memorandum basis.

Service centers should be established whenever it is economically feasible to do so. For example, in the case of a large motor pool which serves an airbase, various aircraft squadrons, and research and development activity, it would be administratively and economically sound to establish the motor pool as a service center. However, a service center would not be worthwhile for a small motor pool serving one predominant activity. It is often desirable to use the service center concept even for a relatively small unit if it serves several customers. For example, a typing pool that provides typing services to several offices might well be set up as a service center.

Since costs for service centers appear in budgets and programs as part of mission center costs, there is a problem in deciding who is responsible for overall evaluation of the service center's effectiveness and efficiency. If the amount of service is a significant component of the costs of one or more of the responsibility centers who receive the service, it is usually safe to count on these responsibility centers to complain if the costs seem to be getting out of line. Indeed, this sort of interaction is one of the great virtues of the service center concept. If, however, the amount of cost charged to any one responsibility center is insignificant, as is often the case with typing pools, this automatic surveillance cannot be counted on. In these circumstances, the system must be set up so that management scruntinizes the service centers as entities, even if they do not appear with dollar amounts in either the program structure or the responsibility structure. It is for this reason that service centers often appears as "memorandum entries;" that is their costs are shown, but are excluded from the totals.

Functional Categories

In order to facilitate the collection of data on the cost of performing functions that are common to several responsibility centers, a set of functional accounts may be prescribed within the responsibility centers. One of these accounts should be designated as a *mission* account, in which the costs of performing the mission are collected. For example, in the various regional and local offices of a job training program, there may be one functional category for the job training mission and others for public relations, training of agency personnel, building operation and maintenance, and administration.

Expense Elements

In order to facilitate analysis, and under certain circumstances to control spending for discretionary elements of expense, a set of expense elements or object classes, are set up and are used in each responsibility center that spends a significant amount for the specified element.

The object classes used throughout the Federal government are:

11   Personnel compensation.
    11.1   Permanent positions.
    11.3   Positions other than permanent.
    11.5   Other personnel compensation.
    11.7   Military personnel.
    11.8   Special personnel services payments.

12   Personnel benefits.
   12.1   Personnel benefits: Civilian.
   12.2   Personnel benefits: Military personnel.
13   Benefits for formal personnel.
21   Travel and transportation of persons.
22   Transportation of things.
23   Rent, communications, and utilities.
24   Printing and reproduction.
25   Other services.
26   Supplies and materials.
31   Equipment.
32   Lands and structures.
41   Grants, subsidies, and contributions.
42   Insurance claims and indemnities.
43   Interest and dividends.

This particular set of expense elements is not well suited to nongovernment agencies, and even government agencies find it useful to eliminate certain object classes and subdivide others. It is given here only as an indication of what expense elements are.

OTHER TYPES OF ACCOUNTS

Cost Accounts

Every organization needs information about the cost of performing various functions or carrying on various activities. To the extent that these functions or activities are set up as program elements, or to the extent they are represented by functional categories in the responsibility structure, this information can be obtained directly from the accounts that have been described above. In some situations, however, such information is too detailed to be of interest to management, other than the manager of the responsibility center directly involved, and hence it is not worthwhile to clutter up the main structure (i.e., the program and responsibility accounts) with this detail. In these situations, the information can be collected through a cost accounting system. For example, the highway departments of municipal governments use a great deal of detailed information on the cost of constructing, repairing, resurfacing, and maintaining roads of various types. They collect this information in a cost system.

The mechanism that accountants use to relate a specialized set of accounts to the general account structure is called a "control account—subsidiary account" relationship. In the general accounts, one account is designated as the control account, and procedures are set up such that the total of all detailed items charged to the subsidiary accounts equals the total charged to the control account. As already noted, a system in which such a relationship does *not* exist is called a "statistical cost system." Such a system is of dubious usefulness because there is no way of verifying the validity of the charges made to the cost accounts. In particular, there is a temptation to "forget" to record costs if to do so would make the amount seem unduly high. In a tied-in system, such lapses of memory are not possible, because of the basic rule of accounting that debits must equal credits; that is, if a cost is incurred, it must appear in some cost account, or the books will not balance.

Usually, statistical cost systems exist because those involved believe that the work entailed in installing a tied-in system is not worthwhile. In most cases, however, the incremental work of tieing a specialized cost system to the general system is less than imagined.

Project Accounts

A set of accounts may exist for each project that an organization undertakes, such as each project in a research and development laboratory. This set of accounts is sometimes viewed as a separate entity, but it is more properly thought of as part of the program structure; that is, as detailed subdivisions of program elements. Information in these accounts is useful to local managers in planning and controlling projects that are carried out to achieve the objectives specified in program elements.

Accounts for Outside Agencies

The accounts described up to this point are those that management needs to plan and control the activities of the organization. Many organizations also must provide information to outside parties. Agencies of the Federal government, for example, must report to the Congress and to the public. The Office of Education, which makes grants to public schools, is naturally interested in knowing what the schools do with those funds and it consequently requires reports on how they were used. State agencies are interested in information about the hospitals that they regulate.

As a general proposition, it seems clear that no outside agency needs a larger quantity of information than that which local management needs for its own purposes; indeed, the outside agency should need much *less* information than internal management needs. Furthermore, it makes sense that the nature of the information that should interest an outside agency should correspond to the information that management finds useful for its own purposes. Reason indicates, therefore, that information furnished to outside agencies should be a summary of the information collected for internal use.

Unfortunately, the real world is not this rational. A great many organizations must collect and report information which they consider useless, simply because an outside party requires it. When the outside party can enforce its request—because it provides funds, licenses the organization, or for similar reasons—the organization has no choice but to furnish the information. It can do so in one of two ways.

The safe, but expensive, way is to create a special account structure to collect the required information. This is the way that Federal government agencies solve the problem of furnishing information to the Congress according to an "appropriation structure" that the agency does not need for its own purposes. In addition to being expensive, such a solution has the great disadvantage of requiring the maintenance of two sets of accounts to collect information about essentially the same phenomena. At a minimum, this can cause confusion within the organization since managers may be uncertain as to which type of information should be used for decision making. A more serious possibility is that operating managers may pay too much attention to the "appropriation" structure and give inadequate attention to the structure which actually best fits the needs of the whole organization.

The alternative to creating a special set of accounts is to prepare reports for outside agencies without relying on accounting information. A skilled and imaginative accountant can construct a plausible list of costs classified in any way that an outside agency specifies. Such a report does not, of course, reveal what the actual spending has been, except by coincidence, but it often satisfies the outside agency. This method is used when the requests from the outside agency seem obviously worthless, particularly when they require an undue amount of detail.

> *Examples:* For many years, the Department of Defense reported annually to Congress on the cost of operating the three service academies. Until an expense accounting system was installed in 1968, there was no accounting foundation for such a report, but it was made anyway. The system did not provide the correct information, but by the same token there was no way of proving that the information submitted on the report was incorrect.
>
> Similarly, the Office of Education requires that each school system which receives grants submit an elaborate cost report. Few, if any, school systems have an account structure that collects the information in the fashion required by this report; the report is therefore made out by an accountant who uses imagination to estimate what the costs probably were.
>
> The reports required of hospitals by some states for rate-making purposes are archaic, and require information of no conceivable use to management; the reports are therefore created (and this word is used intentionally) by skilled accountants. Such reports are unreliable, to put it mildly.

Fund Accounts

A unique feature of the accounting systems in nonprofit organizations is the use of what are called *fund accounts*. Indeed, a study of accounting in such organizations is often called "fund accounting" as if this were the central feature of the system. Actually, the fund accounts play a relatively minor role in the management control process. For our purpose, therefore, it is unnecessary to describe their intricacies. A general understanding of their nature and purpose is nevertheless desirable.

In a business accounting system, all the available resources are, in effect, in one "pot", that is, the balance sheet lists the assets for the whole entity. In a nonprofit organization, by contrast, the resources may be accounted for in several separate pots, each of which is called a fund. Each fund has its own set of accounts, that are self-balancing, and each fund is therefore a separate entity, almost as if it were a separate business. The purpose of this device is to insure that the organization uses the resources made available to each fund only for the purposes designated for that fund.

Some years ago, this segregation by funds was carried to great extremes. It is said, for example, that the Post Office had one fund for first-class postage, another for third-class postage, another for money orders, and so on, and that each post office had to maintain a separate bank account for each fund. In recent years, there has been general recognition of the fact that the necessary control over spending can be obtained without an elaborate fund mechanism, and the number of separate funds has been greatly reduced. In general, those funds that remain do serve a useful purpose, although in many cases it is quite possible that the same objective could be accomplished without the fund mechanism.

Omitting several highly specialized funds, the funds we are principally interested in are: (1) general funds, (2) capital funds, (3) endowment funds, (4) sinking funds, and (5) working capital funds.

The *general fund* comprises the resources made available to operate the organization for a specified period of time, usually a year; that is, there is one operating fund for 1974, another for 1975, and so on. Preferably, there should be a single fund for all operating activities combined, but in some organizations there are several operating funds in a given year. In some municipalities, for example, there may be a separate operating fund for each department, and in many municipalities there is a separate operating fund for the school system. Separate operating funds are warranted when management responsibility is divided (as in a community in which a school committee is responsible for education and selectmen for all other activities), or in situations when revenues can be used only for a specified purpose; but even in these situations adequate control usually can be attained without the use of separate funds.

Other funds correspond roughly to asset categories on the balance sheet of a profit-oriented business.

A *capital fund* provides for the construction or acquisition of approved capital assets. Usually, money is added to this fund for each approved acquisition, amounts spent are accounted for separately for each project, and the money remains available until the project is completed. This separation between capital investment and operations is essential, for reasons already discussed.

An *endowment fund* holds money entrusted to an organization for endowment purposes. The principal is supposed to be held intact, usually forever, and the earnings on that principal are made available for current use. There are obvious advantages in erecting a strong barrier between monies that can be spent in the current year and monies that are intended to be held intact as a basis for generating future earnings.

Sinking funds are maintained in association with bond issues. Many such issues provide that the organization set aside a certain amount each year to provide for the systematic retirement of the bonds, and the sinking fund provides the mechanism for doing this.

Working capital funds, also called "revolving funds," are used to finance inventories and other consumable assets. Their function corresponds to the function of the inventory accounts in a business, namely, to hold assets in suspense until they are consumed and hence become costs. There are two types of working capital funds, which are often called "stock funds" and "service funds." Stock funds finance inventories. Service funds finance the work in process at large service centers, such as shipyards and aircraft overhaul facilities. These are revolving funds in the sense that the benefiting agency reimburses the fund for the value of the material or services that it receives from the service center, and this reimbursement permits the service center to acquire more material. Thus, once a working capital fund has been created, the service center does not need to be financed by external sources unless the rate and/ or amount of its activities increases.

To the extent that fund accounting forces a clean separation between operating transactions and capital or endowment transactions, it is a useful device, corresponding essentially to the separation between income statement items and other balance sheet changes in a business. Conversely, to the extent that funds are further segregated as a device for enforcing detailed decisions on spending, they are unnecessary. The same results can be achieved with less effort by other means. The use of fund accounts in controlling current operations will be discussed in Chapter 12.

Social Accounts

Some have suggested that a nonprofit organization should prepare a "social" income statement, showing how well it has achieved its service objectives, analogous to the conventional income statement which shows how well a profit-oriented organization has attained its profit objective.

The accounts required for such a statement are not included in the above description because no feasible, objective way of doing this has been proposed, nor does it seem likely that one will be developed in the foreseeable future. The proposals that have been made smack strongly of being public relations gimmicks rather than as a means of communicating information of substance.[9]

Even though the social income statement may not be feasible as such, management of a nonprofit organization should recognize that statements of services rendered, even if subjective, are a more essential part of a report of accomplishment than are income statements.

Possibilities do exist, however, for developing and reporting overall performance in a way that, although not in the form of an income statement, provides much more useful information than currently exists. These will be discussed in Chapter 6.

---

[9] Also, many such proposals do not actually involve the creation of formal accounts for recording social costs. For example, Beans and Fertig propose a *disclosure* of what an organization spends for pollution control, but do not go so far as to recommend that the social cost of pollution be included in the accounts, despite the title of their article. Floyd A. Beans and Paul E. Fertig, "Pollution Control through Social Cost Conversion" (*Journal of Accountancy*, November 1971).

appendix

A Program Structure for Public Schools[*]

This Appendix describes a set of accounts that are suggested for use by school districts as a part of their total accounting system, in order to (1) meet the needs of the Office of Education for financial information and (2) enable a given school district to compare its costs with costs in other school districts. Using this design, a school district can structure a detailed program-oriented accounting system that both meets its own needs and, except for requirements that may in the future be mandated by the Congress, also meets the needs of the Office of Education.

The set of accounts shown here has *not* been adopted by the Office of Education. Instead, the Office of Education recommends a much more elaborate set. Our purpose in presenting this alternative is to show that, for the purposes stated above, the account structure can be fairly simple.

OVERVIEW OF THE STRUCTURE

The structure collects operating costs, as distinguished from capital outlays, and also as distinguished from information on assets and liabilities. Operating costs are, in general, the cost of resources consumed in operations, as measured in accordance with the accrual concept. Certain exceptions to the strict interpretation of the accrual concept are made, as described subsequently.

The structure classifies operating costs by programs and within most programs by subprograms and program elements.

[*] An excerpt from a report prepared under Contract No. OEC-0-70-5127 between the Department of Health, Education, and Welfare and Harvard University.

107

The basic program structure consists of the following major programs:

1. Elementary Schools, regular session.
2. Elementary Schools, summer session.
3. Middle Schools, regular session.
4. Middle Schools, summer session.
5. High Schools, regular session.
6. High Schools, summer session.
7. Vocational and Technical Schools, regular session.
8. Vocational and Technical Schools, summer session.
9. Junior College, regular session.
10. Junior College, summer session.
11. Adult Education.
12. Community Services.
19. System-Wide Expenses.
20. Nonprogram Costs.

The program structure enables managers to think of trade-offs within each program, and focuses on what the school system does, that is, its outputs.

Under each of the instruction programs are the following subprograms:

x.1 Regular Instruction.
x.2 Other Instruction.
x.3 Instruction Support.
x.4 Pupil Support Services.
x.5 Other Pupil Support Services.
x.7 Plant Maintenance and Operation.
x.8 Administration and General.

Under all of these subprograms except x.7 are program elements, which are the actual accounts to which charges are to be made.

CONSIDERATIONS GOVERNING THE CHOICE OF PROGRAMS

Programs 1 through 10

The main instruction programs are intended to conform reasonably closely to organization units, i.e., elementary schools, middle schools, high schools, vocational and technical schools, and junior colleges.

These organization units are defined in such a way that the traceable costs of operating a given school are classified into one, and only one of these categories. This avoids the necessity of prorating costs incurred in a given school, thus greatly simplifying the recordkeeping problem. It does not mean that the schools included in a given category are identical, but they are believed to be sufficiently alike to permit valid comparisons among the schools in each category. Because the official definition of types of school varies among states, often because of State law, there is no way of constructing definitions that exactly fit all schools.

Programs 1 through 6. Schools that have any of grades K through 12 are classified as follows:

Elementary is a school that includes at least grades 1–3, and/or kindergarten. By this definition, schools with grades 1–3, 1–4, 1–5, 1–6, 1–7, and 1–8 would be included, as would those few schools that have grades 1–12. The latter type is admittedly not homogeneous with the others, but it is such an insignificant part of the total school spending that the disparity is not important. Furthermore, such schools are usually small; they need, and can afford, only a simple set of accounts. In this category and in the other categories, provision is made for classifying ungraded schools according to the age of the pupils that attend them.

Secondary is a school, other than an elementary school, that includes at least grades 11 and 12. By this definition, schools with grades 7–12, 8–12, 9–12, and 11–12 are defined as secondary schools.

Middle is any other school. By this definition, schools with grades 4–6, 5 and 6, 7 and 8, 7–9, 8 and 9, and other similar patterns would be included. For local purposes, a school district might well want to divide this category into subcategories, such as (a) 5 and 6 and (b) 7–9, if it is organized in this fashion.

Regular Session and Summer Session

For each type of school, there is one program for the regular school year and another program for the summer. The decision to segregate the cost of summer programs in such detail was arrived at reluctantly because it almost doubles the number of accounts in the structure. Nevertheless, it appears that an increasing number of school districts operate summer programs and incur significant amounts of cost for them. Since the amount of such costs varies widely among school districts, the per-pupil costs of education during the regular school year might be significantly distorted if summer program costs were lumped in with regular-session costs.

Two other alternatives for solving the summer problem were considered: (1) A single program for summer instruction of all types; (2) subprograms for summer instruction. The first would not provide all the information needed to administer categorical grants. The second turned out to be more cumbersome than the alternative decided upon.

Programs 11 through 20

In addition to the main instruction programs, there are other programs, as follows:

11. *Adult Education.* This collects the expenses of educational act-

ivities carried on for other than regularly enrolled pupils. The expenses of such programs must be separated from those of regular programs so as not to distort the per-pupil cost of these programs. No breakdown is prescribed unless required by grantors.

12. *Community Services.* This program is for the expenses of non-educational activities carried on by the school, such as community recreation, civic activities, public library, custody and care of children, and welfare.

19. *System-Wide Expenses.* This program is for expenses that are incurred for more than one type of school and which cannot feasibly be traced directly to one type of school. Use of this separate program category avoids the necessity for allocating such costs to individual types of schools.

20. *Nonoperating Costs.* This program is used for capital expenditures, debt service, and other costs not associated with operating the school system.

Subprograms and Program Elements

The subprograms are defined consistently under each of the instruction programs. Comments about each are given below.

x.1. Regular Instruction. For elementary schools, no breakdown is prescribed, except in those schools that have grants requiring such a breakdown. Because most elementary schools are organized by grade, the only feasible breakdown would be by grade, and the value of such a breakdown is judged not to be worth the cost. A breakdown by subject area would require time cards or some similar elaborate method of apportioning salary costs. For other schools, this program is broken down by subject area.

x.2. Other Instruction. The program elements given under this subprogram in Exhibit 5–4 indicate its content. These program elements, however, would be prescribed only in those schools in which the information is required by fund grantors.

x.3. Instruction Support. This subprogram includes the costs of activities that directly support the instructional program: libraries, central audio/visual services (i.e., services that cannot be charged directly to an instructional program), and guidance activities. Detailed accounts are provided to meet the needs of certain fund grantors.

x.4. Pupil Support Services. This subprogram includes expenses that are incurred for the benefit of pupils, but not directly in support of instruction: athletics, health, and attendance.

x.5. Other Pupil Support Services. This subprogram includes expenses for food services and transportation.

x.7. Plant Maintenance and Operation. Although this subprogram would contain many detailed accounts to meet the needs of local management, no breakdown is believed to be necessary for the centrally prescribed structure.

x.8. Administration and General. This subprogram includes the expenses of administration and of personnel and program development for individual types of schools and corresponding expenses that are traced directly to a given level of instruction. (System-wide administration and general expenses are in Program 19.)

Program Elements

The program elements, detailed in Exhibit 5–4, are structured in sufficient detail to provide the information required by the Office of Education.

Expense Elements

All expenses can be classified as labor, material, or services. For most purposes, the Office of Education is interested only in the total cost of a program element, but for some purposes it needs a breakdown by type or object of expense. The structure provides for eight types: three for labor, three for material, and two for services.

Labor is by far the largest element of cost in a school district, so it seems appropriate to classify total labor costs in some useful way. There are two main alternatives: (1) by type of payment (regular, overtime, fringe benefit, etc.) or (2) by type of employee. The latter is more useful.

Most management control systems attempt to classify labor costs in a way that indicates employee status, such as professional and other, exempt and nonexempt, or salary and wage. In view of the importance of teachers, our structure classifies them separately from other professionals, and therefore has three categories: teachers, other professionals, and nonprofessionals.

Material costs are classified as either books and periodicals, other materials and supplies, or equipment.

The *equipment* item is often not found in an expense accounting system. Instead, purchases of equipment are capitalized and are charged off periodically as an expense through a depreciation mechanism. At some future time, it may be desirable to include such a mechanism in the accounting systems for public schools, but this time has not arrived. In the absence of depreciation, there are two ways of handling equipment purchases; (1) omit them, or (2) charge them as if they were an expense when acquired. In our structure, the initial equipment of new school facilities and major items of equipment are omitted, whereas relatively minor equipment purchases are included. Since those items that are included tend to be replacements, the effect is roughly the same as charging depreciation. It is not exactly the same because the amount of equipment purchases is not constant from one year to the next, and because there is a tendency to make equipment purchases for other than replacement purposes.

In drawing the line between equipment to be included as an expense and that to be excluded, the distinction made is similar to the one school districts use in deciding on whether an item should go in its operating budget or in its capital budget. Since practice varies, of course, the distinction will not fit all cases precisely, but it is believed to be adequate for the intended purpose.

Data for Comparability Purposes

The structure provides three types of information that are useful in establishing comparability.

First, it provides information on total spending for instruction and for instruction support, for elementary, for middle, and for secondary schools, and with spending for the regular session separated from spending for the summer session. Each of the subprograms and types of schools listed above is carefully defined so as to minimize ambiguity as to how transactions are to be classified. This information is the best overall way of comparing schools which receive Office of Education grants with other schools.

Second, the structure provides program elements that are intended to correspond to the principal projects for which Office of Education funds are requested and for which they are expected to be spent. The structure, for example, provides elements for special activities for the handicapped, transportation, library, and cultural programs. Spending as recorded in these program elements provides a direct way of assuring that within a school which receives grants from the Office of Education, the funds were spent in the manner intended.

Third, the expense elements in the structure provide amounts spent for teachers, textbooks, library books and periodicals, audio/visual materials, and similar objects of expense that have been mentioned as being desirable in examining the details of spending.

Data for Local Management

The management of an individual school district needs more detailed information on costs than is provided in a centrally prescribed system. The structure has been constructed in such a way that this detail can be obtained by creating additional program elements or subprogram elements in the program structure and by creating additional expense detail under the expense elements. For example, if a school district wishes to collect the cost of instruction in reading, it will simply establish

a Reading account under English Language Arts (x.11); if it wishes
costs on individual foreign language instruction, it will create as many
accounts as are necessary under Foreign Languages (x.12).

Outputs for Budgeting Purposes

A budget consistent with the structure is fundamentally different from
the traditional "line-item" budget in which the primary basis of classification is by object of expenditure: salaries, textbooks, supplies, and the
like. The structure given here is a program structure. The focus is on
the amount that is to be spent for each program, rather than on the
types of resources that are to be used. More and more school districts
are adopting the program budget approach. By relating proposed spending to the purposes for which the funds are to be spent, decision makers
have a much sounder basis for applying their judgments than is the
case with line-item budgets.

This does not mean that a classification by object of expense is not
needed. It is needed, but primarily by those who are analyzing the
details of proposed budgets. At the decision-making level—the superintendent and school board—the focus should be on programs: What
programs do we intend to carry out? How much can we afford to spend
on each of them?

Because their cost characteristics are likely to differ from one another,
there is a separate program for each type of school. The programs are
also arranged so that discretionary and peripheral activities, such as
adult education, summer programs, and community services are separated from the programs for the central mission of the organization,
that of educating children. This facilitates making judgements about the
appropriate spending level for each of these activities.

There is a separate program for system-wide overhead costs, and
within each program, there is a program for the administrative costs
of individual types of schools. Budget analysts and decision makers
usually find that a clear separation of these costs from other costs is
useful. As a general tendency (to which, of course, there are many
exceptions), as large a fraction of available resources as possible should
be allocated to instruction and related programs. The decision maker
needs to be aware of proposals that may shift emphasis away from
the central mission of the school system. The structure encourages this
type of analysis.

At the level of program elements and expense elements, accounts
in the structure are intended to be useful to the staff analysts who
do preliminary work on preparing and analyzing budget requests; these
accounts are less likely to be of interest to the decision makers. Proposed
changes in funds required to carry on a continuing program (as distinguished from proposals for changes in emphasis of programs, or for

EXHIBIT 5–4

Program Elements

x.1 Regular Instruction (†for elementary
     schools and system-wide expenses)
    x.11 English Language Arts
    x.12 Foreign Languages
    x.13 Social Sciences/Social Studies
    x.14 Sciences
    x.15 Mathematics
    x.16 Cultural
    x.17 Occupational
    x.18 Physical Education
    x.19 Other
x.2 Other Instruction†
    x.21 Remedial
        x.211 English
        x.212 Reading
        x.213 Social Sciences/Social
               Studies
        x.214 Natural Sciences
        x.215 Mathematics
        x.216 Cultural
        x.217 Foreign Languages
        x.219 Other
    x.22 Special Education
        x.221 Gifted and Talented
        x.222 Mentally Handicapped
        x.223 Physically Handicapped
        x.224 Socially and/or Emotion-
               ally Handicapped
        x.229 Other
    x.29 Other
x.3 Instruction Support
    x.31 Libraries
    x.32 Audio/Visual
    x.33 Other Education Media
    x.39 Other Instruction Support
x.4 Pupil Support Services
    x.41 Attendance and Social Work
    x.42 Guidance
        x.421 Vocational Guidance and
               Counselling
        x.422 Testing
        x.429 Other Guidance and
               Counselling
    x.43 Psychological Services
    x.44 Health Services
    x.45 Special Services for the Handi-
        capped

    x.46 Athletics
    x.47 Student Activities
    x.48 Student Subsidies
    x.49 Other
x.5 Other Pupil Support Services
    x.51 Food Service
    x.52 Transportation
    x.59 Other
x.7 Plant Maintenance and Operation
x.8 Administration and General† (applies
    to programs 1–11)
    x.81 Instructional Administration
        x.811 School-Wide Direction
               and Management
        x.812 Instructional Supervision
        x.819 Other Instructional
               Administration
    x.82 Personnel Development
    x.83 Program Development
        x.831 Research and Develop-
               ment
        x.832 Planning
        x.833 Evaluation
        x.834 Demonstration
19.8 System-Wide Administration†
    19.81 Instructional Administration
        .811 System-Wide Direction
              and Management
        .812 Instructional Super-
              vision
        .819 Other Instructional
              Administration
    19.82 Personnel Development
    19.83 Program Development
        .831 Research and Develop-
              ment
        .832 Planning
        .833 Evaluation
        .834 Demonstration
    19.84 General Administration
        .841 Information Dissemina-
              tion
        .849 Other
20. Nonoperating Costs

---

    1. Program elements marked by a dagger (†) are necessary only if required by an agency that grants funds for the specific functions listed. No program elements are prescribed for Program 11 unless required by a grantor.

    2. Some of the program elements listed here are, in most school districts, treated a system-wide costs. Such school districts should record *all* such costs under the appropriate system-wide program elements in Program 19, and should *not* allocate to individual schools.

The elements are repeated in the program elements for individual schools solely for the convenience of those school districts in which the costs are easily identified with individual types of schools. For example, most school districts will record transportation costs in system-wide program element 19.52, rather than under, say, elementary schools, as program 1.52. Most of the program elements under "Pupil Support Services" and under "Other Pupil Support Services" should be treated in this fashion.

new programs) need to be analyzed in detail. The program elements and expense elements provide raw material for such an analysis. In general, this level of detail would not appear on the documents that the decision makers use.

Data for Reporting Purposes

Summary reports of spending might well have a format that was consistent with the program structure. Control reports prepared for individual schools and other responsibility centers probably would *not* follow the program structure, however. Instead, they might contain data only for controllable items. Such reports, for example, might have no detail on salaries—indeed, the salaries expense element might be omitted entirely—but would have much detail on operation and maintenance of facilities, even though our structure has no detail on these items. Reports on spending thus would have quite a different format from that used in the budget request.

BIBLIOGRAPHY

General

Gross, Malvern J., Jr.   *Financial and Accounting Guide for Nonprofit Organizations.* New York: Ronald Press, 1972.

Hay, Leon B. and Mikesell, R. M.   *Government Accounting.* Homewood, Ill.: Richard D. Irwin, Inc., 1974.

Kerrigan, H. D.   *Fund Accounting.* New York: McGraw-Hill Books, Inc., 1969.

Education

American Council on Education.   *College and University Business Administration.* rev. ed. Washington, D.C.: American Council on Education, 1968.

American Institute of Certified Public Accountants.   *Audits of Colleges and Universities.* New York, 1973.

National Association of Independent Schools.   *Accounting for Independent Schools,* Boston, 1969.

Peat, Marwick, Mitchell & Co.   *Planning, Budgeting and Accounting.* Washington, D.C.: National Association of College and University Business Officers, 1970.

Ryan, L. V.   *An Accounting Manual for Catholic Elementary and Secondary Schools.* Washington, D.C.: National Catholic Education Association, 1969.

U.S. Department of Health, Education, and Welfare, Office of Education. *Financial Accounting: Classifications and Standard Terminology for Local and State School Systems.* State Educational Records and Reports Series: Handbook II, rev. ed. Washington, D.C.: U.S. Government Printing Office, 1973. (DHEW Publication No: OE73-11800)

————. *Principles of Public School Accounting*. State Educational Records and Reports Series: Handbook II–B. Washington, D.C.: U.S. Government Printing Office, 1967.

Federal Government

Comptroller General of the United States (General Accounting Office), *Manual for Guidance of Federal Agencies*.

————. *Illustrative Accounting Procedures for Federal Agencies: Application of the Accrual Basis of Accounting . . . , 1962, Accounting for Accrued Expenditures, 1969*. Washington, D.C.: Government Printing Office, 1969.

————. *Frequency Asked Questions About Accrual Accounting in the Federal Government, 1970*.

————. *Accounting Principles and Standards for Federal Agencies, 1972*.

Health Care

American Hospital Association. *Accounting Manual for Long-term Care Institutions*. Chicago, 1961.

————. *Chart of Accounts for Hospitals*. Chicago, 1966.

————. *Cost Finding and Rate Setting for Hospitals*. Chicago, 1968.

American Institute of Certified Public Accountants. *Audits of Voluntary Health and Welfare Organizations*. New York, 1974.

————. *Hospital Audit Guide*. New York, 1972.

U.S. Department of Health, Education, and Welfare. *A Guide for Non-Profit Institutions. Cost Principles and Procedures for Establishing Indirect Cost Rates for Grants and Contracts with the Department of Health, Education, and Welfare*. Washington, D.C.: 1970. DHEW Publication No. (OS)72–28.

Private Nonprofit

Englander, L. *Accounting Principles and Procedures of Philanthropic Institutions*. New York: New York Community Trust, 1957.

Holt, D. R. II. *Handbook of Church Finance*. New York: Macmillan Co., 1960.

State and Local Government

American Institute of Certified Public Accountants. *Audits of State and Local Governmental Units*. New York, 1974.

National Committee on Governmental Accounting. *Governmental Accounting, Auditing, and Financial Reporting*. Chicago: Municipal Finance Officers Association, 1968.

chapter six

The Control Structure: Inputs and Outputs

Chapter 5 described the "accounts" that were appropriate for the management control system in a nonprofit organization. Each of these accounts may be thought of as a box containing data that match the name of the account. In the case of historical data, each transaction gives rise to bits of data which are placed in the appropriate boxes. The contents of each box are periodically totalled, and the totals are reported, usually in summary form, for management's use. Chapter 6 deals with the nature of the data that are put into each box. There are two general types of such data: (1) inputs, or costs, which are discussed in the first part of this chapter, and (2) outputs, which are discussed in the second part.

The relative emphasis given to topics in Chapters 5 and 6 of this book differs considerably from that in most books on management control in profit-oriented organizations. In such books, there would be only a few pages dealing with the account structure, which was the whole of Chapter 5 in this book, and there would be only a few pages on output measures, to which considerably more than half of Chapter 6 will be devoted. The latter difference is especially significant. In a profit-oriented organization, the measurement of output is relatively straightforward, because output is measured by revenue or by gross margin. In a nonprofit organization, there is no such convenient measure, and the task of finding acceptable substitutes is one of the most difficult ones in the design of a management control system.

PART I: INPUT MEASUREMENT

Inputs are measured by cost. *Cost is a monetary measure of the amount of resources used for some purpose.* This is as true in a nonprofit organization as in a profit-oriented company; however, not all systems in nonprofit organizations take account of this basic fact. Instead of measuring the costs of their operating activities, some organizations attempt to measure inputs in terms of obligations (i.e., orders placed), accrued expenditures (i.e., resources received), or outlays (i.e., bills paid).

ACCRUAL ACCOUNTING

The costs of operating a responsibility center for a given period of time, such as a month, are the *expenses* of that responsibility center. The principles for the measurement of expenses—as distinguished from obligations, accrued expenditures, or outlays—are called accrual accounting. Nearly all profit-oriented businesses use accrual accounting. Amounts recorded for a responsibility center under accrual accounting differ from amounts recorded under obligation accounting in two respects: they differ as to time, and they differ as to place.

The unit for which costs are collected, which may be either a program element or a responsibility center is called a cost objective. Under obligation accounting, an amount is recorded at the time that a contract to *acquire* resources is entered into, whereas under accrual accounting, the amount is recorded at the time these resources *are consumed*. Under obligation accounting, the amount is recorded for the responsibility center that *places the order* for resources, whereas under accrual accounting the amount is recorded for the responsibility center that *consumes the resources*.

> *Example:* Consider $1,000 of supplies to be used by an operating agency, but purchased by a supply depot. The supplies are purchased in March and consumed in April. Under obligation accounting, the $1,000 is recorded as a charge to the supply depot and in the month of March; it is never recorded as an expense of the operating agency. Under accrual accounting, it is recorded as an expense of the operating agency in the month of April.

These differences can have a tremendous influence on the amount of resources reported as being consumed. For example, the accounting system in the Department of Defense did not, until recently, record the cost of the services of military personnel in the responsibility centers for which they worked. These costs represented almost half of the total operating cost of the Defense establishment. It was argued that "military personnel have enlisted for a fixed period of time, so there is no cost involved in using them," or "military personnel are paid from a central pool of funds, so they are not a cost to the base on which they work." Neither of these arguments is valid. The military personnel who work on a given base are a part of the cost of operating that base. They are a resource which is used, along with other inputs, to carry on the work of the base.

Similarly, materiel which, although consumed at a military base, was purchased by some agency outside the base and paid for from funds that the base did not control, was not counted as a cost. This was also an incorrect practice because the consumption of such materiel is a cost, regardless of where the materiel was purchased and regardless of the source of funds used to acquire it.

Exhibit 6–1 shows the effect of these policies on the recorded cost

EXHIBIT 6–1
Costs Recorded in Defense Department System at
Naval Air Station, Quonset Point, 1966
(000s omitted)

	Actual Direct Costs*	*Accounted for*	
		Dollars	*Percent*
Personnel	$19,726	$10,730	55
Materiel	6,696	1,403	21
Services	3,945	3,945	100
Total	$30,367	$16,078	53

* Estimates made by a special study; data were not available in the accounting system.

of operating the Air Station, Quonset Point, R.I. As a result of these policies the accounting system recorded only 53 percent of the *direct* cost of operating that base; it recorded no indirect costs.

Reconciling Accrual and Obligation Accounting

Agencies of the Federal Government, and of most state and municipal governments are required to keep their accounts on the obligation basis of accounting. This is long-standing tradition, reflecting a legislative desire to prevent an agency from contracting for goods and services in excess of the agency's appropriated funds. In a profit-oriented business, no accounting entry is made when orders are placed. The first entry is made when goods are received, and this entry is made to an inventory account. The cost of the goods are held in the inventory account until the goods are withdrawn for use, at which time they become an expense. Similarly, services are first recorded in the period in which the services are rendered, for it is then that an expense is incurred.

With the introduction of working capital accounts, an agency can record *both* obligations and expenses. This procedure is illustrated in

Exhibit 6–2. In the month of April, labor services of $100,000 were used, and orders were placed for $80,000 of material and $60,000 of services (e.g., a contract was let for painting buildings). Total obligations for the agency in April were therefore $240,000.

Labor on an obligation basis is essentially the same as labor on an expense basis, with some exceptions to be noted later, so labor expense is here assumed to be $100,000. In order to record material expense and services expense, however, two types of working capital accounts are necessary. One is called *Undelivered Orders*. As orders are placed, they are debited to this account, and as the services are rendered or material received, the account is credited. Thus, for $70,000 of services performed in April (e.g., the buildings were painted), a credit is made to Undelivered Orders, with a corresponding debit to an expense account. The undelivered orders account has no counterpart in a profit-oriented company.

The other working capital account is *Inventory*, and it has the same nature in a nonprofit organization as in a profit-oriented business; namely, it records the amount of material that is on hand at any time, which, by definition, is an asset at that time. In other words, it holds the cost of material between the time of acquisition and the time of consumption. In the above example, $50,000 of material was received in April, reducing Undelivered Orders by $50,000 and increasing Inventory by the same amount. In April, $40,000 of material was issued from inventory for use in current operations, so Inventory was credited $40,000, with a corresponding debit to an expense account.

As Exhibit 6–2 shows, total expenses for April can be reconciled to total obligations for April by measuring the changes in the two working

EXHIBIT 6–2
Reconciliation of Obligation and Accrual Accounting
Transactions for April
(000s omitted)

Obligation Basis		Working Capital Undelivered Orders				Expense Basis	
						Labor	100
Labor	100	Balance	200	Services	70	→ Services	70
Material ordered	80 →	Material	80	Material	50	↱ Material	40
Services ordered	60 →	Services	60			Total expenses	210
Obligations	240	Balance	220			Change in working capital	30
		Inventory					240
		Balance	90	Used	40 ←		
		Received	50				
		Balance	100				

Change in:

Undelivered orders	20
Inventory	10
Change in working capital	30

capital accounts. Undelivered Orders increased by $20,000 and Inventory by $10,000, so the total change was $30,000, and this $30,000 is the difference between obligations and expenses.

WORKING CAPITAL FUNDS

For obligations and expense transactions that take place within a single accounting entity, such as a single military base or a single office of a civilian agency, the working capital transactions can be handled simply as accounts, as in Exhibit 6–2. When obligations are incurred in one entity and the related expenses in another, as when a central unit purchases and stores material for use by several operating units, it is usually more convenient to use working capital *funds* to accomplish the same purpose. A working capital fund can be used to finance the "wholesale" inventory of a whole supply system. A working capital fund can also be used to finance goods that are manufactured by one unit for the use of another or for services furnished by one unit for another. In these latter situations, the working capital fund corresponds to Work in Process Inventory in a profit-oriented company.

Importance of Accrual Accounting

The shift to accrual accounting is generally regarded as the most important single technical development currently taking place in accounting in nonprofit organizations. Little improvement can be made in other planning or control techniques unless reliable expense data are available, and such data can come only from an accrual accounting system. The movement, significantly enough, started in relatively new agencies, such as the Atomic Energy Commission and the National Aeronautics and Space Administration. All Federal agencies are required by a law passed in 1956 (P.L. 84–863) to make the shift to accrual accounting as soon as practicable, but there has been a great deal of footdragging. The Department of Defense installed an accrual accounting system in 1968. The Department of Labor, Interior, and the Forest Service of the Department of Agriculture are among those that have installed, or are planning to use, accrual accounting.

PROBLEMS OF EXPENSE MEASUREMENT

The unit for which costs are collected is called a cost objective. Cost objectives include program elements, responsibility centers or any other purpose for which costs are collected. Costs incurred for operating purposes in a given period of time are called expenses. Some of the considerations involved in measuring expenses are discussed below.

Measurement of Full Costs

The full cost of a responsibility center, a program element, or any other cost objective is the sum of its direct costs plus an equitable share of its indirect costs. Direct costs are costs that are directly traceable to a single cost objective. For a responsibility center, they include the labor services used in the responsibility center, the cost of materials and services consumed in the responsibility center, and also resources used elsewhere on behalf of the activities of that responsibility center.

Indirect costs are costs applicable to several cost objectives, one of which is the cost objective in question. An equitable share of total indirect costs is allocated to each cost objective on some reasonable basis. To the extent feasible, costs are allocated according to either of two criteria: (1) in proportion to the benefits received by the cost objectives, or (2) in proportion to the extent that each cost objective caused the cost to be incurred. Those costs which cannot be allocated according to either of these criteria are allocated on some basis that represents the relative magnitude of the cost objective.

Full Costs versus Direct Costs

There is no question about the desirability of collecting the direct expenses of each responsibility center, that is, the wages and related costs of the personnel who work in the center, the cost of the materials consumed in the center, and the costs of utilities and other services that are furnished to the center, to the extent that such measurement is feasible. There is considerable question about whether indirect expenses should be collected, however, even though conceptually they are part of the full cost of the responsibility center. Omission of indirect expenses simplifies the accounting task since the process of allocating these expenses can be complicated. Consequently, a system that does not allocate indirect expenses is often used when a control system is first installed, on the grounds that managers who have been unaccustomed to using full cost data may have difficulty in understanding and using information on indirect expenses. Additionally, for many management decisions, only the direct expenses are needed.

The omission of indirect expenses from *program* costs may hamper the work of planners, however, for planners usually need to know the full costs of programs, which includes both the direct and indirect costs. In some situations the needs of planners can be met by a mechanism that provides estimates of indirect costs; this mechanism is not part of the formal accounting structure. Rough estimates, in the form of dollars of indirect cost per dollar of direct cost, for example, may be adequate for the analyses that are made by the planners.

In some organizations, a strong case can be made for collecting the full costs of responsibility centers or program elements. This is especially the case when costs are to be used as a basis for pricing the agency's services, as in TVA, St. Lawrence Seaway, hospitals, and universities; or when judgments need to be made about the extent to which each of several programs should "pay for itself," which is conceptually almost the same problem. Full cost information may also facilitate the comparison of the cost of performing certain services in government with the costs of comparable services in private organizations, although the innate difficulties of making such comparisons should not be minimized.

Whether or not the system is a "full cost" system—that is, whether or not it records both direct and indirect costs—it is essential that all parts of the system be consistent with one another. For example, if for programming purposes the system includes full costs, but for operating purposes it collects only direct costs, the two types of information cannot be compared directly. It is also essential that persons who use information from the system understand the nature of this information; for example, they must be careful not to assume that it records full costs if some or all of the items of indirect cost are in fact omitted.

Controllable Expenses

It is sometimes argued that an item of expense should be charged to a responsibility center only if it is controllable by the head of the responsibility center. The arguments in favor of this practice are weak, however. It seems generally preferable to charge direct expenses to responsibility centers whether or not they are controllable at that level. This practice corresponds to the needs of the cost analysts, who are not interested in controllability. It also obviates the necessity of trying to make an operational distinction between controllable and noncontrollable expenses when amounts are being recorded.

Controllability is always a matter of degree. Even for direct labor, which is usually cited as an example of a controllable expense, rates of pay are set by organization policy often based on negotiation, employees are hired by the personnel department, their skill level is influenced by training they received in the training department, and the most that the operating manager can control is what the person does while on the job.

When all direct expenses are charged to a responsibility center, the question of controllability must be taken into account whenever past performance is being analyzed. This suggests that a clear *separation* between controllable and noncontrollable costs is desirable.

It follows that all direct expenses normally should be charged to a responsibility center, even if there is a debate about whether they are controllable at that level. For most practical purposes, it is usually appropriate to think of direct expenses as being substantially synonymous with controllable expenses. Even though an element of expense may not be controllable directly—in the sense that the manager of the responsibility center cannot vary it at his or her discretion—nevertheless, the manager often can influence the decision maker who does control the expense if the manager judges that the directly indentifiable expenses are excessive or inadequate. The concept of controllability should include all expenses which the manager of the responsibility center can directly or indirectly influence.

Variable and Fixed Expenses

The distinction between variable and fixed expenses is an essential one for many purposes, but in the interests of simplicity many control systems do not explicitly separate variable from fixed expenses, nor are budget amounts adjusted for volume changes. As is the case with indirect costs, such a refinement in the system may be desirable at a sophisticated stage of development, even though not warranted in the early stages of a control system.

Personnel Costs

Some organizations record as personnel costs only the wages and salaries paid to employees. This far understates the true costs of personnel services because taxes, fringe benefits, and other elements of compensation can easily amount to 25 percent or more of wages and salaries. Wrong decisions are made when the total compensation of personnel is not charged to program elements or responsibility centers. For example, the understatement of such costs can lead to too much work being done by an organization's own personnel, rather than by an outside organization, and to too much use of manual labor rather than machinery.

Retirement costs are one large element of compensation that is often omitted. Although retirement benefits may not be paid for many years in the future, the costs are incurred because of the time that the employee currently works and are properly an expense of current operations. There is a temptation to omit this element of current cost and let the next generation worry about it. "No one wants to do anything except increase pension benefits and duck the cost," said the mayor of Harrisburg, Pa.[1] Because they have the power to finance retirement benefits by taxation, government agencies often do not fund these costs currently, but the amount of such costs nevertheless should be included in the measurement of personnel costs.

In some organizations, calculating the total amount of compensation for an hour, a week, or a month of personnel services is a complicated

---

[1] *The Wall Street Journal* (June 25, 1973), p. 1.

matter. The greatest complications arise in the Department of Defense, where the amount earned by individuals varies with their rank or rating, their length of service, where they are stationed, their marital status, the type of job they have, whether or not they eat in a military mess, whether or not they live in military housing, whether or not they patronize a military exchange or commissary, and a number of other factors. In these circumstances, recording of personnel costs is greatly simplified by using an average or standard cost. In the Department of Defense, for example, personnel costs are recorded at an average amount for each rank and rating, with a few special increments that are related to the specific job being performed.

Depreciation

Capital (i.e., investment) costs can be converted to operating expenses by means of a depreciation mechanism. Depreciation expense is needed primarily in connection with computations used as a basis for pricing the services rendered by the responsibility center; therefore, it may not be necessary to include depreciation as an item of expense when no charge is to be made for such services or when the charge intentionally excludes the recovery of capital costs.

An argument can be made that the purpose of depreciation is not to provide for the recovery of the cost of fixed assets, but rather to match the cost of an asset to the periods which it benefits. By this line of reasoning, the inclusion of depreciation expense is important in measuring the resources consumed by an operating manager in the accomplishment of the job. In many situations, however, such a matching is not necessary for good control.

When capital assets are financed by bond issues, as is the case with many municipal assets, the amount of debt service often corresponds roughly to depreciation plus interest and therefore can be included as an operating expense in lieu of a depreciation charge.

Capital outlays should be converted into operating expenses of programs for analytical and evaluation purposes so that the amount of capital assets being used for a program can be measured; however, this need not be a part of the formal program structure. On the other hand, some control mechanism is needed to make operating management "capital conscious," that is, to motivate them to conserve capital. A formal conversion of capital outlays into operating expenses via the depreciation mechanism tends to foster such an attitude. This leads to problems of allocation since a single capital outlay, like a building, may relate to several program elements.

If the operating expenses do include depreciation, care must be taken to insure that double counting of investment (i.e., both as an acquisition, and as depreciation expense) is avoided.

Mixed Expenses

Expenses that are incurred predominantly for one program element should ordinarily be charged to that program element, even if a minor part of the expense is incurred for other program elements. This sacrifice of purity in the interest of simplicity should be made clear to the operating managers who are responsible for the program element. These managers should understand that they are being charged with some expenses for which they are actually not responsible. Allowance for this fact must also be made in analyzing performance.

Transfer Prices

When one responsibility center receives goods or services from another responsibility center and is charged for them, the amount of the charge is called the *transfer price*. A transfer price is therefore used for transactions within an organization, as contrasted with the *external* price which is used for transactions between the organization and its clients. Chapter 7 contains a discussion of external pricing. Following are some comments that relate specifically to transfer prices.

In all organizations, the primary purposes of a transfer pricing mechanism are: (1) to encourage the optimum use of the resources subject to transfer and (2) to facilitate decisions on external prices. The transfer price, supplemented by some other form of cost transfer if necessary, should assign all of the costs of service centers to the various using responsibility centers.

In general, the transfer price that is used to charge the cost of goods or services rendered to benefiting responsibility centers should be the market price. If a market price is not available, the transfer price usually should be based on the standard full cost of the service center. In some situations the transfer price should be based on the standard *direct* costs of the service center.

> *Example:* The audio-visual center of the University of Puerto Rico charged users on the basis of full costs, including depreciation. These prices stimulated some using departments to acquire their own audio-visual equipment. Consequently, the audio-visual resources of the center were only partially utilized. In such a situation, transfer prices based on direct cost would probably stimulate optimum use of the audio-visual equipment.

In other situations, the transfer price might be higher than full cost in order to discourage certain undesirable practices, such as excessive use of the facilities or services subject to transfer.

When a competitive market exists for the service, the transfer price should be no more than the market-based price in order not to discourage use of services furnished by the service center. If the service center were to charge a price that was higher than the market price, those needing the service would be motivated to seek it from an outside source. If the service center cannot provide the service at a cost that is no greater than the price charged by an outside organization, there is a serious question as to whether the service center should even exist. The transfer price for outsiders, if they are allowed to buy the services of a service center, should normally be a competitive price.

In some circumstances, in order to encourage the using responsibility centers to make the proper use of the service centers, and at the same time absorb the total costs, a standard direct cost should be used as the primary transfer price, and the balance of the service center costs should be apportioned to the using responsibility centers as a fixed amount per period.

Standby Costs

In some situations, it may be desirable to include a separate classification of "standby costs" to distinguish these from recurring operating expenses. Standby costs are costs incurred in order to be ready to carry out some possible future mission, but which are not necessary for current operations. Examples are the cost of air raid shelters, and costs incurred in order to maintain a "surge" capability in the Military Airlift Command, that is, the capability to increase its airlift rapidly and significantly in the event of an emergency.

If significant, standby costs should be shown separately, both (1) to facilitate management decisions about how much should be spent and (2) to permit valid comparisons with other operating activities that do not have such costs. For example, without such a separation, Military Airlift Command operating costs cannot be validly compared with costs of commercial airlines. Such a separation also facilitates the comparison of operating expenses with outputs (i.e., work accomplished). It is difficult to separate standby costs from normal operating costs, however.

Opportunity Costs and Imputed Costs

In most control systems, costs are measured by monetary outlays. Conceptually, costs are measured by opportunity losses, but this is rarely practical.

> *Example:* The use of water is often controlled by public agencies, sometimes through public investment in public works, and sometimes (at least under western states' water law) because the agency is the legal holder of original water rights. As water becomes an increasingly scarce resource, the expense of some programs, such as waterfowl refuges, may come to be measured as the opportunity cost of water con-

sumption rather than solely in terms of monetary outlays. Similar instances can be cited for public lands, and public controls of private land.

Rather than estimating an opportunity cost, the above problem might be approached in another way. A monetary price provides a measure of value to both the seller and buyer. It reflects the rational decision of the buyer as to how best to allocate resources among various alternative expenditures. The price also is affected by the supply that the seller has to distribute among buyers. Another method of measuring the value of a good such as water is to measure the quantity sought by the buyer relative to the total supply available.

> *Example:* In the case of water, the ratio of water consumed for a waterfowl refuge to the total supply of water available for use is a measure of the allocative importance of the refuge. The value may be expressed not in monetary terms but in comparative terms. A state or an agency can decide whether a price of .1 (or .01 or whatever) of the available water supply is too high for a waterfowl refuge. If only .001 of the total is used, the "price" is relatively low, but if .1 is used then a watering place for ducks is "expensive" (a high toll on the total supply). This measure of value is variable depending upon the supply and the number of "purchasers," but dollar values are variable for the same reason. If the price is low there will be many "buyers," but if the quantity is scarce and the cost is high in terms of percent of total consumed, then buyers will be few.

In certain situations, *imputed* costs, which are a form of opportunity costs, need to be incorporated into the system. For example, in hospitals and educational institutions operated by certain religious organizations, many members of the staff receive no salary. In comparing the expenses of these institutions with those of other organizations, and in setting selling prices for services, it can be argued that costs are understated unless these personnel services are valued at their market value rather than the monetary amounts paid. On the other hand, there is room for much difference of opinion in determining the market value of such services, and many people question whether the effort is worthwhile. For example, most hospitals obtain a substantial amount of services from volunteers, and comparisons are not distorted if the proportion is roughly the same among hospitals. The nonmonetary cost of volunteers should not be included in selling prices, it is argued.

Control is facilitated if imputed costs are converted to actual monetary outlays. For example, in religious orders, the nonmonetary costs of members can be converted to monetary costs by making a charge, at market rates for the services, which reverts to the order.

> *Example:* In the United States, the cost of polluting water is usually an imputed cost, that is, companies are not charged for the social cost

of the rivers that they pollute. In the Ruhr Valley in Germany, by contrast, polluters pay a charge which is based on the effect of the effluent on the river's need for dissolved oxygen, that is, its biochemical oxygen demand. The revenue derived from this charge is used to provide for water treatment. The effect is to convert an imputed cost into a monetary cost. The amount involved is about $60 million per year.[2]

Materiality

Insignificant amounts of expense should not be charged to a responsibility center, even though they are direct. The cost of the paperwork required to do so exceeds the benefits. Sticky problems arise in deciding what expenses are insignificant enough to be disregarded. This is an important problem which must be carefully considered in working out the details of a system.

Nonmonetary Input Data

The principal input data should be in terms of cost because cost is the common denominator that permits the various kinds of resources used in a responsibility center to be aggregated. Nonmonetary measures of input are also useful, but strictly as a supplementary measure; they are not a substitute for costs.

Since labor cost is a high percentage of total cost in many nonprofit organizations, measure of the quantity of labor used is the most common nonmonetary measure. Two precautions need to be observed in using such a measure, however: (1) the quantity of labor—number of work-hours, workdays, work months—may not be an accurate measure of the labor input, and (2) too much emphasis on labor may distract attention from total costs.

As an example of the first problem, consider two elementary schools, one predominantly with White pupils, and the other predominantly with Black pupils. The question is raised as to whether the school system discriminates against the latter school. The Superintendent responds, "No, we don't discriminate. Each school has 500 pupils, and each has 27 teachers; this proves that we are treating the schools similarly." The Superintendent is using the number of teachers as a measure of inputs. Further analysis may reveal, however, that the total salary cost is significantly higher in the White school than the salary cost in the Black school because the teachers in the Black school are younger and less experienced, and hence receive lower average salaries. Salary cost is a better measure of the labor input than is number of teachers because

[2] From Barbara Ward and René Dubos, *Only One Earth*, an official report commissioned by the secretary general of the United Nations Conference on Human Environment, (New York: W. W. Norton & Co., 1972), chap. 7.

salary tends to reflect the quality of teachers. This conclusion is qualified, of course, by the fact that the best teachers do not necessarily receive the highest salaries, but the tendency for a relationship between salary level and ability nevertheless exists.

The second problem is illustrated by a situation that has been documented on many occasions in the federal government and which is probably common in other environments as well. Money becomes tight, so a freeze on personnel is put into effect; that is, agencies are forbidden to hire additional personnel, and sometimes they are forbidden even to replace those who retire or quit. The freeze order is obeyed, but after a period of time it is observed that costs are increasing. The explanation is that an agency has several alternative ways of obtaining labor services or their equivalent: (1) It can pay overtime, thus increasing the number of hours of service obtained from each employee; (2) it can add labor-saving equipment, thus substituting a capital cost for the labor cost; (3) it can hire a contractor to do the work, thus substituting contract costs for labor costs, and (4) in the military establishment, it can use military personnel for work previously done by civilians (the freeze usually is stated in terms of civilian jobs). Presumably, these alternatives are, on balance, less efficient than the use of additional personnel; otherwise, the manager would have adopted one of them voluntarily rather than being forced to do so because of the freeze. Thus, the net result of the freeze is an increase in cost.

A personnel freeze has its uses, however. It is a device that can be implemented quickly and that is easy to monitor. If the agency does not have a good cost control system, it may be the only effective way of putting a short-run damper on costs. But, because personnel is only one input, a more effective control is one that encompasses all the inputs, and that means cost.

CAPITAL COSTS

The foregoing comments related to operating costs. As pointed out in Chapter 5, it is essential that a clean separation be made between capital costs and operating costs because the two types of costs are managed in different ways. The rules for collecting capital costs in a nonprofit organization are similar to those in a profit-oriented company, and most nonprofit organizations follow these rules in their accounting systems. The focus is on the individual capital item, and the system collects the total cost of acquiring or constructing the item. By contrast, with respect to operating costs the focus is on a specified period of time, such as a month or a year.

Although management needs operating information classified by responsibility centers and program elements, it is not always feasible to classify capital costs in this fashion. If an investment is planned that benefits more than one program element (for example, a multipurpose building or the procurement of office equipment and furniture) it may be desirable to set up separate program elements for such investments, rather than allocating them to each program element that benefits from the investment. This does result in an understatement of the cost of the benefiting program elements, but it avoids the necessity of allocating the investment, which may be a complicated job not worth the accompanying effort. Also, this practice may correspond to the way in which management makes decisions about investments. There may be little or no value to management in allocating certain investments to each benefiting program element.

Capital costs can be converted to operating costs by the mechanism that is called depreciation, as discussed in a preceding subsection.

COST MEASUREMENT IN CERTAIN ORGANIZATIONS

Described below are some general characteristics of the measurement of operating costs in the three largest types of nonprofit organizations: government, education, and health care.

Government Organizations

In the federal government, a movement toward the accrual basis of accounting is underway. The Comptroller General and the Joint Committee for Improvement in Financial Management are strongly encouraging this movement. However, progress is not rapid. Complete conversion to the accrual basis would be made easily and quickly if the Congress required that this be done. Although, as has been mentioned above, PL 84-863 requires that it be done, the Appropriations Committees have not yet instructed the Departments and Agencies to implement this law. Even in those agencies that already have installed an accrual accounting system, considerable time is still required for managers to learn how to use the better information that such a system generates.

Few state or local governments have a full accrual accounting system. Many of them, however, make increasing use of working capital accounts or funds to handle inventory of materials and supplies between the time of purchase and the time of consumption, which has the effect of permitting expenses to be recorded properly for this substantial element of cost.

Education

Since primary and secondary schools are usually local government organizations, the comment made above applies to them. Many states attempt to exercise control over primary and secondary education by a cumbersome, obligation-oriented (or expenditure-oriented) accounting system, and this is another cause of the failure of school accounting systems to provide good information for management.

Colleges and universities generally do not have adequate systems for measuring operating expenses, although there has been considerable improvement in recent years, particularly in certain state systems. In general, however, comparisons of costs among institutions of higher education can be made only at the level of the institution as a whole, and the validity of even such gross comparisons of cost-per-student is lessened by a failure to make a good separation between education costs and other costs, such as research. Comparisons at a more detailed level, such as among functions, or between undergraduate and graduate education, are practically worthless.

Those institutions that receive government contracts or grants, either for education or for research, are required to use cost principles prescribed by the General Services Administration, and these do provide a sound basis for measuring costs. These prescribe in some detail which items of cost are allocable to government contracts and which are not, they define direct costs, and they state principles for allocating indirect costs to specific cost objectives.

Health Care

Most private nonprofit hospitals use accounting systems that conform to principles suggested by the American Hospital Association, and therefore are able to measure costs on a basis that is comparable from one hospital to another. Government hospitals, including Veterans Administration and military hospitals, typically do not use such a system, however, nor do other government sponsored health care organizations, such as community health centers. The Department of Health, Education, and Welfare has prescribed principles for cost measurement for reimbursement under Medicare and similar programs, and these have tended to produce comparable data. On the other hand, many states require elaborate cost reports and elaborate methods of allocating indirect costs that are not useful to hospital management and that tend to inhibit the use of good systems. In some cases, however, these reports can be prepared from estimates made outside the formal accounting system.

Influence of Reimbursement Principles

In general, the increase in cost reimbursement by government and by other third parties such as Blue Cross in the case of health care, has led to the establishment of cost measurement principles by the fund-providing agencies, and these have increased the comparability of costs. These principles are substantially similar to one another in their definition of direct cost and the rules for treating direct costs, and their general approach to the allocation of indirect costs is also similar in that they usually use benefits received or cost incurrence as general criteria. They differ considerably in the details of cost allocation procedure, however. At one extreme is the rule that permits an educational institution with annual government business of less than $1,000,000 to use a single allocation rate for all indirect costs. At the other extreme are certain state systems for hospitals whose allocation requirements are complicated to the point of being unworkable.

PART II: OUTPUT MEASUREMENT

Output information is needed for two purposes: (1) to measure efficiency, which is the ratio of outputs to inputs, and (2) to measure effectiveness, which is the extent to which actual output corresponds to the organization's goals and objectives. In a profit-oriented organization, revenue or gross margin provides a measure that is useful for both these purposes. In a nonprofit organization, no such monetary measure exists. Some nonprofit organizations do generate revenues, but, as explained in Chapter 3, these revenues often do not reflect output in the same sense as do revenues in a profit-oriented company. This section discusses alternative ways of measuring outputs in nonprofit organizations. Despite the importance of devising good measures of output, current management control systems tend to give inadequate attention to this problem.

The problem of measuring output is not unique to nonprofit organizations. The same problem exists in those responsibility centers in profit-oriented organizations in which discretionary costs predominate (e.g., research, law, personnel). Conversely, output of many individual activities in nonprofit organizations can be measured as readily as corresponding activities in profit-oriented organizations (e.g., food service, vehicle maintenance, clerical activities).

GOALS AND OBJECTIVES

Since actual output is, or at least should be, related to an organization's goals and objectives, we begin with a discussion of these topics.

Goals

A goal is a statement of intended output in the broadest terms. It is normally not related to a specific time period. Goals normally are not quantified, and hence cannot be used directly as a basis for a measurement system. The purpose of a statement of goals is to communicate top management's decisions about the aims and relative priorities of the organization, and to provide general guidance as to the strategy that the organization is expected to follow.

Example: From the Department of Health, Education and Welfare:

To increase substantially the number of students from low income families participating in higher education student aid programs.

To stimulate changes in organization and delivery of health services particularly for the poor, with priority to: preventive measures, prepaid group practice, use of subprofessional and paraprofessional personnel, ambulatory care services, and neighborhood care delivery units.

Example: From Department of Defense:

To determine what forces are required to support the political objectives of the United States.

To procure and support these forces as economically as possible.

Goals alternatively, but less desirably, may be expressed as constraints, as indicated in the following comment:

> The operational goals of an organization are seldom revealed by formal mandates. Rather, each organization's operational goals emerge as a set of constraints defining acceptable performance. Central among these constraints is organizational health, defined usually in terms of bodies assigned and dollars appropriated. The set of constraints emerges from a mix of the expectations and demands of other organizations in the government, statutory authority, demands from citizens and special interest groups, and bargaining within the organization. These constraints represent a quasi-resolution of conflict—the constraints are relatively stable, so there is some degree of resolution; but the constraints are not compatible, hence it is only a quasi-resolution. Typically, the constraints are formulated as imperatives to avoid roughly specified discomforts and disasters.
>
> For example, the behavior of each of the U.S. military services (Army, Navy, and Air Force) seems to be characterized by effective imperatives to avoid: (1) a decrease in dollars budgeted, (2) a decrease in personnel, (3) a decrease in the number of key specialists (e.g., for the Air Force, pilots), (4) reduction in the percentage of the military budget allocated to that service, (5) encroachment of other services on that service's roles and missions, and (6) inferiority to an enemy weapon of any class.[3]

Every organization has one or more goals, but in many organizations little attention is given to articulating these goals. Managements in many organizations will find it worthwhile to devote significant effort to thinking about what the organization's goals actually should be and to expressing them as concretely as it can. Such an exercise will greatly facilitate later steps in the management control process. This is not to say that management should try to state *all* the goals of the organiza-

---

[3] Graham T. Allison, *Essences of Decision: Explaining the Cuban Missile Crisis* (Boston: Little, Brown and Company, 1971), p. 82.

tion; it should rather focus on the principal ones. The intention is to delineate the predominant goals, not to make an exhaustive list of them. Also, every organization carries on some activities that are not directly or obviously related to its stated goals.

> *Example:* The stated goals of the Philadelphia School District are listed below:

1. *Learning goals*
    1.1. To develop in each student, by relevant, interesting, and diversified instruction, a command of the basic skills and the ability to think clearly, communicate effectively, and learn easily.
    1.2. To help each student to be creative and make cultural and recreational activities a part of life.
    1.3. To give each student a clear and honest understanding of the United States, including contemporary urban problems, historical interpretation, and international relations.
2. *Community goals*
    2.1. To provide each student with an awareness of career alternatives and with the skills, motivation and assistance to choose a future.
    2.2. To make our schools as freely integrated and diversified as possible and to develop greater harmony among different ethnic groups.
    2.3. To develop more direct and effective systems of communication and involvement with the community and with government agencies at all levels.
    2.4. To improve adult educational opportunities.
    2.5. To improve mental and physical health so that each student learns self-respect and respect for others and so that the student can cope with the environment constructively.
3. *Enabling goals*
    3.1. To develop an efficient, responsive and flexible organization with the motivation, ability and resources to meet the needs of each student, each teacher, each administrator, and each school.
    3.2. To engage in every effort to attract, train, and retain the most competent personnel.
    3.3. To improve the effectiveness of educational program planning.
    3.4. To provide functional physical plants, in which teachers can utilize modern teaching methods and to which community residents will come.
    3.5. To improve short- and long-range planning and decision-making.

Although thinking about goals and attempting to express them in words is often a useful exercise, beyond a certain point the exercise can become frustrating and not worth additional effort. For example, if a hospital has decided that it wants to be a general hospital, there may be no need to reduce to words an exact statement of the goals of a general purpose hospital. Similarly, although many committees have spent long hours attempting to state the goals of a liberal arts college, the results sometimes have had little operational impact.

Objectives

An objective is a specific result to be achieved within a specified time, usually one year or a few years.[4]

If feasible, an objective should be stated in measurable terms. Since measurement is always quantitative, if an objective is not stated in quantitative terms, performance toward achieving the objective cannot be measured, although it can be judged, evaluated, appraised, or "weighed." If a statement of a particular objective in measurable terms is not feasible, the objective should be restated with sufficient clarity so that there is some way of judging whether or not it has been achieved. Exhibit 6–3 is an example.

EXHIBIT 6–3
Programs and Objectives, Fairfield Baptist Church, Chicago, Illinois
(excerpts)

Programs

1. To proclaim the Gospel to all people.
    Objectives:
    a. To establish a church evangelism committee by April 15.
    b. To contact every person within the city limits (for whom we can find record) who ever attended a church function, but no longer does with a personal visit from this church by 5/1/71.
    c. To contact every home in our immediate census tracts by 5/1/71.
    d. To adopt a comprehensive church-wide missionary education program by 9/1/70.
2. To Promote Worship
    Objectives:
    a. To establish a church worship committee by April 15, 1970.
    b. To implement systematic membership participation in the church worship services by May 8, 1970.
    c. To involve all institutionalized (elderly and otherwise) members in regular church worship by June 1, 1970.
    d. To provide a sanctuary suitable for worship by May 1, 1971.
                          *   *   *   *   *
6. Community Service
    Objectives:
    a. To establish a church community service by 4/15/70.
    b. To define the meaning of "service" and the extent of "community" by May 8, 1970.
    c. To establish communication with all community service agencies by May 1, 1970.
7. Administration

Source: Contributed by Dennis W. Bakke.

An objective should be consistent with the goals of the organization. Usually, the ordinary, ongoing activities that require little management judgment as to the amount of emphasis that is to be given to them

---

[4] Some writers use "goal" for the idea that is here described as "objective," and vice versa. Care must be taken to deduce the intended meaning from the context.

are not included in a statement of objectives; that is, objectives are nonroutine.

Examples: From the Department of Health, Education and Welfare:

HSMHA: To organize and staff the National Center for Family planning by June 1970, while offering family planning services to 900,000 women who otherwise could not obtain services.

NIH: To increase the output of schools of medicine and osteopathy, by awarding grants to augment the present commitments for first-year enrollments by 400 in Fall 1970 and by an additional 600 in Fall 1971, and by awarding construction grants to increase capacity for 1973–75 first-year enrollments by 300.

Example: An unsatisfactory statement of objectives from City of Long Beach Department of Community Development (these are *not* properly worded objectives because they are not stated in measurable terms and there is no way of judging whether or not they have been achieved):

Completion of the City's Community Analysis Program and development of a schedule of programs to prevent and correct blighted areas as well as predisposing and precipitating factors.

Expansion of the federally approved low income housing program for additional housing units.

With some effort, it is often feasible to state objectives in a measurable way. For example, the following is a vague objective for third-grade instruction in geography:

To learn to use the vocabulary, tools, skills, and insights of the geographer in interpreting and understanding the earth and our relation to it.

This objective becomes more useful if it is recast as follows:

That 90 per cent of the third grade students attending the Booth Elementary School, by June 30, 1975, will score between 90 and 100 percent and the remaining 10 percent will score between 80 and 90 percent on a wide evaluative instrument and/or process which measures their ability:

a. To understand why we have maps and why they are important.
b. To understand the importance of the globe being marked with horizontal and vertical lines which represent degrees of longitude and latitude and that the earth consists of hemispheres, continents, and oceans.[5]

TYPES OF OUTPUT MEASURES

There are a wide variety of ways of classifying output measures. The most important of these are listed below. The purpose of such

---

[5] From Larry Pauline, Education Systems Consultants.

a categorization is to provide a convenient way of commenting about the nature, advantages, and limitations of measures of various types.

Subjective or Objective

An output measure may result from the subjective judgment of a person or a group of persons, or it may be derived from data that (unless consciously manipulated) are not dependent on human judgment. A judgment made by a qualified person is usually a better measure of the quality of performance than any objective measure because humans incorporate in their judgment the effect of circumstances and nuances of performance that no set of objective measures can take into account. (Numerical ways of measuring beauty, for example, are far inferior to a visual judgment.) Hospitals are usually reluctant to measure the performance of physicians by any means other than peer review. Professors also prefer peer review judgments but will increasingly accept ratings made by students; many will not accept number of students electing a course, or number of articles published as valid measures of performance, however.

Subjective judgments are, however, subjective; that is, they depend on the person making the judgment and may be affected by the prejudices, attitudes, and even the person's emotional and physical state at the time the judgment is formed. Objective measures, if properly obtained, do not have these defects.

Quantitative or Nonquantitative

Strictly speaking, a measure is, by definition, quantitative; nevertheless, much information about output is nonquantitative, expressed in the form of words. Information in control systems is usually quantitative, so that it can be summarized or compared. Subjective judgments can be expressed in quantitative terms. Grades in schools, even though numerical, are an expression of the instructor's judgment as to where the student's performance is located along some scale. Performance in figure skating contests, ski jumping, and certain other athletic events is measured by the subjective judgments of the judges; the performer is ranked along a numerical scale by each judge and these ranks are then averaged.

Discrete or Scalar

A measure of performance may be either a dichotomy ("satisfactory/unsatisfactory" or "go/no-go"), or it may be measured along a scale. For example, in measuring performance of a reading program in a school, a target could be established, such as "80 percent of students should read at or above grade level on a standardized test." If the measure were discrete, any performance of 80 percent or higher would be counted as success, and any performance below 80 percent would be counted as failure. If the measure were scalar, the percentage of students reading at grade level on a standardized test would be used as the measure of output. Each of these types of output measures has its place.

Quantity or Quality

Performance has both a quantity and a quality dimension. Usually it is more feasible to measure quantity (e.g., number of students graduated) than to measure quality (e.g., how well the students were educated). Despite this difficulty, the quality dimension should not be overlooked. Indeed, the indicator that is chosen to measure quantity usually implies some standard of quality. "Number of lines typed per hour" usually carries with it the implication that the lines were typed satisfactorily in order to be counted, and there may even be an explicit statement of what constitutes a satisfactory line of typing, such as the requirement that it be free of errors. Similarly, the measure "number of students graduated" implies that the students have met standards of quality that are prescribed for graduation.

In some situations, judgments about quality are limited to such "go/no-go" statements as those given above; either a line of typing was error-free or it was not; either a student met the requirements for graduation or did not. In these situations, it is not feasible to measure quality along a scale; for example, to determine that this year's graduates received a better education than last year's.

In a nonprofit organization, measures of quality are more important than in a profit-oriented company, however, so it is worthwhile devoting considerable effort to finding usable scalar measures. This is because in a profit-oriented company, the market mechanism provides an automatic check on quality. If the perceived design and construction of a pair of shoes is shoddy, people will not buy them. The factory will then have to lower prices and/or raise quality in order to stay in business. If it doesn't do so, other factories will take its customers away. There is no such mechanism for consumer reaction to the output of many nonprofit organizations, however. If the organization's program does not fulfill consumer ideas of quality, there is little they can do.

Further, in most public programs, the private motive for the program and the social motive for sponsoring it may diverge; i.e., private and social measures of quality differ. Thus, even if Head Start produces indifferent results or neurotic children, mothers may still send their children to the program just to get them out of the home. Similarly, if a personnel program neither trains nor places its clients properly, unemployed people may still participate in it out of boredom or because of the stipend for participation. In such circumstances, unless there are adequate measures of quality in the program's management control system, the program will continue to operate without challenge.

The total absence of quality measures in management control systems may lead to a detrimental emphasis on quantity, e.g., people's being rapidly pushed through an education program; a number of quick and careless pollution inspections; quick, shoddy construction jobs.

Quality measures are usually available, even in the short run. For example;

In Head Start, one can measure a child's degree of literacy, social acclimation, etc., before and after the program.

In personnel training, one can ask employers to rate the graduates.

In construction, one can test stress, fulfillment of construction standards, and so on.

Even though these measures are crude, and even though they may not even contain the "proper" attribute of quality, they may, if nothing else, serve as good motivators for the program's management.

If, however, there is no demonstrable relationship between inputs and the quality of outputs, it may not be worthwhile to attempt scalar measurements of quality for either planning or for control purposes.

Example: The Peace Corps sponsored an attempt at a scalar measurement of the qualitative effectiveness of its program in Peru, using measures that purported to show the change in the well-being of Peruvians during a two-year period. Since there was no plausible way of relating the measures of well-being to the efforts of Peace Corps workers, this effort was probably a waste of time and money.

In the absence of objective data, judgmental estimates of quality may be useful. For example, in a university, subjective comparisons can be made between the standing of a college or department within its professional discipline, or its position currently with its position at some specified time in the past.

Measurements of quality may require so much elapsed time and be so expensive that they are unwarranted for management control. The same measures may nevertheless be warranted, at least on a sampling basis, as an aid in strategic planning.

Example: In 1969, the Westinghouse Learning Corporation reported on an intensive evaluation of Head Start programs in various cities The technique used was to measure the performance of Head Start pupils a year or two after they had left the program. This measurement, at best, reflected the performance of Head Start schools at least a year previously, and therefore was of no use in making decisions about the current performance in such schools. Nevertheless, it was undoubtedly useful to those responsible for making strategic decisions about continuing, dropping, or redirecting the Head Start program.[6]

Results, Process, or Social Indicators

Many different terms are used to classify output measures according to what it is that they purport to measure. For our purposes, three terms will suffice: (1) results measures, (2) process measures, and (3) social indicators.

Results Measures. A results measure is a measure of output expressed in terms that are supposedly related to an organization's objectives. In the ideal situation, the objective is stated in measurable terms, and the output measure is stated in these same terms. When this relationship is not feasible, as is often the case, the performance measure represents the closest feasible way of measuring the accomplishment of an objective that cannot itself be expressed quantitatively. Such a measure is called a *surrogate* or a *proxy.*

> *Example:* From Department of Defense:
>
> An *objective* under the second goal of the Department of Defense (see above) is: Buy at the lowest sound price. *Surrogates* used to measure this objective are:
>
> 1. Percent of contracts let after competition.
> 2. Percent of incentive-type contracts.

A results measure relates to the impact that the organization has on the outside world. If the organization is client-oriented, a results measure relates to what the organization did for the client. Organizations that render service to a class of clients, such as alcoholics or unemployed persons, may measure output in terms of the results for the whole class, or *target group.*

Process Measure. A process measure relates to an activity carried on by the organization. Examples are the number of livestock inspected in a week, the number of lines typed in an hour, the number of requisitions filled in a month, or the number of purchase orders written. The essential difference between a results measure and a process measure is that the former is "ends oriented," while the latter is "means oriented." An ends-oriented indicator is a direct measure of success in achieving an objective. A means-oriented indicator is a measure of what a responsibility center or an individual does. There is an implicit assumption that what the responsibility center does helps achieve the organization's objectives, but this is not always a valid assumption. For example, in an air pollution program, the change in the amount of SO_2 in the atmo-

---

[6] Westinghouse Learning Corporation for the Office of Economic Opportunity, and Ohio University, *The Impact of Head Start: An Evaluation of the Effects of Head Start Experience on Children's Cognitive and Affective Development* (1969).

sphere is an ends-oriented results measure, while the number of inspections made of possible violators is a means-oriented process measure. There is an implication of a causal relationship between the number of inspections made and the amount of air pollution, which may or may not be valid. The terms "performance oriented" and "work oriented" are other names for the same distinction between ends-oriented and means-oriented indicators.

Process measures are most useful in the measurement of current, short-run performance. They are the easiest type of output measure to interpret because there presumably is a close causal relationship between inputs and process measures. They measure efficiency, but not effectiveness. Being only remotely related to goals, they are of little use in strategic planning. They are useful in constructing relevant parts of a budget, but only for those activities for which it is feasible to obtain process measures. They are useful in the control of lower-level responsibility centers.

Process measures should not be used if results measures are available. For example, the U.S. Air Force measured performance of certain squadrons by the number of hours flown, which is a process measure. Sometimes squadrons would build up performance based on this measure simply by flying in large circles around a base, without any real accomplishments.

A *productivity* measure is a type of process measure which may or may not be a good measure of efficiency. Productivity means output per man hour. An increase in output per man hour is equivalent to an increase in efficiency; if, but only if, input factors other than personnel remain constant. This point was not well recognized in the 1971–2 study of productivity of Federal agencies, which is probably the broadest attempt ever made to collect output information.[7] The study attempted to measure the change in output for the period 1967–71 for functions employing 1.5 million persons in 17 Federal agencies. Outputs in these agencies were measured in 605 different ways, and the separate measures were then combined into an overall index.

An example of misconceptions in output information appears as Exhibit 6–4 taken from this Federal Productivity Study. This exhibit shows production per work hour for each of 10 different methods of preparing checks and bonds in the Bureau of Accounts in the Treasury Department. The report draws attention to the heavy line, which is the weighted average of the ten methods. This line shows a dramatic increase in checks per work hour from 1949 to 1962. Careful inspection will show, however, that this increase results entirely from the introduction of automatic equipment, and that the output per man hour of manually typed checks actually decreased during the period. There was

---

[7] *Measuring and Enhancing Productivity in the Federal Sector*, Joint Economic Committee, August 4, 1972. (Government Printing Office 81-339).

EXHIBIT 6–4

Measures of Productivity

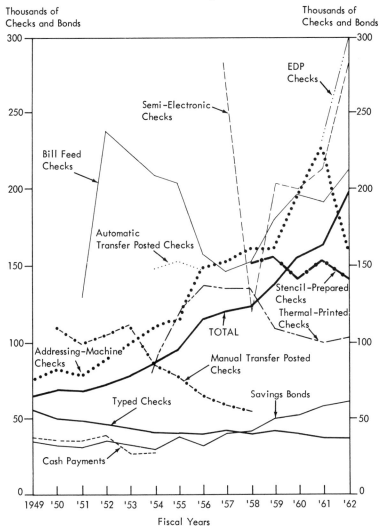

Division of Disbursement
CHECKS AND BONDS PER MAN YEAR BY PROCESS
OF PREPARATION, 1949–1962

an increase in *productivity* (which means output per man hour) but not necessarily in efficiency.

Social Indicators. A social indicator is a broad measure of output which is significantly the result of the work of the organization, but which is also affected by exogenous forces, and which therefore is at best only a rough indication of the accomplishment of the organization itself.

Social indicators are often stated in broad terms (e.g., "the expectation of healthy life free of serious disability and institutionalization"). Such statements are generally not as useful as those expressed in more specific, preferably measurable, terms (e.g., infant mortality rates, life expectancy).

Social indicators are useful principally for long-range analyses of strategic problems. They are so nebulous, so difficult to obtain on a current basis, so little affected by current program effort, and so much affected by external influences that they are of limited usefulness in day-to-day management.

Social indicators tend to relate to the overall objectives of the organization rather than to specific activities, hence, they are most likely to be useful in strategic planning. Valid social indicators are difficult to collect. They are also difficult to use properly because there is no demonstrable cause-effect relationship. Some social indicators may be collected fairly easily, but such measures are likely to be of dubious validity. The proportion of youth from a certain school district who fail to pass the armed forces qualifying test may indicate the quality of the educational program in that school district, but only in a tenuous way. Likewise, proxy indicators for intangible factors, such as percentage of registered citizens voting as an indicator of citizenship, or crime and disturbance statistics as an indicator of social unrest, may be collected fairly easily, but are of limited reliability.

Alternative Terminology.   As already indicated, various terms are used for types of output measures. For example, in New York City the three measures are referred to as (1) program output measures, (2) program impact measures, and (3) social impact measures. Program output measures relate to the number of units of output produced (e.g., the number of cubic yards of rubbish collected in the city). Program impact measures refer to the effect of program outputs on the objectives of that program (e.g., the contribution of the collection of an incremental cubic yard of garbage to a reduction in the number of cubic yards of garbage collected on a collection day. It is assumed that this ratio gives some indication of the general cleanliness of the city). Social impact measures, if they can ever be developed, will relate the program's objectives to the objectives of society as a whole.

These are by no means the only ways of classifying output. Exhibit 6–5, for example, gives a four-way classification system for measuring the output of schools.

Output Vectors

It is rarely possible to find a single overall measure of the performance of a nonprofit organization that is analogous to the profit measure in a profit-oriented company. The goals of nonprofit organizations are usu-

EXHIBIT 6–5

Dimensions of School Output

Level I: Leading Factors	Level II: Testing Measures	Level III: Subjective Measures	Level IV: Social Indicators
Classroom time	1. Grades and grade point averages	1. Citizens surveys: what do people think?	1. Increases in income
Use of students' time	2. Achievement test scores	2. Opinions of outside experts	2. Performance on AFQT
School days/year	3. Test batteries on attitudes	3. What do students and recent graduates think?	3. Citizenship voting behavior
Number of school graduates	4. Other testing instruments	4. What do employers of students think?	4. Adaptability in job setting; i.e., ease in training
Number and kind of jobs obtained	5. Behavioral objectives		
Salaries earned			
Drop-out rates; juvenile delinquency			

Source: Unpublished paper by John L. Moore, Harvard Graduate School of Education.

ally complex and often of an intangible nature. The outputs of such organizations are accordingly complex, and many separate devices are used to measure them. It is sometimes feasible to combine a multidimensional array of indicators into an aggregate which provides patterns, trends, and indicators of output quality and organizational performance. This may be called an *output vector.*

The value weights placed on each component of this output vector should reflect the values of the policy makers, not of the systems analysts or accountants. There are few programs which could not satisfactorily be described by such a weighted output vector; the question is whether the effort to do so is worthwhile. The Strategic Air Command, for example, for many years measured the performance of each of its wings by an output vector computed by weighting scores for each of several dozen measures of performance. Some observers judged this system to be highly valuable; others were dubious as to whether it was worth its cost.

Dennis Gillings describes an elaborate way of measuring performance in terms of objectives which he (with the assistance of Priscilla Gould) devised for the Lincoln Community Health Center.[8] The nature of this measurement plan is suggested by Exhibits 6–6 and 6–7. Exhibit 6–6 shows the eight goals that were established for this organization. Under each goal, specific activities were identified, and

---

[8] Dennis Gillings, "Evaluation: A Methodology for Determining the Effectiveness of a Social Program in Terms of Goal Fulfillment" (Department of Biostatistics, School of Public Health, University of North Carolina, Chapel Hill: October 1972).

EXHIBIT 6-6

Goals and Activities in a Primary Care Organization

Program Level 1: **Program**

Goals Level 2	Activities Level 3
Target Population	Define; Check Target Population Being Served
Operation of Center	Building; Staff; Facilities; Courtesy; Pleasant Decorations; Appointment System; Walk-Ins; Patients Encouraged to Make Appointments; Reimbursement; Registration and Encounter Forms; Reporting System; Evaluation
Accessibility of Health Care	Registration; Family Care; Encourage Enrollment; Transportation of Patients; Opening Hours; Keep Appointments; Transport for CHW's; Map
Improvement of Health	Adult Health Assessments; Child Health Assessments; Immunization; Sickle Cell; EKG; Chest X-Ray; GYN Exam; Prenatal Screening; Hypertension Follow-Up; Follow Up External Referrals; Ensure Patients Keep Appointments; Health Education; General Improvement of Health
Quality of Care	Review Health Assessments; Encourage Patients to Keep Appointments; Follow Up External Referrals; Ensure Patients Keep External Referrals; Patients Have No Difficulty Making Appointments; Waiting Time; Opening Hours; Patients Comfortable Expressing Health Needs; Understand Doctors
Contribution to Quality of Life	Employment; Training; Youth Employment; Services Helpful; Other Centers; Arrange Compensation for Specialty Care
Relation to Other Programs	Liaison with Voluntary Primary Health Care Facilities; Liaison with FOOD Project; Liaison with Local Health Agencies
Catalyst for Social Reform	Liaison with Agencies and Corporations for Training; Other Health Centers

EXHIBIT 6–7

Activities, Targets, Measures, and Weights

(goal V: deliver high quality health care   goal weight = 5)

Activity	Assessment Regime				Achieve-ment	Effec-tiveness
	Target	Outcome Measure	Weight	Outcome		
Establish a routine series of tests and examinations for a complete health assessment.	September 1971.	$x = \begin{cases} 0.4 \text{ if no} \\ 0.6 \text{ if yes} \end{cases}$ Achievement = x	4	Yes	0.60	1.00
Encourage patients to keep appointments.	65 percent of appointments should be kept.	$\left[\begin{array}{l} \text{Proportion of appointments} \\ \text{that are kept January–June} \\ 1972 \end{array} \right] \times \frac{12}{13}$	2	61 percent	0.56	0.93
Establish mechanisms to facilitate follow-up of patients referred to other institutions.	Mechanisms established by March 1972.	$x = \begin{cases} 0.4 \text{ if no} \\ 0.6 \text{ if yes} \end{cases}$ Achievement = x	3	Yes	0.6	1.00
Ensure that patients referred to other institutions appear for a consultation.	50 percent of externally referred patients appear for a consultation at the institution to which they are referred and notification of results sent to center.	$\left[\begin{array}{l} \text{Proportion of externally} \\ \text{referred appointments} \\ \text{kept about which center} \\ \text{notified} \end{array} \right] \times \frac{6}{5}$	3	161 appointments. Notification received for 60 i.e., 37.3 percent	0.45	0.75
Ensure that patients have no difficulty making an appointment at the center.	85 percent of a sample of patients answer negatively to the question: "Have you every had any difficulty making an appointment at this center."	$\left[\begin{array}{l} \text{Proportion of a sample} \\ \text{of patients who answer} \\ \text{negatively} \end{array} \right] \times \frac{12}{17}$	2	97 percent	0.68	1.14

a measure of accomplishment, or target, was agreed to by Center management for each activity. Some of the activities for one goal are listed in Exhibit 6–7. The outcome measures were set so that an outcome of 0.6 was rated as satisfactory performance, and the relative effectiveness of activities for the whole goal was determined by weighting each of the separate outcomes and adding them. Note that some of the activities were measured on a "yes-no" basis, and others were rated along a scale such that accomplishment of the designated target resulted in an achievement of 0.6.

Many managers decide that such a plan of measuring outputs is more time-consuming than the results justify, but greatly simplified versions of this general approach may be eminently worthwhile.

SELECTION OF OUTPUT MEASURES

In the following subsections, some factors that should be considered in selecting output measures are discussed.

General Propositions

Three obvious, but often overlooked, general propositions about output measures follow:

1. *Output measures are useful both for planning and for control.* For planning purposes, output measures provide a focus that facilitates analysis. The whole idea of "benefit/cost analysis" which will be discussed in Chapter 8 rests on the foundation of some measure of "benefits," which means output. For control, measurement of both effectiveness and efficiency depends on some measure of output. It follows that a considerable expenditure of effort in finding and developing output measures is worthwhile.

2. *Output measures that are not used for planning or control should ordinarily not be collected.* This is the converse of the first proposition. More information is not necessarily better than less information. An increment of information may be dysfunctional. It may swamp the system, increase the "noise" level, draw attention away from useful information, and lessen the credibility of the system as a whole.

3. *Some measure of output is usually better than none.* Valid criticisms can be made about almost every output measure. Few, if any, of them measure output perfectly. There is a tendency on the part of some managers to magnify the imperfections and thus downgrade the attempt to collect and use output information. In most situations a sounder approach is to take account of the imperfections and to qualify the results accordingly, but to recognize that some output data, however crude, is of more use to management than no data at all.

Example: In New York City, municipal office workers were once given one hour off per day with pay in the summer because their offices were not air conditioned. Later on, the offices were air conditioned on the grounds that this would improve output, but the employees continued to receive the hour off with pay. In the absence of any output measure, there was no good way of making an analysis of the desirability of installing air conditioning. If such information existed, the installation of air conditioning probably could have been traded off for a decrease in the summer bonus pay.

Continuum of Output Measures

The types of output indicators that are appropriate for use in a given organization tend to be arranged along a continuum. At one end are unmeasurable social indicators that are closely related to the goals of the organization, and at the other end are precisely stated process measures that are only remotely related to the goals of the organization.

Example: For the U.S. Information Agency, one extreme is the degree to which the agency influences international behavior through its activities. A second level indicates the extent to which specific attitudes and opinions of the governing members of other nations have been changed by the agency's work. A third level represents a measurement of the increase of understanding of people overseas in regard to specific issues. A fourth level is a count of the number of times people have been reached by media of different kinds. A fifth and lowest level is a count of the number of "media products" produced by the agency.

It is useful to think of output measures in terms of this continuum for two reasons. First, higher level output indicators are better indicators of program effectiveness than are lower level measures. The latter tend to be surrogate measures that often are not closely related to program objectives. Second, lower level indicators are easier to specify and quantify than are higher level indicators. This fact explains the prevalence of measures of project efficiency or effectiveness which are irrelevant to overall program objectives.

The continuum also corresponds to the relative usefulness of types of output indicators at various levels in the organization hierarchy. Social indicators and results measures are most useful to top management, whereas process measures are most useful to first-line supervisors.

Example: A regional Air Pollution Control Administration headquarters has a broad variety of measures. It is concerned with its own efficient functioning; that is, it has its own process measures (how fast a request is considered, how quickly budget and project requests can be handled, etc.). At the other end of the spectrum, it has objectives for air quality in each region. The progress toward these objectives can be measured by the appropriate instrumentation.

In between these process measures and results measures there is a variety of measures related to the functioning of the regional administrator and the state programs within a region. For example, the agency may establish as an objective the improvement of air quality in the New England region by more vigorous antipollution efforts on the part of the Commonwealth of Massachusetts.

In comparing the output measurement problem of various agencies, it is useful to think of another continuum, one which is expressed in terms of the degree to which the goals and the means of reaching those goals are understood. At one extreme are agencies (e.g., Head Start) in which there is disagreement among policymakers as to what the goals should be and as to the relative importance of various goals, and in which the effectiveness of various techniques is not well understood (e.g., little is known about the relative effectiveness of various methods of teaching preschool children). At the other extreme are agencies where goals and the optimum means of reaching these goals are reasonably clearcut (e.g., U.S. Postal Service). In agencies of the former type determination of what the program should be trying to accomplish is itself one of the objectives of the program, and the management control system should facilitate this process of discovery.

Variety of Measures

In a single organization, there can be a variety of measures, each used for a different purpose. For example, with respect to health care in a community:

1.   There can be a measure of the total cost of the health care system, as a basis for comparison with the cost of other community services; this measures the relative emphasis given to each service. Expressed as a cost per person in the community, this can be compared with costs per person in other communities as another expression of relative emphasis.

2.   There can be an overall cost per patient day in each hospital, as a basis for detecting gross differences in the operating characteristics of each hospital. Per patient costs for each service (medicine, surgery, pediatrics, psychiatric, etc.), are useful for similar reasons.

3.   At a lower level, information can be collected on the cost per episode of each type of admission.

4.   At a still lower level, costs per unit of service rendered, such as cost per meal served, can be collected.

Timeliness

A timely, but less accurate, output measure is usually preferable for management control to an accurate, but less timely, measure. The converse is often the case in strategic planning. Timeliness is not equivalent to speed in this context, but rather is related to the time-span of the task.

> *Example:* Mortality from emphysema, which can be measured only years after the occurrence of the cause of the disease, is less useful for control of air pollution programs than less accurate but more timely measures, such as the number of persons with eye/ear/nose/throat irritations, or the number who are advised by physicians to move to another locality, or the amount of effluent in the air.

The problem of timeliness is different in nonprofit organizations (especially government) than it is in profit-oriented organizations for several reasons. The first is that output often cannot be measured immediately after the effort has been applied. The results of funds invested in a school program in September may not be measurable until the following June. The effect of interest rate subsidies on low-income housing stock may not be measurable for two or three years because of the time necessary to design and construct buildings.

Second, reports on a program may work their way through several organizational layers. Thus Title I, an HEW educational program, provides grants through a state educational agency, then through a local educational agency, and ultimately to the local Title I administrator. The data which work their way back through this chain could well be several months old by the time they reach program analysts at HEW.

Third, some data although not timely may indicate a situation which is not likely to have changed since the time of measurement. Thus, the data are as important as if they were current. School segregation data is an example of data that need not be collected frequently.

Strategic Planning and Management Control

The control system should provide output information that is useful both for strategic planning and for management control. The criteria governing output measures that are useful for making strategic plans tend to differ from those that are useful for management control in the following ways:

Precision. For strategic planning, rough estimates of output are satisfactory. For management control, the measure must be more precise in order to be credible.

Causality. For management control, there should be a quite plausible link between the effort (i.e., inputs) of the organization and the output measure. For strategic planning, the connection can be more tenuous. Even for strategic planning, there should be a plausible connection between inputs and outputs if output measures are to be used in analyzing a proposal for a specific program. To include noncorrelating output figures in an analysis is not only a waste of time, but it may do more harm than good because it leads people to believe that there is a causal connection when none in fact can be assumed.

The fact that a causal connection cannot be demonstrated is no reason for abandoning an attempt to make an analysis or to recommend a certain program. It simply means that the decisions must be based on judgments unaided by this kind of quantitative information. For example, it seems obviously desirable to spend money on a judiciary system even though no good measure of output is available. Similarly, although there is no conclusive measure of educational effectiveness which demonstrates that the Head Start program is worthwhile, this fact is not sufficient reason for abandoning the Head Start program.

Responsibility. For management control, the output measure must be related to the responsibility of a specific person or organization unit. For strategic planning, this is unnecessary. It follows that strategic considerations can require that operating personnel collect data for which they themselves have no use.

> *Example:* In Title I Education programs, central planners in Washington may require the collection of data (e.g., test scores) which will be of no use to operating managers, but which are necessary for reformulating program goals and methods.

Timeliness. For management control, data on output must be available shortly after the event. For strategic planning, this is less important.

> *Example:* Measures of the subsequent performance of Head Start students in school are useful for strategic planning, but they cannot be part of a management control system.

Cost. For both strategic planning and management control, the benefits of obtaining information about inputs and outputs must always exceed the costs of obtaining such information. For strategic planning purposes, it may be possible to obtain certain data on an *ad hoc* or sampling basis, whereas the continuous collection of these data for management control may be prohibitively expensive.

Relation to Program Elements

Output measures are desirably, but not necessarily, related to individual program elements. They may also be related to program subcategories, or even to overall goals or objectives.

> *Example:* In education, an output measure may be the number of students with a specified reading skill level. This probably cannot be related to costs or to program elements, except possibly in the primary grades where the development of reading skills may constitute an impor-

tant specific objective. In other grades and classes, teachers may spend only a fraction of their time on reading skills. Nevertheless, it, along with a number of similar measures, may be a good way of measuring the overall performance of a school.

It would be possible to allocate teacher salaries, and other costs, to reading, for example, but (*a*) it would be an expensive job to do so, and, more importantly, (*b*) students learn reading indirectly as well as directly from reading instruction.

Just as the economy has many indicators of "healthiness" which various people interpret differently in our complex society, nonprofit organizations have numerous ways of looking at their complex outputs. The results in the social field are often indirect and unexpected. To peg indicators directly to program elements or categories may totally overlook some of the lasting results of a program. Thus, a variety of output measures, including a number of surrogates, are often necessary in order to obtain a valid impression of the effectiveness of a program. A series of indirect output measures may make it difficult for top management to measure the effectiveness of a responsibility center, but it is unfair and depressing to morale when "output" is defined in terms that are too narrow.

Inputs as a Measure of Outputs

Although generally less desirable than a true output measure, inputs are often a better measure of output than no measure at all. For example, it may not be feasible to construct output measures for research projects. In the absence of such measures, the amount spent on a research project may provide a useful clue to output. In the extreme, if no money was spent, it is apparent that nothing was accomplished. (This assumes that the accounting records show what actually was spent, which sometimes is not the case.) When inputs are used as proxy output measures, care must be exercised to avoid undue reliance on them, and the organization should try to develop usable measures of output.

Caution on Use of Surrogates

A surrogate should be closely related to an objective. By definition, however, a surrogate does not correspond exactly to an objective, and it should be used with this limitation in mind. If the lack of correspondence is not recognized, the organization may focus too much attention on the surrogate, and this may be dysfunctional. Achieving the *surrogate* should not be permitted to become more important than achieving the *objective.* The following examples illustrate the principle that caution must be exercised in the selection and use of surrogates.

Example: Body count.[9]

A competitive program involving the deduction of "points" from units losing men in combat was established recently by an American battalion commander, but abandoned under criticism.

Three weeks ago, Colonel Bradley, of Arlington, Va., started a competition in which the winning rifle platoon would get three duty-free days in a rest center and the winning weapons platoon get two days. Points were awarded to platoons for enemy soldiers killed, for weapons captured and rice caches discovered. Points were deducted from platoons suffering battle casualties.

The last part of the program touched off an angry letter from one of the infantrymen. "The morale is low enough without a stupid contest that only shows us what little is thought of what we're already doing," he wrote home. "We don't need to be playing games in a combat zone. I wouldn't like to think that because one of my buddies gets killed it only means we lose points."

Example: Lines typed.

The number of lines typed measures the typists's output, but this says nothing about whether what was typed had any relationship to the organization's objectives.

Example: Incentive Contracting.

The Defense Department's surrogate on percent of incentive type contracts as an indicator of buying at the lowest sound price (see above) reached the field level buying offices as a virtual command to make contracts of the incentive type. Each buying organization had its target percentage. While the original objective was well communicated and understood, it became secondary to meeting the target. The surrogate became the basis for a decision rule: when in doubt, make the contract an incentive type.

The reasoning that incentive-type contracts are more advantageous for the government than cost-type contracts is generally true, but there are numerous exceptions; however, the circumstances in which exceptions were appropriate were not subject to measurement. Because the surrogate was tangible, it became more important than the objective.

Example: Small Business Administration.[10]

Consider some of the loan programs of the federal government. Many of these programs, rightly or wrongly, have supposedly the objective of providing loan capital to small enterprises which are too risky for investment by commercial lenders. The Small Business Administration is a case in point. Measures have not been developed, however, which can be used to judge the performance of various regional loan offices in terms of overall program objectives. Defaulted loans, on the other hand, are easily identified; and a significant default rate is sure to invite congressional questions. Therefore, loan officials tend to avoid

---

[9] An AP dispatch from Dautieng, South Vietnam in the *Boston Globe*, May 4, 1969.

[10] Charles L. Schultz, Brookings Institution, in testimony before the Joint Economic Committee, October 6, 1969.

risky loans. As a consequence, far from meeting their original objectives, the programs end up (in many cases) simply in making loans of commercial quality at less than commercial rates. It is difficult to expect public officials to pursue the basic objectives of a program unless they are judged on the basis of performance measures which have some relevance to those objectives.

Example: Number of Complaints.

A city used "number of complaints" as a surrogate measure for the performance of the agency that managed low-cost rental housing units. It was later discovered that the agency was spending considerable effort to persuade tenants not to make complaints. This made performance as measured by the surrogate appear to improve, whereas service to tenants had actually deteriorated.

Example: Job Corps.[11]

When "effectiveness" of a Job Corps training program was being calculated by the contractor, "completions" were the mark of success; "dropouts" were the failures. When the latter appeared to be on the increase, "certificates of completion" were issued every other Saturday instead of the diploma originally given at the end of some previously designated period, such as six months. Immediately, the number of "completions" rose; "dropouts" declined; the "effectiveness" of the enterprise was assured, and so was its continued funding.

Example: Hospital Beds.[12]

It may sound plausible to measure the effectiveness of a mental hospital by how well its beds—a scarce and expensive commodity—are utilized. Yet a study of the mental hospitals of the Veterans' Administration brought out that this yardstick leads to mental patients' being kept in the hospital—which, therapeutically, is about the worst thing that can be done to them. Clearly, however, lack of utilization, that is, empty beds, would also not be the right yardstick. How then does one measure whether a mental hospital is doing a good job within the wretched limits of our knowledge of mental diseases?

The inappropriateness of an output measure may cause the discontinuance of a useful program, but more likely it will support the continuance of a useless one with a corresponding waste of resources. Inappropriate measures also cause agencies to be self-satisfied even though they are not reaching their objectives.

Reactions to Output Measurement

Attempts to measure output in nonprofit organizations are relatively new, especially attempts to measure the output of professionals. They tend to be resisted by those whose output is to be measured.

---

[11] Ida R. Hoos, *Retraining the Workforce; Analysis of Current Experience* (Berkeley and Los Angeles: University of California Press, 1967), p. 173.

[12] Peter Drucker, *The Age of Discontinuity* (New York: Harper and Row, 1969), p. 196.

Example: Following is a summary of a paper prepared by the Academic Council of the University of California objecting to a proposal to measure and control faculty workload:

A standard workload for the system, the professors said, would encourage large lectures, discourage individual tutorials, demean the status of the faculty, undercut its morale, and inhibit the recruitment of outstanding scholars.

Trying to measure faculty output is an extremely complicated matter, they said, because of the variety of campuses, departments, disciplines, and teaching methods. Simple formulas would be meaningless and misleading, they maintained.

The professors did not address the auditors' specific suggestions that a formula be developed to measure faculty effort in terms of classroom contact hours, type of course, number of tutorial students, number of student credit-hours generated, and the participation of teaching assistants. However, they did analyze and reject two of the most important elements in the proposed formula—contact hours and credit hours produced.

Their biggest objection was that the measures did not take into account the growing number of hours spent on field trips and tutorials as well as time spent on class preparation, grading exams, reading term papers, keeping up with the literature, and supervising teaching assistants.

Further, the council's paper said, neither of those measures gives any clue to the quality of teaching.

All such complexities make generalizations about faculty workloads suspect, the professors said.[13]

This problem will be discussed in more detail in Chapter 13 on Implementation.

BIBLIOGRAPHY

U.S. General Service Administration. *Cost Principles for Educational Institutions.* Federal Management Circular 73–8 (December 19, 1973) 34 CFR 254. Obtainable from General Services Administration (AMF) Washington, D.C. 20405. (Supersedes OMB Circular No. A–21).

U.S. Cost Accounting Standards Board. *Cost Accounting Standards.* (Published in the *Federal Register* as Parts 400 *et. seq.*)

---

[13] *The Chronicle of Higher Education* (April 24, 1972), p. 1.

chapter seven

Pricing

In a profit-oriented company, pricing policies and practices are within the jurisdiction of the marketing organization; the topic would ordinarily not be included in a description of management control practices. In a nonprofit organization, however, the prices charged for services rendered are an important consideration in management control. An analysis of pricing policies in nonprofit organizations is fascinating because many of the considerations that make a discussion of market pricing so frustrating (e.g., the fact that consumers do not act like "economic persons") do not complicate the picture. Indeed, a study of nonprofit pricing policies can illuminate some of the underlying forces that govern market prices. Many nonprofit organizations have not given enough thought to their pricing policies; they tend to regard all activities that come under the general heading of marketing as something that they need not worry about.

This chapter is organized around five principles of pricing. All of these principles have exceptions, and none is universally accepted as being valid. These exceptions and disagreements are included in the discussion. The five principles are that, as a general rule:

1. Services should be sold, rather than be given away.
2. The price should affect the consumer's actions.
3. The price should be equal to full cost.
4. The unit of service that is priced should be narrowly defined.
5. Prospective pricing is preferable to cost reimbursement.

WHEN SERVICES SHOULD BE SOLD

Advantages of Selling Services

This section discusses the advantages of selling services, rather than giving them away, and particularly selling them at a price that approximates full cost. It also describes situations in which the sale of services is not feasible.

Output Measurement. If services are sold at prices that approximate full cost, the revenue figure that is thereby generated is a measure of the quantity of services that the organization supplies. As has been pointed out in Chapter 6, in the absence of such an output measure, it is difficult to measure either efficiency or effectiveness.

Motivate the Client. Charging clients for services rendered makes them more aware of the value of the service and encourages them to consider whether the services are actually worth as much to them as their cost. If revenues generated by full-cost prices are not sufficient to cover total expenses, there is an indication that the service is not valuable enough to society to warrant the cost of providing it.[1] It may be that the organization's costs are higher than necessary, or that a lower-cost service would satisfy the clients' needs.

Motivate Managers. If services are sold, the responsibility center that sells them can become a "revenue center," that is a unit whose output and input are both measured in monetary terms. The manager of a revenue center becomes responsible for operating the unit in such a way that revenue equals expenses.

The manager of a revenue center is motivated to think of ways of rendering additional service that will increase revenue, to think of ways of cutting costs to the point where the corresponding price is one that clients are willing to pay, to become more vigilant in controlling overhead costs, and in general to behave like a manager in a profit-oriented company.

> *Example:* On a military base, an organization known as the Motor Pool furnishes trucks and passenger vehicles for the use of other organization units on the base. Until recently, these services were furnished without charge. Consequently, users had no inhibition about asking the Motor Pool for all the transportation they could get; users were not motivated to consider how much transportation they actually needed.

---

[1] The notion that societal approval of a firm's activities can be deduced from the size of its profits has come under attack, most notably from J. K. Galbraith in *The New Industrial State* (Boston: Houghton Mifflin Co., 1967). Galbraith asserts that all one can deduce from corporate profits is the acumen of the corporation's marketing department. For a rebuttal and an argument in support of the "immaculate conception of preferences," see Robert M. Solow's discussion "The New Industrial State or Son of Affluence" in *The Public Interest* (New York: National Affairs Inc., Fall 1967), pp. 100–108.

Allocation of motor vehicles was the responsibility of the manager of the Motor Pool; allocations were made according to the manager's perception of need (and in some cases according to friendship with users). There was no way of measuring the overall efficiency of the Motor Pool.

When the Motor Pool was set up as a revenue center, all these conditions changed. Users now were motivated to think about how much transportation services they needed; they weighed such needs against other possible uses of available funds. One immediate consequence of this was that users requested smaller trucks than previously, with a resultant saving in both operating costs and in the purchase cost of new vehicles. No longer were users at the mercy of the Motor Pool manager's perception of need; if users had the money, they could have the vehicles. There was an income statement for each Motor Pool; if it showed that revenue was inadequate to cover costs, there was an indication that costs were out of line or that the scale of operations was larger than necessary. It was possible to compare prices with those charged by commercial rental companies, and if they were out of line, questions needed to be answered (especially since prices charged by rental companies included depreciation and profit, which were not included in the calculation of motor pool costs).

Services that Should Not be Sold

Notwithstanding these advantages of charging for services rendered, there are many qualifications and *caveats* to the general principle stated above.

Public Goods. The most important class of services that normally should be furnished without charge to the client is *public goods*. Public goods are services which are for the benefit of the public in general, rather than for an individual client. Examples are police protection, as contrasted with a police officer who is hired by the manager of a sporting event; and foreign policy and its implementation, as contrasted with services rendered to an individual firm doing business overseas. Public goods are well described in the following passage:

> These are goods and services that simply cannot be provided through the market. They have two related qualities. First, they inevitably have to be supplied to a group of people rather than on an individual basis. Second, they cannot be withheld from individuals who refuse to pay for them.
>
> Take national defense, for example. The national security provided by our military forces is extended to all persons in the country. They all receive the same protection, whether they are willing to pay for it or not. There is no way of withholding the service, of creating a market which separates those who pay from the freeloaders. In fact, in this type of situation, rational consumers who are interested only in economics will never pay since they will get the benefit in any event.

In the case of ordinary private goods, this difficulty does not occur. If one person likes some item of food or clothing or a service, and another does not, one will pay for it and receive it, and the other will not. If someone should refuse to pay yet wishes to obtain the product, the sellers would simply refuse to give the item or service. . . .

Defense is not the only collective good. Other expenditures for foreign policy objectives—foreign aid, space exploration, and so on—exhibit the same quality. Some domestic cases are flood control, where a dam protects all the persons in a valley whether each agrees to pay or not, police and fire protection and the administration of justice.[2]

The classic example of a public good is a lighthouse. One ship's "consumption" of the warning light does not mean that there is less warning light for other ships to "consume." There is no practical way by which the lighthouse keeper can prohibit ships from consuming. On the other hand, a ship cannot refuse to consume the light; it is there. No private individual could make a living by selling lighthouse protection since there is no way of refusing service to noncontributors. Nor, in general, could lighthouses be financed by voluntary collections among shipowners since every shipowner has powerful incentives not to contribute. If one can "let George do it," all of the benefits are obtained without the attendant costs. If each person acts in a similarly rational manner, the lighthouse will never get built, even though all would prefer that it be built.

Charging for Public Goods. The concept that no price should be charged for any public goods is being challenged increasingly. Even in the classic "lighthouse" example, it is argued that shipowners, as a class, should pay for lighthouses, and that this will lead to at least some of the benefits listed in the first section of this chapter. For example, if lighthouse costs become too high, the objections of shipowners may help to bring them back into line. The point is closely related to the practice of charging users of highways for the cost of these highways via a tax on gasoline and diesel fuel, and to the possibility of charging airlines and owners of private aircraft for the cost of operating the air traffic control system.

A useful way of thinking about this problem is to separate the question of whether a price should be charged from the question of who ultimately should pay this price. Thus, it is generally agreed that all children are entitled to an education and that the community as a whole is responsible for providing this education whether or not the child's parents are able to pay for it. Education is therefore a public good—not because it is impossible to withhold the service, but because it is against public policy to do so. Nevertheless, it may be possible to accept this principle and still charge for education.

---

[2] Otto Eckstein, *Public Finance*, 2d ed. (Englewood Cliffs, N.J.: Prentice-Hall, 1967), p. 8.

This is the idea behind the "tuition voucher" plan for education with which some communities are currently experimenting. Every child is provided with a voucher that provides the right to obtain an education without charge. On the voucher is a dollar amount, which generally is the average cost per pupil in the public school system. Within certain limits, the voucher can be used at any school that the parents elect, including private schools (but perhaps not parochial schools because of constitutional prohibitions). The purpose of such a price mechanism is not to affect clients' decisions as to *whether* to obtain the services, but rather to permit a consumer choice as to *what school* will provide the service. By using the tuition voucher at the school of their choice, parents can express their pleasure or displeasure about individual schools and thus introduce an element of competition among schools. Care must be taken to avoid the possibility that parents will "vote" for schools that are publicly popular rather than educationally sound, but this is no more serious a problem in public schools than in colleges where tuition *is* charged.[3]

Charges Within Public Organizations. Even when the principal service of an organization is a public good which must be given away, there may be opportunities to charge for certain peripheral services rendered by the organization. For example, the Congress recently instituted the policy of charging for the copying of certain documents in its files. Although in this particular case the price was deliberately set higher than cost in order to discourage copying of these documents, which is an unconscionable abridgement of the public's right of access to information, the principle is nevertheless economically sound.

Other Free Services. In addition to the general class of public goods, there are other situations in which prices should not normally be charged for services. These include the following situations:

1. Clients cannot afford to pay for services which it is public policy to provide them with (e.g., welfare investigations; legal aid services).

2. It is public policy not to ration the services on the basis of ability to pay. (*Example:* Legislators do not charge fees for assisting constituents, even though their time is a scarce resource.)

3. The cost of collecting the revenue exceeds the benefits. This is an argument used against levying toll charges on automobiles under normal circumstances. (But note how the benefit/cost balance changes, as on toll bridges and toll highways, and how it might, upon analysis,

---

[3] In Alum Rock, California, where the voucher plan is being tried in six schools, the school board says that in addition to the advantages of providing more choices, that absenteeism and truancy have been sharply reduced and that parents participate more actively in school activities. This school district decided to expand the program in 1974 after the initial experiment in 1973. (*Wall Street Journal,* June 4, 1973, p. 1). *See also* Milton Friedman, "The Voucher Idea," *New York Times Magazine* (September 23, 1973), pp. 22 ff; and *Education Vouchers,* Cambridge, Mass:, Center for the Study of Public Policy, 1970.

be found worthwhile to levy a toll on automobiles using inner city streets.)

4.   A charge is politically untenable (e.g., public tours of the White House and the Capitol). The public clamor over such charges can be so harmful to overall organizational objectives that the services should be provided without charge, even though a charge would be equitable and would promote management control. A similar situation exists with respect to taxation. Even though an indirect tax may be relatively less equitable than a direct tax, the indirect tax may have a better chance of passage by the legislature and of acceptance by taxpayers because it is less visible.

5.   Client motivation is unimportant. A nominal charge to a public park or bathing beach will not measure actual output, nor will it influence clients' decisions to use the facilities. A charge equal to full cost may be inconsistent with public policy.

6.   There is a tax saving to the client. This situation must be viewed circumspectly; it is not to be confused with tax evasion. An example is parking charges at universities. Some students finance their education by fellowships, which in normal circumstances are tax exempt. If a separate charge were made for student parking, this charge would be outside the amount covered by the fellowship, and the income earned to pay this charge (either by students or by their parents) would be taxable income. If instead of a separate parking charge the cost of parking was included in the tuition charge, the students or parents would save the corresponding amount of income tax.

IMPACT OF PRICES ON CONSUMERS

In some situations, although prices are set forth for services rendered, the price does not actually affect clients as strongly as would the price they pay for goods or services in the marketplace. Such a price has some value, but it is unlikely to be as effective a control device as a price that directly affects the client's pocketbook.

One such situation occurs when the charges are paid by a third party, such as an insurance company, which has become the predominant way of paying for hospital costs. There are sound reasons for such third-party payment systems, and no criticism of them is here implied. The fact is simply noted that they are not as effective a motivating device as would be a direct charge to the client. The third party, acting on behalf of the whole class of clients, can be motivated by such prices, of course, even though the motivation is not as strong as a direct charge to the individual client would be. It is in the interests of third parties to keep costs down, and increasingly insurance companies, Blue Cross, and Medicare officials recognize their responsibilities in this regard. It must also be recognized that hospital patients cannot, as a practical matter, decide what services they need; clients must rely in large part on the expertise of their physicians.

In other situations, the price is a mere bookkeeping charge with no direct effect on the client's resource allocation decisions. Some universities, for example, allocate computer resources by providing students and faculty members monetary "allowances" which entitle them to a certain amount of computer time. The allowances may be set so high or may be so easily supplemented that they do not motivate at all, although they nevertheless may be a useful way of keeping track of computer usage. Even if they are set low enough so that they do have an impact on computer usage decisions, the motivating force would be much stronger if computer users had the opportunity of trading off "dollars" of computer time for other resources, or if there was a reward of some sort for time not used. (Some universities intentionally provide liberal allowances or provide computer service at no cost in order to encourage computer usage.)

The National Commission on the Financing of Post-secondary Education supports the position that "funds to reduce tuition would accomplish less in improving people's access to education than would the same amount spent on student grants awarded on the basis of financial need."[4] Its reasons were that direct grants provide students with a better means of making choices about higher education, and also that a given amount of aid would be used more efficiently in this way than by direct grants to institutions.

The influence of pocketbook impact as a motivating force is illustrated by the situation that has arisen in certain state universities in which the legislature provides funds based on the number of student credit hours. In these universities, some administrators encourage an increase in the number of credit hours for which students could register by authorizing extra credit hours for dissertation work, informal seminars and the like, and thus obtained additional funds from the legislature. Graduate students were willing to sign up for these extra credit hours because it had no impact on their workload or their graduation requirements and because their tuition was a specified amount per semester, regardless of the number of credit hours they signed up for.

> *Example:* In 1973, after introduction of a credit-hour funding plan, one state university campus reported a drop in the number of graduate students by headcount but an *increase* in the number of credit hours. All of the increase came in nonclassroom courses, such as "supervised teaching," "supervised research," and "directed dissertation."[5]

---

[4] *Report of the National Commission on the Financing of Post-Secondary Education,* submitted to the President and Congress, January 1974.

[5] See "A Scholar's Explosive Memo," *Chronicle of Higher Education* (July 8, 1974), p. 10.

In those universities in which tuition is based on the number of credit hours taken, however, there is a much greater reluctance for students to sign up for such credit hours, even though the tuition charge may be quite low. Every additional credit hour affects their pocketbooks.

THE BASIS FOR PRICES

The general principle is that prices should be equal to full costs. In this section, we discuss both situations in which this general principle is applicable, and also situations in which other pricing practices are more appropriate.

Full-Cost Pricing

The rationale for full-cost pricing is as follows: A nonprofit organization often has a monopoly position. It should not set prices that exceed its cost, for to do so would be taking unjustifiable advantage of its monopoly status. Furthermore, the organization does not need to price above cost. If it does so, it generates a profit, and by definition no person can benefit from such a profit. (Some organizations do need a small margin above costs because this is the only way they can generate funds needed for expansion.) Neither should a nonprofit organization price below full cost because that would be providing services to clients at less than the services are presumably worth; this can lead to a misallocation of resources in the economy.

> *Example:* The General Services Administration purchases and stores thousands of items of equipment and supplies which it sells to government agencies. Its selling prices include the invoice cost of the items but do not include an allowance for procurement, storage, recordkeeping and other costs of operating the program. In 1971, these costs came to $83 million, which was 18 percent of the invoice cost of merchandise sold.[6] This percentage is approximately the same as the markup added to cost by profit-oriented wholesalers and distributors. It seems likely, therefore, that if GSA charged prices equal to full cost, its prices for some items in some localities would equal or exceed prices charged by commercial sources and that government agencies would be motivated to procure these items from commercial sources.

Recent developments that also further the tendency for full-cost pricing are lawsuits against nonprofit organizations that price below full cost on the grounds of unfair competition. In 1971 and 1972 more than 30 complaints on such grounds were lodged with universities and affiliated

---

[6] Estimates prepared by Federal Supply Service, General Services Administration, at the authors' request.

research institutes for performing research services that commercial laboratories argued should be handled in the private sector.[7]

Peripheral Activities. A full-cost pricing policy should normally apply to services that are directly related to the organization's principal objectives, and to services that clients ordinarily take as a necessary concomitant to the organization's principal objectives; but it does not necessarily apply to peripheral activities. Prices for these activities should ordinarily correspond to market prices for similar services.

> *Example:* In a university, board and room charges should be based on full cost because students live in dormitories and eat in dining rooms as a necessary part of the educational process. Textbooks, laboratory supplies, and the like, should be priced at full cost (if furnished by the university) for the same reason. But rental of space to outside groups, the price of special programs furnished at the request of outside groups, prices at soda fountains, etc., are not closely related to the main objective of the university. The university does not have a monopoly with respect to these services, and their prices should be market based. The price for research projects conducted to accomplish the university's objectives should be based on full cost, as contrasted with the price of research for the benefit of a commercial client, which should be market based.

> *Example:* In a hospital, prices for hospital care, surgical procedures, laboratory procedures, X-rays and meals come within the general rule, but prices in the gift shop in the hospital should be market based.

Mix of Prices. Although the pricing strategy should normally be to recover full cost for the organization as a whole, it may be desirable to price specific services above or below full cost. The relevant considerations are essentially the same as those that profit-oriented companies consider when they depart from full-cost pricing. For example, electric utilities charge a lower than average rate for energy used during nonpeak hours; this shifts demand away from peak hours and allows the utility to meet its total demand with a smaller capital investment than otherwise would be required. Off-hour prices on subways and buses are useful for similar reasons.

> *Example:* The New York Port Authority charges fifty cents for a trans-Hudson crossing. The same charge is made for the George Washington Bridge as for the Holland Tunnel. Full costs per vehicle are different for the bridge than for the tunnel because the bridge has twice the traffic of the Holland Tunnel and their maintenance and repair costs are different. Tunnel users in effect receive a subsidy from Bridge users, but the Port Authority, for sound transportation reasons, has decided to charge the same price for each service.

---

[7] *Chronicle of Higher Education* (January 29, 1973), p. 1.

Similarly, some public bathing beaches or other nonprofit recreation areas charge a higher price for weekends and holidays than for less busy times. Adequate attention has not been paid by other nonprofit organizations who have opportunities to encourage off-peak use of facilities by charging a lower price. If peaks of demand can be levelled off, the total demand can be satisfied with a smaller investment in facilities and lower fixed operating costs.

Tuition

The price charged for higher education is perhaps the outstanding example of a price that intentionally, but unnecessarily, is set below full cost. The essential reason is that the price leaders (Stanford, Harvard, Yale, Princeton, etc.) keep tuition below the level of full cost, and other colleges and universities believe, rightly or wrongly, that their clients are unwilling to pay higher prices than those charged by the price leaders.

The principal argument against full-cost tuition is that it would deprive worthy students of an opportunity for education. The counter-argument is that students who are unable to pay full costs can be financed by loans or grants, which are provided from endowment or current gifts. Unless constrained by competition, a university will have a net increase in income if it increases tuition to an amount that is equal to full cost. This is so because additional revenue will be generated by those students who can afford to pay. Even though students who cannot afford to pay the higher tuition receive commensurately higher financial aid. and although this may be only a bookkeeping transaction, the revenue generated from these students certainly will be no less than it was before.

> *Example:* Assume that a college of 1,000 students charged $2,000 tuition, and therefore had gross tuition revenue of $2,000,000. Assume that of this amount endowment income provided $300,000 in the form of financial aid, and $1,700,000 came from cash received from students. If the college increased tuition to $2,500, its gross revenue would increase to $2,500,000. Even if it had to use as much as $200,000 of this revenue for additional financial aid, it would have more net revenue from students than before; that is, the $300,000 of endowment income would remain as before, and if $200,000 of the remaining $2,200,000 were used for additional financial aid, $2,000,000 would come from students, a net increase of $300,000. In short, students who are able to pay, pay; and other students can continue to attend because of the increased financial aid.

Another, but entirely specious, argument is the following:

> Clearly, if universities were to function efficiently as the means by which donors "produced" attitudes for a certain set of students, it was necessary to avoid a competitive market situation in which consumer

preferences would be catered to. This could only be guaranteed if the education was offered at a "bargain" price, that is, below full cost. If schools began to cover all costs by tuition, students or their parents would have been converted into "consumers" and would have exercised normal market controls over competing sellers. Only by maintaining the form of a nonprofit institution, subsidizing as it were the students who could take advantage of the program, could the donors continue to control the substance of what was taught, who taught it, and to whom it was taught. Thus there were no "consumers" who could be sovereign, since no school was established to "sell" their product on a competitive, business-like basis.[8]

The argument is also made that the government should subsidize higher education because it provides social benefits; that is, it benefits society (by making the gross national product higher than it otherwise would be, by making the electorate better informed, etc.), as well as the person who is being educated. There are two counters to such an argument.

First, it seems unlikely that any reasonable basis for a subsidy can be devised. If one attempts to relate the subsidy to social benefits, and measures social benefits in terms of the incremental income earned by college graduates, then the government subsidy would be high for business schools and medical schools and low for education schools, theological schools, and art schools; this would seem to be contrary to public policy.

Secondly, if instead of attempting to relate social benefits to types of education, the subsidy was a flat amount per student, the real cost of education would be obscured, and students, their parents, and other interested parties would have less reason for challenging the costs that the institution incurs. One of the important reasons for charging full cost tuition is that it leads clients to question the necessity for the costs, thus providing a check and balance system.

For these reasons, it is unlikely that the concept of "social benefits" should become a consideration in pricing higher education.

The argument is sometimes made that when tuition is less than full cost, the subsidy will be recouped later on from alumni contributions. This assumes a causal relationship between current subsidies and future gifts, which is at best a tenuous assumption. It also tends to neglect the low present value of future contributions.

Implementation of Full-Cost Tuition. Two important problems must be solved before a full-cost tuition policy can be adopted. First, competitive prices must be raised, and secondly, a method of making a gradual transition must be worked out.

The most important aspect of the first problem is that state universities

---

[8] Henry G. Manne, "The Political Economy of Modern Universities," *AGB Reports* (October 1972) p. 5.

and other public institutions charge tuition that is far below full cost. The argument for this practice is that residents of the state are entitled to a college education. This argument is weak in the case of residents because the tuition of needy residents can be provided by financial aid, rather than with low tuition; the argument is not relevant at all for nonresidents. Nevertheless, the practice of low tuition is firmly established, and legislators perceive that voters would not like to see it changed. Because of the existence of these low tuitions, a policy of full-cost tuition is feasible only in those private colleges and universities that are able to compete successfully with state institutions on other than a price basis.

The problem of transition is easier to solve. Having decided that a full-cost price is appropriate and feasible, a program can be devised to make a gradual transition to that price over a period of years.

In some institutions a plan like that adopted by Yale University offers an opportunity to ameliorate the financial aid problem. In that plan students who take out loans to finance their education repay them in proportion to their actual gross income. Each graduating class is treated as a group and the loan is held open until the principal is repaid by the group as a whole. Thus, those whose income after graduation is high, pay relatively more than those whose income is low.

Pricing at Other than Full Cost

Situations in which a full-cost price is not appropriate can be grouped under two headings: (1) situations in which the price should be market based, and (2) situations in which the price should be set to encourage or to discourage the use of a certain type of service. These may be called subsidy and penalty pricing, respectively.

Market-Based Prices

A market-based price is a price set in accordance with the same factors that would be considered if the organization were profit-oriented. These factors include competitive prices, the elasticity of demand, incremental costs, and so on. A market-based price may be higher or lower than full costs. If a nonprofit organization operates in a competitive environment, it usually should use competitive pricing practices. Nevertheless, if the institution is the "price leader" in a market, its prices should be set so as to recover full costs. The importance of market-based pricing is related to the necessity of providing management of these nonprofit organizations with information regarding the relative efficiency and effectiveness of their operations.

  Example: A hospital with an outstanding reputation for the quality of its service is, in the sense intended here, the price leader in its community. It should set its prices so that they equal cost, even though its reputation would permit a higher price. If this price is lower than the prices charged by competing hospitals, there is an indication that some of society's resources are being channelled to support inefficient facilities. An awareness of this fact may lead to a redirection of those resources; at least it should alert the managers of competing hospitals to the fact that a problem exists.

As indicated above, a market-based price is also appropriate for services that are not closely associated with the principal objectives of the organization.

> *Example:* In addition to the university services mentioned above, educational programs designed for clients other than those for which the university exists should be market based. However, it is difficult to draw the line between programs that are closely related to the organization's objectives—such as adult education programs in a municipal school system or university extension courses—and programs where a market-based price is appropriate—such as executive development programs.

A market-based price higher than cost is also appropriate for the principal services of a nonprofit organization if these services are of a type that the private sector could furnish, such as research and development services. The fact that clients are willing to pay the price demonstrates that the service is valuable, and the "profit" thus generated can be used to offset losses on services which cannot pay their own way. Thus, in some situations, the policy should be "cost or market, whichever is higher." Such a policy is appropriate only when adequate competition exists. If an organization is a monopoly, it abuses its nonprofit status if it charges prices in excess of cost.

Subsidy and Penalty Prices

In certain situations an organization may depart from both the cost-based and the market-based concepts of pricing in order to facilitate the achievement of its objectives. It may deliberately price below full cost in order to encourage the use of certain services, or it may deliberately price above full cost in order to discourage the use of other services. The former is called a "subsidy" price, and the latter a "penalty" price.

Subsidy Prices. An organization may use a subsidy price to encourage the use of its services by certain clients who are unable or unwilling to pay a price based on full cost, or when as a matter of policy the organization wishes to allocate its service on a basis other than ability to pay (e.g., new drugs; low-cost housing; socialized medicine). Unless the service is a public good, a price that is less than cost is preferable to providing the services free, for a low, even a nominal, price motivates clients to give some thought to the value of the service they received. Such a subsidy price should preferably be a fraction of the cost of the services rendered, rather than a flat per-client amount, in order to increase the clients' motivation to be concerned about the quantity of services that they consume.

It should be recognized, however, that when clients are charged less than full cost, this is equivalent to stating that it is public policy to provide the service at less than its value. In these circumstances, the danger of a misallocation of resources exists. If a service cannot generate enough revenue to cover its costs, questions should be raised about the desirability of continuing it. As each of the following examples exemplify, the issues are not simple, and policy questions are raised regarding the desirability of continued subsidy of operations.

> *Examples:* 1. A university discovered that the cost of operating its nuclear reactor was $50,000 per student using the reactor. The reactor probably should be closed unless other uses can be found, or unless increased utilization is expected to develop.
>
> 2. The pediatric department of a hospital operated at a loss when a price equal to that of other hospitals in nearby communities were charged. It was nevertheless decided to continue the department because no other pediatric facility existed in the community. The deficit was made up by the municipality.
>
> 3. There is a dual education system in France: the state one that is free, and the private one that is not. The private system is generally not able to sustain itself financially, and it is subsidized in part by the Government on the basis that this is still less expensive for the community than being obliged to admit all the students from private schools to state schools. Closing the private schools would require a substantial increase in investments and operating expenses in state schools without any increase in revenues.

Even if clients are unable or unwilling to pay a price based on full costs, there are advantages in stating a *gross* price at full cost, and providing the subsidy separately to those who need it, or to those whose use of the service should be encouraged. This policy focuses attention on the true cost of providing the services and thus (1) motivates clients to ask questions if they judge the services received to be worth less than their cost, which facilitates management control; and (2) motivates managers to consider whether available resources are properly allocated.

Penalty Prices. An organization may charge more than full costs, in order to discourage clients from using a certain type of service. This may be because the organization is required to provide this service and finds it disadvantageous for some reason, because it is ill-equipped to provide the service, or because providing the service has certain corollary adverse effects on the organization or its other services.

Examples: 1. A nonprofit regional stock exchange and clearing corporation charged proportionately more for small transactions because it wanted to encourage another type of business indirectly and because the small transactions were a nuisance to its members.

2. A hospital charged appreciably more for providing outpatient services to nonemergency patients than other hospitals in the area because its staff and facilities were fully utilized providing for its in-patients' requirements.

3. The civil aviation department of the Government of India charged one rupee for every person not making a flight but coming to the major airports in Bombay, Calcutta, and other cities to see friends and relatives off, even though zero cost was incurred for these persons. The reason given was to discourage the crowds of people around the airport.

Some organizations deliberately set normal prices above full cost so as to generate a surplus that can be used for what are considered to be worthwhile purposes, even though they do not directly benefit the client. For example, a hospital's fees may provide a surplus that can be used for charity patients or for research. This raises an interesting question: should a hospital force its solvent patients to make an involuntary contribution to charity or to research? Arguments can be advanced for and against this position.

Prices may also be set high in order to discourage certain socially undesirable activities. Thus, user fees are proposed to be levied against polluters of rivers. The price could be either high enough to totally stop the practice, or it could be high enough to cover the cost of providing water treatment plants to repair the damage done. In the latter case, it is essentially a price based on full cost.

When it is public policy to include, in effect, a tax in the price, the price may be regarded as being higher than full cost (e.g., prices in state liquor stores). Alternatively, this practice may be regarded as full-cost pricing, with the "tax" as an element of cost.

MEASUREMENT OF COST

Assuming that an organization has decided to price its services at full cost, the question arises: What exactly, is full cost? The general answer to this question has been discussed in Chapter 6: Full cost is the sum of (a) the direct cost of providing the service, plus (b) an equitable share of common costs. Common costs are elements of cost that are incurred because of, or for the benefit of, both the service that is being costed and also other cost objectives. Common costs exclude cost elements that are in no way associated with the service that is being costed; for example, the cost of athletic facilities may be a common cost for the several educational programs whose students use them, but this cost is not a cost of a university research project.

Not everyone recognizes that the techniques of cost accounting provide a reasonable approximation to full cost even when common costs are present, and that profit-oriented businesses rely on such costs in making pricing decisions.

> *Example:* In an otherwise excellent article on pricing blood services, the statement is made, "Since there can be no precise measurement of cost, there can be no sure correspondence between cost and price. Therefore, administrative decisions about prices must be made on the basis of criteria other than cost."[9] This statement is used as an argument for basing prices on public policy considerations, and specifically for setting the price of whole blood well above the prices of blood components—red cells, plasma, platelets, and Factor VIII. The case made for such pricing differentials is strong, but it is a case that should rest on its own merit, and not on the premise that cost-based pricing is impossible.

Many problems arise in measuring full costs in any organization. Certain problems that are peculiar to pricing problems in nonprofit organizations are discussed below; namely, (1) depreciation, (2) capital costs and fees, (3) gifts and endowment income, and (4) imputed costs.

Depreciation

Under some circumstances, costs used as a basis for pricing should include depreciation based on historical cost; in other circumstances, cost should include depreciation based on replacement cost, and in still other circumstances, depreciation should be excluded from cost. A useful way of deciding on the appropriate treatment is to assume that the organization will have an indefinitely long life and ask the question: How will new fixed assets be financed?

One possible answer to this question is that new fixed assets will be financed by gifts generated by a capital-fund drive or by capital funds supplied by the legislature. This is the way most church and college capital assets have been financed and, until recently, this was the source of funds for most hospital buildings. If it is prudent to conclude that funds for future buildings and other fixed assets can be raised in a similar manner, then depreciation need not be included as an element on the cost that is used to calculate prices; that is, revenue from services need not provide funds for the replacement of assets.

Some organizations, however, believe that it is dangerous to assume that fixed assets can continue to be financed by such outside sources. Other organizations foresee special fund drives as a method of financing new buildings, but not of replacing other fixed assets. Under these circumstances, funds for some or all of new fixed assets must come from

---

[9] D. M. Surgenor *et al.* "Blood Services: Prices and Public Policy," *Science* (April 27, 1973), p. 387.

clients, and this means that depreciation must be included as an element of cost in the price charged to clients.

Either of two classes of clients may pay for tomorrow's capital assets: (1) today's clients or (2) tomorrow's clients, that is, those who use the new assets. There is considerable controversy over the question of which of these two groups should pay. If today's clients are to pay for tomorrow's assets, then the depreciation charge should be related to replacement cost; the historical cost of the assets now in use is irrelevant. But *what* replacement cost? A current estimate of the replacement cost of present assets is conceptually incorrect for two conflicting reasons. On the one hand, new fixed assets will cost more when they are acquired than the current replacement cost of the existing assets both because inflation will continue to increase replacement costs and also because new equipment tends to be more complex, and hence more expensive, than existing equipment. Increased complexity of equipment is particularly noticeable in health care organizations, but it is also a factor in universities and research organizations. On the other hand, if funds generated from depreciation are invested until they are needed, the income from this investment can be used to help finance the new assets. In view of the uncertainties of all the estimates involved in this problem, some people believe that it is safe to assume that the two forces listed above will approximately offset one another, and that depreciation should therefore be based on current replacement cost.

The other possibility is that tomorrow's clients should pay for tomorrow's assets. If this approach is adopted, today's clients pay for today's assets, and depreciation is therefore based on the historical cost of these assets. This sounds like an eminently reasonable solution: these are the people who benefit from the new assets; why shouldn't they pay for them? And why should today's clients be asked to pay for assets they are not going to use?

There are complications involved in this solution, however. Where does the money come from to finance a new building? If an organization could borrow 100 percent of the cost of the building, this would solve the problem, but a loan of this magnitude is ordinarily not available. If today's clients are paying off the cost of the current building, the funds generated by the depreciation included in the price charged is not available to pay for the new building.

These considerations suggest that depreciation based on historical cost is unlikely to provide a flow of funds sufficient to finance the acquisition of new fixed assets if these funds must be used to pay off loans used to acquire the existing assets. Some part of the depreciation charge will be available to finance the "equity" portion of the new assets because the loan on existing assets was probably less than the total cost of these assets, but this portion will not be adequate to provide an allowance for inflation and increased complexity. Thus, even if the policy is that today's clients should pay for the facilities they use, the depreciation charge should probably be somewhat greater than an amount based on historical cost.

Several observations can be made on the basis of the above analysis.

First, the answer to the question of whether or not depreciation should be charged does not depend on whether or not *existing* capital assets were acquired by gift. The relevant consideration is the financing of the next buildings, not the source of funds for the current building. (Of course, if no debt exists on the present buildings the provision of the necessary "equity" portion of the new building is easier than if there is a loan to be paid off.) If this fact is not taken into account, a long-established organization that now uses donated buildings may be unable to continue.

Second, if an existing building was provided by gift and there is no intention of replacing it, there is no need to charge depreciation on it.

Third, it is desirable to give special attention to the increasing complexity of equipment. Many hospitals, for example, include a "growth and development charge," as an element of cost, which is specifically intended for this purpose.

Fourth, since the purpose of depreciation in this context is to provide for new assets that may not be needed for several years, it is desirable that depreciation be funded, that is, that an amount equal to the depreciation charge be invested in a separate fund and kept completely shielded from current operations. The funds that are necessary to build the new building are unlikely to be available when they are needed if funds from depreciation are comingled with regular operating amounts because there is a strong temptation to use them to meet current emergencies.

The foregoing used a building as an example of fixed assets. The same type of analysis applies to all capital assets. It applies even more strongly to equipment, furnishings and relatively short-lived assets because donors are less likely to provide for the replacement of these assets than they are to provide new buildings.

Capital Employed and Fees

In a profit-oriented company, the full cost of a capital asset is greater than the amount of money paid for the asset. The use of the company's capital that is tied up in the asset also is an item of cost, even though a charge for the use of capital is not currently identified as a cost item in most accounting systems. If a nonprofit organization borrows money to finance the purchase of an asset, the interest on that money is correspondingly a cost. There are other situations in which a cost of using capital exists, but is not so obvious.

Suppose a university uses $1,000,000 of its unrestricted endowment funds to finance the construction of a building. Some would argue that there is no capital cost associated with this transaction because the university is merely using its own money. This argument is weak. If the university had not used the $1,000,000 to finance the building, it would have continued to invest it and earn perhaps $50,000 a year on it. It now foregoes that $50,000, and the $50,000 is therefore appropriately part of the annual cost of using the building.

Similarly, all organizations need working capital with which to operate. This working capital has a cost, just as the funds tied up in a building have a cost.

These cost elements are important in situations in which it is mutually agreed that the client will reimburse the organization for the full cost of the service rendered as, for example, in a research contract between the government and a nonprofit research organization. Unless the reimbursement includes an allowance for items such as the above, the organization is not in fact "kept whole" by its revenue.

Because of the difficulty of calculating such costs exactly, many cost-reimbursement contracts include provision for a small fee to cover this cost. Sometimes this fee is regarded as a profit, and the question is raised: Why should a nonprofit organization be entitled to a profit? The answer is that a fee, if properly set, is not a profit; it is a recovery of unmeasured costs.

If the parties so intend, such a fee, in addition to covering the cost of capital, can provide for (1) other legitimate but unmeasured costs, (2) a reserve against future uncertainties, and (3) a provision for growth. The latter point is vital in organizations which have no source of income other than from revenues received for services. Such an organization has no way of growing unless some part of the price provides for this.

Gifts and Endowment Income

If an organization has revenue from gifts and endowment income, should the amount of such revenue be deducted from costs before calculating the charge made to clients? This is an important question, and the answer depends largely on the intention of the donors. If donors intended that their gift be used to help finance general operations, then it is appropriately deducted from the cost of those operations; but if they intended that the gift be used for some special purpose not of direct benefit to current clients, then no such deduction need be made. Among such special purposes are research and specialized equipment in universities and hospitals; financial aid, libraries, and athletic facilities in unversities; and missionary activities in religious organizations.

If the intention of the donors is not clear, then it is desirable that management formulate a specific policy as to how such revenue is to be treated. In this connection, it is often useful to make a distinction between annual gifts, which are "soft money," and endowment income, which is "hard money." If annual gifts are used to finance educational operations of a university, for example, and if the tuition charge is lower than it otherwise would be because of these gifts, the university could easily have a crisis situation in a year in which annual giving declined. If, by contrast, the tuition charge was high enough to finance educational costs, and if the annual gifts were used to finance research, additions to the library, or other costs which could be temporarily reduced if the need arose, such a crisis might be averted.

Opportunity and Imputed Costs

The cost accounting systems of profit-oriented companies generally exclude imputed costs; that is, costs that do not, did not, or will not require actual outlays of cash or its equivalent. In general, this is a good practice for nonprofit organizations to follow, but there are situations in which such costs should be included in calculating prices. Schools and hospitals associated with religious organizations pay less than the market rate for personnel services. Many nonprofit organizations do not pay property taxes or income taxes. Should prices reflect these costs?

In the case of low-paid, or nonpaid religious personnel, it would seem appropriate to value their services at the market rate, when the intention is to charge full cost, with the difference between market value and actual cost representing a contribution of the individual to the religious order.

Conversely, consider a government-sponsored day care center that hires unemployed women at prevailing wage levels, even though these women undoubtedly could be induced to work at lower rates. The cost to society of having the day care center is overstated if the cost of these employees is measured by the amounts paid to them. Clients of the day care center should pay a price that reflects the market rate of employee services, which is less than the money cost; the difference should be made up by a direct subsidy.

In situations in which the price charged by a nonprofit organization is supposed to be a yardstick for profit-oriented organizations, as is the case with Tennessee Valley Authority, or when users are explicitly expected to pay such costs, as in St. Lawrence Seaway, the imputed costs of taxes are also properly recognized.

In other situations, the case is not so strong. If a tax-exempt hospital should include an allowance for property taxes in its prices, what does it do with the money that this fee generates?

THE PRICING UNIT

The fourth principle of pricing can be stated more specifically than was done in the introductory section: *In general, the smaller and more specific the unit of service that is priced, the better the basis for decisions about the allocation of resources and the more accurate the measure of output for management control purposes.* An overall price is not a good measure of output because it masks the actual mix of services rendered. An annual flat charge for the use of water (as was the case in New York City) is not as effective as a charge that reflects the quantity used. With an annual charge, the consumer is not motivated to be careful in using water.

Qualifications

There is considerable disagreement about this principle, and there are some who reject it entirely. They argue that price should reflect an average mix of services and the needs of more detailed information for management control purposes can be met by other devices. Even those who support the validity of the basic principle accept two important qualifications.

The first is the obvious one that beyond a certain point, the paperwork and other costs associated with pricing tiny units of service outweigh the benefits. The precise location of this point is of course uncertain.

The second qualification is that the pricing policy should be consistent with the organization's overall policy. It is a fact that undergraduate English instruction per student costs less than undergraduate physics instruction, and it would be feasible to reflect these differences in cost by charging different prices for each course that a student takes. Indeed, this has been advocated, as in the following:

> In the final analysis, consumers are the ones who will accept or reject any price. This realization of the marketing man requires him to focus on how the consumer perceives price. Consequently, he may price some items lower, because of low demand and/or cost, and other items higher. He works on an averaging process over a number of items to give him a reasonable or better return. It has been shown repeatedly that if his price becomes too high (i.e., too much profit) an efficient competitor will eventually enter the market, reducing the former's share.
>
> Applying this principle to college and university pricing, one perceives a rigidity in pricing approach that may have worked against the growth of some divisions. Is it fair and "market wise" to charge the same price to English major "X" as to chemistry major "Y", when it costs much more (through fixed overhead) to educate the latter than the former? In reality, the English program, in this example, is carrying the burden for the chemistry program.[10]

Despite the superficial plausibility of this argument, a separate price for each course may well lead students to select courses in a way that

---

[10] Eugene Fram, "We Must Market Education," *Chronicle of Higher Education* (April 17, 1972), p. 8.

the university administration does not consider educationally sound. Since the total cost of a course may be essentially a fixed cost, such a pricing policy would lead students to shun courses with low enrollment, such as Greek and Latin, which have a high cost per student, and it would increase the enrollment in popular, but perhaps less valuable courses that have a low cost per student.

By contrast, there are good reasons for charging higher tuitions to graduate students than to undergraduate students, so as to reflect the differences in the overall cost of graduate and undergraduate programs. These differences do not motivate individual students to make unwise choices.

Hospital Pricing as an Example

Exhibit 7–1, which shows some of the approaches that could be used in pricing the various services furnished by a hospital, is used as a

EXHIBIT 7–1
Pricing Alternatives in a Hospital

A All Inclusive Rate	B Daily Charge plus Special Services		C Type of Service		D Detailed Costing
$150/day	Patient care	$110/day	Medical/Surgical		Admittance
	Operating room	xx	1st day	$140	Work-up, per hr.
	Pharmacy	xx	other days	110	Medical/surgical bed
	Radiology	xx	Maternity		per day
	Special nurses	xx	1st day	110	Maternity bed per day
			other days	90	Bassinet per day
			(Plus special ser-		Nursery care, per hr.
			vices as in B)		Meals per day
					Discharge
					(Plus special services
					as in B)

basis for discussing considerations involved in selecting the unit of pricing.

At one extreme, the hospital could charge an all inclusive rate, say $150 per day. This practice is advocated by some people both on the grounds that patients then know in advance what their bill will be (assuming that the length of stay can be estimated) and also on the grounds of simplicity in recordkeeping. Its advocates point out that the more detailed information required for management purposes can be collected in the management control system, even though they are not reflected in prices charged. The difficulty with this latter argument is that if detailed information is going to be collected for management purposes anyway, the all inclusive price does not in fact result in significant savings in recordkeeping unless shortcuts and estimates are substituted for sound data collection methods. The only savings would be in the billing process, which is a small part of the total accounting function. As to the arguments that patients will know the amount of their bills in advance, it is questionable whether this is more important than charging each patient for the services that he or she receives.

Another, and common, pricing practice is to charge separately for the cost of each of easily identifyable special services and make a blanket daily charge for everything else. Radiology prices, for example, are customarily calculated according to a rather detailed point system that takes into account the size of the radiology plate and the complexity of the procedure. There is some incongruity in calculating prices for radiology in terms of points which are worth a few cents each and lumping everything else into an overall rate of, say, $110 per day.

Column C indicates one approach to breaking the daily charge into smaller units. Different charges could be made for each department, and it would also be possible to charge more for the first day, to take account of admitting and workup costs, than for subsequent days.

Column D indicates the job-cost approach that many profit-oriented businesses would use in situations of this type. In an automobile repair shop, for example, each repair job is costed separately. It is charged with the services of mechanics according to the number of hours they work on the job, and it is charged with each part and significant item of supplies that is used on the job. The sum of these separate charges is the basis for the price the customers pay, and customers would not tolerate any other approach. They would not, for example, tolerate paying a flat daily rate for repairs, regardless of what services were provided. Hospitals, by contrast, rarely use the job cost approach to pricing, except for specialized services as indicated in Column B. They lump large amounts of services together into a daily rate, and they charge this daily rate to each patient regardless of the amount of services that the patient receives.

As one moves from left to right across Exhibit 7–1, the practices involve (1) an increase in recordkeeping, (2) a corresponding increase in the amount of output information for use in management control, and (3) charges to clients that more accurately reflect services rendered. Management gives thought to such factors in selecting the appropriate unit of pricing.

PROSPECTIVE PRICING

As a general rule, management control is facilitated when the price is set prior to the performance of the service, as contrasted with the alternative of reimbursing the service provider for the actual amount of costs incurred. When prices are set in advance, they provide an incentive for the organization to keep costs down, whereas no such incentive exists when the organization knows that whatever the level of costs, they will be recouped.

This principle can be applied, of course, only when it is possible to make a reasonable advance estimate of what the services should cost. For many research or development projects, for example, there is no good basis for estimating how much needs to be spent in order to achieve the desired result, and the reimbursement for such work is necessarily based on actual costs incurred.

Currently, the question of prospective pricing is a controversial one in health care organizations. Until fairly recently Blue Cross, Medicare, and other third parties that account for a large fraction of payments, reimbursed hospitals essentially for actual costs incurred. Although the actual payment plan usually specified that tentative reimbursement would be made on the basis of a schedule of prices, nevertheless at the end of each year or shorter period an adjustment would be made that in effect equated the total amount of reimbursement to actual costs incurred. Such a system provided little incentive to keep costs under control. In the 1960s and 1970s, hospital prices increased at a rate that was about twice as high as the increase of prices in general. In some states, including Connecticut and Pennsylvania, experiments with a quite different approach to pricing are being conducted. In this approach, which is called prospective pricing, the third party and the hospital agree in advance to a budget of costs for the forthcoming year, and prices are determined on the basis of this budget. The hospital is paid on the basis of these prices, adjusted in some cases for unforeseen changes in labor rates, material prices and/or for changes in volume. If the hospital can keep its cost below the budgeted amount, it retains part or all of the saving. If its costs exceed budget, it must absorb some or all of the excess.

The argument for this approach is the incentive for cost control. An argument against it is the difficulty of making reliable budgets, and especially of forecasting a reliable volume figure, which is necessary in order to arrive at sound unit prices. Some opponents also assert that prospective pricing may lead to too much emphasis on cost control, with a consequent lowering of the quality of patient care. Price control regulations in 1971–74 had the effect of stimulating hospital managers to give much more emphasis to the preparation of sound budgets, and had the indirect effect of lessening the opposition to prospective pricing.

An organization that knows that it is going to recover its costs, whatever they are, is not likely to do much worrying about cost control. When reliable methods of setting prices in advance can be worked out, the incentive is much stronger.

chapter eight

Programming:
New Programs

Programming is the process of deciding on the nature and size of the several programs that are to be undertaken in order to achieve an organization's goals. In view of the importance of the programming process, we discuss it in two chapters. In Chapter 8, we describe the process in general and discuss considerations that are relevant in deciding on proposals for *new programs.* In Chapter 9, we discuss the analysis of *ongoing programs,* and also describe the operation of a formal programming system.

The process of programming involves two related but separable activities. The first activity involves the preparation and analysis of individual program proposals and making decisions on these proposals. The second is the system for facilitating the flow and coordination of the separate proposals. An organization should do a good job at both these activities, but many organizations are effective at one of them and not the other. Some organizations are effective at formulating and analyzing individual program proposals, but they have no formal programming system; whereas other organizations have a well-developed programming system, but they do an inadequate job of analyzing the individual proposals that flow through the system. The latter is characteristic of many government organizations, who have been sold on the virtues of a system (usually with the initials "PPBS" or some variation), or who have had a programming system thrust upon them, but who have not recognized the importance of good analysis. Such organizations are in general less well managed than organizations which make good analyses of individual proposals but have no formal system.

Nature of Programs

The following is a good description of the program concept, and the distinction between a program and a policy, as stated by Daniel Moynihan:

> The defining characteristic of a program is that it is directed to a specific situation with the purpose of maintaining or changing that situation in some desirable fashion. We have programs to build roads, subsidize the growing of cotton, cure cancer, retrain the unemployed. To be sure there are programs that are quite general in their outlook but here, with respect to the Federal Government and to all levels and forms of government within the United States with which I am familiar, any tendency toward universality is immediately constricted by the structure of government. Doubtless there are even programs that would wish to evolve into policies, but reality is quickly enough imposed on them by the fact that one bureau in one department is responsible for performing the function involved; that one branch of one division in the Bureau of the Budget handles the appropriation request; that one super specific subcommittee of one special committee of the Congress handles the substantive legislation, and an equivalent subcommittee handles the provision of funds. These are the constituencies of the program, and also its masters. It is a wise program that knows its place, and does not aspire beyond its station.
>
> By contrast, a policy approach to government does at least begin by seeking to encompass the largest possible range of phenomena and concerns. This has its dangers, its difficulties. But I shall argue that increasingly there is no respectable alternative. Knowing what we do about the nature of society and of social interventions, we have no option but to seek to deal in terms of the entire society, and all the consequences of intervention. One might wish for a simpler time when such knowledge was not available, but the loss of innocence is an old experience to mankind, and not perhaps to be avoided. Certainly not to be reversed.[1]

Programming and Budgeting

In many organizations, the programming process is combined with the process of budgeting. Both programming and budgeting involve planning, but the types of planning activities are different in the two processes. The budgeting process focuses on a single year, whereas programming focuses on activities that extend over a period of several years. A budget is, in a sense, a one-year slice of the organization's programs although, for reasons discussed in Chapter 10, this is not a complete description of a budget; the budgeting process involves more than simply carving out such a slice.

---

[1] Daniel P. Moynihan, *The Concept of Public Policy in the 1970s* (Speech at Hendrix College, Conway, Arkansas, April 6, 1970).

Many organizations do not make an explicit, formal distinction between the programming process and the budgeting process. Since the two processes are conceptually different, it is useful to think about these differences even if no formal distinction is made.

Relation of Programming to Strategic Planning

In Chapter 2, we drew a line between two management processes, labelled respectively strategic planning and management control. Programming, although part of management control, is close to the line dividing these two processes, and it is therefore of some importance to distinguish between them. The distinction is not crucial, however, and as is the case in most matters relating to organizations, the line is not a sharp one. In fact, some authors use the term "long-range planning" to encompass both strategic planning and programming.

In the strategic planning process, management decides on the goals of the organization and the main strategies for achieving these goals. Conceptually, the programming process takes these goals and strategies as given and seeks to identify programs that will implement them effectively and efficiently. In practice, there is a considerable amount of overlap. Studies made during the programming process may indicate the desirability of changing goals or strategies. Conversely, strategic planning often includes some consideration of the programs that will be adopted to achieve goals.

An important reason for making a separation in practice between programming and strategic planning is that the programming process tends to become institutionalized, and this tends to put a damper on purely creative activities. A separate strategic planning activity can provide an offset to this tendency. Strategic planning should be an activity in which creative, innovative thinking is strongly encouraged.

Although the following comment makes no distinction between strategy formulation and programming, it provides a good rationale for the necessity of giving adequate management attention to the process:

> Nonprofit institutions need strategy far more than profit-making organizations. Their goals are more complex, their sources of support are more complex, and the interaction between their support and performance is more complex. Consequently, the problem of identifying optimal policies and potential strategies must be inherently more complex. In fact, most institutions would find their planning and policy formulation much easier if they were profit-making organizations. Then at least they would have a common denominator for their objectives and strategies.
>
> Strategy has many definitions but all definitions imply a goal, a set of constraints, and a firm plan for allocating resources. All of these

factors interact and affect each other. Therefore, they must be considered simultaneously. Change one, and you may change them all.

The goal of most nonprofit institutions is clear enough. Be it a hospital, a school or a governmental unit, the intuitive goal is this: "Get as much as possible in the way of resources; do as much as possible with these resources."

But if the resources available are not enough to do everything, the definition of goals becomes more complicated. Which objective should be given priority? Should a school or hospital provide service to those who are willing to pay for its full cost; or should it be provided to those who can benefit most? . . .

Any strategy requires a compromise between the choice of goals and the resources available. To this extent every institution or organization is profit-making. It must attract resources at least equal to the requirements of its goals. . . .

Whether the organization is a nonprofit institution or a profit-making business, the strategy problem is the same: "How do you produce an economic equilibrium between costs and incomes that is stable at a sufficiently high level?" Stable means that any reduction in services will cut cost more than it will reduce resources. . . .

In a society of competitive institutions and philosophies, an explicit statement of strategy is one of the prerequisites for a productive and honored future.[2]

ORGANIZATIONAL RELATIONSHIPS

Four principal parties have roles in the programming process: top management, the planning staff, the controller, and operating managers.

Top management makes the decisions, at least the decisions on programs that affect the whole organization. If a program affects only one segment of the organization, then the management of that segment can make the decision on it.

The staff unit involved in the programming process is here called the planning staff, but it also is called the program office, the systems analysis office, or the operations research office. The planning staff provides information and analyses that can be used by management as an aid in making decisions.

The staff may either originate proposals, or it may only analyze proposals originated by others. Its role is stronger if it originates proposals. For example, in the Department of Defense under Secretary McNamara, the Systems Analysis office both originated proposals and analyzed proposals submitted by the individual Military Departments. It was a strong organization, as evidenced by the fact that there

---

[2] *Strategy for Institutions,* The Boston Consulting Group, Inc., 1970. Used by permission.

was much heated discussion about the activities of its "whiz kids," inside the Pentagon, in the Congress, and in the news media. In the next administration, Secretary Laird prohibited the Systems Analysis office from initiating proposals, and its influence was much weaker, as evidenced by the almost complete lack of controversy about it, both inside and outside the Pentagon.

The planning staff should be close to the top of the organization hierarchy. It should report directly either to top management or to the controller. If the planning staff reports to the controller, there is a danger that it will become involved too much in the budgetary process, which is also a function of the controller organization. The budget process has a short-range focus, and is carried out under considerable time pressure. If the planning staff gets too involved in this process, or if the "budgeteers" in the controller organization are permitted to have too much influence on the programming process, the long-range view that is essential to good programming is likely to suffer. Thus, if the planning staff is a part of the controller organization, it probably should be kept separate from the part of that organization that is responsible for the budget process.

If an appropriate separation between programming and budgeting activities can be achieved, there are good reasons for having the planning staff as part of the controller organization. This reduces the number of staff units reporting to top management, increases the likelihood that planners will be aware of the existence of, and have easy access to, available data, and tends to even out the workload in the controller organization.

Whether or not the planning staff is part of the controller organization, the controller's office should be responsible for the flow of programming information, for it should be responsible for *all* information systems. If there is a formal programming system, as described in Chapter 9, the controller's office should oversee the operation of this system; that is, it should set up procedures governing the flow of information through the system, and it should assure that these procedures are adhered to. In some agencies, the planning staff has taken over this function, but this leads to unnecessary duplication of data and to a lack of coordination and consistency between programming data and other data.

The operating organization may be the source of some ideas for new programs or changes in programs, but unless operating managers have their own planning staff, it is unlikely that operating managers will develop an idea in the depth that is required to permit a sound judgment to be made about it. Thus, it often happens that the rough outline of an idea originates in the operating organization and is turned over to a planning staff for development into a full-blown program proposal.

In the Federal government and in other organizations where the idea of a formal programming effort is relatively new, there tends to be friction between the planning staff and the operating organization. The planning staff may consist of young, technically oriented, bright, but inexperienced persons, who tend to be unaware of, or to minimize the importance of, the rules of the "bureaucratic game." Such a staff underestimates the value of experience and the importance of the pressures of day-to-day operations. It tends to use a jargon that is unfamiliar to operating managers. To the operating organization, the planning staff may represent a threat, a challenge to the established way of doing things.

In order to minimize such conflicts, it is desirable to build up a planning staff gradually, starting with a small group and increasing size only as resistance from operating managers subsides. If feasible, at least some members of the initial staff should come from the existing organization. The planning staff should never forget that it *is* a staff; it does not make decisions itself. It should spend considerable time—much more time than it usually prefers to spend—working with the operating organization, explaining the approaches it uses and attempting to establish good working relationships. The planning staff must gain and maintain the firm support of top management. The operating organization must perceive that the programming effort is not a "trial" or a "fad," but a permanent part of the management process.

ANALYZING PROPOSED NEW PROGRAMS

The approach used to analyze proposed new programs is here called *benefit/cost* analysis. The underlying concept is the obvious one that a program should not be undertaken unless its benefits exceed its costs, and the approach therefore involves an attempt to measure benefits and costs. The term *cost/effectiveness* analysis is also used, sometimes as a synonym for benefit/cost analysis, and sometimes for a special version of the general approach.[3] Systems analysis is another term with approximately the same meaning.

Status of Benefit/Cost Analysis

The idea of comparing the benefits of a proposed course of action with its costs is not new. Techniques for analyzing the profitability of proposed business investments involve essentially the same approach. Certain government agencies, such as the Bureau of Reclamation, have made such analyses for decades. Proposals to build new

---

[3] If two programs have approximately the same benefits, but one has lower costs, that one is said to be more cost effective than the other.

dams were justified on the grounds that their benefits exceeded their costs. Interest in the approach grew rapidly in the 1960s when the Department of Defense applied the concept to problems for which no formal analysis previously had been attempted. It then became fashionable to apply benefit/cost analysis to all sorts of proposed programs in nonprofit organizations. The results of these efforts have been mixed, and there is now considerable controversy about the merits of the whole approach.

At one extreme are indictments, such as that in Ida Hoos' *Systems Analysis in Public Policy*. Following is a sample that suggests her attitude:

> Their scholarly conferences and compendia of papers having bravely thrashed the straw man of conventional statistics for being unreliable and inadequate, they try to develop "social indicators," which will somehow provide macro-insights into the multiplicity of changes still to come. Ignoring the perils of linear curve extrapolations, they repeat old mistakes by establishing their conception of a firm and reliable data base which then becomes their springboard into the future. Their literature stoutly affirms that the indicators need not necessarily be quantitative, and, in fact, that it is desirable that the qualitative be considered. But their focus and emphasis belie their heroic assertions. They start ambitiously with the universe or Planet Earth but soon whittle out a few variables which they and their computers can handle comfortably.
>
> The mythology of systems analysis accompanies its forward march into the future. Presented as though it had accomplished wonders and taken the guesswork out of planning, the technique is represented as the key and clue to the salvation of mankind on this planet. Those who sell this notion believe their own sales story and they are finding buyers among decision-makers in the far flung corners of the earth. What is new and portentous here is that invocation of "scientific" tools and techniques, which provide a dutiful and convenient rationale for whatever cause of action seems politically expedient, may stifle thoughtful research and experimentation. Heady with heterogeneous facts and shy of theory, the futurists may be directly or indirectly abetting the anti-intellectualism that has already gained considerable momentum in this country and abroad.[4]

At the other extreme are promotional brochures, journal articles, and proposals by certain individuals and organizations that imply that benefit/cost analysis does everything: "it takes the guesswork out of management." For example, a proposal for a $275,000 research project submitted to the National Institute of Education promised to "address the Cost-Effectiveness Benefit questions by making a Macro Management and Policy analysis of alternate Cost opportunities in Elementary-Secondary and Post-Secondary Education" and to

---

[4] Ida R. Hoos, *Systems Analysis in Public Policy* (Berkeley: University of California Press, 1972), p. 240.

provide the results in nine months; which translated means that the proposer promised to find the optimum amount and character of educational programs from kindergarten through college, in nine months and for $275,000.

Although overexuberant persons and outright charlatans do exist, and their works are properly criticized, there is no doubt that benefit/cost analysis has produced useful results. There are two essential points:

1.   Benefit/cost analysis focuses on those consequences of a proposal which can be estimated in quantitative terms. Since there is no important problem in which *all* the relevant factors can be reduced to numbers, benefit/cost analysis will never provide the complete answer to any important problem.

2.   However, if *some* of the important factors can be reduced to quantitative terms, it is often better to do so than not to do so. The resulting analysis narrows the area within which management judgment is required, even though it does not eliminate the need for judgment.

> *Example:*   Until 1961, top officials in the Defense Department and in the Executive Office of the President, agreed that the Navy should have 15 aircraft carriers. The reason for this judgment was that the United States was party to a treaty that permitted 15 aircraft carriers. The new Systems Analysis office, under the leadership first of Charles J. Hitch and then Alain Enthoven, undertook an analysis of the need for aircraft carriers in achieving the goals of the Defense Department. For what type of operation were they needed? Where should they be stationed in order to be able to participate in probable operations? How many were needed in each theater, and how many were needed for training and to provide for overhaul? Was the additional endurance provided by nuclear power worth the enormous additional cost of nuclear power? Analysis did not provide a complete answer to any of these questions, but it provided the decision maker with a better basis for deciding questions relating to aircraft carriers than the previous dogma, which was based on no analysis at all. Enthoven's book [see bibliography] gives many other examples of analyses that unquestionably aided the decision maker.

Charles Schultze, at the time Director of the Bureau of the Budget, summarized the middle ground in a statement which has become a classic:[5]

> Much has been published on PPB.[6] Learned articles have treated it sometimes as the greatest thing since the invention of the wheel.

---

[5] From his Statement to the Subcommittee on National Security and International Operations of the Committee on Government Operations, U.S. Senate, 90th Congress, 1st Session, August 23, 1967.

[6] PPB stands for Planning, Programming, Budgeting, which was the name given to the overall approach of which benefit/cost analysis was one part.

Other articles attack it, either as a naive attempt to quantify and computerize the imponderable, or as an arrogant effort on the part of latter-day technocrats to usurp the decision-making function in a political democracy.

PPB is neither. It *is* a means of *helping* responsible officials make decisions. It is *not* a mechanical substitute for the good judgment, political wisdom and leadership of those officials. . . .

While our approach to the PPB in the past may, perhaps, legitimately be criticized for lack of precision about forward planning, there is another frequently heard criticism of PPB which stems, I believe, from a straight misconception as to what PPB is all about.

This criticism takes a number of forms. But basically it charges that PPB and cost-effectiveness analysis set up a bias in decision making: by concentrating on the cost accounting elements of an issue and ignoring those human factors and intangibles which cannot be quantified; or, conversely, by naively attempting to put numbers on these essentially imponderable elements, thereby misleading the decision maker.

Often this criticism is expressed in terms of an attack on PPB for trying to "computerize" what is essentially a political and judgmental process. Or sometimes it is expressed in terms of "not letting the statisticians and cost accountants take over."

I might interpolate, Mr. Chairman, that on the basis of my experience in government, which is limited, I will admit, this fear of the statisticians and analysts taking over ranks about 28th on my list of fears, perhaps just below my fear of being eaten alive by piranhas. I have many fears of government, and this is not one of them so far.

Quite frankly, Mr. Chairman, these kinds of criticisms—however sincere—reflect a complete misunderstanding of the issue. And sometimes they simply reflect chagrin that particular pet projects do not show up well under the light of cost-effectiveness analysis.

PPB *does* call for systematic analysis of program proposals and decisions, concentrating upon those decisions which have budgetary consequences. But systematic analysis does not have to be and is not coextensive with quantitative analysis. The word "analyze" does not, in any man's dictionary, have the same meaning as the words "quantify" or "measure," although analysis often includes measurement.

Systematic analysis is an aid to policy debate. Too often these debates revolve around a simple list of pros and cons. There are no means of making progress in the debate, since participants simply repeat, in different words, their original positions. Systematic analysis is designed to improve this process by:

Uncovering the irrelevant issues.

Identifying the specific assumptions and factual bases upon which alternative recommendations rest, and,

Tracing out the knowable consequences and costs of each alternative.

By this means, systematic analysis is designed to narrow the debate, to focus it on the important issues, and—I underline and stress this—to separate those points about which the judgments of reasonable men can disagree from those which are demonstrably true or false.

Now such analysis often does, and must, involve quantitative estimates. Most of our decisions—in fact, all of our budgetary decisions—willy-nilly involve quantitative consideration. For example, take the question of how many doctors to train and how much aid to give to medical schools. We can debate this simply in terms of arguing more or less budget dollars for the program. Alternatively, we can calculate the current and projected ratio of doctors to population, examine the relationship between the doctor/population ratio and various indices of health, review the distribution of doctors throughout various areas in the nation, estimate the costs of training doctors, and a host of similar factors. We cannot, of course, measure precisely, or even close to precisely, the national advantages to be gained from a program of aid to medical schools, nor can we account for all of the costs. But we can isolate, in a quantitative form, a number of the key elements involved in the program. The debate then can proceed in terms of weighing fairly specifically the advantages the nation gains from alternative increases in the supply of doctors against the costs of achieving each alternative.

Handled properly, a well constructed numerical estimate can be worth a thousand words. And, in PPB, we seek to encourage quantitative estimates, as part of the systematic analysis of budgetary issues.

But this, most emphatically, does not mean that quantitative estimates are the only elements of systematic analysis. The latter is far broader than the former. Human factors and intangible elements in a decision must not be ignored. And that which cannot reasonably be measured should not be.

In short, Mr. Chairman, PPB does not represent an attempt to "computerize" decision making or to measure the immeasurable or to ignore the intangible. It merely seeks to subject to systematic analysis both the tangible and the intangible elements of a program decision.

In short, the issue is not whether benefit/cost analysis is a panacea or whether it is a fraud, for in general it is neither. The issue rather is to define the circumstances under which benefit/cost analysis is likely to be useful. Some aspects of this question are discussed below.

Clarifying Goals

Since the "benefit" in a benefit/cost analysis is related to an organization's goals, there is no point in making a benefit/cost analysis unless there is some measure of agreement on what the goals are. Hoos[7] summarizes a report made by the General Accounting Office of three successive study contracts made by the same consulting firm on the "problem" of civil defense. The studies cost $600,000, and in the opinion of the General Accounting Office, they were worthless.

---

[7] Hoos, op. cit., p. 117.

The reason was that no one, either prior to the study or in the course of the study, had defined what the goals of a civil defense program should be.

Thus, at the outset, there should be a fairly specific statement as to what the study team should do. If at this stage the goals themselves are not clear, the first task may be to formulate tentative goals for the consideration of top management. Moreover, as the study progresses, analysis may indicate that the original statement of goals needs to be changed because the goals are not feasible, or for other reasons. But at every stage of the study, there is no point in expending effort on the wrong problem, and the right problem is how to achieve whatever top management decides the goals should be. The basic purpose of a benefit/cost analysis is not to formulate goals, but rather to suggest the best alternative way of reaching a goal. The formulation of goals is largely a judgmental process.

In some situations, various members of management and various staff people may have different ideas of what the goals are. These ideas should be reconciled as much as possible. Failure to clarify goals and failure to agree as to what the goals are, obviously makes it difficult to formulate programs to achieve these goals.

> *Example:* People associated with the Head Start program say variously that its goals are some, but not all, of the following: (1) to prepare disadvantaged children for elementary school, (2) to provide a child care center for working parents, (3) to improve child health, (4) to train teachers and teachers' aides, and (5) to educate parents. When there is a great difference of opinion as to the relative importance of these goals, programming is difficult.

> *Example:* The Peace Corps defined its objectives from the Statute which created the Corps. These were: (1) to provide trained personnel to other countries, (2) to increase the understanding of Americans by other people and (3) to increase the understanding of other countries by Americans. Such a statement is not sufficiently concrete to provide an adequate basis for making decisions on programs.

Clarifying the goals also helps to clarify the specific activities necessary to reach them. For example, an agency may decide: "We should do something about the rat problem." But "rat problem" has many possible meanings, such as:

1. There are too many rats.
2. Rats are too destructive.
3. Rats cause disease.
4. People are upset about rats.
5. Rats are appearing where they are not supposed to be.

The magnitude and nature of activities designed to solve the "rat problem" depend on precisely how the problem is perceived.

National Goals. On July 13, 1970, President Nixon established a National Goals Research Staff. Since then, not much has been said publicly about the work of this staff. In due course, it undoubtedly will produce a report that contains some words about national goals, but it seems unlikely that this statement will actually be a result of a rational analysis of priorities for the nation as a whole or that the statement will actually be used as a basis for making an optimum allocation of resources. However desirable such an analysis may be, it seems unlikely that an analytical process will have much influence in determining priorities at the national level, at least in the foreseeable future. The problem is simply too complicated for rational analysis. Rather, decisions on priorities at this level are likely to continue to be made according to a political, rather than an analytical, process.

Nevertheless, overall analyses are worth pursuing as an aid to the political process. The French economic plan does make an attempt to integrate the analytical and the political aspects of decisions. This is done at three stages. First, "Commissions" that include business leaders, unions, and professionals formulate proposals; second, these proposals are analyzed by the Plan Administration that prepares several (generally three) alternative plans with their implications, documented with extensive economic analyses; third, the final decision is voted by the National Assembly. There is no corresponding process in the United States.

Surrogates for Goals. In preparing programs, attention may be focused on surrogates for goals (as defined in Chapter 6) rather than on the goals themselves, since the goals may not be quantifiable. Such a focus may add a desirable precision to the programming process, but care must be taken to insure that the surrogates are in fact consistent with the real goals; otherwise, wrong actions may be taken.

> *Example:* A program designed to increase the number of suspects jailed may be consistent with a surrogate used to measure public safety activity, but this surrogate may be inconsistent with the objective of reducing crime. Many experts believe that there is no causal relationship between the number of persons jailed and the incidence of crime.

Proposals Susceptible to Analysis

In benefit/cost analysis the general principles are that (1) a program should not be adopted unless its benefits exceed its costs, and (2) as between two competing proposals the one with the greater excess of benefits over costs, or the one with the lower costs if benefits are equal, is preferable. In order to apply these principles there must be some way of relating benefits and costs.

"Economic" Proposals. For many proposals in nonprofit organizations, it is possible to estimate both costs and benefits in monetary terms.

These proposals are similar to the capital budgeting proposals that are discussed extensively in the literature for profit-oriented companies, and the method of analysis in nonprofit organizations is essentially the same as the method described in that literature. A proposal to convert the heating plant of a hospital from oil to coal involves the same type of analysis that would be used for the same problem in an industrial company. Problems of this type are numerous in nonprofit organizations. Unfortunately, they are also relatively unimportant. For most of the important problems a reliable monetary estimate of the benefits cannot be made.

Alternative Ways of Reaching the Same Objective. Even if the benefits cannot be quantified, a benefit/cost analysis is useful in situations in which there are two or more ways of achieving a given objective. If there is a reasonable presumption that each of the alternatives will achieve the objective, then the alternative with the lowest cost is preferred.

This approach has many applications, simply because it does not require that the objective be stated in monetary terms, or even that it be quantified. All that is necessary is a judgment that any of the proposed alternatives will achieve the objective. We need not measure the *degree* to which a given alternative meets the objective; we need only make the "go/no-go" judgment that the results are adequate.

> *Example:* The output of an educational program is difficult to measure, and it is especially difficult to find a causal relationship between a certain teaching technique and the resulting quality of education. Nevertheless, it is possible to compare alternative teaching techniques, such as team teaching, computer assisted instruction, and conventional tests and workbooks, in terms of cost. In the absence of a judgment that one method provides better education than another, the technique with the lowest cost is preferred.

> *Example:* A calculable number of passengers arrive and depart Washington, D.C., by air. The objective of a certain analysis was to provide the optimum ground transportation and airport facilities for these passengers in the Washington area. The costs of various airport locations and associated ground transport services were estimated. The proposal that provided adequate service with the lowest cost was preferred. There was no need to measure the benefits of "adequate service" in monetary terms.

> *Example:* It was assumed that in a major war in the European theater, X aircraft sorties per day would be required. The analysis sought to find whether these sorties should be provided (*a*) by carrier-based Navy aircraft, (*b*) by land-based Air Force aircraft, or (*c*) by some combination. The lowest cost alternative is preferable. (Note that this problem is susceptible to analysis only if the number of sorties per day is taken as given. The estimate of the optimum number of sorties

per day is a quite different problem, which has not been found susceptible to benefit/cost analysis.)

Equal Cost Programs. If two competing proposals have the same cost, but one produces more benefits than the other, it ordinarily is the preferred alternative. This conclusion can be reached without a measurement of the absolute levels of benefits. Such an approach is often used in deciding on the best mix of resources to be used in a program. The question is raised, for example: will $100,000 spent on teachers' salaries produce more educational benefits than $100,000 spent on a combination of teachers and teaching machines, or $100,000 spent on team teaching rather than individual teaching? The analysis involves an estimate of the amount of resources the stated amount of money will buy and a judgment of the results that will be achieved by using this amount and mix of resources, but it does not require that the benefits be expressed numerically.

Different Objectives. A benefit/cost comparison of proposals intended to accomplish different objectives is likely to be worthless. An analysis that attempts to compare funds to be spent for primary school education with funds to be spent for retraining of unemployed adults would not be worthwhile because such an analysis requires that monetary values be assigned to the benefits of these two programs, which is an impossible task.

Causal Connection between Cost and Benefits. Many benefit/cost analyses implicitly assume that there is a causal relationship between the benefits and the costs, that is, that spending X of cost produces Y amount of benefit. If this causal connection does not exist, such an analysis is fallacious.

> *Example:* An agency defended its personnel training program with an analysis which indicated that the program would lead its participants to new jobs which would increase their life-time earnings by $25,000 per person. Thus, the average cost per person trained of $5,000 seemed to be quite justified. However, the assertion that the proposed program would indeed generate these benefits was completely unsupported; it was strictly a guess. Without some plausible link between the amount spent and the results obtained, such an analysis is worthless.

Benefit/Cost as a Way of Thinking. Benefit/cost *analysis* is feasible in only a small proportion of the problems that arise in nonprofit organizations, and these tend to be the well-structured and less important problems. By contrast, a benefit/cost *way of thinking* is feasible in approaching a great many problems. One of the characteristics of competent managers is that they look at proposals, at least in a general way, in terms of whether the benefits are probably worth more than the costs. They may not be able to quantify the relationship, nor do they need to do so in many cases. This way of looking at problems tends to distinguish the factors that are relevant from those that are not relevant. Each of the following examples describes a situation in which the benefit/cost way of thinking aided the decision maker.

Example: The president of a liberal arts college was considering a proposal that the college join a consortium of three other colleges in the general area. Those advocating the proposal argued that the consortium movement originated in Oxford in the 15th century, and the idea was therefore good because it had a long and noble history; that there were 67 American consortiums in 1970 compared with only 7 in 1967, and that the idea was therefore good because it was growing rapidly; that it was good for college faculties to cooperate with one another; that central purchasing is more efficient than having each college do its own purchasing; and so on. The president said that although these statements were interesting none of them directly addressed the questions that were on his mind. These questions were: How many students were likely to be benefited by the activities of the consortium? Was the benefit likely to be worth the cost per student benefited (the annual fee was $15,000)? What would a central purchasing office cost? Would it be likely to reduce costs sufficiently to pay for itself plus the cost of the consortium? Could a central purchasing office be created without having a formal consortium?

For some of these questions, such as those related to central purchasing, quantified information could be developed that was sufficiently accurate to aid in making the decision. For other questions, such as the number of students benefited, no reliable quantified estimate was possible, but the process of thinking about these questions was nevertheless important. It drew attention away from irrelevant matters such as generalities about the history of consortiums, and focused it on relevant matters: namely, the objectives of the college. In this situation it became apparent that the number of students likely to be interested in the specialized courses that a consortium could develop was so small that it did not warrant a $15,000 cost. The president reached this conclusion without any elaborate numerical calculations. When he looked at the problem in benefit/cost terms, the irrelevant arguments faded away, and the relevant arguments came to the foreground.

Example: Dr. Sam Peltzman of UCLA sought to measure the social benefits and costs associated with the 1962 Amendments to the Food, Drug, & Cosmetic Act—a piece of legislation which some people regard as one of the great triumphs in the history of the consumer movement.

This legislation required that drug manufacturers provide "proof-of-efficacy" as well as the already required proof of safety when filing for permission to market a new drug. No new drug could be marketed until the Food and Drug Administration (FDA) determined that there was substantial evidence not only that the drug was safe, but that it was also effective in its intended use.

Professor Peltzman concluded that while the effects of the 1962 Amendments are difficult to ascertain—there have been no new-drug disasters in the U.S. nor were there any major therapeutic innovations since 1962—the relevant costs appear to exceed the benefits by a large margin. The Amendments led to higher prices for existing drugs, reduced competition from new drugs and increased the possibility of enormous losses of benefits to the consumer—the potential loss from a delay in the introduction of a major life-saving drug. Partially offsetting these costs was a reduction in consumer outlays for ineffective new drugs. But according to Peltzman's calculations these were trivial compared with the losses from reduced innovation. The authors of the legislation obviously *assumed* that it was worth sacrificing potential return from innovation for reduced risk. Peltzman's calculations indicate that the sacrifice was probably not worthwhile.[8]

Listed below are fallacies that often are urged in support of proposals when the benefit/cost way of thinking is absent:

1. An activity is important; therefore we should spend a lot of money on it. (This is a *non sequitur*. It is not importance *per se*, but the relation between additional spending and additional benefits that is relevant. An appreciation of ethics is important, but schools should not spend money on teaching ethics unless they believe that the program will increase ethical perceptions sufficiently to be worth its cost.)

2. We should do it because others do it.

3. We should do it because we always have done it.

4. We should do it because an outstanding authority recommends it.

Overreliance on Benefit/Cost Approach. The benefit/cost way of thinking can be carried to extremes, however. If the decision maker rejects all proposals in which no causal connection between costs and benefits have been demonstrated, the total program is unlikely to be innovative. This is because a primary characteristic of many new, experimental, promising schemes is that there is no way of estimating benefit/cost relationships in advance. Undue insistence on benefit/cost analyses can therefore result in overly conservative programs. Although the risk of failure of an innovative proposal may be high, it may be a risk worth running.

As is the case in profit-oriented companies, a proposal to change or discontinue an ongoing program is more susceptible to analysis than a proposal to institute a new program. This may be attributed to the historical data that have been accumulated for the ongoing program and because of the inevitable uncertainties associated with doing something new.

As in profit-oriented organizations, quantitative analysis of a problem rarely if ever provides a complete solution. The most it does

[8] *Argus Weekly Staff Report* (Argus Research Corp., November 6, 1972).

is to reduce the number of factors about which judgment must be exercised and thus make the judgment process easier.

SOME PROBLEMS IN ANALYTICAL TECHNIQUES

The literature on benefit/cost analysis is voluminous, and we do not attempt to summarize here the various techniques that are described in it. Selected references are given at the end of this chapter. In this section, we limit ourselves to a few of the particularly difficult problems that arise in making an analysis for a nonprofit organization.

Use of Models

All benefit/cost analyses at least imply that there is an underlying model that describes the essential variables in the situation being studied and the relationships among these variables, and many studies explicitly attempt to construct such a model. The construction of a model often helps in estimating the benefits and costs of each alternative. These models can be extremely complex. The model that depicts the consequences of a nuclear exchange between the United States and the U.S.S.R. or between the United States and China is perhaps the most elaborate model ever built. It is also extremely useful, as evidenced by the fact that most of those who are involved in discussions about the appropriate size and composition of strategic forces accept without question the amount of destruction that the model predicts under a given scenario, and use these numbers as a starting point in arguing for the particular course of action that they recommend.

In many situations, attempts to construct models have turned out to be fruitless. Persons contemplating model building for public-oriented problems should read Brewer's *Politicians, Bureaucrats, and the Consultant*[9] to be forewarned about what can go wrong. Brewer made an intensive analysis of attempts to build models of the demand for housing in San Francisco and Pittsburgh. Over $1,000,000 was spent on each of these models, but no useful results were forthcoming. Some of the reasons for the failure were: (1) the goals were not clearly set forth at the beginning of the study (essentially, they consisted of the vague statement: "Provide the best housing at the lowest cost for all our citizens"); (2) the consultants did not understand the housing problem; (3) the historical data used in the model were so voluminous and detailed that a single run of the model required two or three weeks of computer time; (4) by contrast, the assumptions about population growth patterns were naive and simplistic; and (5)

---

[9] Gary D. Brewer, *Politicians, Bureaucrats and the Consultant: A Critique of Urban Problem Solving* (New York: Basic Books, 1973).

the output of each computer run was several inches thick, and decision makers could not comprehend it.

In order to develop useful models, one needs reliable data, and such data are often not available. Califano, with only slight exaggeration, described the situation as follows: "The disturbing truth is that the basis of recommendations by an American Cabinet officer on whether to begin, eliminate, or expand vast social programs more nearly resembles the intuitive judgment of a benevolent tribal chief in remote Africa than the elaborate, sophisticated data with which the Secretary of Defense supports a major new weapons system."[10]

Quantifying the Value of a Human Being

In the analysis of proposed programs in nonprofit organizations, a factor is frequently encountered that rarely is relevant in proposals originating in profit-oriented organizations, namely, the value of human beings. Some programs are designed to save or prolong human lives, such as automobile safety programs, accident prevention programs, drug control programs, and medical research programs. In these programs, the value of a human life, or of a work-day lost to accident or illness, is a relevant consideration in measuring benefits. Analysts are often squeamish about attaching a monetary value to a human life since there is a general belief in our culture that life is priceless, but such a monetary amount often facilitates the analysis of certain proposals. In a world of scarce resources, it is not possible to spend unlimited amounts to save lives in general (although there are circumstances in which society is willing to devote unlimited resources to saving a specific life; for example, hundreds of people may hunt for a child who is lost in the woods).

> *Example:* In an interesting article,[11] Sagan shows how relating costs to lives can be applied fruitfully to many problems involving nuclear energy. For example, he estimates that a recent reduction in the permitted radiation levels in uranium mines increased operating costs by $7 million per year in order to save 1.54 cases of lung cancer among miners. He estimates the value to society of the reduction of 1.54 lung cancer cases at $462,000 and therefore questions whether the new safety standards are sound.

Great care must be used in calculating the value of a human life. If, for example, the value of a life is taken as being the present value of a person's lifetime earnings, calculations using such an ap-

---

[10] Presidential Assistant Joseph A. Califano, Jr., in testimony before the Senate Labor Subcommittee, 1969, as quoted in Paul Dickson, *Think Tanks* (New York: Ballantine Books, 1971), p. 226.

[11] L. A. Sagan, "Human Costs of Nuclear Power," *Science,* 11 (August 1972), pp. 487–93.

proach will discriminate against programs aimed at persons with relatively low expected life-time earnings: women, elderly people, members of minority groups, ministers.

In order to overcome such discrimination, it has been suggested that programs which involve saving or prolonging human lives be evaluated by favoring the alternative which saves the most lives per dollar spent, independent of the economic characteristics of the target group. This procedure makes the problem of choosing among alternatives much more complex than the procedure which quantifies the monetary value of human lives. If the valuation criterion is replaced by that of saving the most lives per dollar spent, one cannot quantitatively compare the benefits and the costs, and the analysis is limited to questioning whether a particular program saves more lives per dollar spent than other life-saving or life-prolonging programs.

Benefits of Social Programs

In undeveloped countries, the present value of the anticipated additions to tax revenue is one way of measuring the benefits of social programs. There are some possibilities in computing the social cost of some types of crime, particularly crimes against property (the direct loss, cost of imprisonment, cost of the court system), and thus estimating the benefits of programs designed to reduce crime, but few worthwhile results of such attempts are now known.

It also has been suggested that public opinion polls might be used to determine the public's judgment as to the relative value of various program objectives, but critics of this approach argue that the essence of leadership is to rise above the vagaries of public opinion and to formulate new programs that the public will endorse after a period of education.

It has been suggested that multi-variate analysis might be used to combine the value of several benefits. The mathematical techniques for doing this are well known; the difficulty is the same as that suggested above, namely, that it is often impossible to find reliable estimates of the value of each benefit. Without these, the mathematical techniques are useless.

Separation of Political Judgments and Analysis

The final decision on a proposed program involves political considerations (such as the predisposition of a member of Congress toward a certain policy, or the desirability of favoring a certain Congressional district), as well as economic and social considerations. Ordinarily it is desirable that political considerations be excluded from the analysis itself. The decision maker takes them into account separately when making a final judgment. The analysis is likely to be less lucid if political considerations are included in it.

Political considerations properly are a part of certain types of analyses, however. If, for example, several political solutions are proposed to a problem, an analysis might be able to show the lowest-cost solution and the incremental cost of other solutions. The decision maker can use such an analysis as an aid in deciding whether the political benefits of a higher-cost solution outweigh the cost.

> *Example:* The Agricultural Stabilization and Conservation Service Peanut Program accomplishes important economic objectives with respect to the supply and price of peanuts, and the economic effect of various program proposals can be estimated with a fair degree of reliability. At the same time, the particular program selected must take into account the desires of peanut growers and of legislators in peanut growing states. This program is likely not to be optimum in an economic sense. It may be desirable to estimate the economic consequences of proposals that are favored for political reasons, so as to judge whether the economic sacrifice is worth the political gain.

Discount Rates

When the benefits of a proposed program are derived in different time periods than those in which the costs are incurred, the proposal cannot be evaluated unless these differences in timing patterns are taken into account. This requires the use of a discount rate. Thus, a proposal to acquire an expensive piece of equipment that requires little annual maintenance can be compared with a proposal to acquire a less expensive piece of equipment that requires higher annual maintenance only if the two streams of outflows have been made comparable by the application of discount rates to the costs of each year. The concept and the procedure is the same in nonprofit organizations as in profit-oriented companies. The special problem in nonprofit organizations is the choice of a discount rate.

In profit-oriented companies the selection of the proper discount rate is also a difficult problem, but it is one that has been analyzed extensively, whereas until recently most nonprofit organizations gave little attention to it.

This problem is particularly important in the Federal government, which considers many proposals for public works and other capital expenditures whose benefits will accrue over a long period of time. Until fairly recently, most government agencies either did not discount at all, or they used the interest rate on government bonds as the discount rate. It is now generally recognized that a government bond rate is too low and that its use results in the approval of projects that actually should not be undertaken.

In the 1960s there was considerable discussion of what the appropriate discount rate should be, and there emerged a concensus that the rate should approximate the average rate of return on private sector investments. There is room for disagreement as to just what this rate is, but the controversy was effectively ended by the revision of Office of Management and Budget Circular No. A-94 in March 1972 which specified that in most circumstances a rate of 10 percent should be used.[12] Circular A-94 also gives concise, useful guidance on applying the discounting principle.

Exhibit 8–1 shows the nature of the errors that result from failure

EXHIBIT 8–1
Characteristics of Investment Proposals

	Project		
	A	B	C
Investment.	$10,000	$10,000	$10,000
Annual benefits	3,000	1,800	1,000
Life (years)	5	10	20
Present Value of Benefits:			
At 0%	15,000	18,000	20,000
At 5% (bond rate)	12,900	13,900	12,500
At 10% (proper rate).	11,400	11,000	8,500

to discount at all and from the use of a discount rate that is too low. The essential characteristics of three projects are listed, together with the present value of the benefits under three assumptions: (*a*) undiscounted, (*b*) at a discount rate of 5 percent which corresponds to an average rate on government bonds, and (*c*) at a discount rate of 10 percent which approximates the real cost of capital to the government. Several conclusions can be drawn:

1. If the benefits are not discounted, Project C, with savings worth $20,000, appears to be the best project of all. Actually, the present value of Project C's benefits is only $8,500 which is less than its cost, so the project should not be undertaken. Prior to 1940 the Soviet Union did not use discount rates, and consequently invested erroneously in projects similar to Project C, that is, in capital-intensive, long-lived projects such as hydro-electric power facilities.

2. If the government is deciding how best to spend a fixed sum of money, and therefore must rank projects in order of desirability, it will favor Project B over Project A if it uses a discount rate corresponding to the interest rate on government bonds. At such a rate, the present value of Project B's benefits ($13,900) exceeds that of

---

[12] The 10 percent rate does not apply to the U.S. Postal Service, to water resource projects, to buy-or-lease decisions, or to certain make-or-buy decisions.

Project A's ($12,900). Actually, Project A is better than Project B ($11,400 compared with $11,000). In general, with a low rate, capital intensive projects and long-lived projects appear to be more attractive than they actually are. In India, the use of a low rate has led to the construction of large cement plants built at infrequent intervals, rather than to smaller plants built more frequently, which was a mistake.

3. If agencies are permitted to use different rates (which until 1972 was the case in the Federal government), an agency that uses a low rate can justify a larger capital budget than an agency that uses a high rate. An agency that uses 5 percent can justify Projects A, B, and C, since in each case the benefits exceed the cost; an agency that uses 10 percent can justify only Projects A and B.

The desirability of long-lived projects is extremely sensitive to the discount rate that is used in the analysis of them. For example, a survey made by the Water Resources Council of 245 authorized Corps of Engineers projects showed that for about one-third of them, the costs would exceed the benefits if the discount rate were raised from the 5⅜ percent actually used in the analyses to 7 percent.[13]

The problem of taking differences in the timing of benefits and costs into account arises in nonprofit organizations of all types. A *de novo* analysis of the appropriate discount rate in a given organization is extremely complex and controversial, however, and most organizations therefore would do well to avoid making such an analysis and to simply adopt the government rate of 10 percent.

Taxes

Some analyses involve the problem of whether a given activity should be performed by the government or by private enterprise. This is a version of the make-or-buy problem that is common in profit-oriented companies, and the analytical approach is the same. In a government analysis, there is the special problem of how to treat income taxes, property taxes, and other taxes that are paid by a profit-oriented company, but not by the government. The amounts involved can be substantial, and must not be omitted from the analysis. A good approach is set forth in Office of Management and Budget Circular A-76.

Content of Proposals

A program proposal can vary in format from a one-page memorandum to a several-hundred-page statement. If the proposal itself is long,

---

[13] Luther J. Carter, "Water Projects: How to Erase the 'Pork Barrel' Image?" *Science* (October 19, 1973), p. 268.

it should of course be accompanied by a summary for the use of top management. Some managers require that such a summary be limited to one page; others permit two pages.

The proposal should describe *what* is to be done but ordinarily it does not contain the details of *how* it is to be done. These details are the responsibility of operating management, to be worked out after the proposal has been approved. Program proposals should include:

1. A description of the proposed program and evidence that it will accomplish the organization's objectives.

2. An estimate of the resources to be devoted to the program over the next several years, divided between investment costs and operating expenses. A principal purpose of this estimate is to estimate the approximate magnitude of the effort; a detailed analysis of the costs usually is deferred until after the program has been approved in principle.

3. The benefits expected from the program over the same time period, expressed quantitatively if feasible. One purpose of quantifying the benefits is to permit the subsequent comparison of actual results with planned results.

4. A discussion of the risks and uncertainties associated with the program.

DECIDING ON PROPOSALS

Few formal staff analyses provide the basis for an automatic decision on a proposal. The decision almost always involves top management judgment; the analysis can aid that judgment, but not obviate the need for it. This is because the analysis contains estimates of variables whose real magnitude cannot be known, and it omits important factors whose magnitude cannot be measured. Also, the analysis is often limited to economic considerations, whereas the decision also involves political considerations.

Advocacy Proposals

The decision maker would do well to consider whether or not a proposal is prepared by, or influenced by, a person who advocates it. An advocacy proposal is essentially a document that is designed to sell the proposal to the decision maker. Most proposals initiated by operating managers are advocacy proposals; indeed, if the manager is not an enthusiastic supporter of the proposal, there is probably something wrong with it. Proposals initiated by a top level planning staff presumably are more neutral, but even staff-generated proposals can incorporate an element of advocacy under certain circumstances.

In general, therefore, it is safe to assume that most proposals reflect someone's advocacy.

> *Example:* In 1967 the Defense Systems Analysis Staff studied the problem of the large size of the U.S. forces in Europe. They evolved the dual-basing concept as a means of solving this problem. Under this concept, approximately ⅓ of the combat forces committed to Europe would actually be based in the United States, and would move to Europe at periodic intervals. The initial proposal was relatively unbiased. Strong opposition to it immediately developed, however, and subsequent drafts of the proposal increasingly had an advocacy flavor. Arguments for the proposal were emphasized, and arguments against it were played down.

A proposal may be biased in any of the following ways:

a. Consequences are asserted without adequate substantiation. (In a benefit/cost analysis, the process may be, first, to estimate the cost and then to plug in a benefit "number" such that the resulting benefit/cost ratio looks good.)

b. Technical matters beyond the comprehension of the decision maker are discussed at length. (This is one of several possible varieties of "snow jobs" that are attempted in proposals.)

c. Opposing views are omitted or not faithfully reported.

The character of such proposals is suggested by the following conjugation:

I am objective.
You are neutral.
They are completely out of touch with reality.
My proposal is based on facts.
Your proposal is based on your best judgments.
Their proposal is based on uneducated guesses backed up with incredible suppositions.

Decision makers naturally attempt to allow for these biases and to minimize them by penalizing persons making deliberate omissions or distortions, but it is unlikely that they have either the knowledge or the time to detect all the elements of bias that are imbedded in the proposal. In reviewing proposals, therefore, they need ways of compensating for the biases. The planning staff provides one important resource for this purpose. Subject to the qualification that a planning staff can develop its own biases, the staff exists to help the decision maker, and it can do this by making a thorough analysis of advocacy proposals. In many circumstances, the staff works with the initiator of the proposal to remove unwarranted assumptions, errors of calculations, or other weaknesses before the proposal is submitted to the decision maker. The staff also may list questions for the decision maker to raise with the advocate, the answers to which will shed light on the real merits of the proposal.

An outside consultant may be hired to make the same type of review. If the consulting firm has special expertise in the topic, its appraisal is especially useful, but in many situations the internal planning staff has built up a background that permits it to do the same job more effectively. A consulting firm is also useful for another purpose; to associate its prestige either for or against a proposal, and thus either aid or hurt the chances of its adoption.

Another approach to the advocacy proposal is to establish an adversary relationship. For every important proposal, there is some group that opposes it, if only because it diverts resources that the group would like to have for its own programs. If arrangements are made to identify such an adversary party and provide for a debate between it and the program advocate, the merits and weaknesses of the proposal often can be illuminated. A danger exists, however, that the adversaries will develop a "back-scratching" relationship; that is, the presumed adversary may not argue forcefully against the proposal, with the understanding, or at least the hope, that when the roles are reversed in connection with some other proposal, the other party will act with equal charity.

In short, for a variety of reasons, there is no such thing as a decision on an important proposal being based entirely on a "rational" analysis. If proposals are arrayed along a continuum, with purely economic proposals at one extreme and purely social or political proposals at the other, the amount of rationality inevitably decreases as one moves along the continuum. Nevertheless, a decision must be made. Because resources are limited, not all worthwhile proposals can be accepted. The decision maker must decide which of the worthwhile projects are the best.[14]

SELLING THE PROPOSAL

Just as program advocates must sell their proposals to the decision maker in each organization, so the decision maker must sell proposals to outside parties who provide the funds for executing programs. These parties include the Office of Management and Budget, the Executive Office, and the Congress for proposals initiated by federal government agencies, corresponding bodies for state and municipal governments,

[14] In 1942, Dr. James Conant, the decision maker with respect to the atomic bomb, was presented with five possible methods of producing fissionable material, each of which required enormous expenditures. He decided to proceed with all five. Two were abandoned a few months later, but the remaining three were actively pursued. There are few problems in which this luxury of adopting several competing alternatives is possible. See Stephane Groveff, *Manhattan Project* (Boston: Little, Brown & Co., 1967).

and Boards of Trustees for hospitals and educational institutions. Aspects of this problem are discussed in Chapter 10. In brief, the agency head is well advised to lay the groundwork for this effort well in advance, to discover, if possible, the likely grounds for opposition to the proposal, and to prepare to meet this opposition, with logical arguments, by enlisting the help of others, or by any other means available.

BIBLIOGRAPHY

Brewer, Gary D. *Politicians, Bureaucrats and the Consultant. A Critique of Urban Problem Solving.* New York: Basic Books, 1973.

Drake, Alvin U.; Keeney, Ralph L., and Morse, Philip M., eds. *Analysis of Public Systems.* Cambridge, Mass.: MIT Press, 1972.

Emshoff, J. R., and Sisson, R. L. *Design and Use of Computer Simulation Models.* New York: Macmillan, 1970.

Enthoven, Alain C., and Smith, K. Wayne. *How Much is Enough: Shaping the Defense Program, 1961–1969.* New York: Harper and Row, 1971.

Ketter, R. C., and Prawel, S. P. *Modern Methods of Engineering Computation.* New York: McGraw-Hill, 1969.

Levey, Samuel, and Loomba, N. Paul. *Health Care Administration: A Managerial Perspective.* Philadelphia: J. B. Lippincott, 1973.

Levin, R. I., and Kirkpatrick, C. A. *Quantitative Approaches to Management.* New York: McGraw-Hill, 1971.

Livingstone, J. Leslie and Gunn, Sanford C. *Accounting for Social Goals: Budgeting and Analysis of Nonmarket Projects.* New York: Harper & Row, 1974.

Lyden, Fremont J. and Miller, Ernest G., eds. *Planning, Programming, Budgeting.* Chicago: Markham Publishing, 1968.

Novick, David, ed. *Program Budgeting.* Washington, D.C.: Government Printing Office, 1965.

chapter nine

Programming:
Ongoing Programs

Although analysis and decision making on proposed new programs is the glamorous part of the programming process, new programs constitute a relatively small fraction of the work in the typical organization. The fact is that most of the activities conducted next year will be similar to those conducted this year. This chapter discusses the review of these ongoing programs. It also describes formal programming systems and in particular the system called PPB.

REVIEW OF ONGOING PROGRAMS

Ongoing programs tend to go on forever unless they are subject to periodic, hard-headed reexamination. There is a need to look at operations in program terms to ascertain whether the benefits of each program continue to exceed its cost, and whether there are ways to improve the effectiveness and efficiency with which these programs are carried on. Opportunities for improvement exist in every organization, but there is a general feeling that these opportunities are especially significant in nonprofit organizations. For example, the Carnegie Commission on Higher Education concluded that "substantial savings—in the order of 20 percent—can be made as compared with continuation of trends of the 1960s—without loss of quality."[1]

---

[1] Carnegie Commission on Higher Education. *Priorities for Action* (New York; McGraw-Hill), Sec. 9, pp. 63–70.

Impetus for Review

New programs have advocates, and these advocates work hard to insure that proposals get favorable consideration by top management. By contrast, unless special steps are taken, it is less likely that operating managers will take the initiative in advocating improvements in existing programs, especially improvements that have the effect of reducing costs. Exhortation alone is unlikely to produce such improvements. For example, the Federal government has had a Joint Financial Management Improvement Program since 1948, which issued statements on at least an annual basis about the need for increased productivity; although these statements were signed by cabinet level officials, their impact has not been great.

One way of involving the operating organization is to conduct a cost-reduction program. Such a program can be effective if adequate incentives are provided for those who achieve results. Money is probably the best incentive, but special recognition, plaques, and other nonmonetary rewards can also be effective if top management demonstrates by deeds that it is genuinely interested in the cost reduction effort. Although there is no way of measuring the exact amount, independent auditors verified that the cost reduction program in the Department of Defense in the 1960s produced savings of several billion dollars.

Another device is to enforce an across-the-board cut in the level of current spending. This is a drastic step, used only in times of financial crisis, but experience has shown that if the need is urgent, most organizations can reduce spending by 5 percent, 10 percent, and in some cases more, without crippling ongoing operations.

The cost reduction program and the across-the-board cut are nonroutine measures, however. In the ordinary conduct of current operations, a staff unit, responsible to the controller or to top management, is usually the most effective means of examining ongoing programs. This staff function may be performed by the programming staff described in Chapter 8, but in large organizations a separate staff, responsible only for examining ongoing operations, may be desirable. Such a staff may be called an operations analysis unit; in a profit-oriented company, it may be called an industrial engineering staff.

A similar function may be performed by an outside consulting firm, but such firms are more appropriately used for occasional studies than for a continuing review. If an organization is not large enough to warrant having a full-time staff member engaged in reviewing continuing operations, hiring a consulting firm to make such a review from time to time is a good alternative.

Some organizations set up a "blue ribbon commission" of well-known citizens to conduct a review of continuing operations. Such commissions have been extremely effective in situations in which they receive the full backing of top management and when they have the necessary expertise on the commission itself or on its staff. In other situations, not much may happen as a result of the Commission's work. Observations like the following are not uncommon: "All the Commission did was to describe the problems that we already knew about; they didn't help us implement solutions to them."

Techniques for Analysis

Asking Questions. The simplest, and often the most effective, method of finding opportunities for improving continuing operations is to ask questions. Procedures which have been accepted for a long time may turn out to have no sound reasons behind them.

> *Example:* The following is the reminiscence of a member of the team from Ernst & Ernst, a consulting firm, that examined the operations of the Louisville, Kentucky, Police Court:
>
> You remember one clerk, in particular, who was industriously banging away at a typewriter. You asked her what she was doing. She looked up briefly from her keyboard to explain that she was typing case dispositions. What happens to them when they're typed? you asked. Why, she answered, they go into the judge's order book. What's the book used for? you asked. She didn't know. So you went to her superior. Why is this done? you asked. You learned why. It's done because a city ordinance says it must be done. But nobody ever uses the book. The same information is available in other records that are easier to use."

> *Example:* The following example is from New York City, which has undertaken a major effort to increase productivity:[2]
>
> In 1968, 38 percent of the garbage trucks were off the streets on the average. The city bought new trucks, but this "down-time" didn't change. So the city asked Andrew P. Kerr, a management consultant who now is the city's housing chief, to look into the problem.
>
> The maintenance system, it seems, had a central repair shop for major overhauls, plus 76 local garages. "But because of union seniority," Mr. Kerr says, "the best mechanics wound up in the local garages doing simple jobs because they were near their homes." The solution: the central shop was replaced with district garages where the senior mechanics could work and still be close to home.
>
> The percentage of trucks in disrepair began to fall. Then another problem came to the surface: Because of fear that any parts kept in district garages would be stolen, needed parts had to be ordered from a central warehouse; trucks were idled for days, waiting for parts.
>
> It was decided that the fear of theft was essentially groundless, that the private demand for sanitation-truck parts was low. "Nobody steals

---

[2] "The Vise Squad," *Wall Street Journal* (April 12, 1973), p. 1.

sanitation-truck parts," Mr. Kerr says. "If they do, we can afford it more than we can afford not having trucks on the streets." The district garages were given their own parts. Downtime dropped to 18 percent.

Comparative Data. Another approach is to compare costs and, if feasible, output measures for similar operations. Such comparisons may identify activities that appear to be out of line, and thus lead to a more thorough examination of these activities. Such comparisons can be useful even though there are problems in achieving comparability, finding a "correct" relationship between cost and output in a discretionary cost situation, and danger in taking an outside average as a standard. For example, they often lead to the following interesting question: If other organizations get the job done for $X, why can't we? As indicated in Chapter 6, good cost data for such comparisons exist on a national basis for only a few types of nonprofit organizations, principally hospitals and certain municipal functions. Nevertheless, it may be possible to find data for activities within a state, or it may be feasible to compare units performing similar functions within a single organization, as in the case of local housing offices.

The comparisons in most cases are simple, such as the cost per student in one school compared with an average cost per student in similar schools. There are particularly good comparative cost data for hospitals as indicated in Exhibit 9–1. In some circumstances, more sophisticated approaches are illuminating. For example, algorithms incorporating a number of interrelated variables have been developed for hospital costs.[3]

Although comparable cost data may be obtainable, data for comparing effectiveness do not exist in many types of nonprofit organizations. In education, reference is often made to the "Coleman effect," a term derived from a report by James S. Coleman and his colleagues,[4] which gave an impressive body of evidence to support the conclusion that no important quantifiable correlation exists between the cost of education and its quality, and specifically between pupil learning and class size, teachers' salary, teachers' experience, age of plant, or type of plant. The effects of these variables were swamped by the influence of the pupil's family environment. Although not everyone agrees with Coleman's conclusions, most people agree that it is extremely difficult to devise experiments that demonstrate quantitatively that one teaching tool or technique is more effective than another.

The use of any quantitative basis of comparison causes concern

---

[3] See, for example, Jonathan Ogur, "The nonprofit firm: a test of the theory for the hospital industry," *Journal of Economics and Business* vol. 26, (Winter 1974), p. 115–120. This article has an extensive bibliography of similar studies.

[4] James S. Coleman *et al. Equality of Educational Opportunity* (Washington, D.C.: U.S. Department of HEW, OE-38001, 1966).

to some people. For example, Sol M. Linowitz, a highly respected business leader and university trustee wrote:[5]

> As to a numerical ratio of students per teacher, I am deeply disquieted—not because I am nurturing a romantic kind of Mark Hopkins hangover, but simply because I think this is the result of regarding a college as first a business operation and only secondarily as an educational institution trying to turn out the right kind of men and women.

Although the faculty-student ratio can be misused, its proper use does not imply that a college is primarily a business operation and

HIBIT 9–1

tement of Operating Revenues and Expenses per Weighted Patient Day
ars Ended 1973 and 1972 (92 Hospitals)

	Any Hospital	1973	1972	Increase (decrease)	Increase (decrease)
oss revenue–patients:					
npatients		$132.06	$118.02	$14.04	11.9
)utpatients		13.48	12.82	.66	5.1
		145.54	130.84	14.70	11.2
owances and bad debts		23.77	22.21	1.56	7.0
Net revenue from patients.		121.77	108.63	13.14	12.1
her operating revenue		4.62	3.53	1.09	30.9
Total operating revenues.		126.39	112.16	14.23	12.7
erating expenses:					
ieneral professional care:					
Interns, residents and supervising physicians.		4.53	3.99	.54	13.5
Medical records.		1.64	1.47	.17	11.6
Central sterile and medical supply expenses.		2.90	2.86	.04	1.4
Pharmacy		3.67	3.29	.38	11.6
		12.74	11.61	1.13	9.7
lursing:					
Administration		1.45	1.17	.28	23.9
General and intensive care.		27.10	24.86	2.24	9.0
School of nursing		1.15	1.12	.03	2.7
		29.70	27.15	2.55	9.4
ousehold and administrative and general:					
Dietary		8.92	8.06	.86	10.7
Housekeeping and maintenance of personnel		4.77	4.41	.36	8.2
Laundry and linen		2.18	1.93	.25	13.0
Operation and maintenance of plant. .		6.60	5.85	.75	12.8
Employee health and welfare		8.44	6.36	2.08	32.7
Administrative and general		14.57	13.17	1.40	10.6
		45.48	39.78	5.70	14.3

---

[5] Sol M. Linowitz, "A Liberal Arts College Isn't a Railroad," *The Chronicle of Higher Education* (February 26, 1973), p. 12.

EXHIBIT 9–1 (continued)
Statement of Operating Revenues and Expenses per Weighted Patient Day
Years Ended 1973 and 1972 (92 Hospitals)

	Any Hospital	*1973*	*1972*	*Increase (decrease)*	*Increase (decrease)*
Special services:					
Operating room, recovery room and anesthesia		6.05	5.21	.84	16.1
Delivery room		1.22	1.05	.17	16.2
Radiology		6.77	6.03	.74	12.3
Laboratory		7.99	7.21	.78	10.8
Physical and occupational therapy . . .		.92	.78	.14	17.9
All other special services.		5.13	4.09	1.04	25.4
		28.08	24.37	3.71	15.2
Outpatient and other services:					
Outpatient department		1.32	1.17	.15	12.8
Emergency service		2.75	2.39	.36	15.1
Social service		.58	.53	.05	9.4
Ambulance and motor service.		.49	.44	.05	11.4
		5.14	4.53	.61	13.5
Total operating expenses		121.14	107.44	13.70	12.8
Net operating revenue before interest and depreciation		5.25	4.72	.53	11.2
Interest.		1.80	1.49	.31	20.8
Depreciation.		4.96	4.51	.45	10.0
		6.76	6.00	.76	12.7
Net operating loss after interest and depreciation		$ 1.51	$ 1.28	$ .23	18.0

Summary of Operating Expenses

Salaries and fees.		$ 76.76	$ 69.43	$ 7.33	10.6
Supplies and expense		44.38	38.01	6.37	16.8
Interest.		1.80	1.49	.31	20.8
Depreciation.		4.96	4.51	.45	10.0
Total operating expenses including interest and depreciation		$127.90	$113.44	$14.46	12.7
Total weighted patient days		7,900,655	8,042,792	142,137	(1.8)

Source: 1974 Review of Hospital Operations, Forty-second Annual Review, Touche Ross and C

only secondarily an educational institution. A college is, in fact, both; neither aspect can be slighted.

Work Measurements. In business organizations much use is made of techniques for measuring the time that should be taken to perform repetitive operations. Nonprofit organizations tend to make less use of these techniques; in fact, there is some question about whether their use in the federal government is legal. They can help to locate opportunities for improving efficiency.

Example: A 1973 work measurement study of the clerical work at the New York City criminal court system demonstrated that the current total of 108 employees could be reduced to 66.[6]

Some effective work measurement studies have also been done in hospitals.[7]

Zero-Base Review. Some organizations have a systematic plan for reviewing all aspects of their operations over a period of years. This approach has come to be called a "zero-base review." According to a regular schedule, each ongoing activity is studied intensively, perhaps once every five years. In contrast with the usual budget review, which takes the current level of spending as the starting point, this more intensive review starts from scratch and attempts to build up, *de novo,* the resources that actually are needed by the activity; it may even challenge the need for having the activity at all. These studies are especially important when costs are of the discretionary cost type. Basic questions are raised, such as: (1) Should the function be performed at all? (2) What should the quality level be? Are we doing too much? (3) Should it be performed in this way? (4) How much should it cost? Although sometimes called a "zero-base budget," such a review actually is not part of the annual budgeting process, for there isn't enough time to conduct it during this process.

A zero-base review is time consuming, and it is also likely to be a traumatic experience for operating managers. This is one reason why such a review is not scheduled annually but periodically so that all responsibility centers are covered once every four or five years. This review establishes a new base for the budget, and the annual budget review attempts to keep costs reasonably in line with this base for the intervening four or five years.

Zero-base review is subject to all the ploys of annual budget reviews, as discussed in Chapter 10, but the game is usually played with much more gusto because more is at stake. Managers under scrutiny will not only do their best to justify their current level of spending, but they will also do their best to torpedo the entire effort. They consider the annual budget review as a necessary evil, but zero-base review as something to be put off indefinitely in favor of "more pressing business." If all else fails, they attempt to create enough doubts so that the findings are inconclusive and the status quo prevails.

---

[6] Economic Development Council of New York City, Inc., Supreme Court Task Force, *Reorganization of Clerical Services at 100 Centre Street,* 1973.

[7] For a description of the technique, see Normal G. Hirsch and Arthur M. Plotkin, "Developing work standards for hospitals—for more effective cost control," *Management Controls* (Peat, Marwick, Mitchell & Co.), vol. 19, July 1972, pp. 153–159.

Privatization. One possible approach to the improvement of efficiency in a nonprofit organization is to have certain activities performed by the private sector, where the spur of competition may result in lower costs. Some organizations explore such possibilities systematically as a part of their zero-base reviews. Opportunities range from such specialized activities as building cleaning and maintenance to activities that are usually thought of as belonging exclusively to the public sector. In Arizona, for example, fire protection for an area that includes 18 percent of the state's population is furnished to municipalities by a profit-oriented company.[8] Organization units whose functions might be taken over by the private sector naturally resist such threats to their continued existence, and studies of these possibilities must therefore be conducted by a high-level staff.

It should not be assumed that a profit-oriented company will perform a function more efficiently than a nonprofit organization, although there are those who act as if this were the case. The proper approach is, of course, to make a careful analysis of the cost of the alternative ways of performing the function. Even if such an analysis leads to the conclusion that the function should continue to be performed by the nonprofit organization, the fact that such comparisons are being made tends to keep the organization on its toes.

Models. If a computer model of an operation can be constructed that gives even a rough approximation of cost and output relationships, this model can be used both as a basis for examining ongoing operations and for predicting future costs under various sets of assumed conditions. Some success has been achieved in the field of higher education. Perhaps the best known models for colleges and universities are those developed by R. W. Judy of the University of Toronto. His model responds to four questions: (1) What are the resource implications (faculty, physical plant, and total budget) of particular enrollment projections? (2) What are the resource implications of meeting established goals in each field of study? (3) What are the resource implications of particular changes in curriculum? (4) What are the resource implications of general policy changes? Models may also be used in the analysis of new programs as described in Chapter 8.[9]

FORMAL PROGRAMMING SYSTEMS

Some organizations have a formal system for the whole programming process. The number of organizations in which such a system is an important aid to management, however, is relatively small. In

---

[8] *Newsweek* (January 1, 1973), p. 37.

[9] For a description of existing educational models, see Colin Bell, "Can Mathematical Models Contribute to Efficiency in Higher Education?" Carnegie Commission on Higher Education, (*Papers on Efficiency in the Management of Higher Education*), 1972.

the period 1967–70, the federal government operated such a system, but it has now been abandoned as a requirement for the entire federal government. Some federal agencies continue to use it, however. Some state governments, a few large municipalities, and a number of other nonprofit organizations also have formal programming systems.

Essentially, such a formal system consists of: (1) procedures prescribing the preparation and analysis of individual proposals and their flow through the organization up to the decision maker, and (2) a document that summarizes the costs, and, if feasible, the outputs of all approved programs for a series of future years. The latter document is usually referred to as "the program" or "the five-year program," or, "the program summary." The program summary differs from the budget in that the former (*a*) often is not related to responsibility centers, (*b*) is less detailed than a budget, and (*c*) covers more than one future year.

There is considerable controversy about the desirability of having such a formal programming system. The preparation of "the program" is an expensive job, and if the process is to be effective, managers at all levels, including top management, must give significant amounts of their scarce time to it.

When such an overall program is prepared, top management is in a better position to make judgments about the overall balance and relative priorities among the separate programs than can be made without such a summary. Furthermore, if the programming process is adequately understood by the operating managers, it can lead them to think in a different and better way about their problems; that is, to take a longer run point of view, to relate activities more closely to objectives, and to consider the impact of their activities on other responsibility centers.

Under what circumstances is such an effort worthwhile? In general, a formal programming system is worthwhile if:

a. there is a need to make a number of program decisions each year;
b. interrelationships among the several parts of the organization are complicated;
c. implementation of program decisions requires a fairly long lead time;
d. complex scheduling of program elements is required to bring activities and capital investments into being in a particular sequence;
e. resources are particularly scarce and the number of desirable programs is quite large.

Steps in a Formal System

Many formal programming systems are described in the literature. Since the use of formal systems is only a few years old, however, most of these books and articles combine a description of how a system gets started with a description of how it is supposed to operate' after its initial introduction. Such descriptions can give an erroneous impression of the headaches and amount of effort involved in the programming process. This is because a large fraction of the effort is involved in creating the initial data base and program descriptions. Once this task has been completed, much less effort is required to keep the data current. The description below assumes that these initial efforts have been completed, and that the system is in operating condition. The problems involved in starting a system are discussed in Chapter 13.

The process involves the following principal steps:

1. Preparation and dissemination of guidelines.
2. Preparation of program memoranda.
3. Staff analysis of program memoranda.
4. Discussion of proposed program with line managers.
5. Discussion with higher authority and approval.

Guidelines

The process starts with the preparation and dissemination of guidelines. These are prepared by the programming staff, discussed with and approved by top management, and disseminated to the operating managers who are responsible for programs. As a minimum, the guidelines contain (*a*) an indication of the constraints, principally resource limitations, within which the program should be prepared, (*b*) a discussion of what constitutes a program, and (*c*) instructions for the format and content of the program memoranda.

In deciding on the overall resource constraints, management and its staff take into account the probable needs of the agency, based on informal discussions and on proposals for major new programs that already may have come to their attention, and the probable amount of funds that will be made available to the agency. It is essential that resource constraints be stated. If this is not done, the initial programs submitted by operating managers are likely to be "wish lists," rather than realistic statements of what is feasible. In particular, managers will be reluctant to come to grips with the difficult problem of priorities; they will tend to recommend *all* worthwhile programs, rather than deciding which are the more important. The initial constraint is of course subject to change in the course of preparing the program.

In some organizations, the resource constraint is stated as a range; that is, managers are asked to prepare programs for three funding levels: (*a*) the most probable level, (*b*) 5 percent (or 10 percent) above this level, and (*c*) 5 percent (or 10 percent) below this level. The purpose of this practice is to identify additional program opportunities and low-priority programs, but the experience has generally not been satisfactory. Managers have a difficult enough time preparing the "most probable" program, and give little thought to the other alternatives.

In the first attempt at a programming effort, programs are likely to be defined in a way that makes them correspond to organization units. Thus each head of a major organization unit is also a program manager, and the "program" consists of what that unit does. As the system becomes more refined, programs tend increasingly to cut across organization units (subject to the limitations discussed in Chapter 5).

Program Memoranda

After receipt of these guidelines, each program manager prepares a document describing the proposed program. This document is called by various names, but "Program Memorandum," is fairly common. The program memorandum describes the objectives that are relevant to the program; the specific activities that are proposed for accomplishing these objectives; and the resources that are estimated to be required in carrying on these activities, including both resources used by the organization itself and services that are required from other responsibility centers. Exhibit 9–2 shows how one such memorandum is organized.

EXHIBIT 9–2
Excerpts from Narcotics Program
Program Goals
- 1.0 Reduce the abuse of narcotics and dangerous drugs in the United States.
- 1.1 Reduce the supply of illicit drugs.
  - 1.1.1 Reduce the amount of legally manufactured drugs available for abuse.
  - 1.1.2 Reduce domestic supply of illicit drugs.
  - 1.1.3 Reduce foreign supply of illicit drugs introduced into the United States.
- 1.2 Reduce demand for illegal use of drugs.
- 1.3 Expand understanding of the problem.
- 1.4 Improve program management and administrative support.

Operating Program Objectives (For Goal 1.1.3)
- 1.1.3.1 Reduce smuggling into U.S. at ports and borders.
- 1.1.3.2 Reduce foreign cultivation, production, and trafficking.

Operating Program Activities (For Objective 1.1.3.1)
- 1.1.3.1.1 Conduct investigations of smuggling.
- 1.1.3.1.2 Arrest smugglers and conspirators and seize smuggled drugs.
- 1.1.3.1.3 Support prosecutions.
- 1.1.3.1.4 Identify international border points vulnerable to smuggling and strengthen them.
- 1.1.3.1.5 Inspect carriers, cargo, persons, baggage, and mail.
- 1.1.3.1.6 Develop and operate a program of mutual exchange of intelligence.

Some people advocate that the first step in the analysis leading to a program memorandum should be a careful definition of the problems that the program is intended to deal with. A description of this "problem statement" approach follows:

> Formulating the problem statement is a most critical, and in some ways one of the most difficult steps of the entire process. The aim is not only to describe the problem—what it is, where it is, how big it is, and whether it is growing or receding—but to break the problem down into components which will make it possible to identify as realistically as possible just where the several different kinds of things a program does are or should be directed.
>
> For example, it would be possible to define the "problem" that a hospital is trying to solve as simply that of caring for sick people. But this "global" problem definition doesn't provide much enlightenment as to the particular nature of the needs the hospital is called upon to meet. The problem becomes much more understandable if "sick people" are further broken down into different kinds—chronically ill, acutely ill, terminally ill, long-term containment, etc. Or, perhaps a breakdown by disease category would be more revealing if substantial differences happen to exist in the types or number of resources needed to treat different disease syndromes.
>
> The basic analytic task is to break out individual components of the problem in such a way as to reflect *real differences* in the way the program approaches those problem components, rather than to divide the problem simply for the sake of dividing it. The key question that must always be asked is whether a breakdown provides *enlightenment*, or just further detail.
>
> An attempt is made to distinguish (in hard numbers) two aspects of each problem segment—the "population size" and the "demand component." The former refers to the total size of the need or problem identified, whether it involves persons, acres of woodland, miles of highway, etc. "Population size" is the total number (of individuals, acres of woodland, etc) which *could* use the program's services. The "demand component," however, is that portion of the problem which is *likely* to present itself for (or require) the services offered by the program, and is a realistic estimate of the particular size of the problem that the program expects to be called upon to meet. Thus, a hospital treating alcoholics would note a "population size" of many thousands of alcoholics in its general service area, knowing that many of them would be treated in other institutions or will not seek treatment at all. Its "demand component" will be what it reasonably expects it may be asked to meet in the coming years—regardless of whether it will actually be able to meet that demand. (Its capacities or its admissions policies may require that a portion of its demand component be turned away.)
>
> In all cases, *numbers* are used to describe the problem components and trends, and an indication is given as to the adequacy of those numbers. In some cases it will be clear that information is insufficient

and should be improved if sharper decisions are to be made. In other cases, the numbers available will describe the problem perfectly adequately, even though they may not always be entirely accurate. The aim here, of course, is to indicate those areas of high uncertainty, where one might consider investing resources to improve data in order to make improved resource allocation decisions.[10]

To the extent that a major shift in activities is proposed, a program proposal, as described in Chapter 8 should be prepared. If feasible, the proposal should be in the form of a benefit/cost analysis. In some organizations, these program proposals are submitted as part of the program memorandum; in others, they are submitted separately.

Although program managers are responsible for the program proposed in the memorandum, a very large percentage of the analysis of data and of the writing should be done by staffs, either their own staffs, or staff assistance furnished by headquarters.

Staff Analysis

When a program memorandum reaches headquarters, the staff makes a preliminary examination of it to insure that it conforms to the guidelines. If it does not, a staff member sits down with the program manager and reworks the document so that it does conform. Next, the separate memoranda are combined into an overall picture of the program for the whole organization. This may be called a "program summary."

This "first cut" at the total program will probably reveal either or both of the following problems: (1) the total of individual program proposals exceeds the resources available, or (2) there is a lack of balance, such as mission units planning to use more resources from service units than the service units can provide, or two managers planning over-lapping programs on the same target group. The staff discusses these inconsistencies with program managers, attempting to resolve as many of them as a staff agency can resolve, but remembering that top management, not the staff, must make the actual decisions. If individual program proposals accompany the program memoranda, these are also analyzed at this time.

Discussion with Line Managers

The purpose of the preceding step is to assemble information in a way that facilitates the discussion of proposed programs that is carried on between top management and the program managers, which is the most important part of the whole process. This discussion

---

[10] From *PMS . . . A Program-Based Management System*, by Modernization Systems Unit, Commonwealth of Massachusetts (1971), vol. 1, pp. 14, 15.

is conducted in various ways. One common method is to have a preliminary general meeting of all program managers, at which overall problems are discussed, and to follow this meeting with a discussion with each manager individually. This discussion must take place between line managers. Although staff people can provide clarification, data, and other assistance, the end product of the discussion is approval of the program, and such approval can only be given by line management.

Discussion with Higher Authority

We have referred to "top management" and "operating management" as if there were only two levels in the organization. Actually, of course, there are likely to be several levels, and the process described above takes place at each level. When it has been completed at one level, it is repeated at the next higher level, with the process concluding at the level of the person or group that has the final say on the allocation of funds.

The approved program becomes an input to the budgeting process, as described in Chapter 10.

The Program Summary

There are two basically different ways of constructing a program summary: (1) The summary is prepared anew each year, as one step in the programming process, or (2) the summary is continuously updated; that is, whenever a program decision is approved, the costs and outputs associated with that decision are incorporated into the program summary.

So far as we know, the only large organizations that used a continuously updated summary are the U.S. Department of Defense and the corresponding agencies in certain NATO countries. The creation of the computer program that is required to maintain a continuously updated summary is a complicated job, but once this program has been developed, the job of maintaining the summary is fairly simple. What is required is that the document that records each program decision set forth the costs and, if feasible, the outputs for each program element affected by the decision. If this is carefully done, the job of updating the program summary is purely a mechanical one.

Taking Account of Inflation. The money amounts in a program summary can be based either on the assumption that prices will not change or on the assumption that a specified amount of inflation is to be expected. Either basis will work; the important thing is that all parties must understand which basis is used and act consistently. If the program summary assumes no inflation, the calculations are easier to make, and the program is easier for users to understand since changes reflect purely physical magnitudes. If estimates of inflation affect the numbers, the user may have difficulty in separating the physical changes from the changes in purchasing power. Furthermore, no one can make reliable estimates of the general rate of inflation over the next five years, and even less of inflation rates for wages, various types of material, and other cost components.

On the other hand, inflation is a fact, and it may be unrealistic to disregard that fact. A program that does incorporate assumed rates of inflation is particularly useful if there is good reason to believe that different cost elements have different rates of inflation.

Relative Importance of Programming

We have referred to three principal types of nonprofit organizations: client-oriented, member-oriented, and public-oriented. Of these, the programming process is clearly most important in public-oriented organizations, especially the government. In such organizations management usually has wide latitude in adopting various types of programs to achieve its objectives, and it needs a formal way of organizing the process for deciding on the best mix of programs.

Certain member-oriented organizations also have this latitude, and the programming process is important to them. Others carry on approximately the same type of activities from one year to the next, and hence do not make many program decisions. Some religious organizations, for example, periodically consider major changes in how they use their resources and hence need a programming process to facilitate such consideration; others carry out essentially the same program year after year, and have no such need.

Corresponding differences exist in client-oriented organizations. If a university is growing, or if the enrollment or the cost characteristics of different departments is changing, or if the balance between instruction and research is changing, the university needs to do the kind of thinking that is facilitated by a formal programming process. If the programs are stable, the need for programming is correspondingly less, although even a stable university would do well to make occasional long-range projections of the major determinants of its costs and revenues.

Nature of the Program Summary

The program summary is fundamentally different from an approved budget. A budget is a bilateral commitment between the budgetee and the supervisor—the former committing to carry on activities with the resources stated in the budget, and the latter agreeing that such action constitutes good performance. A program summary does not represent a commitment; it is an estimate or best guess as to what will happen over the period covered. Also, it is likely that actual spending will be quite close to the budgeted amounts, whereas actual spending in the later years of a program will probably vary considerably from the amounts set forth in the program summary. Both of these differences stem from the fact that the budget relates to the next year whereas the program covers several years in the future; the longer the time period, the greater the uncertainty.

A program summary therefore does not state what *will* happen, nor is it a management commitment. Rather, it shows what is *likely* to happen if presently approved policies are continued unchanged.

Robert Bartnik highlights the purposes of the program summary in this statement about the "Working Memorandum" used at the Franklin Institute (which corresponds to the program summary as used here):[11]

> The Working Memorandum breaks the shackles of one-year planning and budgeting by emphasizing the horizon five years from now. It permits unit aspirations to be expressed creatively, with a minimum of budgeting and a maximum of activity in thinking through the future, selecting from alternatives through informed management estimates rather than precise pencil pushing. To promote realism, the Working Memorandum includes provision for thinking through funding sources.
>
> A focus on a single year tends to keep the manager's thinking fettered by the shortness of each year and by an acute awareness of things that have had to be postponed before. Long-range planning is *not* planning each year at a time; it *is* developing a five-year program during which realistic objectives can be attained *and then planning appropriate checkpoint and milestones during intervening years.* The manager is then able to do free, unfettered, yet realistic thinking, not frozen by existing organizational structures.

THE PPB SYSTEM

The most widely known acronym in the programming literature is PPBS, which stands for Planning—Programming—Budgeting System. PPBS has three central ideas; first, it is a formal programming system, essentially like that described in the preceding section; second, it uses a program budget, as contrasted with a line-item budget;[12] and third, it emphasizes benefit/cost analysis. The concept of a program budget has been discussed in Chapter 5, and the process of

---

[11] Excerpted from "The Franklin Institute: Where we are going and how we plan to get there" (May 22, 1974).

[12] The idea of a program budget is much older than PPBS; PPBS gave the idea publicity. See, for example, the 1954 book by Frederick C. Mosher, *Program Budgeting: Theory and Practice* (Chicago: Public Administration Service).

preparing it will be discussed in Chapter 10. The "P" for Planning suggests that there is another central idea, but this is not so. Programming and budgeting are both forms of planning, and no third type of planning is involved in the PPB system; the inclusion of the first "P" in the acronym has led to some unnecessary misunderstandings.

The PPB system is well described in the following statement by Charles Schultze, who was Director of the Budget at the time it was introduced in the Federal Government:[13]

As the *first* step, PPB calls for a careful specification and analysis of basic program objectives in each major area of governmental activity. The key to this part of the operation is forcing federal agencies to back away from the particular program they are carrying on at the moment and to look at their objectives. What are they really trying to accomplish? The objective of our intercity highway program, for example, is *not* to build highways. Highways are useful only as they serve a higher objective, namely transporting people and goods effectively and efficiently and safely. Once this is accepted as an objective, it then becomes possible to analyze aviation, railroads, and highways to determine the most effective network of transportation. But so long as we think of the ultimate objective of the highway program as simply laying concrete, this comparison of different transportation systems is impossible.

At the same time, while we want to view our objectives broadly we are not helped at all by stating them too broadly. Highways or transportation, for example, generally may contribute to the good life and to national unity, but to take these as our sole stated objectives does not tell us much, if anything, useful about the desirable rate of highway building, the character of the highways, their locations, or their relations to other elements of our transportation system. In the case of highways, we want a specification of objectives broader than "laying concrete" but narrower than "improving our national life." As a matter of fact, there is a constant interaction between the decision process and our knowledge of our true objectives. Often, the more we learn about *how* to reach an objective, the more clearly we begin to understand the objective itself.

The *second* step, under the PPB system, is to analyze insofar as possible, the *output* of a given program in terms of the objectives initially specified in the first step. Again, for example, in the case of highways, we must ask not primarily how many miles of concrete are laid, but more fundamentally what the program produces in terms of swifter, safer, less-congested travel—how many hours of travel time are eliminated, how many accidents are prevented.

The *third* step is to measure the *total costs* of the program, not just for one year, but over at least several years ahead. In this year's

---

[13] U.S. Congress, Senate, Committee on Government Operations, *Planning-Programming-Budgeting*. Hearings, 90th Congress, 1st session. (Washington, D.C.: Government Printing Office.)

budget, for example, $10 million in budget funds are requested for the Atomic Energy Commission to design a 200 billion electron volt atom-smasher. But the total cost of constructing this machine will amount to $250 million or more. We have commonly had some estimate of the total capital cost in mind when we have embarked on construction projects. This has not happened systematically, however. And we can't stop here. Once the machine is built, the annual operating costs will run $50 to $100 million per year. This is not to say that because of these costs we should decide to abandon the project. But it does mean that we should be aware of all the costs when we make the initial $10 million decision, not just the capital costs but the follow-on operating costs as well. Or, to cite the highway example again, in deciding to build an expressway through a downtown area we must take into account not only the cost of the expressway, but also the cost of relocating the displaced residents and, in a qualitative sense, the effects of the freeway on the areas through which it is to run.

All of this sounds obvious. Yet, too often large federal investment decisions have been made on the basis of the first-year costs alone—or made without taking into account all of the indirect associated costs.

The *fourth* and crucial step is to analyze *alternatives,* seeking those which have the greatest effectiveness in achieving the basic objectives specified in the first step or which achieve those objectives at the least cost. In the highway case, for example, we should be comparing the effectiveness of additions or improvements to highways with that of additions or improvements to aviation and railroads as a means of providing safe and efficient transportation. This does not mean that we pick only one. Of course, we should not. But we do need to decide, at least roughly, which combination of alternatives is the preferred one.

By this process we hope to induce federal agencies to consider particular programs not as ends in themselves—to be perpetuated without challenge or question. Rather, they must be viewed as means to higher objectives and subjected to competition with alternative and perhaps more effective programs. It is this competition among alternatives which is crucial as a means of testing the effectiveness and economy of existing and proposed programs.

The *fifth* and final element of this approach is establishing this method and these analytic techniques throughout the government in a *systematic* way, so that, over time, more and more budgetary decisions can be subjected to this kind of rigorous analysis.

Merely writing up academic papers is not enough. The analysis has to be an integral part of the budgetary decisions. The programming concept is the critical link that relates planning to budgeting, converting planning from paper exercise to an important part of the decision process.

PPBS was first discussed in the 1950s, was first applied in practice in the Defense Department in 1962, spread to other government agencies in 1966, and by 1971 had been abandoned by the federal government. Because of its short life in the federal government, PPBS has become a dirty term. Its basic ideas, however, live on. They live, under other labels, in some federal agencies, in a number of state and municipal governments, and in other types of nonprofit organizations. A 1972 study of 1,873 public and private institutions of higher education found that 30 percent had implemented PPB systems.[14] The system continues essentially unchanged in the Department of Defense.[15] Because of the controversy surrounding the name, those interested in the field should have some understanding of what went wrong.

In essence, the poor acceptance of PPBS was the result of faulty implementation. In August 1965, President Johnson directed wide use of PPBS. Instructions for implementing PPBS were issued in Bureau of Budget Instruction 66-3, dated October 12, 1965, which required that work on the new system begin immediately with implementation within a year. Doctor Schultze, the Director of the Budget, well recognized that this was a dangerously short time period, but President Johnson decided that it was preferable to get something started and then improve it, rather than to go through a long period of preparation when nothing happened.

PPBS received little support. Few Bureau of the Budget analysts were convinced that the new system was an improvement, and they paid little attention to it.[16]

In the Congress, the Appropriations Committees refused to examine a budget that was cast in program terms, and extensive hearings which had a generally critical tone were held by the Government Operations Committee. Members of Congress felt comfortable with the old budget format, and were suspicious of a new arrangement of the data, especially since its principal advocates were regarded as impractical "whiz kids." In retrospect, it was unreasonable to expect Congress to accept this new approach, without a thorough educational program, even though it gave a demonstrably better basis for making decisions. Some educational efforts were made, but they were inadequate.

There was inadequate time to educate Agency heads as to the advantages of PPBS, let alone the techniques involved in it. Agency heads therefore gave little personal attention to PPBS, did not at-

---

[14] Lawrence Bogard, "Management in Institutions of Higher Education," in *Papers on Efficiency in the Management of Higher Education* (Carnegie Commission on Higher Education, 1972), p. 11.

[15] See, for example, Burton B. Moyer, Jr., "Evolution of PPB in DOD," *Armed Forces Comptroller* (Spring 1973), vol. 18, pp. 21–26.

[16] In his article, "The Demise of PPBS" *The Federal Accountant,* vol. 21 (June 1972 pp. 4–13), Carl W. Tiller gives a lengthy catalog of the reasons that PPBS failed, but he omits the rather important factor of his personal opposition to this new way of doing things. Tiller was an executive in the Bureau of the Budget at that time.

tempt to build up adequate programming staffs (without which the system could not function), and permitted the traditional budget process to continue essentially unchanged. Agency operating personnel regarded PPBS as a threat since it challenged established ways of allocating resources. The few new people who were brought in to operate PPBS were no match for the knowledgeable experienced budgeteers who had a proprietary feeling about the established budget apparatus. The requirements for program memoranda and program summaries were perceived as additional paperwork with no commensurate benefit. Few managers, from the top on down, were persuaded that PPBS was a way of helping them do a better job.

In most agencies, the PPB system was no more than window dressing. A few people were assigned the task of designing a program structure, and they did this by thinking up new labels for the work that was done by existing organization units. Other people wrote Program Memoranda, which were essentially narratives of what the Agency was currently doing, and others prepared five-year summaries of costs and outputs, mostly by straight extrapolation from current experience. The PPBS effort was divorced from the traditional planning apparatus, and, what is just as important, it was divorced from the systems for collecting information on actual spending and actual outputs. (One of the conceptual weaknesses of PPBS was that it did not emphasize the necessity for a close tie between programming, budgeting, and accounting; it would have been preferable if an "A" for Accounting had been included in the acronym.)

This experience with PPBS does not demonstrate that the basic concepts of the system are unsound. It does tell us much about the necessity for a proper program of implementation, a topic discussed in Chapter 13. Allen Schick sums it up succinctly, as follows:

> "PPBS is an idea whose time has not quite come. It was introduced government-wide before the requisite concepts, organizational capability, political conditions, informational resources, and techniques were adequately developed. A decade ago, PPB was beyond reach; a decade or two hence, it, or some updated version might be one of the conventions of budgeting. For the present, PPB must make do in a world it did not create and has not yet mastered."[17]

[17] Allen Schick, "Systems Politics and Systems Budgeting," *Public Administration Review*, vol. 29 (March/April 1969), p. 150.

chapter ten

Budgeting

The general character of the budgeting process in a nonprofit organization is similar to that in a profit-oriented organization, but there are significant differences in emphasis. This chapter focuses on these differences.

NATURE OF THE PROCESS

A budget is a plan expressed in monetary terms. There are several types of budgets, including the *capital budget* which lists and describes planned capital acquisitions; the *cash budget,* which summarizes planned cash receipts and disbursements, and the *operating* or *expense budget* which describes planned operating activities for a specified period of time, usually one year.[1] The discussion in this chapter relates primarily to the operating budget because the capital budget is derived more or less automatically from decisions made during the programming process and the cash budget is derived from the operating budget, just as in a profit-oriented company.

Relation to Programming

In concept, the budgeting process follows, but is separate from, the programming process discussed in Chapters 8 and 9. The budget

[1] Some states prepare a biennial (once every two years) budget, but this practice is declining. In nongovernment organizations, the budget year is usually the calendar year. Until 1977, in the federal government, the fiscal year ends on June 30 (Fiscal Year 1975 ended June 30, 1975), but thereafter in accordance with P.L. 93-344 the fiscal year ends on September 30. Most states and many local governments have a fiscal year that ends on June 30. Because state and municipal governments rely increasingly on funds from federal sources, it seems likely that many state and local governments will change their fiscal year so that it ends September 30.

is supposed to be a "fine tuning" of the program for a given year, incorporating the final decisions on the amounts to be spent for each program, and making clear who is responsible for carrying out each part of the program. These decisions are supposed to be made within the context of the basic decisions that were made during the programming process. In practice, no such clean separation between programming and budgeting exists, nor can it exist. Even in organizations that have a well-developed programming system, circumstances may be discovered during the budgeting process that require revision of program decisions. In organizations that have no recognizable, separate programming process, program decisions are made as part of the budgeting process.

Despite this overlap, it is useful to think about the two processes separately because they have different characteristics. The purpose of the programming process is to make decisions about programs. As such, it involves more creativity and imagination than does the budgeting process, it does not require as accurate estimates of costs and revenues, it is less constrained by considerations of the resources that are available, and it often does not require decisions on which responsibility centers are to be responsible for carrying out each program.

By contrast, the purpose of the budgeting process is to decide on the actual operating plan for a year. The budgeting process requires careful estimates of costs and revenues, and the budget must be constructed within a ceiling that represents estimated available resources. Since the budget will be used during the year as a plan against which actual performance will be checked, it is essential that the budget be related to individual responsibility centers. Thus, the budget provides a basis for control of responsibility center managers; the program does not.

The approved program is a starting point in preparing the budget. It provides a framework within which budget estimates are made. Nevertheless, even with an excellent programming process, budget estimates will differ from amounts shown in the program for any of a number of reasons. Prices of input factors may have changed since the program estimates were prepared. Budget analysts should scrutinize estimates more carefully than is necessary in order to reach program decisions, and this leads to revisions of the amounts shown in the program. Furthermore, conditions change, and a need for changing the program itself may become apparent during the budgeting process.

Two-Stage Budgets

Although this chapter will generally refer to "the" budget, as if there were only one, in the federal government and also in many other nonprofit organizations, there actually are two budgets. One, which may be referred to as the *legislative budget,* is essentially a request for funds. It does not correspond to the budget that is prepared in a profit-oriented company. Its closest counterpart is the prospectus that a company prepares when it seeks to raise money. Most of the media reports about government budgets relate to the legislative budget, and many textbook descriptions of government budgeting focus on this budget. The purpose of this budget is to convince the legislative branch that the agency needs the funds that it requests.

The second budget, which may be called the *management budget,* is prepared after the legislature has decided on the amount of funds that is to be provided (or, if the legislature is dilatory, it is prepared as soon as the executive branch can make a good estimate of what the legislature will eventually approve). This budget corresponds to the budget prepared in a profit-oriented company; that is, it is a plan showing the amount of spending that each responsibility center is authorized to undertake.

Importance of Budgeting

Budgeting is an important part of the management control process in any organization, but it is even more important in a nonprofit organization than in a profit-oriented company. There are several reasons for this.

In a profit-oriented company, particularly a manufacturing company, a large fraction of the costs are engineered costs; for example, the amount of labor and the quantity of material required to manufacture products are determined within rather close limits by the specifications of the products and of the manufacturing process. Consequently, little can be done to affect these costs during the budgeting process. By contrast, in most nonprofit organizations a large fraction of the costs are discretionary; that is, the amount that is to be spent can be varied within wide limits according to decisions made by management. The most important of these decisions are made during the budgeting process.

In a profit-oriented company, a budget is a fairly tentative statement of plans. It is subject to change as conditions change, and such changes, particularly in the level and mix of sales, can occur frequently during the year. Furthermore, there is general agreement on the way in which managers should react to such changes; they should make revised plans that are consistent with the overall objective of profitability. In most nonprofit organizations, conditions are more stable and predictable. In a university, the number of students enrolled in September governs the pattern of spending for the whole year. A hospital gears up for a certain number of beds, and although there may be temporary fluctuations in demand, these ordinarily do not cause major changes in spending patterns. A government agency has a certain authorized program for the year; it operates so as to execute that program. Under these circumstances, the budget can be, and should be, a fairly accurate statement of what is to be done during the year and of the resources that are to be used. It is therefore important that it be prepared carefully.

As is the case with most such statements, these differences between nonprofit and profit-oriented organizations are matters of degree, and there is considerable variation among different types of organizations. It is nevertheless safe to say that in general the budgeting process is a key part of the management control process in a nonprofit organization. Much time, including much top management time, should be devoted to it.

GENERAL DESCRIPTION

Many aspects of the budgeting process are the same in nonprofit organizations as in profit-oriented companies. In order to focus on those aspects that are especially important in nonprofit organizations, but to show where these aspects fit in the whole process, a brief description of the process is given in this section. In the following sections, certain topics that are important in nonprofit organizations are discussed in more detail.

Guidelines

The process begins with the formulation of guidelines and the communication of these guidelines to operating managers. If a formal program exists, one guideline is, of course, that the budget should be consistent with the approved program. This does not necessarily mean that the budget should consist only of approved programs. Frustrations of operating managers may be minimized, and desirable innovations may sometimes (although not frequently) come to light if managers are permitted to propose activities that are not part of the approved program. These unapproved activities should be clearly distinguished from those in the approved program, however, and operating managers should understand that the chances that new programs will be approved during the budget process are small. Any other impression downgrades the importance of the programming process.

Even if there is no formal program, operating managers should be made aware of the constraints within which the budget should be prepared. These constraints can be expressed in an overall statement, such as "budget for not more than 105 percent of the amount spent this year," or they can be given in much more detail. Guidelines should be approved by top management. Considerable top management attention to them is warranted since if the budget is formulated on the basis of unrealistic assumptions, it may have to be redone with consequent wasted effort.

In addition to the substantive guidelines, there are also guidelines about format and content of the proposed budget. These are intended to insure that the budget estimates are submitted in a fashion that both facilitates analysis and also that permits their subsequent use in the comparison of actual performance against planned performance. Some useful format guidelines are:

1. Whenever feasible, dollar amounts should be broken down into physical quantities and unit costs. Such a breakdown facilitates analysis of the budget request and also provides the basis for the subsequent analysis of the reasons for the difference between actual and budgeted expense, particularly, how much was caused by price and how much by efficiency.

2. Output measures should be shown, even if they are rough. A cost-per-unit of output can easily be computed if output measures are included, and this is a good starting point in analysis.

3. Data for the current year, and possibly for one previous year, should be included as a basis for analyzing how the proposed budget differs from current spending patterns. These data should be strictly comparable in terminology and content with the budget data.

Initial Budget Preparation

The operating organization prepares a proposed budget in accordance with the guidelines issued by top management. Most of the detailed calculations are made by staff persons, but the important judgments are made by operating managers, that is, by the heads of responsibility centers.

Budget Review

The operating manager, or "budgetees," discuss their proposed budgets with their supervisors, and they negotiate a budget. Next the supervisors, who now become the budgetees, discuss the proposed budget for all the responsibility centers that they supervise with *their* superior, and so on up the line, to top management.

Budget Approval

The final set of discussions is held between top management and whatever body has ultimate authority for approving the organization's plans—the trustees or a similar group for private, nonprofit organizations, or the legislature for a public organization. (As noted above, this is the case with respect to the "legislative" budget, but the process of formulating the "management" budget takes place separately from this.) After being approved, the budget is disseminated down through the organization, and becomes the authorized plan to which the organization is expected to adhere unless compelling circumstances warrant a change.[2]

The Budget Timetable

In the federal government, the budgeting process starts about six months before the budget is submitted to the Congress. In less complex organizations, the period is shorter, about one to three months. The problem of timing is a delicate one. If the budget is prepared too far in advance, it will not be based on the most current information. If, on the other hand, not enough time is allowed, the process may be rushed and hence superficial. The budget process should be arranged so as to allow adequate time for:

1. *Dissemination of instructions,* often through several levels of the budget organization, to the personnel who will prepare the budget. Each level may have additional specific instructions for organization units that it supervises. Time must be allowed for the preparation of these instructions.

2. *Preparation of the initial budget.* If adequate time is not allowed, the budget may be put together by the budget staff without adequate participation by line managers. This creates the feeling among lower level managers that they are divorced from budget decisions.

3. *Review and adjustment.* Time must be allowed and specified for adequate review at each level of the organization.

4. *Appeal* (called "reclama" in the federal government). In order for lower level managers to appeal a budget decision, they must be informed of the results of the next higher headquarters' decisions before these decisions are passed on up the organization hierarchy.

Late Budget Submissions. Late submissions should be avoided, if at all possible, at each level of the organization. Acceptable reasons for late submissions are:

a. Late changes in critical programs that cannot be delayed until the next financial period;

b. Late changes due to last minute changes in instructions;

c. Rewrites necessary to stay within budgetary ceilings which

---

[2] Some people refer to actual operations as "executing the budget." This is an unfortunate term because it implies that the operating manager's job is to spend whatever the budget says can be spent. A better term is "executing the *program.*" This implies that the primary job is to accomplish the program objectives; the budget shows the resources that are available for this purpose.

have come to light only after review of the combined programs of several lower-level responsibility centers.

MATCHING SPENDING WITH AVAILABLE RESOURCES

A budget that is prepared without adequate recognition of the resources that are likely to be available to the organization is unrealistic, and hence of little use to management. The guidelines should set forth the probable amount of available resources. In government organizations this requires an estimate of the funds that are likely to be provided by the legislature. In other organizations it requires an estimate of revenues to be derived from fees charged to clients, from gifts and grants, from endowment earnings, and from other sources.

In many of these organizations, the total amount of such revenue in the budget year is, for all practical purposes, fixed within quite narrow limits. In these "fixed revenue" organizations, the budgeting process is fundamentally different from that in a profit-oriented company. A profit-oriented company considers both revenue and cost together; it is willing to "spend money to make money," that is, to incur additional costs in order to earn increased profit. A fixed revenue organization must ordinarily take its revenue amount as a given. Its approach to budgeting is therefore to decide how best to spend the available revenue; that is, it should budget costs that are equal to revenues in such a way that the maximum output is achieved from available resources.

This is a fundamental philosophical point. If current costs are less than current revenues, current clients are not receiving the services to which they are entitled. They are entitled to these services partly by virtue of the fees (tuition, church pledges, hospital charges) which they paid, or which were paid in their behalf by a third party, and partly by the intention of donors of endowment funds or other givers. On the other hand, if current costs exceed current revenues, some of the endowment principal is consumed, or a deficit is incurred which must be made up out of future revenues; in either case the effect is to favor current clients at the expense of future clients, thus cheating future clients. The management of fixed-revenue institutions should be proud of a balanced budget; they should *not* be proud of either a surplus or a deficit.

The Treasurer of Yale University wrote: ". . . An Operating Surplus evidences lack of achievement rather than good management if educational quality can be improved."[3] The thrust of the statement is sound, but the conditional clause is unnecessary because educational quality can *always* be improved, provided there is money to

[3] *Report of the Treasurer of Yale University* (1967), p. 2.

do so. There is an inexhaustible number of ways to spend money productively at a university.

The Yale treasurer further states, "Even if quality is good, an Operating Surplus above a reasonable reserve evidences failure of the President and Fellows to discharge the duty of their trust." Failure to use available resources for current needs penalizes current students.

> *Example:* In 1962, New York University embarked on a major expansion program. Substantial amounts of additional revenue were obtained from additional enrollments, fund-raising campaigns, and government grants. Beginning in 1968, funds from all these sources began to shrink. Instead of cutting costs to meet the lower level of revenues, however, deficits were permitted. They reached a peak of $14 million in 1973. In 1972, drastic steps were finally taken to bring costs in line with revenue, but by then a considerable fraction of the university's capital had been dissipated.[4]

Sometimes churches budget their expenses without regard to anticipated revenue. They justify the deficit with the argument, "God will provide." Such a policy can lead to disaster. Although somewhat different words are used, a similar approach is sometimes followed by organizations other than churches. The results can be equally disastrous.

One great advantage of the policy of budgeting anticipated revenue first and then budgeting expenses to equal revenue is that this approach provides a bulwark against the arguments, often made by highly articulate and persuasive people, for programs that the institution cannot in fact afford. (Especially pernicious is the argument: "We can't afford *not* to do this.")

If the first approximation to the budget indicates a deficit, the least painful course of action is to anticipate additional sources of revenue that will eliminate this deficit. This is also a highly dangerous course of action. Presumably, all feasible sources of revenue were thought of when the revenue estimate was initially made. New ideas that arise subsequently *may* produce the additional revenue, but the evidence that they will do so is usually not strong. If they do *not* produce the revenue, then operations may proceed without taking the steps that are necessary to provide a balance between revenues and costs.

The safer course of action is to take the steps that are necessary to bring costs into balance with revenue.

> *Example:* In 1971, the initial budget of the Metropolitan Museum indicated a $1.5 million deficit. Various proposals were made to increase revenue to offset this deficit, such as increase the admissions charge, rent paintings, earn a higher return on endowment, obtain more new

---

[4] Condensed from a report in *Science,* (December 8, 1972), pp. 1072–5.

members, and obtain more help from New York City. Top management decided that the more prudent course of action was to reduce costs.

Discretionary Revenue

It can be argued that the revenues of organizations of the type being considered here are not in fact fixed, and that the top management can increase them by appropriate tactics. For example, it may be possible to increase the revenue from current gifts by an intensified fund-raising effort. This is "spending money to make money" in the same sense that a profit-oriented company considers its marketing budget. To the extent that this argument is valid, it is appropriate to speak of "discretionary revenue" as well as "discretionary costs." Such opportunities are ordinarily not of major significance, however. In most situations, the organization has already used all the fund-raising devices that it can think of, and it must take the probable revenues from such efforts as a given, not subject to major alteration.

Hard Money and Soft Money

The nature of the cost commitments should correspond to the nature of various types of revenues. A college with a reasonable expectation of meeting its enrollment quota can count on a certain amount of tuition revenue; this is hard money. Income from endowment is also hard money. It is prudent to make long-term commitments, such as tenure faculty appointments, when they will be financed by hard money. By contrast, income from annual gifts or from short-lived grants for research projects is soft money. In a recession, gifts may drop drastically; the donors of grants may decide not to renew them. The institution must be careful about making long-term commitments that are financed with soft money. For example, if a major new research program is financed with a special grant, it is dangerous to hire tenured personnel for that program because it may be difficult to find funds for these tenured people if the grant is terminated. A preferable alternative is to hire nontenured personnel, or to so arrange the personnel schedule that appropriate slots are available elsewhere should the special program be terminated.

Every Tub on Its Own Bottom

Not only should the organization as a whole budget so that costs equal revenue, but so should each principal revenue center in the organization to the extent that this is feasible. The principle that every tub should stand on its own bottom is said to have been originated by A. Lawrence Lowell, President of Harvard from 1909 to 1933. His philosophy was that Harvard College and each of the dozen or so graduate and professional schools should operate within the resources available to them and should in addition help to finance the general administration of the university. He was willing to make exceptions to this rule in the case of new schools, and for certain schools that could not conceivably pay their own way, such as the Divinity School; he provided support for these schools from the general university endowment. A similar policy is applicable to hospitals, and to other nonprofit organizations that have identifiable revenue-producing departments. Care must of course be taken to insure that justifiable circumstances that may prevent a revenue center from breaking even are taken into account.

Exceptions to the General Rule

The policy that budgeted revenue sets the limit on expenses is not applicable under certain conditions. Some of these are discussed below.

Short-Run Fluctuations. When it is expected that there will be short-term fluctuations around an average, it is appropriate to budget for the average revenue, rather than for the level of revenue in a specific year; that is, in some years expenses may exceed revenue if in other years revenues exceed expenses by a corresponding amount. Reserves are provided for equalization. This averaging process is difficult. If the policy is overly conservative, the effect is to deprive current clients of services that are rightfully theirs. Conversely, if it is assumed that next year will be better, and when this doesn't happen it is assumed that the following year *surely* will be better, the institution may be headed for disaster.

The Promoter. Occasionally, the amount of resources available can be increased by a dynamic individual. The governing board thereupon authorizes a budget in excess of current revenues in anticipation of the new resources that the promoter will provide. Such a decision is obviously a gamble. If it works, the institution may be elevated to a permanently higher plateau. If it doesn't work, painful cutbacks may shortly be necessary to bring the budget back in line with revenues.

Deliberate Capital Erosion. There are situations where the current revenue is deliberately not regarded as a ceiling, and part of the permanent capital is used for current operations. This may represent a gamble in anticipation of new resources as described above, or it may reflect a conscious policy to go out of existence after the capital has been consumed. Decisions to use permanent capital for current operations are made with great care because no organization can live beyond its means indefinitely.

Special Effort. The organization may deliberately budget a loss as a psychological device to induce its supporters to provide more funds than they normally would, or to convince prospective benefactors that their support is vitally needed. Such a device must be used sparingly. If it does not produce the desired result, management must be prepared to adjust the budget to available resources.

Resources Not Needed. Occasionally an organization may estimate that it will receive more funds than it needs, and hence will budget a surplus. This rarely happens, because nonprofit organizations usually could render more service or better quality service if funds were available to do so. A surplus does occur when the need for the organization's services has declined but those who provide the funds are not yet aware of this fact. (The March of Dimes is an example both of an organization whose need for funds declined with the decline in polio cases and of an organization which found new services to render in order to use available revenue.) In a new organization, especially when its output is glamorous, the management may be unable to organize rapidly enough to spend wisely all funds that become available; in these circumstances, the budget should be determined by opportunities for spending money wisely rather than by the amount of available revenue. A recent example was the situation in the National Institute for Cancer Research when an enthusiastic Congress appropriated more money than could prudently be spent. An organization may also budget a current surplus in anticipation of future needs for funds, but this policy is warranted only if due regard is given to the rights of current clients.

BUDGETING REVENUES

From the above, it is apparent that the budgeting process should begin with a realistic estimate of revenues that are to be earned or received during the budget period. In client-oriented organizations, this may involve a process similar to that of making a sales budget in a profit-oriented company. In public-oriented organizations, it may involve extensive soundings of the mood of the legislature and analysis of the appropriate tax burden that the public should be asked to bear. One aspect of the revenue budgeting part of the process will be discussed here; namely, the special problem of measuring endowment earnings.

Measurement of Endowment Earnings

Many nonprofit organizations obtain resources for current operations from earnings on endowment funds. Endowment is created when donors give to an institution with the intention that the principal will be kept intact forever (or for a very long time) and that earnings on that principal will be used for the current needs of the institution. In recent years, the measurement of these earnings has become a problem.[5]

As a simple way of visualizing the problem, assume that an organization controls two separate pools of money. One pool is available to finance current operations, and the other pool will be used to generate earnings that finance both current and future operations. The problem is to decide how much of the total funds controlled by the organization belongs in each pool.

Unless this problem is solved correctly, the current level of the organization's activities will be wrong. If too much is assigned to the "operating" pool, current clients will receive more services than they are entitled to, and the endowment that is supposed to finance services for future clients will gradually disappear. If too little is assigned to the "operating" pool, current activities are unnecessarily curtailed; in effect, the organization will not carry on the level of activity that donors to the endowment fund presumably intended. At the extreme, some policies can result in a growth of endowment just for the sake of growth; that is, there is no intention of benefiting clients, either now or in the foreseeable future. Instead, those responsible for endowment management derive satisfaction from observing the growth of the fund. Such a policy cannot be defended.

Until two or three decades ago, endowment funds were invested mostly in bonds and real estate. The earnings available for current operating expenses clearly consisted of the interest on these bonds and the net rentals from the real estate. Since bonds were often held to maturity, appreciation in market value was not a significant factor, and real estate typically was not sold so no measure of its appreciated value was readily apparent. Two developments altered this situation:

a. Institutions began to invest in common stocks as well as in bonds. The nature of dividends on common stock is roughly similar to, but by no means identical with, the nature of interest on bonds.

b. In recent years, many companies adopted the policy of paying no dividends or of paying dividends that were significantly less than the company's income. In these companies, earnings are reinvested in additional assets, with the expectation that these new assets will produce additional earnings which will be reflected in an appreciated market price for the stock. This policy was adopted partly because it was viewed as an efficient way of obtaining equity capital for

---

[5] This problem was brought to public attention primarily by the 1967 report of the Treasurer of Yale University. Subsequently, the Ford Foundation published two useful reports on the subject: *Managing Educational Endowments* (1969), and William L. Cary and Craig B. Bright, *The Developing Law of Endowment Funds:* "The Law and the Lore," rev. ed., 1974.

expansion, and partly to permit stockholders to have earnings taxed at the capital gains rate rather than at the ordinary rate on dividend income, which is about twice as high.

If a university continued to adhere to the historical definition of endowment earnings, it did not count the increased market value of the stock as revenue, but rather added the proceeds from the sale of such stock to the principal of its endowment. It counted as endowment earnings only the interest from bonds, rental income from real estate, and the dividends from stock; only these amounts were available to finance current expenses.

One consequence of this definition of earnings was that universities tended to avoid investments in stock in companies that did not pay out a large fraction of their earnings in dividends because the earnings on such investments were inadequate to support the current operating needs of the university. Such a policy required that endowment fund managers pass up some excellent investment opportunities, opportunities which were clearly in the long run best interests of the university. With an increasing emphasis on long run results, university endowments have increasingly been invested in common stock of companies which pay shareholders a smaller portion of earnings in dividends. This has intensified the problem of measuring the earnings on such investments.

It seems clear that the endowment problem should be divided into two parts. There is, first, the problem of how best to invest funds so as to provide the greatest benefit to the university. This is the problem of investment policy, and the same factors are relevant as in any investment policy: diversification, risk *vs.* return, and the like. The other problem is to define how much of the total increase in endowment in a year constitutes earnings that are available for current operations. The first problem does not concern us here. The important point is that investment policy should have no bearing on the question of defining current earnings.

The problem of measuring earnings arises primarily in connection with common stock. If only a part of a company's income is paid out in dividends, that part which is retained presumably adds to the company's earning capacity and hence increases the price of its stock. The increased stock price represents income which would be specifically identified as such if an equivalent amount had been paid out as current dividends. But the price of the stock also fluctuates for a number of other reasons, including general business conditions, the market's evaluation of the company's future prospects, and so on. The question is: How much of the change in the market price of the stock arises because of retained earnings? Unfortunately, no one knows how to answer this question. Lacking a direct answer, universities seek indirect methods of assigning a part of the change in market price as earnings available for current operations. There are two general approaches, which may be called respectively the "need" approach and the "formula" approach.

The "Need" Approach. In its pioneering report, mentioned above, the Treasurer of Yale University described the first approach. He said that a "prudent portion" of the appreciation in the market value of stock should be considered as being current earnings. Yale defined "prudent portion" on the basis of an historical analysis. The increase in university costs over the years was analyzed, and it was assumed that costs would continue to increase at about the same rate. Revenue from sources other than endowment were also estimated, and endowment earnings were calculated as being equal to the gap between the amount needed and the amount of revenue likely to be obtained from tuition and other sources, subject to an upper limit related to the total currently unused amount of appreciation in the endowment.

If the principle that budgeted costs should equal revenue is accepted, the first step in budgeting is to measure revenue and the second step is to match expenses to this revenue, rather than vice versa. The original Yale approach was inconsistent with this principle, for it let revenue be determined, in part, by expenses. The dangers of such an approach have been described above. Yale itself has now shifted to a formula approach.

Formula Approach. Although many variations in detail exist, the general rule for most of the formula approaches to measuring endowment earnings is simple: Take X percent of the average market value of the endowment and call it earnings. The problem is to decide on what X should be. The above formula is based on the *total return concept* of endowment earnings. The total return concept recognizes that over a period of time the earnings on endowment consist not only of interest, rents, and dividends, but also of the growth in market value of the endowment portfolio. It would be possible to regard this total return as available for current operations, and if this were done, the principal of the endowment would remain intact, as measured in current monetary amount. Thus, if the total return were found to be 9 percent, and the endowment principal were $1,000,000, then $900,000 could be used for current operations each year, and the principal would remain at $1,000,000. Because of fluctuations in market value, there would be practical problems in applying this rule, but with proper averaging and reserve devices, one could come close.

The difficulty with this concept, however, is that although the principal would stay intact at $1,000,000, in a world of inflation its purchasing power would decline. Although there is no way of ascertaining exactly what the intentions of donors were, it seems likely that they wanted to keep the *purchasing power* of the principal intact. In order to do this, the absolute size of the principal must grow, so that it will generate an increasing amount of earnings in current dollars, sufficient to provide a constant amount of purchasing power.

For this reason, the formula approach does *not* take the estimated total return as earnings available for current operations. Instead, it subtracts from this total an allowance for inflation, and takes only the difference as current earnings. By leaving the inflation allowance in the endowment fund, the principal continues to grow, and if the estimates work out correctly, the principal will provide annual earnings of constant purchasing power, forever.

In calculating total return, no distinction is made between realized gains and unrealized gains; both are part of earnings. This is in sharp contrast with the older approach, in which only realized gains (i.e., the difference between selling price and cost for those securities actually sold) were recorded, and many accountants still argue that unrealized gains should be disregarded. Most practitioners now agree that there is no important difference between an unrealized and a realized gain. An unrealized gain can be turned into a realized gain by one telephone call, but the proceeds from the sales transaction must be reinvested in some other security which, like the security sold, can fluctuate in market value.

Both the total return to be expected in the future and the amount of inflation that should be allowed for, are estimates. There is a surprisingly small variation in the net result of these two estimates as adopted by various endowment funds. In general, few organizations take less than 4.5 percent or more than 5 percent of market value as current earnings. It does not matter whether the 5 percent was arrived at by judging total return to be 8 percent and inflation to be 3 percent, or by judging total return to be 9 percent and inflation to be 4 percent; the net result is the same. It is also likely, of course, that after the first organizations to adopt this concept settled on a rate of 5 percent or a little below, those who came later chose such a rate without a careful analysis of total return and inflation.

Whatever the percentage, it is always applied to an *average* market value; a three-year average, a five-year average, or even a longer average. Appropriate adjustments are made for new gifts received during the period over which the average is computed. If an average were not used, the endowment earnings would swing widely from one year to another, because of cyclical changes in the market value of the portfolio; this would result in variations in budgeted revenue. The average dampens, but does not eliminate, the effect of these swings.[6]

When the total return approach was first introduced, questions

---

[6] For further details, see J. Peter Williamson, *Performance Measurement and Investment Objectives for Educational Endowment Funds* (New York: The Common Fund, 1972).

were raised about its legality in view of state laws that often stated
or implied a narrow definition of endowment income. These concerns
have largely abated. Many states have changed their laws to provide
specifically for the total return concept. In others, it is usually possible
to accomplish the desired result by using funds on which donors
placed no legal restriction.

BUDGETING EXPENSES

As indicated earlier, the expense budget is constructed essentially
by fine tuning the estimated program costs. For new programs, this
involves assigning program responsibility to responsibility centers and
constructing careful cost estimates in each responsibility center. For
example, a research/development *program* may be costed at $200,000
simply by estimating that it will require four professional work years
at $50,000 a work year. In constructing the *budget*, the salaries of
professionals and the other support costs that make up the overall
estimate of $50,000 per work year will each be stated. The total
amount will usually approximate $200,000 but will vary somewhat
from this estimate as the costs are examined in more detail.

For ongoing programs, the current level of spending is usually taken
as a starting point, with an upward adjustment to allow for inflation.
These historical data can be expressed in either of two ways. Some
items are budgeted as absolute dollar amounts. If the current level
of spending is, say, $10,000 per year, the budgeted amount might
be $10,400, assuming a 4 percent inflation allowance. Other items
are budgeted by the use of "estimating relationships" which shows
the relationship of costs and volume. If experience shows that food
service costs $100,000 plus $2 per day per client, and if it is estimated
that the volume in the next year will be 200,000 client days, the
food service budget is $500,000.

Variable Budgets.   In profit-oriented companies, the budget allowance for an item whose costs vary with volume, as in the food service
example above, would actually be stated in terms of a fixed amount
plus a variable rate per unit of volume (e.g., $100,000 + $2 per client
day). This practice is also appropriate in a nonprofit organization *if*
revenue also varies with volume. Thus, it would be appropriate to budget
food service in a hospital or a school in this fashion because the revenue
from patient care or student board varies with volume. In other circumstances, however, it is doubtful that a variable budget provides adequate
control. For example, the snow removal budget in a municipality may
be arrived at by estimating costs at $10,000 per inch of snow, which
would be $300,000 if 30 inches of snow is estimated. Since the actual
amount of snow probably will be more or less than 30 inches, actual
snow removal costs are likely to be more or less than $300,000. Neverthe-

less, it usually is desirable to set the snow removal budget at the fixed amount of $300,000, and require a budget revision when the snowfall exceeds or falls short of the budgeted amount. If the budget were permitted to vary automatically with the amount of snowfall, there would be no way of assuring that the total amount of funds appropriated were not exceeded. With budget revision, an offsetting change can be made in some other item or, if necessary, supplemental funds can be sought.

Advanced Techniques.   Various analytical techniques, such as the use of subjective probabilities, preference theory, multiple regression analysis, and models, have been advocated as an aid to budget preparation, but few of these have been used in practice. One experiment that may turn out to have wide applicability is Roche's use of preference theory in the preparation of a budget for a public school.[7] In this experiment, the heads of the language arts, science, mathematics, and social studies program in an elementary school system were asked to estimate what the effect on student learning would be if the budgets for each of their programs were increased by stated amounts. Safeguards were set up to minimize the biases in these estimates. Decision makers (the superintendent and the school committee) were asked to state their preferences as to the relative importance of increased learning in each of the four programs. Preference theory was then used to arrive at the optimum way of spreading an increment of funds among programs. Although this method has actually been used in the preparation of a budget, and although those involved in the process found it to be helpful, it is complicated, and for this reason probably will not become popular in the near future.

FORMULATING OBJECTIVES

In addition to estimating costs, operating managers should also state, as specifically as possible, the objectives that they expect to attain during the budget year. This part of the budgeting process is relatively new, or at least the organized effort under the label "Management by Objectives" is relatively new, but it is being increasingly emphasized in the federal government,[8] and is spreading to other types of nonprofit organizations.

If at all possible, the objectives should be quantified so that actual performance can be compared with them. Objectives are output mea-

---

[7] James G. Roche, *Preference Tradeoffs among Instructional Programs; An Investigation of Cost-Benefit and Decision Analysis Techniques in Local Educational Decision-Making* (Boston: Graduate School of Business Administration, George F. Baker Foundation, Harvard University, 1972, ICH #9–175–079).

[8] For a description of the federal program, see Rodney Brady, "MBO Goes to Work in the Public Sector," *Harvard Business Review*, vol. 51 (March/April 1973), pp. 65–74.

sures; problems of finding appropriate measures of output are discussed in Chapter 6. These statements of objectives take the place of the profitability objective which is a key part of the budgeting process in a profit-oriented company. The appropriateness of the revenue and cost estimates in such a company can be judged in terms of whether or not they produce a satisfactory profit. In a nonprofit organization, such an overall yardstick of judging the estimates in the budget does not exist. In the absence of some substitute, the budgeted costs can be judged in terms of what was spent last year, but this is not a very satisfactory basis for judgment. What the supervisor wants to know is what results will be obtained from the use of the budgeted resources. A statement of objectives that is related directly to the budgeted costs provides this information.

Some organizations use a "management by objectives" procedure that is quite separate from the budgeting process. This separation came about usually because the technique happened to be sponsored by persons who were outside the controller organization. The controller is usually responsible for the budgeting process. Such a separation is undesirable. In discussing plans for next year, both the costs and the results expected from incurring these costs should be considered together.

THE BUDGET REVIEW

In any organization, and especially in nonprofit organizations, the budget review is the heart of the budgeting process. The review has both technical aspects and, more important, behavioral aspects.

Technical Aspects

An important, but sometimes overlooked, fact about the review process is that not much time is available for it. The proposed budgets for every responsibility center must be examined in the space of, at most, a few weeks. This is in contrast with the programming process, in which one program, covering only a small fraction of the organization's activities, can be examined in depth. Because there is not enough time to do otherwise, the level of current spending is typically taken as the starting point in examining the proposed budget. Although the burden of proof to justify amounts about that level is on the budgetee, there is an implication that budgetees are "entitled to" the current level. This "blight of incrementalism" is widely criticized, but there is little that can be done about it as a practical matter, simply because of the time pressure. The place for a more thorough analysis of spending needs is the programming process.

"*Zero-Based Budgeting.*" Several recent articles have described an activity called zero-based budgeting. A brochure published by the State of Georgia describes this activity:

> The first step requires the preparation of a "decision package" for each function or activity. It includes an analysis of the cost, purpose, alternative courses of action, measures of performance, consequences of not performing the activity, and benefits. The second step requires that each decision package be ranked in order of importance against other current and new activities. This first year we are analyzing about 10,000 decision packages.

A photograph in the brochure shows the Governor and his staff reviewing one of these decision packages. A moment's reflection should convince anyone that it simply is not possible to review 10,000, or any reasonable number, of "packages" in any depth during the budget process. Zero-based budgeting is a propaganda phrase. On the other hand, a zero-based *review* during the programming process, as discussed in Chapter 9, is a feasible and worthwhile activity.

Technical Analysis. In addition to last year's figures, the budget is also reconciled with the program, if there is a program. If comparable data are available on similar activities in other organizations, these are used for comparisons. Comparisons are also made among the unit costs of similar activities within the organization. The budget is checked for consistency with the guidelines; wage rates and costs of significant materials are checked for reasonableness, and other checks—including the simple but important check of arithmetical accuracy—are made.

This work is done by budget analysts. The nature of the operations listed above suggests an important distinction between the ideal budget analyst and the ideal program analyst. The former must work under great time pressure, possess a "feel" for what is the right amount of cost, and be able and willing to get to the essence of the calculations quickly. The latter is less interested in accuracy and more interested in judging, even in a rough way, the relation between costs and benefits of the proposed program.

Budgeting for Service Centers. Service centers provide services for other responsibility centers. Service centers should prepare budget estimates, and they should be examined as carefully as are the estimates of mission centers; in fact, since service centers usually perform functions whose output can be measured (e.g., typing pools, maintenance shops, computers), the scrutiny of their budget requests can be more thorough than that of the typical mission center.

Whenever it is feasible to do so, the units that receive the service should "pay" the service center for it. Thus, the costs of the service center also appear in the cost of the units receiving the service. This creates two problems in budgeting.

The first is the avoidance of double counting. Unless care is taken, summaries of responsibility center budgets can include the service center costs twice, once in the budget of the benefiting unit and once in the budget of the service center. The easy solution to this problem is to exclude service center costs from budget totals, except for that fraction of the cost, if any, for which the service center is not expected to receive reimbursement from its customers.

The second, and much more difficult, problem is to reconcile the amount that the service center budgets for its own operations with the sum of the amounts that other responsibility centers include in their budget requests for these services. Often, an exact reconciliation is not possible, nor is it necessary. Nevertheless, it is important that top management ascertain that there is an approximate balance between the scope of the service center's activities as assumed in its own budget request and the probable demand for services as indicated in the budget requests of its customers. In order to do this, budget requests of customers should specifically identify the estimated cost of the services that customers expect to receive from each significant service center. An analysis of these amounts may indicate the need for either enlarging or shrinking the size of the service center, or for planning to obtain comparable services from outside the organization.

Behavioral Aspects

In estimating the labor cost of making shoes, there is little ground for disagreement on the part of well-informed people because the cost of each operation can be estimated within close limits, and the total labor cost can be found by adding the costs of each operation and multiplying by the number of pairs of shoes. As noted above, such engineered costs constitute a relatively large fraction of the costs of an industrial company. By contrast, discretionary costs—costs for which the optimum amount is not known, and often not knowable—constitute a relatively large fraction of the budget of a nonprofit organization. Since there is no "scientific" way of estimating the amount of discretionary costs, the budget amounts must be determined through negotiation. Negotiation is also required because there is no objective way of deciding which requests for funds have the highest priority.

This process of negotiation has been described as a two-person nonzero sum game.[9] The players are the budgetee, who is advocating a proposed budget, and the supervisor, who must approve, modify, or deny the request. Except for the lowest echelon, all managers are

---

[9] See G. H. Hofstede, *The Game of Budget Control* (Assen, The Netherlands: Van Gorcum & Comp., N.V., 1967).

supervisors at one stage in the budget process, and they become budgetees in the next stage. Even top management becomes a budgetee in presenting the budget to the outside agency or Board that is responsible for providing the funds. Although in one sense a new game is played each year, there are important carryover consequences from one year to the next. The judgment that each party develops in one year, about the ability, integrity, and forthrightness of the other party affects attitudes in subsequent years.

As in any negotiation, the two parties have a common interest in reaching a satisfactory outcome, but they have antagonistic interests in what that outcome should be. The essence of this antagonism is that budgetees want as large a budget as possible, and supervisors want to cut the proposed budget as much as they safely can.

Thus, the points of view of supervisors and budgetees in the budget negotiation are naturally in contradiction. The supervisor has the "reach" approach and tries to pull the goal upward, i.e., to expect large results from a given expenditure or to expect that a given result can be obtained with a relatively small expenditure. The budgetee tries to be conservative and leave a safety margin. Unless the parties are permitted to uphold their point of view they may not feel committed to the final budget.

The attitude of professionals is also an important factor. For example, in a hospital, the budgetee may be a physician and the supervisor a hospital administrator. Physicians are primarily interested in improving the quality of patient care, improving the status of the hospital as perceived by their peers, and increasing their own prestige; their interest in the amount of costs involved is secondary. By contrast, hospital administrators are primarily interested in costs although they realize that costs must not be so low that the quality of care or the status of the hospital is impaired. Thus, the two parties weight the relevant factors considerably differently.

Sometimes, however, the budgetee and the supervisor act as though their interests were similar. A university administrator writes:

> Department chairmen who are elected and reviewed by their colleagues are unwilling to pass harsh judgments on their constituents. Deans who hold office by similar process are no more likely to challenge vested interests in establishing academic priorities. Presidents, insofar as they are captives of the populist practice, hold an empty power whether they are "political" presidents or not.[10]

The budget process is most effective when the supervisor and the budgetee behave in a certain manner. In general, effective behavior by supervisors is as follows: They trust their subordinates. They as-

---

[10] Robert L. Payton, Long Island University, in a letter to *Science* (July 9, 1971), p. 103.

sume that subordinates are competent and that they have goodwill and honesty. They feel secure enough, have enough self-esteem, so that they do not frequently impose their own solutions. They do not feel overly threatened if the budgetee does not always agree with them. They repress in themselves, and in their subordinates, signs of what could be interpreted as disrespect or rebellion against authority. They do not hide information in order to get leverage on subordinates. They do not force goals onto subordinates.

Effective budgetees also trust their superiors. A plan is necessarily based on certain assumptions about the external world, assumptions which often prove to be wrong. If budgetees do not trust supervisors to recognize this fact, they will be reluctant to make realistic estimates. They may be so afraid of their bosses that they cannot negotiate, that is, enter a give and take collaboration with them.

Rules of the Game

It is usually not considered polite to refer to the budget process as a game; therefore, many of its rules are unwritten. Nevertheless, as in any game, rules do exist. They vary considerably from organization to organization. They depend in large part upon the size of the organization and on the relationship between the two participants, the supervisor and the budgetee. In a small organization, the chances are good that the two persons can establish a close relationship, with considerable understanding and trust. As a result they can be more frank with each other. In larger organizations, with attendant greater separation between budgetee and supervisor, and a larger number of distinct sources of demands for resources, the relationship between parties is likely to be more formal and the rules of the game therefore become more complex and more important.

Some of the unwritten rules in the Department of Defense are the following:

a. The game is to be played entirely inside the Pentagon. Outside pressures, such as Congressional intervention, are not permitted to exert an influence on the formulation of a budget, and any attempt to use them would be frowned upon.

b. There must be a reason for every action. One cannot request $100,000,000 for aircraft operations next year without substantiating data on how many hours the aircraft will fly, and the cost-per-hour for operation. These data are not necessarily verifiable because at some point they are derived from an educated guess regarding a crucial factor.

c. Neither side ever admits that its reasons are not sound, and as a matter of sportsmanship it is bad form to accuse the other party of using illogical arguments if the arguments are in fact the best that can be made. It is also bad form to treat historically derived formulas lightly, however shaky they might be.

BUDGET PLOYS

In order to play the budget game well, each party should be familiar with its ploys and the appropriate responses to these ploys. Ploys can be divided into two main categories: (1) those used primarily within an organization, and (2) those used primarily externally, that is, between the head of the organization and the legislative body or governing board that authorizes funds for the organization. External ploys are so well described in Wildavsky's *The Politics of the Budgeting Process*[11] that it would be redundant to repeat them here. (Anyone involved in external negotiations, on either side, would do well to read this book.) The following list is therefore limited to internal ploys. These can be roughly divided into four categories:

1. Ploys for new programs.
2. Ploys for ongoing programs.
3. Ploys to resist cuts.
4. Ploys primarily for supervisors.

There is some overlap among the categories. Some ploys relate to programming as well as to budgeting. Each ploy is described briefly with an appropriate response.

PLOYS FOR NEW PROGRAMS

1. Foot in the Door

Illustration: During the Vietnam War, the Navy proposed reactivation of the battleship New Jersey with a budget estimate of approximately $8,000,000. At $8,000,000, there was a slightly favorable trade-off when compared with delivery of the same firepower by aircraft or artillery, so the program was approved. The Navy then proceeded to enhance the program so that the actual cost became $32,000,000. For example, instead of consuming old ammunition, new munitions were specified.

Response: This ploy can elicit either of two responses: (*a*) detect the ploy when it is proposed, consider that it is merely a foot in the door and that actual eventual costs will exceed estimates by a wide margin, and therefore disapprove the project (but this is difficult to do); *or* (*b*) hold to the original decision, limiting spending to

---

[11] Aaron Wildavsky, *The Politics of the Budgetary Process* (Boston: Little, Brown & Company, 1964).

the original cost estimate, despite pleas for enlarging it. (The latter is effective only if the ploy is detected in time.)

2. Hidden Ball

Illustration: Some years ago it was difficult to get Air Force funds for general purpose buildings but easy to get funds for intercontinental missiles, so there was included in the budget for the missile program an amount to provide for construction of a new office building. Initially this building was used by a contractor in the missile program, but eventually it became a general-purpose Air Force office building.

Response: Break down programs so that such items become visible. Discourage recurrence by special punishment.

3. Divide and Conquer

Illustrations: (*a*) The City Planning Commission in New York City was so organized that each member was supposed to be responsible for certain specified areas. The distinctions were not clear, however, so budgetees would deal with more than one supervisor, hoping that one of them would react favorably.

(*b*) A military service requested 13,000 trainees in excess of the number that could be supported by an analysis of actual needs. So many offices in the Office of the Secretary of Defense became involved in the discussion that an agreement among them could not be reached by the budget deadline. The 13,000 extra trainees were therefore retained in the budget.

Response: Responsibilities should be clearly defined, but this is easier said than done.

Caution: In some situations, especially in research, it is dangerous to have a single decision point. It is often desirable to have two places in which a person with a new idea for research may obtain a hearing. New ideas are extremely difficult to evaluate, and a divided authority, even though superficially inefficient, lessens the chance that a good idea will be rejected.

4. Distraction

Illustration: At a big meeting, the Navy presented arguments as to why some buildings at a training base should be replaced with a new set of buildings in order to implement an "approved plan" for doubling the capacity of the training base. The argument was that newer buildings would be more useful and efficient than the existing buildings. The merits were discussed in terms of the return on investment arising from the greater efficiency of the new buildings. This discussion went on for some time until a supervisor thought to ask who had approved the plan for expansion of the training base in the first place. It turned out that the expansion had never been approved; approval of the new buildings would have *de facto* approved the expansion.

Response: Expose the hidden aims, but this is very difficult.

5. Shell Game

Illustration: The budgetee was head of the Model Cities program for a certain city. He wanted available funds to be used primarily for health and education programs, but he knew that his superiors were more interested in "economic" programs (new businesses and housing). He drew up the following chart:

	Source		
Purpose	Federal	Other	Total
Health and education.	$2,000,000	$ 15,000	$2,015,000
Economic	50,000	2,300,000	2,350,000

He emphasized to the Mayor and interested groups that over half the funds were intended for economic purposes. The catch was that the source of "other" funds was not known, and there were no firm plans for obtaining such funds. This was not discovered by the supervisor until just prior to the deadline for submitting the request for Federal Model Cities funding, at which time the budgetee successfully used the delayed buck ploy (No. 14).

Response: Careful analysis.

6. It's Free

Illustrations: (*a*) A state decided to build a highway, reckoning the cost as low since the Federal government would reimburse it for 95 percent of the cost. The state overlooked the fact that maintenance of the highway would be 100 percent a state cost.

(*b*) Title III of the Elementary and Secondary Education Act of 1965 provided for grants of money to school districts for a variety of experimental programs. Many districts rapidly expanded or began instructional and special service programs that would fit under this Title. As funds have become less readily available in recent years, School Boards have had to decide whether to discontinue programs or pay the bill from their own pockets. In the instance of special service programs, the choice has been expensive, and experimental grants are now being explored carefully to determine their long-run financial implications.

Response: Require an analysis of the long-run costs, not merely the costs for next year.

7. Implied Top-Level Support

Description: The budgetee says that although the request is not something that he personally is enthusiastic about, it is for a program that someone higher up in the organization asked to be included in the budget. Preferably this person is not well known to, and is more prestigious than, the budgetee's superior. The budgetee hopes that the supervisor will not take the time to bring this third party into the discussion.

Response: Examine the documentation. If it is vague, not well justified, or nonexistent, check with the alleged sponsor.

Note: In a related ploy, the end run, the budgetee actually goes to the supervisor's boss without discussing the matter with the supervisor first. This tactic should not be tolerated.

8. You're To Blame

Illustration: It is alleged that the supervisor was late in transmitting budget instructions, or that the instructions were not clear, and that this accounts for inadequacies in the justifications furnished.

Response: If the assertion is valid, this is a difficult ploy to counter. It may be necessary to be contrite, but arbitrary, in order to hold the budget within the guidelines.

9. Nothing Too Good for Our People

Description: Used, whether warranted or not, to justify items for the personal comfort and safety of military personnel, for new cemeteries, for new hospital equipment, for research laboratory equipment (especially computers), and for various facilities in public schools and colleges.

Response: Attempt to shift the discussion from emotional grounds to logical grounds by analyzing the request to see if the benefits are even remotely related to the cost. Emphasize that in a world of scarce resources, not everyone can get all that is deserved.

10. Keeping Up with the Joneses

Illustration: New Haven must have new street lights because Hartford has them.

Response: Analyze the proposal on its own merits.

11. We Must Be Up to Date

Description: This differs from Ploy #10 in that it does not require that a "Jones" be found and cited. The argument is that the organization must be a leader and must therefore adopt the newest technology. Currently, this is a fashionable ploy for computers and related equipment.

Response: Require that a benefit be shown that exceeds the cost of adopting the new technology.

Caution: Sometimes the state of the art is such that benefits cannot be conclusively demonstrated. If this leads to a deferral of proposals year after year, opportunities may be missed.

12. If We Don't, Someone Else Will

Illustration: A university budgetee argued that a proposed new program was breaking new ground, was important to the national interest, and that if her university didn't initiate it, some other university would start it, obtain funds from the appropriate government agency, and thus make it more difficult for her university to start the program later on.

Response: Point out that a long list of possible programs have this characteristic, and the university must select those few which are within its capabilities.

13. Call It a Rose

(*a*) Defense policy discourages the procurement of aircraft for the personal use of commanding generals because their transportation is supposed to be furnished by the Military Airlift Command or by commercial airlines. Budgetees therefore describe such aircraft as "administrative aircraft," "support aircraft," "logistics aircraft," or "evacuation aircraft." (The latter term, implying transportation of wounded, also uses the "nothing too good for our people" ploy.)

(*b*) In the early 1960s the National Institutes of Health were unable to obtain approval for the construction of new buildings, but were able to build "annexes." It is said that Building 12A (the annex) is at least double the size of Building 12.

Response: Look behind the euphemism to the real function. If the disguise is intentional, deny the request and, if feasible, discourage recurrence by special punishment.

14. Outside Experts

Description: The agency hires outside experts to support its request, either formally in hearings, or informally in the press.

Response: Show that these experts are biased, either because of a present connection with the agency or because they are likely to benefit if the request is approved.

PLOYS FOR MAINTAINING OR INCREASING ONGOING PROGRAMS

15. Show of Strength

Illustration: In the summer of 1966 when the Community Development Agency of New York City was trying to decide which 50 of the 500 summer programs would be funded for the full year, a director of one of these programs got the entire staff of about 150 people to come down to the central office to sit in. The director had told the staff that for no apparent reason the city had not forwarded the last reimbursement, and therefore the payroll could not be met. On leaving the central office, the director dropped the hint that the sit-in might recur if his program was not extended.[12]

Response: Have fair criteria for selecting programs and have the conviction to stand by your decision.

16. Razzle-Dazzle

Illustration: In 1967 both the Army (budgetee) and the Defense Department (supervisor) knew that the amount of supplies needed in Southeast Asia could not be estimated within close limits because of the inadequacies of the data. Records of shipments were inaccurate, and the existing system did not separate material consumed from material added to inventory. Nevertheless, the budgetee made elaborate calculations of "requirements" for thousands of individual items of material, so voluminous that Defense Department analysts could not possibly examine them in detail.

Response: (*a*) Make equally voluminous (and equally unsubstantiated) calculations using lower consumption factors, and require the budgetee to substantiate the difference between the two estimates; i.e., shift the burden of proof. (*b*) Find a single soft spot in the original analysis and use it to discredit the whole analysis. (Note: Both of these responses cannot be used together, for the former assumes that the approach is worthwhile, whereas the latter assumes it is not.)

17. Delayed Buck

Illustration: The Army had a procurement category called "minor procurement," which consisted of thousands of items, no one of which was very expensive, but which were substantial in total. The total

---

[12] This ploy is developed in depth in Tom Wolfe, *Radical Chic and Mau-Mauing the Flak Catchers* (New York: Farrar, Straus, and Giroux, 1970).

budget estimate was obtained by estimating broad categories of items. In 1967, the Army proposed a refined method of calculation, which would estimate the requirements of each item, using a computer. Once the computer program started to operate, the Army lost the capability of doing the job manually. The computer program developed bugs, however, and it did not produce output by the October deadline. Indeed, it did not produce output until December, too late to permit analysis by the supervisor.

Response: This is a difficult ploy to counter. Complaining about the delay may make the supervisor feel better, but will not produce the data. One possible response, designed to prevent recurrence, is to penalize the delay by making an entirely arbitrary cut in the amount requested, although this runs the risk that needed funds will be denied.

18. Reverence for the Past

Description: Whatever was spent last year must have been necessary in order to carry out last year's program; therefore, the only matters to be negotiated are the proposed increments above this sacred base.

Response: As a practical matter, this attitude must be accepted for a great many programs, because there is not time to challenge this statement. For selected programs, there can be a zero-base review (see Chapter 9).

19. Sprinkling

Description: "Watering" was a device used in the early 20th century to make assets and profits in prospectuses for new stock offerings look substantially higher than they really were. Sprinkling is a more subtle ploy, which increases budget estimates by only a few percent, either across-the-board or in hard-to-detect areas. Often it is done in anticipation that the supervisor will make arbitrary reductions, so that the final budget will be what it would have been if neither the sprinkling nor the arbitrary cuts had been made.

Response: Since this ploy, when done by an expert, is extremely difficult to detect, the best response is to remove the need for doing it; that is, create an atmosphere in which the budgetees trust the supervisor not to make arbitrary cuts.

PLOYS TO RESIST CUTS

20. Make a Study

Illustration: On the basis of a study, the supervisor proposed to the budgetee (Army) a fairly large reduction in spending in a certain theatre of operations. This proposal was based on an analysis of spending at dozens of bases in this theatre. The proposal was submitted to the budgetee for comment several months prior to the time of budget submission. At budget time, the budgetee asserted that the proposal was too superficial, and that a new study was required to determine whether the reductions were actually possible. (Note: Supervisors can use the same ploy as counters to ploys for new programs.)

Responses: (*a*) Reject the request. (*b*) Agree to have the study made but broaden its scope so that it scrutinizes areas not covered in the original proposal. This places the budgetee in the difficult position of deciding whether to accept the smaller, certain reduction, or to run the risk that the new study will lead to a larger reduction.

21. Gold Watch

Illustration: This well-known ploy derives its name from an incident in which Robert McNamara was involved when he was with the Ford Motor Company. In a period of stringency, all division heads were asked to make a special effort to cut costs. Most responded with genuine belt tightening; however, one division manager, with $100 million sales, reported that the only cost reduction opportunity he had found was to eliminate the gold watches that were customarily given to employees upon their retirement with 30 or more years of satisfactory service. The ploy encompasses any situation where the budgetee attempts to defeat the purpose of the request by taking actions that do more harm than good.

Response: Reject the proposal. (In the illustration, disciplinary action was also taken with respect to the division manager.)

22. Witches and Goblins

Description: The budgetee asserts that if the request is not approved, dire consequences will occur. It is used often by the House Armed Services Committee in its reports to Congress. For example, in 1968, an antiballistic missile system was recommended as a counterdefense to the "Talinin System" that the Soviets were supposed to be building. In fact, the Soviets were not building such a system.

Response: Analysis based on evidence rather than on emotion.

23. We are the Experts

Description: The budgetee asserts that the proposal must be accepted because he has expert knowledge which the supervisor cannot possibly match. This ploy is used by professionals of all types: military officers, scientists, professors, physicians, and clergy.

Response: If the basic premise is accepted, the budget process cannot proceed rationally, for the supervisor tends to be a generalist and the budgetee a specialist. The supervisor should insist that the expert express the basis for his judgment in terms that are comprehensible to the generalist.

24. Agreement in Principle

Illustration: In 1967 the Secretary of Defense obtained written agreement from the Services on an inventory policy which in principle was intended to maintain the inventory, consisting of some 5,000,000 items, at about its current level. One Service submitted a budget request that included increases in inventory levels totalling $4 billion. The increases in particular items were substantiated on the grounds that they were exceptions to the basic policy or were not covered by the wording of the policy statement.

Response: Prevent this from occurring by wording policy statements with great care. Wherever feasible, express the policy in numbers as well as in words. Numbers are more difficult to evade.

PLOYS FOR THE SUPERVISOR

25. Keep Them Lean and Hungry

Illustration: The supervisor tells the budgetee that the latter's organization will work harder, and possibly more effectively, if it doesn't have to carry so much fat.

Response: Show that the analogy with human biology is false, or go along with the analogy, and show that the cuts represent muscle rather than fat.

26. Productivity Cuts

Description: It is assumed that many capital expenditures are made with the intention of cutting operating costs. Although few systems permit individual cost reductions to be identified, it is reasonable to assume that they, together with continuing management improvements, should lead to lower operating costs in the aggregate. In the Defense Department, for this reason, personnel-related costs were automatically reduced by about $1\frac{1}{2}$ percent from the previous year's level. In the entire economy, productivity increases by about 3 percent annually; the lower percentage assumes that nonprofit organizations are only half as susceptible to productivity gains as the economy as a whole.

In some organizations, the cost reductions can be specifically traced. When an organization makes a large capital expenditure to convert its recordkeeping to computers, this presumably results in lower operating costs, and the planned savings should be specifically identified. When a program in 1969 reflects a decision to convert to a computer operation by 1971, the programmed clerical costs for 1971 should reflect a cost reduction.

Response: Point out that dismissals are politically inexpedient, and retirements and resignations may not be rapid enough to permit costs to be reduced to the desired level.

27. Arbitrary Cuts

Illustration: The supervisor, who was director of research of a large company, followed the practice of reducing the budget for certain discretionary items (travel, publications, professional dues) in certain departments by approximately 10 percent. The supervisor was careful to do this at random and achieved a reputation for astute analysis.

Response: Challenge the reason for the cuts (but the items tend to be so unimportant and difficult to defend that such challenges may consume more time than they are worth).

28. I Only Work Here

Description: The supervisor says she cannot grant the budgetee's request because it is not within the scope of ground rules that her superiors have laid down.

Response: Carry the issue to higher authority (although never by an *end run*—see No. 7).

appendix

Building a Defense
Budget

On January 27, 1968, the Secretary of Defense transmitted to the Director of the Bureau of the Budget (now the Office of Management and Budget) the final set of numbers for the FY 1969 budget. (FY 1969 means the fiscal year ending June 30, 1969.) The amount of New Obligational Authority requested in that budget, and presented by the President to the Congress, was $79,576,357,000. This was, except for the total budget for the United States Government itself and possibly that for the USSR, the largest single budget ever put together by any organization up to that time. This note describes the main steps in the process that culminated in that final figure, as perceived by the author, then the Controller of the Department of Defense.

Nature of the Budget

It is quite important that the reader understand just what the Defense figures in the 1969 President's budget were, and what they were not. They were *not* a statement of how the funds made available to the Department of Defense would actually be spent in 1969. They had the appearance of being such a statement, and in justifying the budget to Congressional Committees there was a tendency to treat the numbers as if they were definite plans, showing exactly what the Defense Department intended to do. But it should be perfectly obvious that even in a relatively placid year—let alone in a war situation—no human being can know in January 1968 what the exact needs are going to be for a period that ends 18 months later, on

June 30, 1969. An individual couldn't make an exact estimate of what his or her personal spending will be that far in the future.

In order to illustrate the difference between what the Defense Department actually does and what the budget suggests that it is going to do, we can look at some data for FY 1964, which is the last year before the Vietnam buildup and hence a year which should have been reasonably stable and predictable.

The 1964 budget as submitted to the Congress in January 1962 totalled $53,661 million. Included in it was $4,385 million for Operations and Maintenance, Air Force. The actual amount obligated in 1964 for Operations and Maintenance, Air Force, was $4,339 million, a slight decrease from the budgeted amount, reflecting primarily a slight reduction made by the Congress.

But although the total remained practically the same, within this total there was significant shifting. The program, Operational Support, for example, grew from $1,394 million to $1,483 million, an increase of $90 million. The Army procurement appropriation included $589 million for ammunition, but the actual amount obligated was $340 million, a drop of over 40 percent. And within the ammunition category the amount for 7.62mm cartridges decreased from $65.5 million appropriated to $35.3 million obligated, and the amount for 155mm projectiles decreased from $67.5 million appropriated to $47.7 million obligated. Although the quantitative requirements for the 2.75" rocket increased above the amount in the budget, the dollar requirement for this item decreased from $25.5 million appropriated to $16.1 million obligated as a result of a sharp reduction in the unit price.

These figures only confirm what common sense suggests; namely, that in a huge, complex, fluid organization no one can make a precise forecast of needs.

Although the forecasts for some categories are necessarily rough, certain parts of the budget are quite specific. The military construction section, for example, does set forth the specific construction projects that are contemplated, and there is a high probability that these projects, if approved by the Congress, will be undertaken and that no other projects will be undertaken. It is in the nature of construction projects that they must be planned considerably in advance. Even here, however, there will inevitably be some shifting, and the cost figures for each project are, of course, estimates which may be changed significantly when actual bids are received.

Except for items like construction projects, there is a general presumption that approximately the amount of money set forth for a specific category will in fact be spent for that category. But that is about the most one can say about the exactness of the budget.

Perhaps the best overall way to describe the budget is to say that it is a request for funds which *in total* are deemed adequate to carry out the mission of the Department of Defense, rather than a detailed statement of how the funds provided to DoD will actually be spent. The budget is therefore more in the nature of the prospectus which accompanies a proposed bond issue, and which gives an approximate idea of what the money will be used for, than it is of the budget of a private profit-oriented company.

A lack of correspondence between actual spending and the budgeted amount for individual items does *not* mean that the Defense Department disregards the will of the Congress. These differences reflect changes in needs, and all significant changes are approved in advance by the appropriate Congressional Committees. Some of these proposed changes are requested during the Congressional review of the budget, which begins in January and goes on for several months. These lead to modifications in the amounts actually appropriated. Changes requested subsequent to the passage of the Appropriation Act are acted on by the Congressional Committees in a formal process that is called reprogramming. Thus, the Congress is always informed as to current plans for the use of resources.

Apportionment

One part of the overall control mechanism does resemble the budget in a profit-oriented company. This is called the apportionment process. It takes place just prior to the beginning of the fiscal year. The apportionment documents are a good description of how the funds are actually going to be spent during the year, as good as is the budget of an industrial company. But the amounts in the apportionment documents can differ substantially from the details in the President's budget, and apportionment is *not* described here.

Overview of the Process

This description should really start with 1963 because certain decisions made at that time had a direct effect on the FY 1969 budget. When these decisions on weapons systems and forces were made, their financial impact was immediately recorded in the Five Year Defense Program (FYDP). Consequently, beginning in 1963, there was a column of numbers in the FYDP labeled FY 1969. These numbers were continually being changed as new decisions affecting FY 1969 were made in the intervening years.

But the really intensive work on the FY 1969 budget began in January 1967, and this description is limited to the period beginning with that date. The principal steps in the process were:

1. Scrubbing the Five Year Defense Program.
2. Preparation of the Joint Strategic Objectives Plan (JSOP).

3. Service field submissions.
4. Program decisions on major issues.
5. Issuance of budget guidelines.
6. Submission of Service requests.
7. Review of Service submissions.
8. Bureau of the Budget and Presidential review.
9. Wrap-up.
10. Budget defense.

Each of these will be described briefly.

Scrubbing the Five Year Defense Program

Early in January 1967, without even a breather to recover from the preparation of the FY 1968 budget, analysts in the Office of the Secretary of Defense and in the headquarters staffs of the Services went over the 1969-and-later columns of the Five Year Defense Program. This was a two-stage review.

The first stage, very much a "quick-and-dirty" operation, focused on certain figures on planned forces for the "out years" (i.e., the years after FY 1968) that the Secretary of Defense needed for the "posture statement," which was his basic presentation to the Congress of the FY 1968 program. This review had to be completed by the middle of January because the Secretary started his Congressional presentations at the end of January.

The second stage was a more thorough review of the program, which extended over a 4-month period. Its purpose was to incorporate in the program the "out-years" effect of decisions made during the final stages of preparing the FY 1968 budget, so as to provide an up-to-date take-off point for the budget cycle that was then beginning. The end product of this review was publication of a complete revision of the hundreds of tables that display the Five Year Defense Program.

This revision was completed and published on May 19 although the various offices were furnished the figures relating to their own work considerably earlier than this. Ideally, this revision should have been completed by the end of March rather than the middle of May.

The total obligational authority for FY 1969 in the May 19, 1967, revision of the Five Year Defense Program was $64.9 billion, but this figure excluded the impact of Southeast Asia operations on 1969. Up through the spring of 1967, the Five Year Defense Program assumed that programs for the years beyond FY 1968 would not provide for financing combat in Southeast Asia. (This was strictly a mechanical device to facilitate a clean separation between Vietnam costs and non-Vietnam costs. It implied no assumption whatsoever about the estimated date of termination of Vietnam hostilities.) Immediately after the spring scrubbing, estimated combat costs were therefore added to the FY 1969 amount. Southeast Asia costs were about $25 billion a year, and when this was added to the $64.9 billion in the FYDP, the total FY 1969 budget estimate became $90 billion.

Preparation of the JSOP

In November 1966, the Joint Staff started to prepare the Joint Strategic Objectives Plan (JSOP), which states the Joint Chiefs of Staff (JCS) position on the forces required to meet Defense objectives in 1969 and subsequent years. Much went into this document, but unfortunately the product was of little use in the decision-making process. This was because the Joint Staff, as it invariably does, requested a force structure which cost much more money than it was reasonable to expect the Congress to appropriate. The JSOP did not contain estimates of how much the recommended force structure would cost, but a rough estimate is that the JSOP submitted in 1967 would have required a 1969 budget well in excess of $100 billion. This amount is more than all other nations in the world, Soviet Bloc and Allies together, currently spent on national defense. It is not an amount that the Administration or the Congress would take seriously.

The Joint Chiefs realized that they were not in fact going to get $100 billion, but they argued that their responsibility is to set down the military requirements as they see them, and that it is the responsibility of the President to adjust the requirements to the funds likely to be available.

The practical effect of a $100 billion request, however, is that it is disregarded. It is simply too unrealistic to warrant serious consideration. It is unfortunate that the Joint Staff has chosen to disregard financial feasibility in preparing its plan, for if it did give adequate consideration to the financial facts of life, the JSOP could be a very valuable aid in the decision-making process.[13]

In any event, the JSOP was received by the Office of the Secretary of Defense on April 1. It was circulated, read by people in various Pentagon offices, and filed.

Service Field Submissions

Each Service headquarters issued a call for budget estimates from its various commands and field installations to be submitted in the spring of 1967. This call had two purposes.

First, it provided the basis for the issuance of FY 1968 program authority in June 1967. This, as mentioned above, is the apportionment process that corresponds to the budget of a profit-oriented company, which states approved plans for the coming year. For this purpose

---

[13] In 1970 the JSOP was prepared within financial guidelines established by the Secretary of Defense and therefore became a much more useful document.

the field submissions are extremely important; they provide the very latest information on which current operating budgets can be based.

The second purpose was to provide data for the FY 1969 budget submission. For this second purpose the submissions from the field organizations were, probably, not worth the time and effort involved in preparing them. To ask each field organization, early in 1967, to state its needs for the year beginning July 1, 1968, when a great many important decisions that affected operations in that year had not been made at headquarters, was simply asking them to do the impossible.

It was, furthermore, to a large extent an unnecessary job because estimates that are sufficiently accurate for the type of decisions being made in the budget process could be made just as well, or better, by the headquarters organization than they could be made by the field. Headquarters did in fact develop estimates for most procurement and Research and Development programs, and the· principle is equally applicable to estimates of operating costs.

The Commanding General of an Army installation could conceivably assemble some estimates of the cost of operating his installation two years in advance, but the way he would make these estimates is about the same as the way the staff at Army headquarters would be making an estimate of the operating costs of all Army General Purpose Forces. The headquarters organization has the advantage of being able to consider the Army as a whole, which is much simpler than trying to decide which units will be at which locations during the budget period and then estimating the costs of operating each of these units. Furthermore, the headquarters organization can reflect in its estimates the very latest judgment as to the proper size and composition of forces, whereas the field organizations must rely on assumptions provided to them when the process began, which was several months previously.

It is desirable that field organizations submit requests for construction projects, for equipment modernization proposals, and the like, because the field has good information on these needs. Service headquarters should preferably restrict their requests for field submissions to that type of information, but they are unwilling to do so. In any event the Office of the Secretary of Defense did not see these field submissions, nor did OSD have any interest in seeing them in connection with the preparation of the FY 1969 budget (although, as pointed out above, similar information was of great use in the FY 1968 apportionment process which went on at about the same time).

Program Decisions on Major Issues

Now we come to a very important part of the process, the discussions between the Services, the Joint Chiefs, and the Office of the

Secretary of Defense that led to the Secretary's decisions on the major issues affecting the FY 1969 budget. This process began in February 1967 with the publication of a tentative list of such issues. Examples are: Should the Army deploy an antiballistic missile system, and if so, of what character? Should the Navy procure an additional aircraft carrier, and if so, should it be nuclear powered? What escort ships should be provided for such a carrier? Should the Army convert an additional division to an airmobile division? How many pilots should be trained by each Service?

The initial list, published in February, was modified by dropping some issues and adding others as the year progressed. There were altogether about 80 of these major issues.

The staff work in resolving these issues was, in the Office of the Secretary of Defense (OSD), mostly the responsibility of the Systems Analysis Office, although the Office of Defense Research and Engineering (DR&E) was responsible for some issues.

The first step in arriving at a decision was a lengthy, but informal, exchange of views between the OSD staff and the staffs in the various Services.[14] Based on this discussion, the Systems Analysis and DR&E staffs prepared a series of what are called "Draft Presidential Memoranda" making an analysis and tentative recommendation on each of the issues. There were about 15 of these Draft Presidential Memoranda. One dealt with Army and Marine Corps Land Forces, another with Tactical Air Forces, another with Naval Replenishment and Support Forces, another with Strategic Forces. They were called "Draft Presidential Memoranda," partly because the final version might actually have been read by the President, but primarily because the name has important psychological implications. It encourages the authors to write in a style that is suitable for submission to the President of the United States, and this helps to prevent the Memoranda from becoming the lengthy, stilted, involved, jargon-filled documents that often are written in large staff organizations.

The Secretary of Defense went over these drafts with great care, and revised them extensively in his own handwriting. The revised drafts were sent to the Services and to all staffs in OSD. In theory, the Services were supposed to have given their comments on these drafts within 30 days, and within another 30 days a revised, and, hopefully, final draft was supposed to have been issued by the Secretary of Defense. Actually this timetable was not adhered to exactly. There was much back-and-forth discussion and an unwillingness to sit down and "bite the bullet," that is, to make a final recommendation. Some argued that a final draft should not be issued until all parties were in agreement. As a practical matter, this is not feasible; there comes a time when top management must say: "This is it."

In theory, also, each Draft Presidential Memorandum was supposed

---

[14] In 1972, OSD(SA) only *reacted* to Service Proposals. This is most unfortunate.

to be accompanied by a document called a Program Change Decision, showing the money, manpower, and force structure authorized by the decision, and this was supposed to provide an automatic basis for preparing the budget. In practice, the Program Change Decisions were actually not prepared in many cases in 1967, and this made the task of tying the Draft Presidential Memoranda to the budget document more difficult.

Issuance of Budget Guidelines

On June 16, 1967, the Comptroller issued guidelines for the detailed preparation of the FY 1969 budget. This guidelines memorandum instructed the Services to prepare their budget requests in accordance with the decisions stated in the Draft Presidential Memoranda, it told the Services to assume that Southeast Asia hostilities would continue for another year, it gave ceilings for the number of military and civilian personnel, and it provided about ten single-spaced pages of other assumptions that were to govern the 1969 estimates. (Incidentally, since these guidelines were not issued until June, it is apparent that the Service field-level submissions prepared the preceding spring could not be based on them, and this is another reason why such submissions are not valuable.)

The budget was to be submitted in two sections, a "basic" budget and an "addendum" budget. The basic budget was supposed to represent the financial implications of program decisions made by the Secretary of Defense, and was constrained by all the assumptions stated in the guideline memorandum. The addendum budget was supposed to represent additional amounts that a Service thought it needed.

The addendum budget is a kind of safety valve. If the budget submission had been restricted only to programs already approved by the Secretary of Defense, then the Services could have argued that they did not have an opportunity to convey their real needs to the Secretary. The addendum budget gave them this opportunity. It also helped the Service headquarters mitigate an important internal problem. The various bureaus and offices in a Service normally request funds far in excess of the amount contemplated in the basic budget, and the people in the headquarters of the Services can include these requests in the addendum budget without too many qualms, knowing full well that the Secretary of Defense will delete these, as he deletes most addendum items, without much analysis. In other words, it can be argued that the addendum budget is a device that permits the Service Secretaries to shift the responsibility for the deletion of "pet projects" to the Secretary of Defense.[15]

---

[15] These arguments for an addendum budget are not especially persuasive. For the FY 1971 budget, the Services' latitude to submit addendum budgets was greatly restricted; this was a desirable move.

Submission of Service Requests

The guidelines memorandum directed the Services to submit their budgets on October 2, except for the plant construction portion which was to be submitted on August 1. The earlier submission of the construction estimates was required to allow time for OSD staff people to visit a number of the proposed construction sites.

It was important that the Services be held quite firmly to this timetable because all the time from October 2 until Christmas was needed to make a good review of the budget submissions. Budget analysts suspect that the Services, for their part, try to think up excuses for delaying the submissions as long as they can, in the belief that the shorter the period in which the budget requests can be examined, the fewer soft spots will be discovered.

Although it may have been inadvertent, the Army procurement people were the most successful in their delaying tactics. In the spring, they announced a wonderful computerized operation that would permit quick, accurate calculations of procurement needs. Then, along about the middle of September, they disclosed the fact that the computer operation was actually consuming somewhat more time than had been anticipated—in fact, it required more time than previously had been required to do the job manually. But by September the computations were so thoroughly mixed up in the bowels of the computer that there was nothing anyone could do to get them regurgitated, so a delay in the Army procurement submission had to be accepted. Such a maneuver works only once, however.[16]

Review of Service Requests

With a few exceptions like the above, the Services did quite a good job in getting their submissions in on time, and the OSD staff immediately set to work to review them. If the system had worked perfectly, the Draft Presidential Memoranda process would have been finished by September 1; this process would have established the decisions and the financial consequences of these decisions on all the major issues; and the Services would then have spent the month of September refining these figures for the final "basic" budget. Actually, since the Draft Presidential Memoranda were not completed on time, and since all of them were not accompanied by Program Change Decisions with specific num-

---

[16] In fairness, note is made of a corresponding maneuver that the Services assert has been used by the Office of the Secretary of Defense for an analogous reason. It is said that OSD budget analysts sometimes ask "Friday night questions" and require "Monday morning answers"; that is, they cut the budget because substantiating evidence has not been received, but do not allow enough time for good rebuttal evidence to be prepared.

bers, the base that the system contemplated was incomplete, and this complicated the job of preparing and reviewing the budget.

The actual budget review is best described as a game between OSD and the Services. It is a fascinating game to play and to watch. It has a quite well-defined set of rules of what constitutes fair play and what is unfair although these rules are nowhere written down. For example, there is a rule that every number submitted by the Service must have some sort of calculation behind it: "We need $12,642,000 of spare parts for such-and-such an aircraft engine because we are going to fly airplanes that use these engines for 116,840 hours, and 108.20 dollars in spare parts is required per hour flown." There may actually be very little support either for the logic of this equation or for the numbers that are in it, but the ground rule is that there must be such a calculation. It would be unthinkable for someone to say for example, "Admiral Smith, who knows more about this matter than anyone else, and in whose judgment both you and we have great confidence, says we need about $12 million of parts for this engine, so that is what we are requesting."

On the OSD side, there is a rule against ever cutting a Service request without a reason. OSD would never say, "Mr. Jones, who has been in this business for a great many years and who has a thorough feel for it, thinks you can get along with $10 million of engine parts, so that is what you are going to get." OSD analysts may know full well from experience that the $12,640,000 looks rather high, but they will express this intuitive feeling by searching through the calculations until they find a weak spot either in the equation or in the numbers plugged into it. If intuitively they feel the final number is about right, they will spend relatively little time on the detail of the calculations.

Both parties know, of course, that in estimating requirements for a gigantic organization that is in the midst of fighting a war and whose nature is in a constant state of flux, one simply can't estimate with any degree of precision the total requirements for a year that begins nine months in the future, much less estimate the requirements for an individual item such as aircraft engine parts. Both sides are nevertheless very careful to give the *appearance* of treating the estimates with great respect, almost as if they had the precision of an engineering calculation.

Program Budget Decision. The key document in the budget review process is called a "Program Budget Decision." For the 1969 budget, 445 of these documents were written, each one covering some segment of the program. At Secretary McNamara's insistence, each of these was written so that the essential facts and a recommendation appeared on a single page, although there could be any number of backup pages of detail, in case the Secretary chose to go into a topic deeply. It is difficult to generalize about these Program Budget Decisions. They ranged in size from a $436,000 request for the National Board for Promotion of Rifle Practice (which was denied) to $6.9 billion for operating expenses of Army General Purpose Forces. A few of the decision documents recommended approval of the Service request without change. Most, however, provided the Secretary with one, two, or even more alternatives, usually lesser amounts, together with a rationale for each.

These documents started flowing to the Secretary early in November, and either he or the Deputy Secretary made a decision to accept either the Service request or one of the alternatives. The top level decisions then went to the Services.

Each Service was permitted to reclama[17] the decisions if it wished. The reclama process is by no means a pro forma one. It resulted in the restoration of $1.3 billion in the 1969 budget.

Bureau of the Budget and Presidential Review

Other government agencies submit their budgets to the Bureau of the Budget after the heads of the agencies have approved them, and they are then reviewed. By contrast, at the Department of Defense, Bureau of the Budget people work side by side with the OSD analysts, so that when the Secretary has made the final decision, that is the end of the Executive Branch review process for all practical purposes. This relationship between the Bureau of the Budget people and the Department of Defense people is unique in government. The Bureau of the Budget has a chance to comment on the draft of each Program Budget Decision, and indeed Bureau personnel write a number of them.

In a few cases, there are differences of opinion between the Defense staff and Bureau staff that are important enough to warrant high-level discussion. Such a discussion is arranged late in November or early in December. There were 10 issues presented for discussion at the 1967 meeting; for example, the level of research and development, the Main Battle Tank, the Minuteman program, and the Sentinel system.

Also, early in December, the Secretary of Defense and the Joint Chiefs met with the President. The principal purpose of this meeting was to resolve differences of opinion between the Secretary of Defense and the Joint Chiefs of Staff on very crucial issues. The 1967 meeting dealt with three such issues.

Wrap-Up

December was a hectic month. Although the schedule called for all decisions to be made by December 18, there were, as is always the case, some matters that had not been resolved at that time. Christmas is a key date. Everyone wants to spend Christmas with his family, and

---

[17] The word "reclama" means essentially "ask for consideration." It is not used widely outside the Department of Defense. Clifford Miller has traced its origin to the Philippines and believes that the Army picked it up during the Philippine campaign around the turn of the century.

everyone knows that this will be impossible if the discussion is prolonged, so there is great pressure to get the job done by Christmas Eve.

In 1967 this target was not met. A few rather important issues were still unresolved, and they had to be held open until January. (But they were issues that could be treated as separate entities, so they were simply put off, and the staff in fact spent Christmas at home. In 1965, the staff worked most of Christmas Day.)

A fantastic amount of work had to be done between the time the last policy decision was made and the time the numbers appeared in printed form as part of the President's budget. The Defense section of the FY 1969 President's budget consisted of about 100 pages of almost the smallest type available in the Government Printing Office, and there were tens of thousands of mistakes that could have crept into these figures. The primary consideration was, of course, that the final figures correspond precisely to the decisions that had been made. But over and above this, there was the extremely complex job of reconciling figures in various tables with those in other tables. Does the total by object classes reconcile with the total by program? Do the reimbursable obligations of the organizations doing the work reconcile with the costs budgeted for the organization that will pay for the work? Do the personnel figures check with the dollar cost for these personnel? This checking is done by people who have worked at it for years and who are the only ones that know exactly how to do it. As of August 1968, no one had discovered an error in the printed President's budget.

The budget emerged from the Government Printing Office on January 29, 1968, and was submitted to the Congress that same day. It requested $82.4 billion of Total Obligational Authority. This contrasts with the going-in figure of $90 billion mentioned earlier.

But even more significant, perhaps, the $82.4 billion represents a reduction of $21.7 billion from the $101.3 billion estimate submitted by the Services, which was the sum of their basic and addendum requests.[18] The $101.3 billion was larger than any single budget ever submitted before, even for the peak year of World War II.

Budget Defense

The next step was the defense of the budget before Congressional Committees. This process is outside the scope of this note, except for one facet of it which does have a bearing on the construction of the budget. Each year before Congressional testimony starts, the Director of the Budget reissues a letter to the heads of all the agencies. While the

---

[18] The adjustments that convert Total Obligational Authority *into* New Obligational Authority, the $79.6 billion mentioned at the beginning of this note, are too complicated to describe here.

details change from year to year, the letter reminds agency heads that they are representatives of the Executive Branch, and that it is the agency head's responsibility to defend the President's budget regardless of personal views. This is an essential policy, but it can work only if agency heads can, in good conscience, defend the President's budget. Thus, throughout the budget process, great care must be taken to insure that the final budget is one that key officials in the organization can "live with." It is invariably smaller than they requested, but it is not so small as to be indefensible. An agency head who felt the budget indefensible would be expected to resign.

Conclusion

This description of how the budget process actually worked for FY1969 does not quite correspond to the way that the textbooks say it works, nor indeed is it quite the same as it was supposed to work. This is, of course, the case with all management processes.

It would be incorrect to conclude that the budget was the result of a completely scientific, rational analysis. It would be equally incorrect to conclude that the budget was a slap-dash set of numbers that had no analytical underpinnings. The correct impression is somewhere in between. Much of the budget is based on sound analysis of data, and the people who make these analyses, both in OSD and in the Services, are among the most highly skilled and hardest working in the government. But for many of the issues, the data are simply not solid enough to permit a good analysis, and these decisions depend on judgment and on a process of negotiation. This may be unscientific, but it is the way life is.

BIBLIOGRAPHY

Burkhead, Jesse. *Government Budgeting.* New York: Wiley, 1966.

Chamberlain, Neil W. *The Firm: Micro-Economic Planning and Action.* New York: McGraw-Hill, 1962.

Heiser, Herman C. *Budgeting, Principles and Practices.* New York: Ronald Press, 1959.

Hofstede, D. H. *The Game of Budget Control.* Assen, The Netherlands: Van Gorcum & Co., NV., 1967.

Steiner, George A., ed. *Top Management Planning.* New York: Macmillan, 1969.

Welsch, Glenn A. *Budgeting: Profit Planning and Control,* 2d ed. New York: Prentice-Hall, 1963.

Wildavsky, Aaron. *The Politics of the Budgeting Process.* Toronto: Little, Brown & Co., 1964.

chapter eleven

Operating
and Accounting

This chapter discusses the operating phase of the management control process. In the operating phase things actually happen: work actually gets done, resources are used, outputs are generated. We describe information that is collected about these activities and the use of information, particularly accounting information, to control spending for these activities. Since many nonprofit organizations use a special kind of accounting, called fund accounting, we describe those aspects of fund accounting that are of interest to managers.

DISSEMINATION OF INFORMATION

A manager, at any level in the organization, needs two types of information. They can be called, respectively, environmental information and internal information.

ENVIRONMENTAL INFORMATION

Environmental (or exogenous) information is data about what is happening in the environment in which a responsibility center operates. In this context, "environment" includes not only the outside world, but also the larger organization of which the unit is a part. The manager needs this information so as to have a basis for reassessing plans and for making decisions on alternative courses of action.

More environmental information exists than any person can possibly assimilate. It is therefore essential that there be some way of deciding what information is important and of making sure that this information comes to management's attention. An important concept in this respect is that of the *key variable*. A key variable is a datum, which, if changed unexpectedly, can have important consequences for the organization. In most organizations, there are perhaps a dozen or so environmental variables that must be watched regularly, and which raise a danger signal if they behave in an unexpected way. The time span between the occurrence of the expected change and the need for action varies widely. It may be very short (a catastrophe requiring the immediate mobilization of emergency room facilities in a hospital), or very long (an upward trend in drug addiction, noticeable only over a period of years, which requires a reassessment of control and treatment plans). In general, however, key variables need to be reported daily, weekly, or monthly, that is, at fairly frequent intervals.

In addition to variables that are known to be important, the system should provide for a process called "scanning," that is, looking over the environment to ascertain whether some important unanticipated force is at work.[1] By its very nature, this process cannot be routinized. Indeed, it is important that the reporting structure not be made so routine that the flow of this type of information is inhibited. The manager picks up much of this type of information from conversations on the general subject: What's new? In large organizations, internal bulletins or newspapers help to convey this information. The contrast between a daily newspaper, whose editor prints what she or he believes is important that day, and a statistical table or graph with a prescribed format that is updated periodically, is a good way of describing the difference between "scanning" information and regularly reported environmental information. Both are important.

Flow of Environmental Information

Many problems arise in attempting to provide the operating managers with the information needed to do their tasks. With the advent of the computer, one obvious problem is overcoming the temptation to provide too much information. Hoos describes several of the many horror stories that abound in the literature and in folklore: (1) A high school in Sacramento, California, has a computerized attendance system, installed at a cost of $100,000 which electronically transmits to the accounting office the attendance of each pupil in each class period. One full-time person is required to operate the system. It provides instantaneous data, but data that no one needs instantaneously.[2] (2) The Bay Area Transportation Study Commission collected information about the movement

---

[1] For a more complete description, *see* Francis J. Aguilar, *Scanning the Business Environment* (New York: Macmillan, 1967).

[2] Ida Hoos, *Systems Analysis in Public Policy,* p. 153.

of people in the San Francisco Bay Area at a cost of $3,000,000 and stored it on 1,100 reels of magnetic tape. The quantity of raw data was so great that no one was able to digest and analyze it.[3]

Less well publicized is the opposite problem, that of the need to provide enough information. In most organizations, particularly large organizations, relevant information exists without the knowledge of all those to whom it would be helpful.

> *Example:* In 1972 the United States government negotiated the sale of a large quantity of wheat to the Soviet Union. In retrospect, it appears that the quantity sold was too high and the price was too low because the negotiators in the Department of Agriculture were not aware that there was going to be a shortage of wheat, both in the United States and world wide. The Department of Agriculture has a large staff of professional economists, and this staff had full knowledge of the impending shortage. The simple, but difficult to explain, fact is that this knowledge did not flow from the economists to the negotiators.

There is no perfect solution to the problem of making everyone aware of all the information that is available in a large organization because the quantity is so vast that no person and no computer program can identify all of it. If one unit, such as the controller's office, is given the responsibility for the collection and dissemination of all information, the problem is mitigated.

The flow of information may be impeded by the reluctance of some managers to disclose freely all the information they have. They operate on the premise that "knowledge is power," and believe that sharing knowledge may dilute power. Dumont, who was an employee of the Department of Health, Education and Welfare, describes this tendency in language which is perhaps overstated but which has an element of truth:

> Power in government resides less in position and funds than it does in information, which is the medium of exchange. The flow of information is controlled, not at the top, but at the middle. There is very little horizontal flow between agencies because of the constant competition for funds, and all vertical flow must be mediated by the GS 14 to GS 17 bureaucrats who make up the permanent government. This concentration of power in the middle is the reason why the national government is essentially unresponsive. It does not respond to the top or the bottom; it does not respond to ideology. It is a great, indestructible mollusk that absorbs kicks and taunts and seductions and does nothing but grow.[4]

---

[3] Ibid., pp. 200, 201.

[4] Matthew P. Dumont, "Down the Bureaucracy!" *Trans-Action,* vol. 7 (October 1970), pp. 10–14.

INTERNAL INFORMATION

Information about the performance of the manager's own responsibility center can take many forms, but the most important usually is a comparison of budgeted outputs and costs with actual outputs and costs; that is, a comparison between what was planned and what actually happened. This information should be structured so that it helps to answer the questions: (1) In what significant respects did actual performance differ from planned performance, both for outputs and for inputs? (2) Why did this happen? (3) Who was responsible? (4) Is corrective action necessary? The first question can be answered numerically. The second question usually requires a written or oral comment on the numbers. The third question can be answered if the budget and related actual data are structured in terms of areas of responsibility. The fourth question probably cannot be answered until the manager has had a conversation with the responsible supervisor.

In addition to information that is directly related to the budget, operating managers need much other information about what is going on in their organizations. Important sources of such information are their own eyes and ears (and in some circumstances, their noses). Personal observation can often reveal matters of more significance than those described in numbers or written reports. A method of insuring that information on complaints from clients and grievances from employees are brought to the manager's attention is also important.

The Accounting System

The central part of the system for reporting internal operating information is an accounting system. It is central because accounting deals with monetary amounts, and money provides the best way of aggregating and summarizing information about the heterogeneous elements of input. (It does not follow that the most *important* information is accounting information.) A few comments about the accounting system are appropriate here.

In the first place, the accounting system should be a double entry system. A sentence like the preceding would never appear in a description of the accounting system of a profit-oriented company because double-entry accounting is taken for granted in these companies. Some nonprofit organizations, however, including some very large government organizations, collect important types of information in single entry systems. Information collected in a single entry system is not likely to be reliable. Technically, it is a simple matter to convert such systems to double entry.

A second important point to make about an accounting system is that it should be consistent with the budget. This is the case with ac-

counting systems in most profit-oriented companies. The budget states
the approved plan for spending. The accounting system should report
actual spending. Unless the two are consistent, there is no reliable way
of finding out whether actual spending occurred according to plan. This
does not mean that the accounting system should contain only the accounts that appear in the budget. Management usually needs more accounting detail than is suggested by the budget items, and it needs
rearrangements of the basic data for various purposes. Nevertheless,
there should be, as a part of the accounting system, accounts that match
each item on the budget.

The usual reason an accounting system does not match the budget
is that the budgeting system has been revised but the accounting system
has not been revised to match it. This is often the case in organizations
which have recently adopted program budgets. The task of designing
a program budgeting system is difficult by itself, but the task of revising
an accounting system is much more difficult—perhaps by a factor of
10 or even 100. It is not surprising, therefore, that the revision of the
accounting system has not kept pace with the revision of budgeting.
Nevertheless, until the accounting system has been revised to match
the budget, the management control process is less satisfactory than
it should be.

Integrated Systems.   Not only should the budget and accounting
data be consistent, but it is desirable that the accounting system be
an integral part of a total information system. Achievement of such
integration is a difficult task, but some organizations are succeeding
in it. The federal government, through its Federal Urban Information
Systems Interagency Committee Program, has been encouraging municipalities to develop such integrated systems, and has provided substantial
sums for this purpose. Such an integrated system includes budget and
accounting information and also information on demography, physical
and economic development programs, and public safety. Accounting
data on costs are integrated with output data throughout the system.

Internal Auditing and Control

The control system should contain its own controls, and there should
be an internal audit staff to insure that these controls are effective.
These controls have three general purposes: (1) to minimize the possibility of loss by theft, fraud, or defalcation; (2) to insure that rules
governing the receipt and spending of money and the use of other resources are adhered to; and (3) to insure that the information flowing
through the system is accurate. Some organizations, including many
state and municipal governments do not have even minimal controls,
as indicated by the fairly frequent newspaper exposés of contracts being
let in an unauthorized manner, persons who are on the payroll but

who do not actually work, or welfare payments being made to persons not entitled to receive them.

Internal controls are not perfect, nor can they be. Their limitations are well described in these standard paragraphs which appear in reports prepared by independent auditors who have been engaged to examine the adequacy of an agency's internal control system:

> The objective of internal accounting control is to provide reasonable, but not absolute, assurance as to the safeguarding of assets against loss from unauthorized use or disposition, and the reliability of financial records for preparing financial statements and maintaining accountability for assets. The concept of reasonable assurance recognizes that the cost of a system of internal control should not exceed the benefits derived and also recognizes that the evaluation of these factors necessarily requires estimates and judgments by management.
>
> There are inherent limitations that should be recognized in considering the potential effectiveness of any system of internal control. In the performance of most control procedures, errors can result from misunderstanding of instructions, mistakes of judgment, carelessness, or other personal factors. Control procedures whose effectiveness depends upon segregation of duties can be circumvented by collusion. Similarly, control procedures can be circumvented intentionally by management with respect either to the execution and recording of transactions or with respect to the estimates and judgments required in the preparation of financial statements. Further, projection of any evaluation of internal control to future periods is subject to the risk that the procedures may become inadequate because of changes in conditions, and that the degree of compliance with the procedures may deteriorate.[5]

In recent years there has been a shift in the focus of internal auditing away from the practice of having the auditor check individual transactions and toward a system that is designed to be largely self-checking. For example, the U.S. General Accounting Office at one time examined each voucher generated in the federal government; today it examines only a few highly unusual transactions. The function of the modern auditor is to see that the system is well designed and to test that it is functioning properly. In a small organization, this function can be performed by an outside accounting firm; a larger organization has its own specialists for this purpose.

Incorrect Charges

Many nonprofit organizations spend considerable effort in assuring that the rules are obeyed precisely (for example, they check each travel voucher to insure that per-diem calculations are accurate and that mile-

---

[5] Committee on Auditing Procedures of the American Institute of Certified Public Accountants, 1973.

ages between points are correctly stated), and they also have voucher systems, locked petty cash boxes, and other devices that inhibit the obvious possibilities for theft. At the same time, they may pay little attention to procedures for assuring the *accuracy* of information.

Some systems which are adequate in other respects do not have safeguards against charging costs to the wrong accounts, that is, to projects or other items that do not correspond to those for which the costs were actually incurred. Such practices even may be winked at by senior officials in some organizations. If the amounts charged to accounts are used as a basis for reimbursement by a client, as is often the case, deliberate mischarging can amount to culpable dishonesty. The situation is even more flagrant when the persons responsible sign their name to a certificate that states that the costs are correctly recorded, knowing full well that they are not. In addition to the illegality of this practice, one obvious consequence is that the recorded data are inaccurate, and reports derived from such data may give management an incorrect impression about current performance and provide a misleading basis for making future plans. Internal auditors generally should pay more attention to the prevention and detection of this type of inaccuracy than they typically do.

An interesting ethical question arises when the rules under which an agency is forced to operate are such that effective and efficient operations are inhibited. Should managers get the job done and cover up the fact that to do the job they had to break rules, or should they use the existence of the rule as an excuse for not getting the job done? Managers with different temperaments answer this question in different ways.

> *Example:* In a certain state the legislature has set maximum rates at which part-time psychiatrists can be employed by state mental health institutions. These rates are about ½ the going rate for psychiatrists, so if these rates were offered, psychiatrists would not work for the state. Administrators therefore hire psychiatrists for half a day and pay them for a full day. This is the only way they can hire psychiatrists. On balance, have they done wrong? Whether or not they have done wrong, it is a fact that the records show that twice as many psychiatrist workhours were provided as actually was the case.

FUND ACCOUNTING

Most nonprofit organizations use a system of accounting that is called fund accounting. This differs from the type of accounting used by business organizations in several respects. Many of these differences are technical and are of interest primarily to the accountants. We discuss here some aspects of fund accounting that are of interest to managers.

A fund is a separate accounting entity, with a self balancing set of accounts. In nonprofit organizations, there are several funds, and therefore several sets of accounts, and this is a major difference between fund accounting and business accounting. In a business, the whole corporation is a single accounting entity, and it has a single set of accounts for all its financial activities. Of the several types of funds, we are here particularly interested in *operating* funds (also called *general* funds). These are the accounts used for general operating activities.

Operating Funds

In government organizations, and in some other nonprofit organizations, accounting for operations requires additional steps that are not found at all in a business accounting system. First, when an appropriation is enacted by the legislature or approved by a governing body, an accounting entry is made to record this fact. Second, when contracts are entered into, a charge is made against this appropriated amount; this is called an *encumbrance* in state and municipal accounting and an *obligation* in federal accounting. For example, if the legislature appropriates $1,000,000 for operations in 1975, this amount is set up in the accounts, and this amount is reduced as contracts are entered into, so the accounts show at all times how much of the $1,000,000 has not yet been encumbered or obligated. Usually, there is a legal prohibition against obligating more than the amount appropriated.

When goods or services are received, the accounts record this fact. This is the initial time at which a transaction is recorded in business accounts, the entry being a credit to accounts payable or cash and a debit to an asset or expense account. From this point on, the accounting process can be the same in a nonprofit organization as in a business. (As pointed out in Chapter 6, however, many nonprofit organizations have not yet adopted accrual accounting, which is an essential characteristic of business accounting.)

The purpose of these additional steps in fund accounting is to provide a strict control over spending. In order to achieve this control, some organizations require that all proposed purchases clear through the accounting organization, which must certify that unobligated funds are available; this of course slows down the purchasing process.

As a practical matter, fund accounting does not guarantee that spending will be held to amounts appropriated. In the federal government, everyone involved in making financial commitments is well aware that Section 3679, RS, requires, as a minimum, repayment of the amount involved from any person who overobligates, and threatens a jail sentence in addition. Nevertheless, no one, so far as we know, has gone to jail, and there are only a few dozen repayments, of a few dollars each, in the typical year. Small errors can be handled in various ways by juggling the accounts; large errors are often admitted, with the knowl-edge that the perpetrator cannot possibly make restitution. For example, in 1972 the U.S. Navy overobligated its military personnel appropriation by $130 million,[6] but no one went to jail and, obviously, no individual paid back the $130 million.

Number of Funds. In the early 20th century, it was common practice for nonprofit organizations to operate with a large number of operating funds, each fund restricted to a narrow purpose. This practice is still followed in some municipalities and state governments. Such a tight, detailed control over spending was a reaction to widespread government corruption in the 19th century. Currently, the trend is to have fewer funds and to exercise control through other devices. Most activities of the entire federal government, for example, operate with a single government-wide General Fund. It is usually desirable that all the operating activities of an agency be financed with a single fund; the alternative of having separate funds for each department or other organization unit within the agency is unnecessarily cumbersome.

When an agency receives financial support from several sources, it sometimes creates a separate fund for each of these sources. This can impede effective control since it may lead to an artificial segregation of the agency's costs. A preferable practice is to have a single fund for all operating costs, with amounts spent for the various purposes intended by the separate grantors being identified by the detailed account structure within the fund. The manager should be held responsible for the overall performance of the responsibility center, but the overall picture can be obscured if the costs of operation are fragmented among the several sources from which resources were obtained.

Appropriations

Although the Federal government operates with a government-wide general fund, spending of individual agencies is restricted by the existence of separate appropriations. In the early 20th century there were hundreds of these appropriations, but the number has been greatly reduced in recent years. Although there are technical differences between an appropriation and a fund, their practical effect is the same; that is, both of them impose a limit on the amount of money which can be spent for a specified purpose. Fewer and broader appropriations are desirable for the same reason that fewer and broader funds are desirable; that is, they lessen the rigidity which can hamper the exercise of appropriate management discretion. The terminology used in connection with the federal appropriation process is described in the Appendix.

---

[6] *New York Times* (January 8, 1973), p. 1., reporting on a report filed by the Navy with the House Appropriations Committee.

Grants

Similar problems arise when an organization operates on grants received from several agencies. In order to minimize these problems, and still assure adequate control, the grantor may prescribe the accounting principles, the internal control principles, the program elements, and the overall expense elements that will govern the accounting system that is to be used by the grantee, but the grantee should be encouraged to develop the details of the system consistent with these general principles and summary elements.

If several grantors finance an agency, the accounting system should nevertheless show the total expenses of the agency. If feasible, one grantor should prescribe the principle of the total system, on behalf of all of them. Chaos can result if each grantor prescribes a separate system applying to each grant. In particular, costs of operating a given activity should not be divided among several funding sources in a way that permits the total costs of important functions to be fragmented. If an administrative office is financed from two grants, and the system is set up in such a way that part of the costs of the office are charged to each grant, it is difficult for management, or for either grantor, to control the total costs of the office. Preferable practices are either to have one grantor finance all the administrative costs, or to require an accounting for all administrative costs under one of the grants with the amount furnished by the other grantor shown as a revenue item, rather than as a reduction in costs.

The accounting system therefore should reflect both the total expenses of activities of the organization, and the amounts spent on the programs financed by each grant, but it should do this in a way that facilitates the analysis of the total cost of operations.

Single System Desirable

In some organizations, a system for fund accounting is maintained separately from the system for management accounting; this is highly undesirable. If there is a separate management accounting subsystem that is inconsistent with the fund accounting subsystem, operating managers will be heavily influenced by the fund accounting subsystem since it represents "where the money comes from," and they are not likely to pay much attention to information from the management accounting subsystem.

This situation arises when the legislature or other governing body prescribes a fund accounting system that is not useful for management purposes; management is therefore forced to set up a separate system for its own needs. Occasionally, it is possible to do the required fund accounting in some central location, and thereby keep the operating organization from being influenced by the fund data. Usually, however, such a segregation is not feasible. In these circumstances, good management control is difficult, especially when the fund accounting system does not use accrual accounting and when costs cannot be related to personal responsibility.

Other Funds

In addition to a fund for operations, nonprofit agencies use a number of other funds. The funds recommended by the Municipal Finance Officers Association are as follows:

1. The General Fund to account for all financial transactions not properly accounted for in another fund;
2. Special Revenue Funds to account for the proceeds of specific revenue sources (other than special assessments) or to finance specified activities as required by law or administrative regulation;
3. Debt Service Funds to account for the payment of interest and principal on long-term debt other than special assessment and revenue bonds;
4. Capital Projects Funds to account for the receipt and disbursement of monies used for the acquisition of capital facilities other than those financed by special assessment and enterprise funds;
5. Enterprise Funds to account for the financing of services to the general public where all or most of the costs involved are paid in the form of charges by users of such services;
6. Trust and Agency Funds to account for assets held by a governmental unit as trustee or agent for individuals, private organizations, and other governmental units;
7. Intragovernmental Service Funds to account for the financing of special activities and services performed by a designated organizational unit within a governmental jurisdiction for other organization units within the same government jurisdiction;
8. Special Assessment Funds to account for special assessments levied to finance public improvements or services deemed to benefit the properties against which the assessments are levied.[7]

Similar lists of funds and their intended use are described by *Audit Guides* issued by the American Institute of Certified Public Accountants for hospitals, for colleges and universities, and for voluntary health and welfare organizations.[8]

---

[7] National Committee on Governmental Accounting, *Governmental Accounting, Auditing, and Financial Reporting* (Chicago: Municipal Finance Officers Association, 1968), pp. 7–8.

[8] These publications are listed in the bibliography with Chapter 5.

There are good reasons for having the fund for operating activities separate from funds for capital investments, and there are also good arguments for having separate funds for the principal of endowments, for grants that the agency passes along to others, for working capital, for the amortization of bond issues, and for other special purposes. It is often possible to accomplish the desired control over spending by devices other than the fund, however, so the case for these separate funds is not open and shut.

FINANCIAL CONTROL OVER SPENDING

The approved operating budget, consisting both of planned expenses and expected outputs, is the guideline for operations. Presumably, management wants the organization to operate in a way that is consistent with this plan, *unless* there is a good reason to depart from it. This qualification is important, for it means that the control process is necessarily more complicated than simply insisting that the organization do what the budget prescribes. The purpose of the management control process is to assure that objectives are accomplished effectively and efficiently. If, because of changed conditions, a different course of action than is contained in the budget will do a better job of attaining objectives, that course of action should be followed. Thus, the control mechanism should have two aspects: (1) It should assure that in the absence of reasons to do otherwise the plan set forth in the budget is adhered to, and (2) it should provide a way of changing the plan if conditions warrant.

Types of Control

The total amount in the approved budget is ordinarily a ceiling that is not supposed to be exceeded; indeed, if there is an appropriation mechanism, it is a ceiling that legally cannot be exceeded. Within this total, more detailed controls are sometimes desirable. These usually take the form of detailed ceilings, but in some cases they are floors.

> *Example:* In 1974 the Congress required the National Science Foundation to spend *not more than* $5 million for construction of a very large array telescope, and *no less than* $25 million on energy research.

Although the budget may contain a detailed listing of amounts for expense elements or object classes, these amounts are normally guides, rather than ceilings which cannot be exceeded. The primary focus should be on the program and on the responsibility center that is charged with executing the program, rather than on what specific resources are to be used. Some years ago, control systems focused instead on individual line items of expense, that is, so much for personnel, so much for supplies, so much for travel, etc. The shift from this "line-item control" to program control is one of the most significant developments in recent years.

The shift, however, should be one of emphasis, for it is desirable that control be exercised over spending for certain line items, even though the primary focus is on programs. A line-item restriction means that operating managers are not given complete freedom to decide the best way to use resources in executing their program. Such restrictions are often for their own protection. If there is a restriction on the amount that can be spent for attendance at conferences, managers have a persuasive answer to requests that professionals tend to make with great frequency. They can simply say, "We don't have the conference money." Without a line-item restriction, it may be difficult to turn down such requests. There is a delicate balance between the restrictions that are desirable in order to curb imprudent spending, and the restrictions that are undesirable because they unduly curb the manager's ability to make decisions on how best to use available resources. Although in older systems the restrictions were much too numerous, there is a danger that over-reaction may result in too strong a swing in the other direction.

One common restriction is on the number of personnel. In most service organizations, personnel not only constitute by far the largest item of direct expense, but also indirectly cause most of the other items of expense. (One additional person requires an additional desk, additional supplies, additional travel, and so on.) Further, if a person is added to the organization, there tends to be a permanent increase in its costs, for it is much easier to increase the size of an organization than to shrink it. Personnel additions therefore need to be carefully monitored. In some situations, the most effective way to do this is with a personnel ceiling. In other situations, as was pointed out in Chapter 5, such a ceiling may unduly restrict management flexibility; it may lead to the wrong mix between personnel costs and costs for contractual services, for example.

Flow of Funding Authority

The flow of funding authority within an organization should generally follow the lines of operating management responsibility; that is, funds should be authorized from higher levels to lower levels according to the formal organizational hierarchy. Difficulties arise when funds are received from sources other than clients or higher authority in the organizational hierarchy. If it does not control the distribution of spending authority, the superior organization often cannot exercise appropriate control over its subordinate elements because it does not have "the power of the purse."

Examples: 1. Some university professors have direct access to external funding sources for research projects. They may operate therefore quite independently of the university, and in a way that is not consistent with top management's plans for the university as a whole; under these circumstances, management control is difficult.

2. In New York City, mental health services are provided to the public on a contractual basis by private institutions. These institutions are supposed to be accountable to the City's Department of Mental Health; however, funds for the operation of these institutions are provided directly by the State, and the institutions therefore tend to disregard the City agency. Conversely, New York City pays the cost of operating the judicial system, but there is no mechanism by which the city can exercise control over the spending of these funds.

If funds are received from staff agencies rather than through the line organization, the staff units tend to have an undue influence on operating management. In the Navy, prior to 1968, staff units (called "Bureaus") had too much power and the Chief of Naval Operations had too little power because the Bureaus controlled most of the funds.

Further, if funds are received from several separate sources rather than through the chain of command, the head of an operating organization is inhibited from making good decisions on the best use of operating resources because the separate funds are compartmentalized. In the Navy, ships have been known to steam on unneeded missions, even though they lacked vital parts for radar, because they had ample funds for fuel, but no funds for radar parts. The overall effectiveness of the ship would have been enhanced if it had spent less money on steaming and had spent an equivalent amount of money to repair its radar.

Also, if there are several funding sources, an operating organization can play one funding source against another. For example, although top management may desire that the overall level of spending be reduced, the operating manager can sometimes defeat this desire by finding one source, among the several available, which provides additional funds.

Finally, if funds are received from several sources, measurement of performance is difficult because each funding source tends to focus on the aspect of operations in which it is interested, but no one may focus on the operation as a whole.

BUDGET REVISIONS AND CONTINGENCY ALLOWANCES

In many nonprofit organizations, the total of the budget for a year constitutes an absolute ceiling which cannot be exceeded except under highly unusual circumstances. Nevertheless, changed circumstances will usually require changes in detailed spending requirements. There is therefore the problem of accommodating these detailed changes within the prescribed ceiling.

There are two general techniques for solving this problem: contingency allowances, and revisions. The choice between them is a matter of personal preference.

Contingency Allowances

In this approach, amounts are set aside at various levels in the organization for unforeseen contingencies. Ordinarily, such amounts are not more than 5 percent of the budget for that level, but if these allowances exist at a number of levels, they can cumulate to considerably more than 5 percent of the total budget for the agency. Under this plan, the budgeted expenses for each responsibility center and program are targets which can be exceeded, if necessary, with the excess being absorbed by the contingency allowance.

An advantage of this approach is that increases in spending can be accommodated without the painful task of finding an offsetting decrease. In this approach, also, the managers who authorize use of the allowance have additional political power over those who must obtain their approval before they can use the funds.

A risk in this approach is that if there is a 5 percent contingency allowance, there may be a tendency to regard the actual ceiling as 105 percent of the target in all responsibility centers, thus defeating the purpose of the contingency allowances.

A variation of the contingency allowance is the practice of releasing somewhat less than the proportionate amount of funds in the early part of the year. For example, in an agency whose spending is expected to be spread evenly throughout the year, only 22 percent of the funds, rather than 25 percent, might be released in the first quarter. As the year progresses, and spending needs become clearer, the contingency allowance thus created is allocated in subsequent releases to those responsibility centers that appear to need it the most.

Revision Procedure

In the second approach, 100 percent of the authorized amount is divided among responsibility centers. Changed circumstances are accommodated by increasing the budget of one responsibility center and making a corresponding reduction in the budget of some other responsibility center(s). Under this plan the budget for each responsibility center is a ceiling; it cannot be exceeded without specific approval.

Although not an authorized practice in the second approach, operating managers nevertheless tend to create an informal contingency allowance (called a *kitty*) so as to avoid the necessity of seeking formal approval for changed spending needs. Thus, allowances exist in both approaches, even though they are not visible in the second plan.

An advantage of the second approach is that at any moment of time the budget states current plans as to how *all* the organization's funds are to be spent.

Whichever approach is used, it is important to recognize the likelihood that changes will be necessary, and that the mechanism for making these changes be well understood. Otherwise, the budget may not conform to the realities of the situation. It will then not serve as a reliable plan against which actual performance can be measured.

Another problem arises when no good mechanism for revising the budget exists. Operating managers do want to get the job done, and if the need is great enough, they will do the job even if the system tells them that no funds are available for this purpose. They simply will charge the costs of the job to some other account in which funds are available. When this happens, the record of actual spending becomes inaccurate.

BEHAVIORAL CONSIDERATIONS

Thus far, we have described technical aspects of the system for controlling operations. These matters are important, but they are far less important than the attitudes of those who use the information that the system produces and those who are affected by this information.

Top Management Involvement

A management control system is likely to be ineffective unless members of the organization's units perceive that it is considered important by their superiors. This requires that the top manager use the system in decision making, in appraising the results of performance, and as a basis for salary adjustments, promotions and other personnel actions. In particular, it requires that superiors at all levels hold periodic meetings with subordinates during which the results of operations are discussed.

Balance between Freedom and Restraint

In any organization, profit or nonprofit, the right balance has to be struck between (*a*) the need for *freedom* in order to take advantage of the ability and knowledge of the person on the firing line, to motivate that person, and to reduce paperwork and (*b*) the need for *restraint,* in order to insure that management policies are followed, and to reduce the effect of poor judgments or self-interest decisions by lower level managers. In nonprofit organizations, because of the absence of profit as an overall basis for measuring performance, there probably should be somewhat less freedom and somewhat more restraint than in a profit-oriented organization.

This is, however, a matter of degree. Many nonprofit organizations, particularly government organizations, impose far too many and too detailed restraints on first-line managers. Sometimes this is caused by the *goldfish bowl* problem. Errors are likely to be played up in the newspapers, and as a protective device top managers prescribe rules, which they can point to when errors come to light: "I am not to blame; he (the sinner) broke my rule." The detailed restraints also result from *encrustation*. A sin is committed, and a rule is promulgated to avoid that sin in the future; but the rules continue even after the need for them has disappeared. No one considers whether the likelihood and seriousness of error is great enough to warrant continuation of the rule.

Motivation

A central purpose of any control system is to motivate operating managers to take actions that help accomplish the organization's objectives efficiently and effectively. The problem of inducing the desired degree and direction of motivation is a difficult one in any organization, but it is particularly difficult in a nonprofit organization.

In any organization, individuals have a series of goals. Some of these goals relate to the overall goals of the organization, but others relate to the career goals of the individuals and the groups that they compose. In a school system, for example, all groups are interested in better education, but teachers as individuals also are concerned with salary, educational advancement and professional status. To make an organization effective and efficient, managers must create the highest possible correspondence between the interests of the individuals and those of the organization. Divergent goals and objectives of individuals should be considered, and to the extent possible reconciled with the goals of the organization.

The Problem of Budget Conformance

The fact that performance in a nonprofit organization is measured in part by how well managers conform to their budget can result in a dysfunctional situation. Suppose a manager has a $1,000,000 budget, and by careful, hard work, performs the required job, and does it by spending only $990,000. In many organizations, the budget for the following year, other things equal, will be $990,000. The manager is punished, rather than rewarded, for reducing costs, for now there is less money to work with than would have been the case if the entire $1,000,000 had been spent. The same attitude, at a higher organizational level, is reflected in this comment in a letter dated January 30, 1970, from the Massachusetts Department of Education to local school superintendents and Title 1 directors:

It is difficult to make the case for increased funding of Title 1 when school districts in Massachusetts allowed the following amounts to remain unused each fiscal year:

FY 66 ...... $1,093,364
FY 67 1,027,243
FY 68 655,839

During this same period Massachusetts Title 1 allocations were $10.8, 14.9, and 15.1 million respectively.

The typical attitude toward budgets is that it is almost sinful not to spend the full amount that is available, as indicated in the following:

Beetle Bailey

It is a difficult matter to create the right attitude in these circumstances. One possibility is to guarantee the manager that if the job can be done at less than the amount budgeted, the budget will not be reduced for the current year and the succeeding year. In order to make this policy work, the definition of operating expenses may be expanded to include minor capital expenditures, for it is on items of this type that the manager will wish to spend the "extra" money. (In government, however, the person who makes such a guarantee may not be in the same job two years hence, and thus may not be able to make good on it.)

On the other hand, such a policy can negate the benefits obtained in reducing costs. Why should a manager be motivated to reduce costs if these savings are not actually realized? Thus, an alternative course of action is to convince operating managers that a budget reduction, *per se*, should not be viewed as a punishment and that there is top management emphasis on recognizing and rewarding cost reduction. A manager is rewarded by a combination of promotion, salary, and the respect of peers, superiors, and subordinates. If top management stresses the importance of cost reduction and rewards, there need not be a negative reaction to reducing the budget.

An alternative device is to release to managers substantially less (say 20 percent less) funds than they probably need. They know that additional funds are available, but they can never be sure of getting them. This may make them more than ordinarily careful in spending available funds. However, this practice may risk stifling their initiative and may result in a reluctance to introduce new programs or in an undermaintenance of existing facilities.

Monetary Incentives. Profit-oriented organizations often make cash payments when savings are realized or profits are high, but a nonprofit organization is not able to do this to the same extent. It can nevertheless take steps in this direction. For example, for cost-saving ideas some federal ˙government organizations pay incentive awards that often are as high as $1,000, and which can amount to as much as $25,000 to one person. However, when the manager of direct mission departments (e.g., Deans of faculty, chiefs of hospital services) do not have opportunities to receive incentive compensation, it is dangerous to provide a significant amount of incentive compensation to the heads of support services. A bonus based on cost performance in the support service may stir up animosity in the mission departments.

Cost-Reduction Programs. Another motivating device is a cost-reduction program, as described in Chapter 9. If properly designed, such a program takes advantage of the knowledge of possible improvements that usually exist in the lower levels of an organization. Possible difficulties should be foreseen. For instance, a suggestion by an employee that a colleague's job should be abolished can be regarded by the supervisor as a personal criticism; it implies that the supervisor should have foreseen this possibility. Also, in a cost reduction program there is a tendency to hold back some ideas for next year so that there will be constant evidence of effort.

In any event, without some incentive, managers are not motivated to reduce costs. Indeed, managers who can successfully negotiate a larger budget expand the scope of their efforts, and this may be viewed favorably and even rewarded by promotion.

Incentives Related to Output. An alternative to reducing a budget is to hold the budget constant and to expect managers to accomplish more work than last year with the same amount of resources. This increases efficiency just as much as a policy of expecting the same amount of work to be done with fewer resources. This approach assumes that there is a genuine need for the organizational unit to accomplish more work. The creation of additional tasks for the same amount of resources is a wasteful way to achieve a higher output/input ratio.

The Special Problem of Government Organizations. As indicated in Chapter 3, Civil Service personnel policies and practices in government organizations are often viewed as inhibiting effective management control. The view is often exaggerated, for with good management many of the evils attributed to Civil Service need not exist. Moreover, there can be no question that detailed rules are necessary in government organizations, not only as a protection against political favoritism, but also as a means of assuring the uniform implementation of policy decisions that is essential in any large organization. Nevertheless, good managers are sometimes frustrated with Civil Service rules, especially those that inhibit the managers' ability to promote and reassign personnel according to their perception of merits. Under some circumstances, managers can bend the rules so as to reward outstanding performance with out-of-step promotions or in other ways.

> *Example:* When a noted urban renewal director became manager of the Boston Redevelopment Authority, he created a new classification for Civil Service employees: temporary employee. Whenever possible, personnel were hired on only a "temporary" basis (although temporary could last for five or ten years) so that some of the disadvantages of the Civil Service could be avoided. Further, he was able to generate the necessary excitement and salary scales in order to attract a particularly fine group of people to work with him.

The implementation of "out-of-step promotion" policies and "incentive" pay scales pose significant problems, however. Such measures are likely to be viewed as threats by the existing organization. Political leaders may be unwilling to institute such programs over the opposition of the existing organization. The best hope for implementation is either in a new organization or in an old organization facing disaster. An attempt at implementation of an incentive system should be coupled with a carefully planned system of increasing rewards to existing personnel so that during the early years no group receives less than it would have received under the old system.

appendix

Federal Government
Terminology and Entries

The terminology used in federal government budgeting and accounting has a highly specialized meaning. The principal terms are here stated in chronological order, that is, in the order in which the events take place. The relationship among them is also indicated in Exhibit 11–1, using data from the 1975 Budget.

The first legislative step in the process is the enactment of *Authorization* legislation, which authorizes the executive branch to carry out specified programs. Authorization legislation is not permission to spend money. Such permission comes only from an *appropriation* act, which is ordinarily enacted after the passage of the authorization act.

An appropriation authorizes an agency to incur *obligations* (also called *budget authorities*). An obligation arises when the agency takes action that legally requires the payment of money either immediately or in the future. The transaction creating an obligation is similar to, but not identical, with the creation of accounts payable in a private business. It differs in that in the government, an obligation is created when a contract is signed, whereas in a business the liability is created when services are performed or when the business takes title to goods. Thus, if in Fiscal Year (FY) 1973, an agency signs a contract to have some buildings painted, this creates an obligation in FY 1975, even though the work may not be done until FY 1976.

Appropriations are either current or permanent. A *current* appropriation is one that is enacted each year. Most of them state a dollar amount, but in a few cases, the appropriation act states only a formula from which the amount appropriated is subsequently calculated. A *permanent*

292

EXHIBIT 11-1
Relation of Budget Authority to Outlays—1973 Budget
Figures in brackets represent Federal funds only.

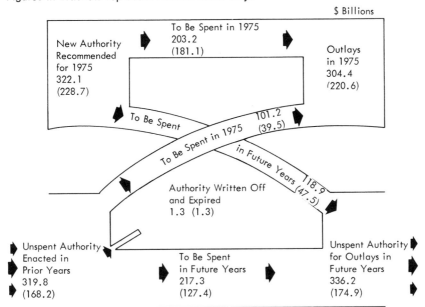

Note: The difference between the total budget figures and federal funds shown in brackets consists of trust funds and interfund transactions between fund groups.

appropriation provides for funds to become available each year, without the enactment of a new appropriation act.

An appropriation may be either annual, multiple-year, or no-year. In an *annual* appropriation, the authority to obligate expires at the end of the fiscal year. Annual appropriations are used for most operating programs. A *multiple-year* appropriation is available for obligation for a specified period of time longer than one year; it is relatively uncommon. A *no-year* appropriation is available for obligation until its purpose has been achieved. It is used for programs involving the construction or acquisition of fixed assets, which may require several years to carry out, for certain research and development programs, and for other programs in which the focus is on a certain end result that is to be achieved, rather than on the authorized level of activity for a given year.

The Congress may also enact *contract authorization*, which is authority to enter into a contract in advance of the appropriation of funds. The Congress guarantees that amounts will subsequently be appropriated to liquidate the contract authorization. Contract authorization tends to provide loose control and therefore is used only rarely now; it was used in a major way during World War II.

The appropriation act normally is stated in terms of *New Obligational*

Authority (*NOA*). The *total obligational authority* (*TOA*) for a program is the sum of NOA plus any unused obligation balances carried forward from prior years.

Many agencies also have working capital funds. The amount of corpus of these funds was originally enacted by the Congress either to provide for the acquisition of inventory (*stock funds*) or for capital needed to finance the manufacture of goods or the provision of services to others (*industrial funds* or *service funds*). When the fund sells goods or provides services, the appropriation of the benefiting organization is obligated, and a corresponding amount is made available to the fund. The fund uses these amounts as a basis for incurring new obligations for its own activities. Thus, these funds are often called *revolving funds.* Congress controls the size of the fund by either adding to or subtracting from the corpus.

When payment is authorized for goods or services that have been received, an *expenditure* (also called *outlay*) is created. The actual payment is a *disbursement*. Thus all transactions go through three stages: obligation, expenditure, and disbursement. For some, such as a cash purchase, the three stages occur simultaneously. For others, such as transactions involving manufacture, the obligation may take place many months prior to the expenditure. The time interval between expenditure and disbursement is only the time required to process the payment and issue the check, normally only a few days.

For current operations, control focuses on the incurrence of *expense* in a specified time period, that is, on the consumption of resources, whereas appropriations are in terms of obligations which have to do with the *acquisition* of resources. The difference between obligation and expense is the result of: (1) inventories, (2) services provided by one organization for another, and (3) accounts payable, principally undelivered orders. The first two of these differences disappear when working capital funds are used. Thus, operating appropriations can actually be stated in terms of expenses, provided there is also an item called *changes in undelivered orders*. Then, expenses ± changes in undelivered orders = obligations. (This is described in more detail in Chapter 6.)

Congress focuses its control on obligations. Sec. 3679 RS makes it a criminal offense for anyone to obligate the government for an amount in excess of that appropriated. Every fiscal officer is so well indoctrinated in the importance of Sec. 3679 that over-obligations occur only rarely, and then almost entirely because of a bookkeeping error. There is no need to exercise a separate control over expenditures because no expenditure can be made in excess of the amount obligated. If actual contract costs appear to be exceeding the amount obligated—the phenomenon called *cost overrun*—additional amounts must be obligated for the contract. They are funded usually by transferring unneeded obligating authority from some other program; occasionally, a supplemental appropriation is required. If no additional obligation were made, the contractor would not get paid.

Accounting Entries

Accounting entries associated with the various stages of the process described above are given below. They illustrate the entries required in fund accounting. Differences between these entries and the entries made in a business accounting system are pointed out. The steps involved in the process are authorization, appropriation, obligation, expenditure, expense, and disbursement.

1. *Authorization.* Since authorizing legislation does not provide funds, no accounting entry is made.

2. *Appropriation.* Assume the Congress appropriates $10,000,000 to an Agency for the fiscal year beginning July 1, 1975. The Office of Management and Budget releases appropriations in quarterly installments, and if it releases ¼ of the amount in the first quarter, the effect on the Agency's account would be:

```
Fund Balances with U.S. Treasury . . . . . . . . . . . . . . .   2,500,000
    Unobligated Appropriation . . . . . . . . . . . . . . . . .             2,500,000
```

This entry roughly corresponds to the entry in business accounting which records the receipt of cash from stockholders.

3. *Obligation.* During the first quarter the Agency entered into obligations for $2,000,000 representing $500,000 of salaries earned and $1,500,000 of materials and services ordered. The entry would be:

```
Unobligated Appropriation . . . . . . . . . . . . . . . . . .   2,000,000
    Unliquidated Obligation . . . . . . . . . . . . . . . . . .             2,000,000
```

This entry has no counterpart in business accounting.

4. *Expenditure.* During the first quarter, $500,000 of salaries were recorded as due employees and $400,000 of materials and services were received. Two entries are required: the first adjusts the status of the appropriation:

```
Unliquidated Obligation . . . . . . . . . . . . . . . . . . . .   900,000
    Expended Appropriation . . . . . . . . . . . . . . . . . . .             900,000
```

The second entry corresponds to the entry in business accounting that records expenses and the related accounts payable:

```
Various Expense Accounts. . . . . . . . . . . . . . . . . . . .   900,000
    Accounts Payable. . . . . . . . . . . . . . . . . . . . . .             900,000
```

5. *Disbursement.* The Agency draws checks on the U.S. Treasury totalling $800,000. The entry which corresponds to the disbursement of cash by a business would be:

```
Accounts Payable. . . . . . . . . . . . . . . . . . . . . . . .   800,000
    Fund Balances with U.S. Treasury . . . . . . . . . . . . .             800,000
```

At the end of the quarter the fund accounts would show the following balances:

Unobligated appropriation (available for
  obligation in future quarters) . . . . $ 500,000
Unliquidated obligations (awaiting receipt
  of materials and services)   1,100,000
Expended appropriation   900,000
                                                           $2,500,000

The accounts would also show that $900,000 of expenses were incurred during the quarter, and that $100,000 of accounts payable had not yet been paid.

These entries are given to show the essence of fund accounting. They omit certain details that are present in the actual system to provide for the processes called apportionment and allotment, and they assume that there are no inventory or other working capital accounts.

chapter twelve

Reporting and Analyzing Performance

This chapter discusses events in the management control process that take place after operations are conducted. Reports on actual performance are analyzed, and action is taken if appropriate. The chapter also discusses other controls in addition to those in these reports. It describes various types of audits that are made of operations. Finally, it describes briefly the control of projects, as distinguished from responsibility centers.

FINANCIAL REPORTS AND THEIR ANALYSIS

In Chapter 11 we described the wide variety of information that flows to the manager of a responsibility center. In the present chapter, we discuss one specific type of information, that describing the performance of a responsibility center. Reports of performance are customarily called control reports since their purpose is to aid the management control process.

It should be emphasized again that the dissemination of reports and the analysis of the information they contain is only one facet of the control process. The whole process consists of a variety of formal and informal devices. The place of reports in the process is well indicated by the diagram in Exhibit 12–1.[1]

Format and Content of Reports

The need for reports is obvious, but in many organizations not enough attention is given to the format and content of reports. In particular,

---

[1] Reproduced by permission from Gene W. Dalton and Paul R. Lawrence, eds., *Motivation and Control in Organizations* (Homewood, Ill.: Richard D. Irwin, 1971).

EXHIBIT 12-1
Types of Control in Organizations

Controls Administered By:	Direction for Controls Deriving From:	Behavioral and Performance Measures:	Signal for Corrective Action	Reinforcements or Rewards for Compliance:	Sanctions or Punishments for Noncompliance
Organization............	Organizational plans, strategies, responses to competitive demands	Budgets, standard costs, sales targets	Variance	Management commendation → Monetary incentives, promotions	Requests for explanation → Dismissal
Informal group.........	Mutual commitments, group ideals	Group norms	Deviance	Peer approval, membership, leadership	Kidding, → Ostracism, hostility
Individual.............	Individual goals, aspirations	Self-expectations, intermediate targets	Perceived impending failure, missed targets	Satisfaction of "being in control" → Elation	Sense of disappointment → Feeling of failure

Source: Gene W. Dalton and Paul R. Lawrence, eds., *Motivation and Control in Organizations*, Homewood, Ill.: Richard D. Irwin, Inc., 1971.

reports should not contain more information than is necessary. System designers should have a basic idea as to what a particular piece of data will be used for before it is included in a report. In designing an information system, there is a tendency to include more information than managers can assimilate (e.g., a system installed in Naval Shipyards in the early 1970s produced 5,000 pages of computer printout per month in each shipyard). Also, it is extremely difficult to eliminate reports, even though they are no longer useful.

The types of data, the levels of aggregation, the reporting period, confidentiality, and other matters about reports are all worthy of careful consideration. Top management needs highly aggregated output data which shows the total results of programs or program categories. Operating personnel, or those responsible for program elements, need a different type of output. They need data more frequently. Their level of management sophistication may be low; consequently, data for their use should be expressed in simple terms. The display format should be easily understood and not formidable.

> *Example: Weaver College.* The formats of control reports used in organizations of various types are so diverse that it is not feasible to describe them here.[2]
>
> We shall instead make some comments about reports based on a single example, the financial report prepared for the trustees of Weaver College (a fictitious name), as shown in Exhibit 12–2. The first quarterly meeting of the Board of Trustees is held in October, so this report summarizes results for the fiscal year to date, that is, from July through September. Similar reports would be prepared for each of the other three meetings. Some comments about it are as follows:
>
> (*a*)   For the year to date, the report compares actual amounts with budgeted amounts. Budgeted amounts are *not* obtained by taking ¼ of the annual budget, but are rather constructed by estimating the correct proportion of the annual budget that is applicable to the current period. (Some organizations compare actual spending for the quarter with ¼ of the annual budget. Others compare actual for the quarter with the *total* annual budget. Neither comparison is of much use.)
>
> (*b*)   The report also compares the budget for the year with management's current estimate of revenues and expenses for the year. This is the most important part of the report. Management should be prepared to explain each of the significant differences and to seek Board approval of controllable differences before the expenses are incurred. (For example, in Exhibit 12–2, management will explain that $113,000 of additional tuition and fee revenue is expected because enrollment is higher than budgeted, and that there will be a corresponding increase in Dormitory

---

[2] Many examples are shown in Leon E. Hay and R. M. Mikesell, *Governmental Accounting* (Homewood, Illinois: Richard D. Irwin, 1974), and Malvern J. Gross, Jr., *Financial and Accounting Guide for Non Profit Organizations* (New York: Ronald Press, 1972).

and Food Service revenue, the food service revenue being offset by additional food service costs; no action is required by these facts. However, management must also explain why the Summer & Special Programs are now expected to generate less than budgeted revenue, and why General Administration and Instruction and Research expenses are now expected to be higher than budgeted. The Board should consider these explanations carefully, and either approve the changes or require that corrective action be taken.)

(*c*) The report is structured so that expenses of auxiliary enterprises are compared with the revenues of these activities, so that the performance of each can be determined at a glance. In many similar reports all the revenues are presented first, and then all the expenses, so that such relationships are difficult to determine. This report is structured so that attention is focused on the revenues of the primary program, education, and the expenses of that program.

EXHIBIT 12–2
WEAVER COLLEGE—
Treasurer's Report July 1–September 30, 1973
(in thousands)

	July–September		Year 1973-74		
Revenue	*Budget*	*Actual*	*Budget*	*Current Estimate*	*Differ- ence*
Tuition	1,906	2,009	3,812	3,918	106
Student fees	244	283	348	355	7
Subtotal	2,150	2,292	4,160	4,273	113
Endowment earnings	231	192	925	925	–
Gifts and grants	54	149	600	600	–
Current investments and miscellaneous	20	24	133	133	–
Auxiliary enterprises					
Dormitory					
Rentals	293	310	575	600	25
Expense	62	71	480	480	–
Food service					
Revenue	495	513	1,010	1,069	59
Expense	40	37	1,008	1,067	(59)
Bookstore					
Revenue	94	95	204	204	–
Expense	79	75	193	193	–
Summer and special programs					
Revenue	278	248	320	275	(45)
Expense	250	255	294	270	24
Athletics and miscellaneous					
Revenue	5	6	37	37	–
Expense	9	10	116	116	–
Auxiliary enterprises, net	725	724	55	59	4
Total Net Revenues	3,180	3,381	5,873	5,990	117
Expenses (see Schedule 1)	1,567	1,538	5,720	5,817	(97)
Difference	1,613	1,843	153	173	20

( ) = Unfavorable.

EXHIBIT 12–2 (continued)
Schedule 1—expenses

	July–September		Year 1973–74		
Expense	*Budget*	*Actual*	*Budget*	*Current Estimate*	*Differ-ence*
Educational and general					
General administration	64	58	275	305	(30)
Student services.	82	83	393	393	–
Public service and information	53	49	293	293	–
General institutional	87	80	281	281	–
Instruction and research	634	638	2,883	2,953	(70)
Instruction and research–special gifts . . .	24	12	47	47	–
Educational plant–operation and maintenance.	120	125	500	500	–
Subtotal	1,064	1,045	4,672	4,772	(100)
Student aid	345	341	871	871	–
Depreciation–furniture and fixtures	6	5	25	25	–
Student government	60	60	60	60	–
Student insurance.	92	87	92	89	3
Total Expenses	1,567	1,538	5,720	5,817	(97)

(*d*) The report is short, and the numbers are rounded so that a maximum of four digits is shown. It nevertheless conveys the significant information that the Board needs to understand what has happened and what is likely to happen. No person needs more than four digits of information, and three digits is usually enough.

(*e*) No mention is made of funds or fund accounting. This is a report of operations, and to structure it according to funds would be an unnecessary complication.

Analysis of Input Information

Reports are designed essentially to help answer two questions: (1) Has something unexpected happened, and if so what should be done? and (2) Are operations proceeding as planned, and if not what should be done? Environmental information and some of the internal information is used to answer the first question. This information can range from a report of a fire, requiring action within seconds, to a report of the possible reversal of a long-term trend that may not require action for months or years. It is therefore not possible to describe systematic methods of analysis.

The second question is related to the appraisal of the performance of operating managers. The budget is a financial plan. In addition to the totals, it shows detailed limitations or guides governing spending by programs, by elements of expense, and by functions. A comparison of actual expense with the budget shows how well these plans were carried out.

Information designed to show the extent to which operations are proceeding as planned is susceptible to systematic analysis. In making this analysis, it is useful to consider separately three types of organizations: those in which the amount of resources is fixed, those in which the nature of the job is fixed, and those in which neither is fixed.

Fixed Resources. In many nonprofit organizations, the amount of resources available in a given year is fixed. This is the case with many religious organizations and other membership organizations whose resources are fixed by the amount of pledges or dues. These organizations should spend the amount of available resources, neither more nor less, and their success is measured by how much service they provide with these resources. In these organizations, there is no such thing as a "favorable" budget variance; any significant departure from the amount of spending specified in the budget, in either direction, is subject to question. Since the amount of service provided is a subjective judgment rather than a measured quantity, the output for the whole organization cannot be expressed in quantitative terms, and measures of efficiency therefore cannot be developed. (Efficiency, it will be recalled, is the relationship between outputs and inputs.) Nevertheless, within such an organization there may well be service units whose output can be measured, and efficiency measures can be developed for these units.

Fixed Job. A fire department has a specified job to do: it must be ready to fight fires. Its performance cannot be measured by how many fires it fights; it fights however many there are to fight. Variances from planned amounts of spending may exist in either direction, because of the nature of the job that had to be done. Similarly, if there are many snowstorms, the budget for snowplowing has to be exceeded. Judgments about the performance of such organizations must therefore be in terms of how well they did whatever they were supposed to do, and whether a minimum amount of resources was used in doing whatever they did. It is more important to consider the cost of snow removal per snowstorm or per inch of snow than the total snow removal cost for the year. Again, the possibility exists for analyzing service units within these organizations.

Other Organizations. In other organizations there are variations in the amount of services rendered and in the amount of resources available. If even a rough measurement of the quantity of services (i.e., outputs) can be made, then analytical techniques similar to those used in profit-oriented companies can be used. Of these, the most important is variance analysis.

Variance Analysis. The analysis of performance consists essentially of comparing actual performance with planned performance; classifying the difference, or "variance," between the two into categories that suggest the causes of the differences; and determining the persons responsible for incurring these variances.

In Chapter 10, we pointed out that some costs vary with volume. Raw food costs and certain elements of food service cost in a hospital, for example, vary with the number of meals served. In these circumstances, we suggested that it is desirable to break costs into variable and nonvariable components and to establish a budget allowance per unit of output (e.g., number of meals served) for the variable component. We also suggested that the budget should show separately the quantity of resources and the price per unit of quantity, if it is feasible to do so; for example, the number of employees and the average cost per employee.

If the budget does contain these details, it is feasible to analyze the total difference between budgeted and actual amounts into the following principal types of variances: volume, price, efficiency, and mix. Techniques for making such analysis are described in books on cost accounting and management control in profit-oriented companies, and only a brief description of their nature is given here.

The *volume* variance shows the difference in expenses or revenues attributable to the fact that actual volume differed from budgeted volume. The revenue variance is presumably proportional with the number of revenue generating units, such as the number of students or the number of meals served. The expense variance is related only to the *variable* cost per unit of service, such as the variable cost per meal served. For cost items that are partly variable in nature, an understanding of the variance requires that the effect of volume be considered.

The *price* variance reflects the difference between actual and budgeted unit prices of the several input factors: wage rates per hour or per month, fuel costs per gallon, and so on. This variance may or may not be controllable by the management. If it is an inevitable consequence of a higher rate of inflation than was anticipated in the budget, nothing can be done about it. It is nevertheless important that the reader of the report understand how much of the variance was attributable to the price factor.

The *efficiency* variance is a residual. Essentially, it is the amount of variance that is not explained by other causes. It is the variance that is of primary interest to management, and the principal reason for identifying the other variances is to segregate them so that attention can be focused, as unambiguously as is feasible, on the efficiency variance.

The *mix* variance results from a difference between the actual and planned proportion of items. For example, a hospital's actual number of total patient days might exactly equal the budgeted number, but it might have a higher than planned proportion of surgical patients to maternity patients. This shift in proportion would create both revenue and expense variances. The mix variance is highly technical, and many well-managed profit-oriented companies make no effort to isolate it formally. Nevertheless, an appreciation of its existence is important in understanding reports of performance.

Other Comparisons

In addition to a systematic comparison of actual and budgeted performance, it is also useful to compare actual performance with that of similar units in the same organization or with other organizations. Such comparison is facilitated when a uniform accounting system is used by all the organizations involved. As indicated in Chapter 5, uniform accounting systems do exist for hospitals, universities, municipalities, and certain other types of organizations. Although no two organizations are identical, the members of a group are sufficiently similar so that valid conclusions can be drawn if significant differences exist between the costs of one organization and the average or other typical figure for members of the group as a whole.

Relative Performance. Although measurement of overall performance in a nonprofit organization may not be feasible, useful indicators of *aspects* of performance may be available. These measures are especially useful in situations where there are a large number of moderately small, discrete, and independent entities with similar clientele, operations, and cost structures (e.g., military dispensaries, urban schools, suburban schools, hospitals, inner city job placement programs). In these cases the indicators measuring parallel aspects of performance (such as pupil-teacher ratio, cost of instruction, cost of supervisory personnel, cost of maintenance and construction, etc.) may be valid indicators of relative performance even though there is no way of expressing what performance should be in absolute terms.

Historical Comparisons. Organizations may also compare this year's performance with performance for the corresponding period last year. Such a comparison represents a holdover from the days when budgets were generally nonexistent or unreliable. A good budget provides a much better basis for comparison than last year's performance because the budget presumably incorporates the significant changes that have occurred since last year. In a dynamic environment, the existence of these changes greatly weakens the usefulness of a year-to-year comparison.

REPORTING AND ANALYSIS OF OUTPUT

The preceding section discussed information about expenses, that is, about inputs. Reporting and analyzing such information is in many respects similar in both nonprofit and profit-oriented organizations. The reporting and analysis of output information, by contrast, is quite different in the two types of organizations. Efforts to provide good output information in nonprofit organizations are relatively new, and great opportunities for improvement exist. Good output measures can lead to a completely different attitude toward the management of such organizations, as is indicated in the following observation:[3]

> The major implication of the development of effectiveness measures for the field of welfare is that "welfare management style" can change. This change in management style can take place because effectiveness measures concentrate on the results of a program, rather than on the operation of a program. Thus, they can alter the traditional focus of welfare managers from emphasis on process to concern with the product turned out by the process. This new welfare orientation can establish a new framework in which goals and objectives buttress a program's intent.
>
> Effectiveness measures can pinpoint program areas where objectives are not achieved. They can cast a spotlight on areas where additional study is needed. The end product will provide an improved basis for decisions on which welfare programs should be maintained, which should be modified, which should be deleted so that a greater impact may be made on defined problems.
>
> The conceptual system undergirding the development of effectiveness measures (and measures of efficiency, as well) also provides the welfare administrator with a basis for assessing the work performance of personnel. The administrator will be in a more knowledgeable position to know whether to modify staff delivery of a program service. He may use agency objectives to establish more specific objectives for units of work or for individual workers. He will also have better information for determining whether he needs more or less staff, or more or less funds to operate programs from year to year.

Analysis of Output

The problems of measuring the output of a nonprofit organization were discussed at length in Chapter 6. In most types of organizations, these problems are severe. Notwithstanding the obvious importance of reporting and analyzing performance, it simply may not be feasible to do so.

In some situations regular reports of output are not necessary. The Weaver College report, Exhibit 12–2, did not contain output information since it could safely be presumed that the student body was in fact attending class, and it was not feasible to report, on a recurring basis, what they learned in class.

In other situations, it is feasible to report at least the process type

---

[3] John J. Foran and Robert Elkin, "A New Approach to Measuring the Effectiveness of Welfare Programs." Paper presented at National Conference on Social Welfare, Chicago: June 1, 1970.

of output measurement, even though all parties recognize that process measures do not reflect the quality of the work done nor are they necessarily congruent with the actual objectives of the organization. Usually such reports are most useful when outputs are related to costs. This is the central idea behind the "Management by Objectives" program described in Chapter 10, a program which currently is emphasized in the federal government.

Reports of output may be useful even though they are separate from cost information. Exhibit 12–3 plots the trend of the "Not Operational

EXHIBIT 12–3
An Output Measurement Report

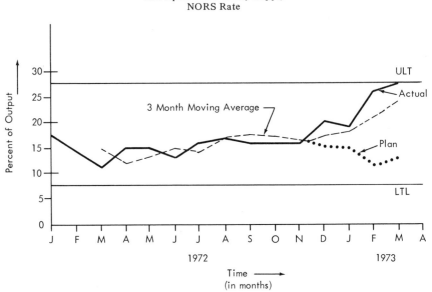

Not Operational Ready Supply
NORS Rate

Source: From a paper by Capt. C. Lewis, USN, Naval War College, Newport, R.I.

Ready Supply Rate" (a measure of the supply department's ability to fill requisitions for parts and other supplies that are necessary to keep aircraft and ships operating) at Point Mugu Naval Air Station. Some interesting features of this chart are: It compares actual performance with plan. In order to smooth temporary aberrations, it has a three-months' moving average. It has both an upper threshold level (UTL) and a lower threshold level (LTL). One indicates an unacceptably poor inventory condition, and the other indicates that inventory is perhaps higher than it needs to be.

The New York City school system measures output at each school by a combination of (1) attendance figures, (2) extracurricular activity participation, (3) number of diplomas, (4) number of scholarships, (5) percent of pupils with five or more major subjects, (6) percent of pupils with an 85 percent grade average or above, (7) standard test results, and (8) number of students discharged.[4] None of these measures reflects true output, which is the amount of education, but they are nevertheless useful as indicators of what is happening in a school.

Reliable reports of true output, that is, accomplishment of the organization's objectives, are extraordinarily difficult to come by.

Example: The Manpower Development and Training Act of 1962 established an institutional program whose objective was to provide training that would increase the future earnings of workers whose jobs had been eliminated for technological reasons and for other groups of disadvantaged persons. It would appear that "earnings" is a quantity that could be measured fairly readily. O'Neill[5] summarized eleven attempts to make such measurements. Three of the studies were well designed, but none of these showed that the program had a significant effect on the earnings of the participants. Of the other eight, six showed an improvement in earnings and two did not. However, O'Neill demonstrates that each of these eight studies had such serious methodological weaknesses that no valid conclusion could be drawn from them. Millions of dollars were spent on these evaluation efforts, and hundreds of millions of dollars were spent annually on the MDTA-Institutional program— $393 million in 1973 alone. If such a large evaluation effort on a program of this magnitude produces such miniscule results, it is clear that true output measurement—that is, results measurement—has a long way to go.

Quality Control

Many control systems provide information about the quantity of outputs: how many patients were in the hospital, how many procedures of various types were given to them, how many meals were served, etc. Few systems can provide information about the *quality* of output, however. For the most part, managers must rely on their judgment, based on bits and pieces of evidence that come to their attention.

Because everyone knows that quality is important, control systems are criticized on the grounds that they omit this important element. Indeed, the absence of quality information is used as a reason for not giving appropriate attention to the information that *is* provided by the system. For example, in a hospital there may be no adequate formal

---

[4] Harry J. Hartley, "Program Budgeting and Cost-Effectiveness in Local Schools," *Budgeting, Programme Analysis, and Cost-Effectiveness in Educational Planning* (Paris: Organization for Economic Cooperation and Development, 1968).

[5] Dave M. O'Neill, *The Federal Government and Manpower* (Washington D.C.: American Enterprise Institute for Public Policy Research, 1973).

mechanism for measuring the quality of care, and this fact leads some people to argue that little attention should be given to the control of costs because of the danger that an emphasis on cost control might lead to a lowering of quality.

Actually, notwithstanding the absence of good data, there are powerful forces at work to insure that the quality of service is adequate, or, if it becomes inadequate, to insure that this fact is brought to management's attention. Physicians, who dominate nonprofessionals and who are vitally interested in patient welfare, will not tolerate reductions in quality. Patients may complain, and when these complaints are about poor food, dirty floors or other matters within the patient's competence, they are relevant; they may even come to the attention of the general public, which management wants to avoid at all costs. The trustees, as representatives of the public, are interested in the maintenance of quality. The presence of competing hospitals may also affect quality, for if quality levels deteriorate in one hospital, physicians will tend to use another. Accrediting and licensing agencies make periodic inspections and check actual conditions against prescribed standards. Thus, physicians, patients, trustees, competition, and outside agencies are all of some help in assuring adequate quality levels, even in the absence of a formal method of measurement.

Peer Review. Currently, there is a widespread feeling that the devices to control quality, as listed above, are inadequate. Consequently, major efforts are underway in several professions to devise new methods of insuring that the quality of service provided is adequate. Although the movements have different labels, they share in common the concept that the work of one professional should be subject to review by his or her peers.

Of these efforts, the most important, and also the most controversial, is the establishment of Professional Standards Review Organizations (PSROs) in the medical profession. Unless opponents succeed in rescinding the law passed in 1972, PSROs will begin to function in 1976 to review the service provided by institutions to Medicare and Medicaid patients, including answers to the following questions:

1. Is the service medically necessary?
2. Is the treatment up to recognized standards?
3. Are the services delivered by the most economical institution or format of care?

PSROs are separate organizations established solely to provide this function. They are staffed by practicing physicians. There will be at least one PSRO in each state, and most states will have several. The HEW Office of Professional Standards Review estimates that the annual cost of each PSRO will be $500,000.

Professionals tend to resist peer review activities, so strong public pressures are necessary if effective measures are to be instituted.

Limitations on Analysis

An analysis of data rarely, if ever, reveals all the significant facts about performance. It must be supplemented with information and impressions received from other sources. It is especially important that the person whose performance is being appraised be given an opportunity to explain what happened.

A quantitative analysis may not only be inadequate; it may also be misleading. If, for example, top management places too much emphasis on certain numerical measures of performance, operating managers may act in such a way that their performance looks good according to the measures that are emphasized, to the detriment of the real objectives of the organization. Examples of such dysfunctional activities were given in Chapter 6. These actions are called "playing the numbers game." They can be avoided only by convincing operating managers that they should concentrate on accomplishing the real objectives of the organization and that they will not be penalized if such efforts do not show up in numerical measures of performance.

Importance of Adequate Staffs

The necessity of having adequate staff assistance was discussed in Chapter 4. Obviously, variance analysis and other devices for appraising performance cannot be conducted unless qualified people are available to make the calculations. Except in small organizations, managers do not have time to make these calculations themselves. Unfortunately, a great many nonprofit organizations, including some very large ones, do not have staffs that are large enough to make such analyses in a thorough and systematic way. One state government agency, with a multi-billion dollar budget, has only six professionals who are engaged in the regular analysis of operating reports. Many states have none at all.

AUDITING

In Chapter 11, we discussed the audit function as it relates to assuring that rules governing the use of funds have been complied with, and that reported data are accurate. This function has been in existence for a long time, but in recent years these "compliance" audit activities have been greatly expanded and new audit functions have been recognized.

The impetus for this change stems from the publication in 1973 by the U.S. Comptroller General of *Standards for Audit of Governmental Organizations, Programs, Activities and Functions.* This booklet contains the following statement:[6]

> A fundamental tenet of a democratic society holds that governments and agencies entrusted with public resources and the authority for applying them have a responsibility to render a full accounting of their activities. This accountability is inherent in the governmental process and is not always specifically identified by legislative provision. This governmental accountability should identify not only the objects for which the public resources have been devoted but also the manner and effect of their application.
>
> This concept of accountability is woven into the basic premises supporting these standards. These standards provide for a scope of audit that includes not only financial and compliance auditing but also auditing for economy, efficiency, and achievement of desired results. Provision for such a scope of audit is not intended to imply that all audits are presently being conducted this way or that such an extensive scope is always desirable. However, an audit that would include provision for the interests of all potential users of government audits would ordinarily include provision for auditing all the above elements of the accountability of the responsible officials.
>
> Definitions of the three elements of such an audit follow.
>
> 1. *Financial and compliance*—determines (*a*) whether financial operations are properly conducted, (*b*) whether the financial reports of an audited entity are presented fairly, and (*c*) whether the entity has complied with applicable laws and regulations.
>
> 2. *Economy and efficiency*—determines whether the entity is managing or utilizing its resources (personnel, property, space, and so forth) in an economical and efficient manner and the causes of any inefficiencies or uneconomical practices, including inadequacies in management information systems, administrative procedures, or organizational structure.
>
> 3. *Program results*—determines whether the desired results or benefits are being achieved, whether the objectives established by the legislature or other authorizing body are being met, and whether the agency has considered alternatives which might yield desired results at a lower cost.

The "financial and compliance" type of audit mentioned in the above statement is the traditional type. Its application to nonprofit organizations has been greatly expanded by several related developments. One of these is the introduction of the revenue sharing program, in which the Federal Government provides funds to some 39,000 state and local governmental units. The use of these funds is subject to audit, either by government auditors or by professional public accounting firms. The

---

[6] Comptroller General of the United States, *Standards for Audit of Governmental Organizations, Programs, Activities and Functions* (Washington, D.C.: U.S. Government Printing Office, 1973), pp. 1–2.

use of professional firms to perform audits on behalf of the federal government is a fairly recent development.[7]

Expansion of the audit function is also a consequence of the publication of audit guides by a number of federal agencies that provide grants, together with the requirement that the accounting systems of applicants for grants be subject to examination by professional accountants prior to awarding the grant and that a statement be made as to the adequacy of the system.[8]

The second and third types of audit that are listed in the Comptroller General's *Standards* quoted above are an outgrowth of a fairly recent development called *operational auditing*. The extension of the audit function beyond that of testing compliance has been practiced in a modest way in some government agencies for a number of years. Moreover, when an agency engages an outside consulting firm to review its activities, the work of such a firm is a form of operational auditing. The effect of the Comptroller General's *Standards* has been to expand greatly this type of work.

The Comptroller General has recognized that operational auditing requires a quite different approach and a quite different type of auditor from that appropriate for compliance auditing. This is evidenced by the fact that in its current recruiting program, the General Accounting Office hires operations analysts, economists, and social psychologists, as well as accountants. In fact, its 1974 program called for the recruitment of an approximately equal number of accountants and nonaccountants. Many other agencies do not yet appear to be aware of the different requirements of operational auditing, and use persons with an accounting background for this work, simply because their current auditing organization consists exclusively of such persons.

When accountants imply that they know how to run a school, a hospital, or any other organization better than the professionals who have spent their careers managing such organizations, their work is resented and, if possible, disregarded.

Operational auditing, if properly conducted, can be a valuable tool in the management of a nonprofit organization. If not properly conducted, however, it can be a source of friction and frustration, with no constructive results. The operational auditor must recognize that all managers make mistakes and that it is easy in any organization to identify, by hindsight, decisions that should have been made differently. There is no point, however, in publicizing such decisions if they were judgments made in good faith, based on the information available at the

---

[7] See Office of Revenue Sharing, *Audit Guide and Standards for Revenue Sharing Recipients* (Washington, D.C.: U.S. Government Printing Office, 1973).

[8] The "Washington Report" section of the *Journal of Accountancy* annually contains a convenient summary of publications describing audit requirements of various government agencies. *See,* for example, the May 1974 issue, page 30 ff.

time. Operational auditing serves a useful purpose if, but only if, it shows how *future* decisions can be made in a better way, that is, if it demonstrates that changes in policies or procedures should be made.

The Comptroller General's *Standards* booklet is sensitive to these problems of operational auditing. For example, it states:

> Efficiency and economy are both relative terms and it is virtually impossible to give an opinion as to whether an organization has reached the maximum practicable level of either. Therefore it is not contemplated in these standards that the auditor will be called upon to give such an opinion.[9]

Also, in its description of the report on an audit, the following statements are made:[10]

> Include only factual information, findings, and conclusions that are adequately supported by enough evidence in the auditor's working papers to demonstrate or prove, when called upon, the bases for the matters reported and their correctness and reasonableness. Detailed supporting information should be included in the report to the extent necessary to make a convincing presentation.
>
> Include, when possible, the auditor's recommendations for actions to effect improvements in problem areas noted in the audit and to otherwise make improvements in operations. Information on underlying causes of problems reported should be included to assist in implementing or devising corrective actions.
>
> Place primary emphasis on improvement rather than on criticism of the past; critical comments should be presented in balanced perspective, recognizing any unusual difficulties or circumstances faced by the operating officials concerned.
>
> Identify and explain issues and questions needing further study and consideration by the auditor or others.
>
> Include recognition of noteworthy accomplishments, particularly when management improvements in one program or activity may be applicable elsewhere.
>
> Include recognition of the views of responsible officials of the organization, program, function, or activity audited on the auditor's findings, conclusions, and recommendations. Except where the possibility of fraud or other compelling reason may require different treatment, the auditor's tentative findings and conclusions should be reviewed with such officials. When possible, without undue delay, their views should be obtained in writing and objectively considered and presented in preparing the final report.

PROJECT CONTROL

In this and the preceding chapters, we have described primarily the management control process as it relates to responsibility centers.

---

[9] *Standards*, p. 12.

[10] Ibid, pp. 42 and 43.

Somewhat different techniques are appropriate for the control of projects, such as the construction of major capital assets. The differences arise principally because in responsibility center control the focus is on the work done in a specified period of time, such as a month, a quarter, or a year, whereas in project control, the focus is on the accomplishment of the project, which in many cases extends over a period of years. Space limitations preclude more than a brief description of project control.[11]

A project control system must take account of three aspects of the project, and of the interrelationships among them: (1) the cost of the work, (2) the quality of the work, and (3) the time required. The essentials of the system for doing this are as follows:

1. As near to the inception of the project as possible, the work to be done, the resources planned to do the work, and the anticipated time required should be estimated. This estimate should be made in terms of "work packages,"[12] which are relatively small units of work. The organization elements responsible for doing the work should be specified.

2. Based on these statements, a work schedule and related budget should be prepared. These should show (*a*) the physical products, milestones, technical performance goals or other indicators that will be used to measure output, (*b*) budgets for the cost expected to be incurred on each work package and for overhead costs, (*c*) the starting and completion time for each work package, and (*d*) the unit responsible for the work.

3. Records should be kept of actual outputs and of actual costs incurred. These records should be entirely consistent with the definitions and accounting principles used in the work plans and budgets. Cost data should be collected in a disciplined accounting system, and should be auditable.

4. Reports should be prepared from these records at frequent intervals, showing, both for the interval and cumulatively, significant differences between:

a. Costs incurred for direct work performed and the budgeted costs of such work.

b. Overhead costs incurred and budgeted overhead costs.

c. Budgeted costs for work actually performed and budgeted costs for work scheduled.

---

[11] For a more complete description, see David I. Cleland and William R. King, *Systems Analysis and Project Management* (New York: McGraw-Hill, 1968).

[12] A "work package" is a measurable increment of work that can be related to a physical product, milestone, or other measurable indicator of progress. It should be of short duration with a discrete start and completion point, and the responsibility of a single organizational unit. Once the work package is begun, its budget and schedule must not change or the performance baseline will be lost.

　　d. Actual and planned schedule.

　　e. Actual and planned technical performance.

　　5.　Based on these reports, revisions in the plans and budgets should be made as necessary, so that the revised budget shows the current estimate of schedule, technical performance and cost. The records should be such that the reasons for significant revisions can be readily identified.

　　6.　Once plans and budgets have been revised, subsequent management reports should show comparisons *both* with the original (i.e., baseline) budget and with the current budget.

chapter thirteen

System Design
and Installation

The installation of a new or substantially revised management control system is a traumatic experience. As a minimum, the new system changes the way in which plans are made, it changes the way in which performance is measured and judged, and it establishes new patterns of communication and discussion between managers at various levels. The new information provided by the system is presumably better information, but it is certainly different information, and it takes some getting used to. Managers who have learned to interpret the information from the previous system, know its virtues, and they also know and make allowances for its limitations. They must now learn how to interpret the significance of the new information, and how to recognize and allow for its limitations. In addition, studies made in the course of developing the system may lead to changes in organizational relationships which are even more upsetting.

The problems involved in introducing a new system are generally more acute in a nonprofit organization than in a profit-oriented company because a new system is likely to represent a greater degree of change from past practice. In a profit-oriented company, many basic concepts are taken for granted: accrual accounting, the idea that results should be related to personal responsibility, the idea that it is important to control costs, and so on. In this environment, a new system essentially is a refinement within the context of existing concepts rather than the introduction of fundamental new concepts. Many nonprofit organizations do not have even the rudiments of a satisfactory management control system, nor is there a good control "climate" which is essential for the functioning of such a system; thus, the introduction of a new system represents a substantial change in the established way of doing things.

These problems, incidentally, are not nearly so severe in the installation of an operating control system, as distinguished from a management control system. A new system for processing payroll, or for keeping track of inventory, may contain technical problems—bugs that must be eliminated—but it is unlikely that such a system will cause serious organizational problems. If the system works technically, organizational members are unlikely to resist its introduction; indeed, they will support it as soon as they recognize that the system helps them do their jobs better.

This chapter discusses the preconditions that are necessary for the successful installation of a new management control system in a nonprofit organization, the problems that must be solved and ways of overcoming them, and the sequence of steps involved in developing and installing the system.

NECESSARY PRECONDITIONS

Top Down or Bottom Up?

There is a difference of opinion as to the essential prerequisites for the successful installation of a new management control system. On the one hand, there are those who believe that the impetus must come from the lower levels of the organization and that a new system cannot be installed successfully unless operating managers request, welcome, or at least support it. On the other hand, there are those who believe that the impetus must come from top management, that it would be nice if operating managers also supported the idea, but that such support is not necessary. The fact that Likert[1] labels the former approach as "participative" and the other as "authoritarian" indicates his support of the former view.

The discussion in this chapter, however, is based implicitly on the latter point of view, namely, that the driving force behind a new system must come from top management, and that it is unlikely that a majority of operating managers will voluntarily embrace a new system in advance of its installation, let alone be enthusiastic advocates of it. However much one might wish it were otherwise, we know from experience of no instance in which the movement for system reform originated with operating managers, and we have heard of only one situation—that of the U.S. Bureau of Reclamation—in which operating managers are said to have enthusiastically welcomed the change. Likert and others feel that a system development effort should not be initiated until a majority of operating managers is sold on the concept. We believe that if systems designers wait until that day arrives, they will be quite old.

---

[1] Rensis Likert, *New Patterns of Management* (New York: McGraw-Hill, 1961).

Some reasons why operating managers are suspicious of new management control systems are discussed in a later section of this chapter.

Top Management Support

Consistent with the point of view expressed above, we believe the prime prerequisite to the successful installation of a new management control system is the active support and involvement of top management. Ideally, this support should come from the Number 1 person in the organization. However, as was discussed in Chapter 4, effective support can come from the Number 2 person if the Number 1 person is "Mr. Outside" who delegates most management authority to the Number 2 person who is "Mr. Inside." Without the support of either the Number 1 or Number 2 person, the effort probably should not be undertaken.

In the late 1960s an attempt was made to install a new control system for the foreign affairs activities of the Federal government. The effort was under the direction of the Deputy Undersecretary of State who was an able person. The system designers were also able people. They were assisted by an illustrious group of advisors, including Charles Hitch, currently President of the University of California and who, as Controller of the Department of Defense, was responsible for the successful installation of a new system in that much larger Department. The President of the United States personally endorsed the effort. Nevertheless, the effort failed.

There were, in our view, two reasons for this failure, both involving top management. First, the leader of the effort, the Deputy Undersecretary, was only the Number 4 person in the Department of State. The Secretary and Undersecretaries of State gave only nominal support to the effort. Secondly, there was in fact no top manager for foreign affairs. In addition to the Department of State, the Economic Cooperation Administration, Department of Defense, Agency for International Development, U.S. Information Agency, Peace Corps, and Central Intelligence Agency were all involved in foreign affairs. A system that encompassed the activities of all these agencies could not be developed successfully unless one person were given sufficient authority over all these agencies to get the job done. The President did not assign this much authority to anyone; indeed, there is no evidence that anyone tried to convince the President that such a step was necessary.[2]

Support means more than acquiescence. Although top management's

---

[2] In his excellent paper "PPBS and Foreign Affairs," Thomas C. Schelling develops the need for a single manager in some detail. He does not, however, stress the fact that the effort was led by the Number 4 person at State, which probably was an equally important reason for its failure. Schelling's memorandum was prepared for the Senate Subcommittee on National Security and International Operations (Senator Jackson, Chairman), January 5, 1968.

time is precious, it must be willing to allocate a significant amount to the systems development effort. It must understand the objectives and general concepts of the proposed system well enough to see the benefits accruing to each individual, and must explain to the principal subordinates how it will help them and the organization as a whole. If roadblocks arise during the development and installation effort, the top management must be prepared to listen to the conflicting points of view and then make a decision which will remove the roadblocks. In some situations, the top manager must also do battle for the system with outside agencies who might otherwise prevent its adoption.

If the systems designers are not convinced that this degree of top management support will be forthcoming, they are not well advised even to begin a systems development effort for the organization as a whole. It is possible, however, that a management control system can be installed in some part of the organization if it has the support of the top management of that part of the organization and if there is good reason to believe that the top management of the whole organization will at least acquiesce.

Support from Outside Agencies

A second essential precondition is that outside agencies who can influence the system either acquiesce in the development effort, or are prevented by some higher authority from blocking it. Several government agencies developed program budget systems in the early 1960s, only to learn that the cognizant House Appropriations Subcommittee was unwilling to look at a budget in the program format.[3] These efforts therefore did not lead to successful systems.

The ideal situation of course is when outside agencies are enthusiastic supporters of the effort. In the federal government effort to install program budgeting in the late 1960s, top management and certain divisions of the Bureau of the Budget and the General Accounting Office were active supporters, but there were so many foot draggers in both organizations that it cannot be concluded that, on balance, the effort had adequate support from these important outside agencies. In many cases, outside agencies do not understand what a good management control system is. Furthermore, they cannot reasonably be expected to endorse the details of a new system until these details have been developed. The most that realistically can be hoped for in many situations, therefore, is that the outside agencies will maintain an open mind and will agree to support the system *if* it fulfills its promise.

In order to obtain this degree of acquiescence, all possible steps should be taken to minimize the impact of the system on outside agen-

---

[3] Reasons for this attitude were discussed in Chapter 9.

cies. This often requires a procedure called "crosswalking," which is discussed in a later section of this chapter.

System Designers

A third prerequisite for success is the existence of an adequate staff of people to design and install the system, and a strong "charter" for this staff. It goes without saying that system designers should have the competence and the expertise that is necessary for the job (and there *is* such an expertise). But they also require a rather special set of relationships with the rest of the organization. System designers are staff persons doing a specialized job, but they need ready access to top management, either in person, or through not more than one intermediary. This is because the system must reflect the style of management that top management wants, and the only way of assuring that the system does this is to discuss the proposed system design with the boss personally.

System designers must spend time with operating managers, who are busy people. Top management must convince operating managers that the system design effort is important enough for them to take time away from the always pressing operating problems to discuss their needs for information. Few, if any, of the other staff specialists require a corresponding amount of an operating manager's time.

In order to do the systems job properly, the system designer should ordinarily work full time, or almost full time, at it. Since a small organization does not need a permanent full time system designer, an outside consultant may provide the full time attention in such an organization. Sometimes even in a large organization, the effort is headed by a part-time person. This is because the major part of the development and installation effort has a finite completion date, and qualified persons in the existing organization are not willing to give up their other responsibilities to work full time on a job of this type. A successful effort under these circumstances is difficult, but by no means impossible, if the part-time leader is backed up by a full-time staff and/or by outside consultants.

One of the problems that affects the organization of the system design and installation program is that the task has several conflicting characteristics. Such a task requires someone who can deal effectively with managers at all levels, including top management, and who has a broad understanding of the management control process; but it also requires someone who will pay careful attention to detail. A large fraction of the development workhours will be spent on tedious matters—the exact definition of accounts, the design of forms, the preparation of computer programs, the preparation of flow charts. Although most of this work can be delegated, the team leader must nevertheless have a sufficient knowledge of the details to be able to detect mistakes which could affect the whole system.

Outside Consultants. Professional system design organizations have existed for several decades, and in the last 25 years all the large public accounting firms have created systems staffs. These firms employ many thousands of professionals. There is a difference of opinion, however, as to whether outsiders should be hired under circumstances other than those mentioned above.

On the one hand, outside system designers have both a general expertise and a specific knowledge that may not be obtainable within the organization. If an outside firm has done a good job of developing a system for one hospital, it is reasonable to expect that it can install a similar system in another hospital with little waste motion, even allowing for the inevitable differences between the two hospitals. Furthermore, outsiders are often perceived by operating managers as being unbiased: they are not associated with an internal faction; they have no axe to grind; they have a detached point of view. This, coupled with their expertise, means that they can add a degree of prestige and respectability to the effort.

On the other hand, outsiders may be expensive. Their daily cost is higher than the cost of insiders of comparable ability although the higher daily cost may well be offset by the fact that outsiders will require fewer workdays to develop the system. More importantly, outsiders *are* outsiders; the new system ultimately should be a vital part of the management process, and some people argue that outsiders can never obtain the essential understanding of "how things really work in our organization."

At most, an outside firm should have only part of the responsibility for systems development and installation. In-house personnel must also be involved. All good systems firms insist on such involvement. At some point in the system's development, outsiders will depart, and when they are gone there must be insiders who will regard the system as "their" system and who will continue to work to insure that it is successful. This attitude can be generated only if in-house personnel are involved in the effort in a substantial way. Such an involvement is especially important if outsiders play a major role in the design of the system and in early phases of its installation, but in-house personnel are responsible for later phases of the installation task; this often happens because of the length of the installation time period. A system that is designed by consultants, described in an impressive report, and then turned over to the organization for installation, is usually soon forgotten; competent outsiders are reluctant to accept a systems engagement if they believe this is likely to happen. In short, competent outsiders are reluctant to do the whole job, but they are equally reluctant to do only the design phase; they prefer to participate, along with in-house personnel, in all phases.

Almost Enough Time

In a large organization, two or three years will elapse between the time a decision is made to proceed with systems development and the date that a cutover to the new system is made. Even after the cutover date, much additional time is required in educating managers in how to obtain maximum use of the new information, and improvements in the system are never-ending. A final precondition to a successful system therefore, is that "almost enough time" be allowed between startup and the cutover date. The time allowed is never quite enough because there are always refinements that could be added and additional educational efforts that would be worthwhile; however, if enough time were allowed for all these worthy endeavors, the system never would go into operation.

It seems clear in retrospect that one of the principal reasons for the failure of the "PPBS" effort in the federal government in the late 1960s was that not enough time was allowed. In August 1965, President Johnson directed almost all federal agencies to install a PPB system as of July 1, 1967, less than 18 months later. The Director of the Budget concurred reluctantly in this timetable, recognizing that it was too short, but hoping that in the time available a beginning could be made, and that improvements would occur later on. As it turned out, the "beginning" was largely window dressing, and provided an inadequate foundation for a satisfactory system. An additional year of preparation probably would have produced a viable system.

It does not seem feasible to be specific about the appropriate time period. In a small organization, with a fairly specific set of objectives, and especially if good systems exist in similar organizations that can be used as models (e.g., hospitals), assuming a vigorous, well-supported effort is made, a new system probably could become operational in a year, perhaps less. It should be recognized that in most circumstances, a year is quite a short period of time, however. Furthermore, it is not necessary, or even desirable, to install all parts of a system at the same time. Possibilities for breaking the total job into phases are discussed in a later section of this chapter.

PROBLEMS

The system designer must address two sets of problems. First, there are technical problems associated with designing a management control system that best meets the needs of the organization. Relevant considerations for this set of problems were discussed in Chapters 5–12. Second, there are the problems that arise because the system designers are "change agents." As a result of their efforts, and assuming they are successful, managers will manage in a different way than before they appeared on the scene. It is this latter set of problems we are concerned with here.

Attitudes

Although life would be more pleasant if this were not the case, it is quite probable that operating managers will resist efforts to introduce a new system, or at least they will be unenthusiastic about it. The reason is *not* that people resist change. After all, a salary increase is a change, and no one resists a salary increase. Rather, the reason is that people resist a change whose effect on them is uncertain.

Even if operating managers perceive that the existing system is inadequate, it is nevertheless a system that they have worked with and are comfortable with. They are uncertain exactly how the new system will affect what they do, and there is no way of removing this uncertainty completely, because there is no way of communicating accurately to them what will happen when the new system becomes operational. Its effect must be experienced to be understood.

More specifically, a proposed new system may raise questions such as the following: Who benefits from it, and who is hurt by it? How will it affect relationships between superiors and subordinates? How will it affect the informal organization structure? Is it designed to help top management at the expense of operating managers (or vice versa)? Will it provide information to politicians or other people outside the organization that can be used to hurt people inside the organization? Is it designed to help accountants or computer specialists rather than operating managers?

A new system can change the style of management and the desired qualifications of managers. It may shift power from operating managers to top management. It often requires professionally educated managers rather than those qualified principally by experience. These tendencies, if perceived by the members of the organization, also create resistance. This is especially the case in a mature organization whose managers are interested primarily in job security.

Even if operating managers understand that the system will provide better information, their worries may not be allayed. Operating managers are part of an organizational hierarchy in which they have subordinates and have superiors. Operating managers may understand that the new system will provide them with better information about what their subordinates are doing, and therefore a better basis for controlling the efforts of their subordinates, and this they welcome. But by the same token, they can perceive that the new system provides better information to their superiors about what *they* are doing and gives superiors a better basis for controlling their efforts, and this they are not so happy about.

Managers who have previously collected information for their own use tend to resist a system in which information is collected, controlled, and furnished to them by an outside, impartial source. They may view their private data system as a source of prestige; other persons must come to them in order to obtain the information. The value of information is that it reduces uncertainty. If a proposed system provides additional information that reduces the uncertainty of superiors about the performance of a subordinate's job, then the subordinate will often resist the system. On the other hand, if the proposed system reduces the uncertainty about the tasks of others on the staff, the manager will support it. This leads to inevitable conflicts in proposing modifications to information systems, for the same proposal may be viewed as a threat by some people and welcomed by others.

As will be discussed in a following subsection, educational efforts can reduce the force of these negative attitudes, but education probably cannot eliminate them. They disappear only after the system has been in full operation for a substantial period of time. The main point is that system designers must not shut their eyes to this resistance, and they must learn to live with it as best they can. They can expect less than full cooperation in obtaining the information needed for systems design, and they can expect that efforts will be made to delay the introduction of the system in the hope that if it is delayed, it may never materialize. They must use the good offices of the top manager who is sponsoring the system to overcome these delaying tactics. They should understand that the installation of a new system is a political process. It involves pressure, persuasion, and compromise in proper proportions as is the case with any important political action.

Aids to Changing Attitudes. Some possible ways of lessening hostility are listed in the following paragraphs.

To the extent that operating managers are convinced that the new system will on balance benefit them, they will support it. Educational efforts should therefore stress the benefits, some of which are: (1) the system will help them to do a better job, which will be perceived as such by their superiors; (2) the system will facilitate smoother coordination with other units; (3) managers can exercise better control over their subordinates; (4) the system permits them to make better decisions about the allocation of resources (this is especially important in periods when budgets are tight), and (5) the system provides a more realistic measurement of performance.

The responsibility center concept should also be stressed. If too much emphasis is placed on programs and if the relationship of programs to personal responsibility is not made clear, operating managers are unlikely to perceive the new system as being helpful. They may instead regard it solely as a mechanism for reporting performance to top management—in the extreme case, as a "spy" system.

One way of reducing hostility is to install the new system when operations are expanding. Operating managers will then associate it with increased budgets, whether or not such an association is warranted. If the system is installed in a period of contraction, it may be associated with the "screw tightening" which is characteristic of such a period, again without regard to whether such an association is warranted.

Developing Information Needed

Notwithstanding the possible resistance described above, the system designer must work with operating managers to find out what information they need to do their job. At one time the recommended approach was that the systems designer should ask managers what information they needed. In recent years, this approach has generally been abandoned because it was found that *operating managers do not know what information they need.* In particular, they are not aware of the existence of certain information which would be of great use to them. The current approach, therefore, is for the system designer to find out what information the operating manager needs by indirect methods. The designer does, if for no other reason than courtesy, ask managers what information they need; but in the interviews the systems designer focuses primarily on the job itself, the relationship of one responsibility center to another, the environmental influences that affect the work in the responsibility center, and so on. Based on this information, a system is designed that provides the information that the manager *should* need.

Operating managers can make important contributions to systems design. For one thing, they are the real experts on feasibility. Higher level managers need, and would like to have, some information that cannot feasibly be collected, and managers on the firing line can demonstrate the impracticability of collecting such information. For example, hospital administrators would very much like to have systematic, quantitative information on the quality of patient care, but the nursing supervisor may be able to demonstrate that reliable information on quality cannot be obtained.

Discussions with operating managers are also necessary to test out proposed reports, both reports intended for their use and reports containing information which they generate. An operating manager can sometimes uncover mistaken assumptions about the availability of data or the exact nature of data.

Finally, the discussions with operating managers are important—second only in importance to the support of top management—in the campaign to obtain acceptance of the proposed system. To the extent that operating managers perceive that they are genuinely involved in the construction of the new system, their willingness to accept it is increased.

Using Existing Data. A study of what goes on in the bowels of the organization is also useful in uncovering operating information that provides raw material for use in a management control system. It is much less expensive to develop management summaries from raw data that are prepared for other purposes than to generate new raw data specifically for management control. The system designer should be prepared to sacrifice some "ideal" type of management information if a slightly less desirable type of information can be obtained from existing data sources. For example, there are dozens of ways in which information on the status of inventories and on inventory movements can be summarized for the use of management. The system designer is well advised to use a way that can be obtained by summary of the existing inventory records, rather than insisting that the operating system for inventory control be changed to provide the information that management needs.

Needs of Program Planners. In Chapter 5, reference was made to two important groups, who may be characterized respectively as operating managers and program planners. The latter is a staff group that plays an important role in the preparation and analysis of proposed programs. Their needs for information are an important consideration in the design of the new system. Unfortunately, as pointed out in Chapter 5, there are inherent differences between the information needed by operating managers and the information needed by program planners. Program planners need approximate costs, full costs, and opportunity costs. Operating managers need more accurate costs, direct costs, and historical costs. It may not be feasible to meet both sets of needs completely, and compromises must therefore be worked out. This may require difficult negotiations with the program planners and operating managers.

Requirements of Outside Agencies

As already noted, it is essential that influential outside agencies, especially those that have the power of the purse, at least acquiesce in the development of the new management control system. In an ideal world, this would not be a problem. Outside agencies do not need more information or different information than management needs to manage the organization; they need the same type of information but in a more summarized form. In the real world, however, many outside agencies may not appreciate this fact. They have grown accustomed to receiving information in a certain format, and they may not perceive that new information is better; this is especially the case when the new system is only a proposal on paper, rather than a functioning system. Under these circumstances, outside agencies may specify that there is to be no change in the information they receive, and the systems designer usually must accommodate them. There are two ways of doing this: crosswalking, and operating a dual system.

Crosswalking. Crosswalking is used by federal organizations to translate management data into the format required by the Appropriation Committees of Congress, it is used by many state and municipal organizations for a similar purpose, and it is used by some organizations that are financed by grants to translate management information into the format prescribed by the grantor. The crosswalking process requires that information in the management accounts be reclassified into the accounts prescribed by the outside agency. In some systems, this reclassification is exact; that is, detailed data exist in the accounts in such a form that they can be rearranged in the prescribed format. More commonly, the reclassification is only approximate; that is, some of the management accounts are subdivided and reclassified, more or less arbitrarily, to obtain the summaries required for outside agencies. Since the whole crosswalking operation is a waste of effort so far as the organization is concerned, the organization devotes as little attention to it as possible.

Dual Systems. Some outside agencies insist that the system of control that they prefer be used as a basis for control inside the organization. Since their requirements may be fundamentally incompatible with the system that is best for management purposes, two systems must be operated simultaneously. This can happen, for example, when the outside agency insists on the obligation basis[4] of accounting, whereas an expense basis is obviously better for management purposes, and the outside agency prohibits the use of working capital accounts that would permit the two bases to be reconciled. Some Congressional appropriations subcommittees impose such requirements on the agencies that they deal with.

When an organization is forced to operate a dual system, there is of course additional bookkeeping, but this is a relatively trivial problem. The much more important problem is behavioral. Top management wants operating managers to obtain their signals only from the management control system, but operating managers also receive signals from the system required by the outside agency. When these signals conflict, which can happen quite frequently, operating managers must decide which signal is stronger. Since they know well that the outside system is associated with the agency that provides them with their funds, they are quite likely to pay more attention to the signals from that system than to the signals from the management control system.

For example, top management in the Department of Defense wants

---

[4] It will be recalled that the obligation basis of accounting focuses on contracts placed, and thus does not provide a record of expenses incurred classified by the responsibility centers that incur them.

operating managers to be concerned about the costs of using military personnel, and military personnel costs are therefore a part of the management control system. Military personnel costs are excluded from the "Operations and Maintenance" appropriation that governs operations, however, and it is consequently difficult to persuade operating managers that these costs are really important. In considering tradeoffs involving a choice between military personnel, civilian personnel or contractor services, inadequate recognition of military personnel costs can lead to wrong decisions. (Readers who have experienced kitchen police duty in the military may be interested to learn that this is the primary reason that military personnel were used in this function.)

Exhibit 13–1 suggests the existence of a similar problem in the Department of Labor. The "Cost Center Detail" report shown at the top of the page contains the information on which top management presumably wishes to focus attention: outputs and costs incurred in attaining these outputs, with a comparison of actual performance against plan. The "Appropriation—Cost Center Report" at the bottom of the page, however, shows that the operating manager must also think in terms of Appropriations, that is, the system specified by the Congress. The two approaches are not reconcilable; in particular, the lower report indicates that $40,000 of incurred costs are "unfunded;" that is, they are not included in the Appropriation system. It is doubtful that operating managers are greatly concerned about these unfunded costs.

In an earlier section, the acquiescence of outside agencies was described as a necessary precondition for a successful systems development. Some people go further and insist that a new system should not be attempted unless the outside agency is willing to accept the information that is provided. They feel that the problems of operating a dual system are too formidable to make the attempt worthwhile. Considerable evidence can be found to support this point of view. For example, both the Air Force and the Army adopted good management systems in the 1950s, but neither was able to convince their Appropriations Subcommittee to adapt its requirements to the information obtainable from these systems. The Air Force consequently abandoned its "Appropriation and Expense Accounting" system; the Army retained its "Command Management" system, but made no important management use of it.

Despite these problems, optimists argue that a dual system is better than the existing one. They hope that as time goes on, the outside agency will appreciate its advantages, to itself as well as to the organization, and will modify its requirements accordingly.

Dealing with the Old System

Except in rare circumstances, a new management control system replaces an existing system. (Even in a new agency, the tendency is to seize some existing system in order to get things going, and this system

EXHIBIT 13–1

Dual Reports in U.S. Department of Labor

COST CENTER DETAIL   September 1969

DEPARTMENT OF LABOR
Mid Atlantic Region
(in thousands of dollars)

Month				Year to Date		
Plan	*Actual*	*Variance*	*Description*	*Plan*	*Actual*	*Variance*
$100	$110	(10)	Salaries and wages	$290	$300	$ (10)
20	20	–	Travel	60	65	(5)
10	12	(2)	Utilities	30	33	(3)
$130	$142	$ (12)	Total Cost	$380	$398	$ 18
			Performance Factors			
			No. of investigations			
100	120	(20)	Investigation A	300	350	(50)
120	80	40	Investigation B	310	280	30
220	200	20	Total	610	630	(20)
$590	$710	$(120)	Cost per investigation	$620	$630	$ (10)
2,700	2,800	(100)	Productive man-days	6,800	7,300	(500)
			DMS Elements			
$ 50	$ 70	$ (20)	Investigation –A	$200	$230	$ (30)
60	70	(10)	Investigation –B	100	110	(10)
20	2	18	Legal actions	80	58	22
$130	$142	$ (12)	Total	$380	$398	$ (18)

APPROPRIATION–COST CENTER REPORT

DEPARTMENT OF LABOR   First
Appropriation–Cost Center Analysis   Quarter
(in thousands of dollars)   1969

Appropriations			*Cost Center*				*Appropriation YTD*		
			QTR			*YTD*			
Description	*Non-current*	*Current*	*Fund*	*Un-fund*		*Fund*	*Un-fund*	*Cur-rent*	*Non-current*	*Descrip-tion*
Wage and Labor Standards			$ 290	$10	Mid-Atlantic Region					
			1,625	25	Pacific Region					
			135	5	Div. of Maritime Safety					
	$100	$2,050	$2,050	$40	Total					

Measurement:
    Assigns costs by responsibility.
    Measures costs by plan and variance.
    Measures performance by workload factors.
    Indicates trend of costs.

is unlikely to be suitable to the needs of the agency.) The system designer has to decide what features of the existing system should be retained, and how the transition from the old to the new system should be made.

It is usually desirable to restrain the natural feeling that the old system should be completely swept away. Operating managers will have much to learn about the new system in any event, and to the extent that it incorporates familiar practices—particularly, familiar terms—it will seem less strange to them. System designers have their own preferred vocabulary; they should, however, be cautious about using these favorite terms if existing terms are almost as good.

Some system designers advocate that a new system should be run in parallel with the existing system until the bugs have been worked out. There are obvious advantages in doing this if it is feasible. In particular, it avoids the terrifying possibility that the new system has a bug that results in the permanent loss of vital data.

It is important that top management use information from the new system as soon as it becomes available. Usually top managers are reluctant to do this because they do not feel comfortable with the new information. Top management should appreciate, however, that operating managers feel the same way, and they are unlikely to take the plunge until top management breaks the ice.

Top management's use of the new system is especially important when a dual system is necessary. Top management should use information from its management system exclusively; it should never use information from the system required by the outside agency, and it should insist that operating managers do the same. This is much easier said than done, for it asks managers to give up something with which they are thoroughly familiar for something which is strange.

If the old and new systems are run in parallel, the old system should be discarded slightly before managers become completely comfortable with the new system. This saves bookkeeping costs, but that is incidental. The principal reason is that opponents of the system may continue to seek a way of sabotaging it until such time as the old data are no longer available and they therefore have no choice but to use the new.

Education

All system designers are intellectually aware of the importance of a thorough educational program as a part of the system installation process. As a practical matter, however, they sometimes do not devote enough time to this effort. There are so many technical problems that have to be solved by prescribed deadlines that often there is not enough time left for the educational campaign. In retrospect, many wish that they had devoted more time to education.

The preparation of manuals, explanations, sample reports, and other written material is a necessary part of the education process, but it is not the important part. The important part is to explain to the managers how the new system can help them do a better job. System experts, who are the only ones with detailed familiarity with the new system, necessarily play a large role in these educational programs, but management should also be involved.

Above all else, operating managers must be convinced that the new system is in fact going to be used. System designers can say this, but they are, after all, only staff people. The most convincing message comes from the lips of the line managers. Thus, within the limits of their knowledge about the system, it is desirable that managers teach other managers; that is, that top management discuss the new system with its immediate subordinates, who then convey the message to their subordinates, and so on. System designers can provide technical support at such meetings, of course, but it is preferable that the meetings be run by managers. Since the teachers must themselves learn, this process aids in the education of those who are involved in it.

Once the system goes into operation, even on a test basis, using the information that it generates is the best educational device available.

Danger of Overselling. In their enthusiasm for the new system, system designers and the sponsors of the system have a natural tendency to state its advantages more strongly than is warranted and to minimize its limitations. A management control system aids management, but it does not lessen the need for management. Even with the best system, managers must analyze and interpret the data, they must allow for its inadequacies, they must take into account much information not available in the system, they must use judgment in making decisions, and they must use behavioral skills in implementing these decisions. If a contrary impression is conveyed in the educational process, hardheaded managers who know the limitations of any system will be skeptical and regard the system effort as the work of impractical theorists.

STEPS IN SYSTEM DESIGN AND INSTALLATION

Details of the system design and installation process are set forth in many books on this subject, and it is not appropriate to describe them at length here. The main steps, assuming that the preconditions listed earlier have been met, are as follows:

1. Planning. Develop a plan for system design and installation, including a timetable (preferably in the form of a PERT diagram or a similar scheduling device), and as careful a statement of responsibilities as is feasible.

2. Analysis of Objectives and Organization. Diagnose the objectives of the organization, the existing control system and the existing organization structure. This analysis may reveal defects in the existing system and organization structure, in part reflecting differences between the real objectives and the objectives as they are perceived by the organization.[5] It may lead to a reorganization.

3. *Inventory of Current Information.* Examine the existing sources of information. Much of the existing information must be collected for operating needs (e.g., payroll, inventory transactions), and its use in the management control system involves little incremental cost.

4. *Develop the Control Structure.* Usually, it is desirable to develop the program structure first, starting with the major program categories. The most important and most difficult decisions involve the choice of program elements and the selection of appropriate output measures, as discussed in Chapters 5 and 6. Feasible output measures initially available will be crude in many cases and nonexistent in many other cases, but the design effort should not be held up unduly because of these inadequacies.

5. *Develop Procedures.*

6. *Test.* Test the proposed structure and procedures, preferably in one part of the organization. This provides a concrete example which is essential in educating people as to what the new system is all about.

7. *Education.* Develop and implement an educational program.

8. *Implementation.* If feasible, run all or part of the new system concurrently with the existing system. As soon as feasible, eliminate all obsolete parts of the existing system.

Gradual Installation

It is often desirable to install a system in stages, allowing enough time for managers to become accustomed to using the techniques available at one stage before proceeding to the next. A possible sequence of stages is:

a. Budget by programs and responsibility centers, using out-of-pocket direct costs, with few service centers, and rough output measures. Do not change the accounting system.

b. Program in the above terms, with perhaps improved output measures.

c. Collect accounting information according to the new structure and educate managers in the use of this information.

d. Continue development of better output measures.

---

[5] Not much time should be spent in defining objectives, however, for it is easy to get bogged down in semantics. For example, although the objectives of a public school system are intuitively fairly obvious, the installation of a system in the Westport, Connecticut school system was delayed for a year or more by attempts to elucidate objectives. *See* John Moore, "The Development of Long Range Plans in the Kirkwood School District (R-7)" (Doctoral dissertation, Harvard University).

e. Add sophistication by
(*1*) extension of service center concept,
(*2*) use of depreciation,
(*3*) use of a capital charge, and
(*4*) use of cost allocations.

Example: State of Pennsylvania. One of the best descriptions of the process of designing and installing a new system is contained in the booklet, *The Design and Implementation of Pennsylvania's Planning Program, and Budgeting System.*[6]

A detailed description is given of a process which began in March 1968 and resulted in a completed program budgeting system in December 1970, which was used to prepare the budget submitted to the legislature in May 1971. The importance of the Governor's commitment to the project is demonstrated. Methods used to educate legislative committees, individual legislators, and managers within the executive branch are described. The system design team consisted of both state employees and outside consultants from Pennsylvania State University. The work of this team is described in considerable detail. Problems and their resolution are discussed with some frankness. This booklet is a useful introduction to the details of the system design and installation process.

ENTRY STRATEGY

In a profit-oriented company, the impetus for a better management control system comes from within the organization, from top management or from the controller. Outsiders, except for consulting firms who occasionally can generate interest with management, play no part in creating the desire for a new system. By contrast, the literature contains many accounts of attempts by outsiders to stimulate interest in better management control in nonprofit organizations, especially public organizations, because every taxpayer has a valid reason for fostering improvements in the management of such organizations. Some suggestions for outsiders who wish to undertake such an effort are given below.

Rather than attempting to install a new system in the whole organization, it is often more feasible to limit the initial effort to one part of it. This should be a part in which there are obvious opportunities for improvement in management and where the results of such improvements will be easily visible. Welfare organizations in both state and municipal governments are examples. Demonstrated success in one area can lead to a general acceptance of the system throughout the organization.

---

[6] Robert J. Mowitz, *The Design and Implementation of Pennsylvania's Planning Program, and Budgeting System* (University Park: Pennsylvania State University, 1970).

If conditions preclude the installation of a true management control system, it may be possible to install an information-reporting system which can be used to gather the data that will be used later on in a management control system. This "back-door" approach is especially feasible in project-oriented organizations or in organizations where output can be quantified relatively easily.

> **Example:** A student went to work at a local redevelopment agency to learn about the management control process. She soon discovered that there were a number of circumstances which made the establishment of a management control system difficult. (For example, budgets were on an overall project basis, rather than on an annual basis.) She therefore proposed an information and reporting system. During system design, an attempt was made to include the necessary information so that it would be possible to "back in the door" to program budgeting. The mayor and the new budget director for the city subsequently became interested in program budgeting, and the available information made the job of installing a program budget system easier.

Following are some perceptive comments about the problem of introducing system improvements in state and municipal governments.[7]

> In state and municipal governments interference from politicians and constituents is likely. Actions taken by managers are clearly visible in the immediate environment. The city resident doesn't need to be told that the street renovation program is failing if there are potholes in front of his house. The hospital patient doesn't need to read that the new facilities program has fallen behind if he finds himself bedded in the hallway. Thus, the opportunities for change are increased because of public perception of the need. By contrast, in the federal government the public is not at all aware, for example, of improvements in the Atomic Energy Commission by the use of PPB analysis.
>
> The strong support of the public is essential to successful implementation, particularly when opposition is likely to be encountered from those who have a vested interest in maintaining the status quo. The political base of partisan political organizations may be firmly rooted in the departments of city administration where the managers are likely to be political appointees. Support for "out of power" parties is not likely because they anticipate the day of their return to dominance.
>
> The current budgeting structure presents another impediment to the introduction of a good management control system. Local governments have adhered to traditional line-item budgeting. Cities, in order to participate in state and federally funded programs, must supply information classified by function, not program. A program budget, then, must overlay a firmly entrenched system. Nor are budget makers likely to be sensitive, particularly at the outset, to methods not related to the source of funds. This does not mean that two systems cannot simultaneously

---

[7] From an unpublished memorandum by David Crow, a Harvard Business School student.

operate. In Illinois, for example, Governor Richard Ogilvy presented his budget message by program, although appropriations are made by function. Nor does it mean that retention of the old system is an immutable fact. The State of Hawaii in one fell swoop adopted by statute a whole new PPB system for all governmment agencies including the school system. It does mean, however, that some fairly tedious crosswalking technique will have to be applied to integrate the systems.

At the departmental level of a city government, the reason for the resistance, other than the usual fear of the unknown, is often the perception that the new system would lessen the autonomy of the departments. The building commissioner likes to think of himself conveniently as the building commissioner, not as one part of the urban redevelopment program. He likes to have direct operating control over all of his budget, whereas program budgeting forces him to cooperate with the other commissioners involved, each of them negotiating their part of the program. The forced interdepartmental cooperation is necessitated by the lack of coincidence between program structures and responsibility centers. The bureaucracy will not yield easily to its own obsolescence.

The level of management sophistication in most municipal and state governments is not high. Many large cities simply don't pay enough to retain competent managers. Smaller cities and towns are usually limited to a staff of one city manager who may have a few assistants.

Recognition of these unique characteristics of local governments dictates certain limited PPB goals and a carefully planned entry strategy. There are several ways to initiate the process.

1. A development of broad government objectives and departmental subobjectives.
2. The transformation of the accounting system into program form.
3. The development of cross departmental program categories.
4. The introduction of systematic analysis without changes in standard practices.
5. A long period of education and training with no innovation until the manager perceives the benefits.
6. A wholesale institution of the total PPB system.
7. Organizational changes into program categories.

All of these and numerous others have been tried with varying degrees of success. Number six, for example, proved successful (so far) in the State of Hawaii. One was tried in Philadelphia, three in New York, and four is likely to be adopted in Boston. There is little question in my mind that the heart of PPB lies in number four particularly when we consider the constraints inherent in municipal government. Four provides the most visible and tangible results, it causes less disruptions, and paves the way for adoption of the whole bag of tools.

There is no logical order for the completion of the changeover to PPB. A possible sequence would be four, one, three, and two. Five, six, and seven are dangerous. Five is obstructionist, six may result in chaos, and seven can cause rebellion.

Concluding Comment

We end this chapter with a comment by Dean Aaron Wildavsky, one of the most perceptive observers of the nonprofit scene. It is the concluding section of his review of Brewer's *Politicians, Bureaucrats, and the Consultant,* a description of tremendous failures in attempts to install new systems:[8]

> Nothing anyone says will stop people from trying an available product; so a few rough rules may be offered to guide government officials contemplating the installation of information systems.
>
> First, the rule of skepticism: no one knows how to do it. As Brewer's account suggests, the people most deceived are not necessarily the clients but may well be the consultants. Their capacity for self-deception, for becoming convinced by listening to their own testimony, should never be underestimated. Thus it may be less important to discover whether they are telling the truth than whether the truth they think they are telling is true. Unless the idea is to subsidize employment of social scientists, the burden of proof should be on the proposer.
>
> Second, the rule of delay: if it works at all, it won't work soon. Be prepared to give it years.
>
> Third, the rule of complexity: nothing complicated works. When a new information system contains more variables than, shall we say, the average age of the officials who are to use it, or more data bits than anyone can count in a year, the chances of failure are very high.
>
> Fourth, the rule of thumb: if the data are thicker than your thumb (skeptics—see rule 1—may say "pinky") they are not likely to be comprehensible to anyone.
>
> The fifth rule is to be like a child. Ask many questions; be literal in appraising answers. Unless you understand precisely who will use each data bit, how often, at what cost, relevant to which decisions they are empowered to make, don't proceed.
>
> Sixth is the rule of length and width, or how to determine whether you will be all right in the end by visualizing the sequence of steps in the beginning and middle. Potential users of information should be able to envisage the length of the data flow over time, that is, who will pass what on to whom. If there are more than three or four links in the chain it is likely to become attenuated; data will be lost, diverted, or misinterpreted. The width of the chain is also important. If the data go to more than one level in the organization, the chances that they will be equally appropriate for all are exceedingly slim. The longer the sequence of steps, the wider the band of clientele, the less likely the information is to be of use.
>
> Seventh, the rule of anticipated anguish (sometimes known as Murphy's Law): most of the things that can go wrong, will. Prepare

---

[8] Aaron Wildavsky, in *Science,* 28 (December 1973), pp. 1335–38.

for the worst. If you do not have substantial reserves of money, personnel, and time to help repair breakdowns, do not start.

Eighth, the rule of the known evil. People are used to working with and getting around what they have, they can estimate the "fudge factor" in it, they know whom to trust and what to ignore. They will have to reestimate all these relationships under a new information system, without reasonable assurance they will know more at the end than they did at the beginning.

Ninth comes the most subtle rule of all, the rule of the mounting mirage. Everybody could use better information. No one is doing as well as he could do if only he knew better. The possible benefits of better information, therefore, are readily apparent in the present. The costs lie in the future. But because the costs arrive before the benefits, the mirage mounts, as it were, to encompass an even finer future that will compensate for the increasingly miserable present. Once this relationship is understood, however, it becomes possible to discount the difficulties by stating the tenth and final rule: Hypothetical benefits should outweigh estimated costs by at least ten to one before everyone concerned starts seeing things.

chapter fourteen

Summary: The Well Managed Organization

By way of summary, we describe in this chapter some management control practices that we believe are characteristic of well managed nonprofit organizations. Our opinion as to what constitutes a "well managed" organization is of course subjective, and others may well disagree with the importance, the relevance, or the validity, of certain of the points made here. The description is intended to be applicable to organizations of at least moderate size, say, at least a few hundred employees and a million dollars of annual operating expenses. Many of the comments apply to smaller organizations as well. The comments are arranged approximately in the order in which the topics were discussed in Chapters 4 through 13.

The principal characteristic that distinguishes the problem of management control in a nonprofit organization from that in a profit-oriented organization is the absence of profit as an objective, as a criterion for appraising proposed alternative courses of action, and as a measure of performance. This makes management control more difficult. The absence of the semiautomatic "red flag" that the profit measure provides also makes it important that much attention be devoted to finding and using other criteria for planning and controlling performance.

From a good management control system, the management of an organization can gain essentially two benefits:

1. It can make better plans: plans that are related to organizational objectives and which, in many cases, are based on an analysis of the relative benefits and cost of proposed alternative courses of action.

2. It can have better control; that is, more assurance that operating managers will act efficiently and effectively to accomplish the organization's objectives.

ORGANIZATIONAL RELATIONSHIPS

The first requisite of good management control is a top management that appreciates the importance of management control, that recognizes that management control is feasible, that understands how to use the management control system, and that is willing to devote enough time to the management control process. Top management appreciates the fact that although control is not as glamorous as planning, and that although criticism is an unpleasant task, control is nevertheless essential. If, by contrast, top management has the attitude that measures to insure the effective and efficient use of resources are relatively unimportant in a nonprofit organization, or, even worse, that such measures are beneath the dignity of the office, then management control will be ineffective, no matter how well designed the system itself may be.

A well managed organization has a strong governing board. Some of its members spend considerable time examining program proposals before they are submitted to the full board and analyzing both formal reports on performance and informal communications from clients and others as to how well the organization is performing. They are assisted in this work by a staff, responsible to the Board.[1] Some members of the board are professional board members, who devote substantial time to board activities in this organization and in similar organizations. In performing these functions, the board is careful not to infringe on the prerogatives of management. The governing board insures that the chief executive's compensation is adequate, that the executive has full authority to execute policies, and that those decisions are backed up by the board.

Top management is assisted by a personal staff, usually not drawn from or with close ties to the bureaucracy, and it looks to this staff for innovative ideas and for the analysis of proposed programs. If the chief executive does not personally know where the levers of power exist and how to manipulate them, there is at least one staff member who has this knowledge about the organization, and the skill to use it.

The controller is more than a chief accountant; the controller is responsible for the operation of all aspects of the management control system. Although the controller is management's principal adviser on management control matters and the principal interpreter of information flowing from the system, the controller is nevertheless a staff person; line management makes the decisions.

There are adequate staffs of experts in personnel, procurement, and similar functions, but, like the controller, they act in a staff capacity

---

[1] In particular, the Congress and legislative bodies in most states need larger staffs than they now have so that they can check on the performance of the executive branch. Although the General Accounting Office does much useful work, there is also a need for staffs directly responsible to Congressional Committees.

and do not attempt to circumvent the decision-making authority of management.

Operating managers are given the authority to use their own judgment as to how results are to be accomplished, but they operate within somewhat closer budgetary and other constraints than is customary in profit-oriented organizations. Operating managers reject the stereotype of civil servants, as a group, as being lazy, incompetent, rule bound, self serving, and immobile. They understand that although job performance in any large organization is influenced by the inherent characteristics of bureaucracy, tolerance of laziness and incompetence is an indication of poor management, rather than a necessary characteristic of the system.

THE CONTROL STRUCTURE

Account Classification

The control system contains two principal account classifications, one structured in terms of programs and the other structured in terms of organizational responsibility. At the lowest level are account "building blocks," each of which relates both to a single program element and to a single responsibility center. Summaries are obtained by aggregating these building blocks by program elements, program subcategories, and program categories in the program part of the structure and by various levels of the organizational hierarchy in the responsibility part of the structure.

The system contains both historical data and also data on estimated future costs and outputs. The historical data are defined and structured in the same way as the estimated future data. Management recognizes, for example, that a program budget that is not supported by an accounting system that collects historical data in exactly the same terms does not provide an adequate basis for control. (Failure to provide accounting support for a program budget is the principal weakness of many of the newly installed program budget systems.)

In order to facilitate control of operating expenses, the structure provides for a clean separation between capital costs and operating costs. The definition of capital costs is unambiguous and is worded in such a way that items of minor importance are excluded, even though they are long lived. If the organization makes grants, a third category of accounts is provided for this purpose.

Management has given much thought to designing the program structure that is most useful in (1) making program decisions, (2) providing a basis of comparison of the costs and outputs of similar programs, and (3) providing a basis for setting selling prices in those situations in which services are sold. (If, however, the organization structure is such that each responsibility center is responsible for a single program, no separate program structure is needed, and no effort is expended in thinking up "program" labels for the work done by these responsibility centers.)

The program structure consists of about ten program categories and as many program subcategories and program elements as are needed for the purposes mentioned above. One of the program categories is administration, so that administrative costs can be collected and analyzed separately from other costs. Program elements and, if feasible, program subcategories are defined in such a way that quantitative output measures can be associated with each of them.

The responsibility account structure corresponds exactly to the organization units in the organization.

Measurement of Inputs and Outputs

In both nonprofit and profit-oriented organizations, inputs are measured in terms of cost. Cost is a monetary measure of the amount of resources used for some purpose. Operating costs incurred in a specified period of time are the expenses of that period. A well managed organization measures expenses on the accrual basis. (Failure to use accrual accounting is a fundamental weakness in some management control systems; without it, other desirable control techniques are not possible.) Even if it is required to keep accounts on an obligation basis, as is the case with government agencies, a well managed organization measures expenses on an accrual basis and uses expense data as a basis for control. It reconciles these expenses with obligations in a separate calculation.

If selling prices are based on cost, or if cost comparisons are made in terms of full cost, the organization measures the *full* cost, that is, direct cost plus a fair share of indirect cost, of the services provided or the activities for which comparisons are made. If costs are not required for these purposes, only direct costs may be collected in the program structure, with the indirect costs required for progam decisions being obtained from estimates made outside the formal accounts. All items of direct cost of a responsibility center (except possibly depreciation) are collected, whether or not they are controllable by the responsibility center manager. Depreciation expense is not charged unless there is a good reason for doing so. Transfer prices are established for services rendered by service centers, and these are based on market prices, if they are available; otherwise, transfer prices are ordinarily based on standard full costs. Imputed costs are not accounted for, except in unusual circumstances.

A well managed organization devotes much thought and effort to finding useful, reliable measures of output. If feasible, its principal objectives are stated in quantitative terms, and performance is measured in these terms. If the attainment of objectives cannot be measured directly, approximately valid surrogate measures are sought. For measuring the day-to-day performance of lower level responsibility centers, it uses process measures, that is, measures of the quantity of work done. If feasible, but not necessarily, output measures are related to the objectives of the organization. It may also use social indicators, although these are of limited usefulness in routine management control activities.

The notion that the search for good output measures is fruitless because output cannot be measured perfectly, is rejected. Instead, the premise is accepted that some measure of output is better than none. There is a never ending search for new, more valid measures. At the same time, the limitations of existing output measures are recognized. In particular, managers are not permitted to emphasize the attainment of a surrogate measure when this detracts from the attainment of the organization's actual objectives. Only those output measures are collected that are actually used in the management control process. Management recognizes that many people, especially professionals, dislike the idea of "accountability," which is associated with the measurement of outputs, but it proceeds with such measurements despite resistance from such people.

The fact that output cannot be measured satisfactorily is not used as a reason for discontinuing a program; the most important results of social programs cannot be measured quantitatively.

PRICING

Except in unusual circumstances, such as "public goods," a well managed organization charges its clients for the services that they receive. In so doing, it generates a monetary measure of the quantity of its outputs, it motivates clients to be concerned about the value of the services they receive, and it motivates managers to be concerned about the cost and volume of services they provide. Even public-oriented organizations seek opportunities to charge clients for certain of the services that they provide.

Prices are charged in such a way that they have a direct impact on the client's pocketbook, if feasible, because this provides a stronger incentive for consumers to question the worth of the services they receive than would be the case if the charge were a mere bookkeeping amount. If clients are unable to pay the regular price, they are nevertheless billed at this price, with the difference between what they pay and the regular price being made up by a gift, a subsidy, or a loan.

In general, the price charged for a service is set equal to the full cost of providing that service. A higher price would take unfair advantage of what may be the organization's monopoly position and is in any event unnecessary. A lower price would provide services for less than they are worth, and hence lead to a misallocation of resources. Although on the average, prices of services are equal to their full cost, the organization may well price some services above cost and others below cost for reasons of encouraging an optimum use of resources, particularly for encouraging the utilization of excess capacity in offpeak periods. As exceptions to the general rule, prices may be based on prevailing market prices when the nonprofit organization competes with profit-oriented companies, particularly in providing services that are not central to its objectives. Also, an organization may use a subsidy price— that is, a price that is below cost—to encourage the use of certain services, or a penalty price to discourage the use of certain other services.

Full cost is the direct cost of providing the service plus an equitable share of common costs. It includes depreciation if funds for the acquisition of new capital assets are to be provided from charges made to clients, rather than from gifts or grants. Cost includes a charge for the use of capital to the extent that the organization's own resources are tied up in working capital or fixed assets. Cost may include imputed costs, such as an amount made in lieu of taxes, particularly when the price is used as a "yardstick" against which the prices of profit-oriented organizations are compared, as is the case with a publicly owned utility. The price may include a fee that provides funds for expansion.

The unit of pricing is made as narrow as is feasible because this provides a better measure of the quantity of services rendered and a better basis for decisions on the allocation of resources. The organization does not, by contrast have a single overall rate, such as a blanket daily charge, regardless of the type of services rendered. An exception to this principle occurs when the pricing of small units would lead to unwise client decisions, as would happen, for example, if the price of each college course were based on its cost.

If feasible, prices are determined prospectively rather than retrospectively; that is, they are set before the fact on the basis of anticipated costs and volume, rather than after the fact on the basis of actual costs incurred. Retrospective pricing greatly diminishes the motivation to control costs.

PROGRAMMING

A well managed organization makes its plans in terms of programs; that is, it decides on the nature of the various programs that are to be undertaken in order to achieve the organization's objectives, and the approximate amount of resources that are to be devoted to each program. The amount of attention devoted to the programming process varies considerably with the type of organization. In a public-oriented organization (that is, an organization that provides services to the public at large rather than to identifiable individual clients) much management and staff effort is devoted to formulating, analyzing, and deciding on program proposals. In client-oriented organizations, paticularly colleges, hospitals, and others whose services are relatively similar from one year to the next, less attention to the programing process is needed.

New Programs

Whenever it is worthwhile to do so, proposed programs are analyzed by comparing estimated benefits with estimated costs. Such a comparison is possible when the benefits can be measured in economic terms, such as in the form of savings in operating costs or increased output. Although many projects are of this character, unfortunately they tend to be of relatively minor importance. A benefit/cost analysis can also be made in comparing two proposals, either of which will accomplish a desired objective satisfactorily; the proposal with the lower cost is preferred. If there is no plausible causal relationship between costs and benefits, however, the organization does not waste time in attempting a benefit/cost analysis.

The organization recognizes that even the best benefit/cost analysis does not provide an automatic signal as to the preferred alternative program. Judgment is required in weighing the importance of considerations that cannot be reduced to quantitative terms. In many problems, political and social considerations may be more important than economic factors. Even when a formal analysis is not worthwhile, however, management takes an implicit benefit/cost approach to all important proposals; that is, it asks: are the benefits probably greater than the costs?

Top management recognizes that most proposals are advocacy proposals and that the accompanying analysis and justification is, at least to some extent, biased. It attempts to offset this bias by having its own staff make a careful review of the proposal (recognizing that the staff itself may develop biases for certain proposals), or by setting up an adversary relationship in which natural opponents of the proposal are encouraged to criticize it.

Ongoing Programs

In many organizations, activities whose character and scope are relatively unchanged from one year to the next are not subject to much top management attention. In a well managed organization, by contrast, a systematic examination of these activities is undertaken. Its purpose is to ascertain whether improvements in efficiency or effectiveness are feasible, and whether the benefits of the program continue to exceed its costs. Such an examination is conducted by staffs that are organized for this purpose, by outside consulting organizations, or, occasionally, by a "blue ribbon commission" of concerned citizens.

The examination can be conducted in various ways. One simple, but often effective, approach is to ask naive questions about why operations are performed in the way they are. Another is to compare costs of an activity with costs of similar activities in other organizations. Another is to apply work measurement techniques that have been developed by profit-oriented companies, and still another is to develop models program. Judgement is required in weighing the importance of consid-

of cost and output relationships. The approach to the review is impersonal and factual.

When these examinations are scheduled in a way that insures that all important parts of the organization are looked at every five years or so, the process is called a zero-base review. The term is derived from the fact that such a review examines each function from scratch, rather than taking the existing level of spending as a starting point, which is necessary in the budgeting process. In making such a review, the possibility that certain functions could be performed more efficiently by a private sector company is carefully explored.

Programming Systems

Some well managed organizations have formal programming systems; others do not. If the organization's programs change in important ways over time, if these changes affect several parts of the organization, and if their implementation requires a considerable period of time, there is need for some systematic method of considering all program proposals together, rather than making decisions on each one separately.[2]

The system used for this purpose starts with the preparation and dissemination of guidelines which specify, among other things, the constraints within which program proposals are to be prepared. Working within these constraints, operating managers prepare program memoranda that describe the activities they propose to undertake and the resources required for these activities. The memoranda cover a period of several future years, often five years. These memoranda are first analyzed by a staff unit and then are the basis of a discussion between top management and operating managers. The approved program that emerges from such a discussion constitute approval in principle to proceed with the program, but its details are subject to refinement and modification in the budgeting process.

BUDGETING

Budgeting is a more important process in a nonprofit organization than in a profit-oriented organization. In a profit-oriented organization, operating managers can safely be allowed to modify plans, provided that the revised plan promises to increase profits. Operating managers of nonprofit organizations, especially those whose annual revenue is essentially fixed, must adhere closely to plans as expressed in the budget. Budgeting is perhaps the most important part of the management control

---

[2] The Planning-Programming-Budgeting System (PPBS) which the federal government tried to implement in the 1960s is an example of such a programming system. The attempt was later abandoned and the PPB System consequently is sometimes characterized as a failure. The flaw, however, was not in the system but rather in the manner in which it was implemented.

process, and well managed organizations devote much thought and time to it.

The first step in the budgeting process is to estimate the amount of revenue that the organization is likely to receive for operating purposes during the budget year. The next step is to budget expenses that equal this amount of revenue. This matching of expenses to revenue differs from the approach used in profit-oriented organizations because in profit-oriented organizations the amount budgeted for marketing expenses can influence the amount of revenue. A nonprofit organization should plan to incur expenses that are approximately equal to its revenue. If its budgeted expenses are lower than its revenue, it is not providing the quantity of services that those who provide the revenue have a right to expect. If its budgeted expenses exceed its revenue, the difference must be made up by the generally undesirable actions of drawing down endowment or other capital funds that are intended to provide services to future generations. If the first approximation of budgeted expenses exceeds estimated revenue, the prudent course of action usually is to reduce expenses rather than to anticipate that revenue can be increased.

Quantitative statements of planned objectives should be included in the budget, as well as planned revenues and expenses.

The budget is structured in terms of responsibility centers. Budget estimates are prepared by responsibility center managers and are consistent with the approved program and with other guidelines prescribed by top management. Budgetees negotiate approval of these estimates with their superiors. Because time does not permit a more thorough analysis, the level of current spending is usually taken as a starting point in these negotiations. The approved budget is a bilateral commitment: the budgetee commits to accomplish the planned objectives within the spending limits specified in the budget, and the superior commits to regarding such an accomplishment as representing satisfactory performance.

OPERATING AND ACCOUNTING

Operating managers need information of two types, environmental and internal. In a well managed organization, the system provides managers with all the environmental information they need (despite attempts by some to inhibit this flow deliberately), but not more information than they can assimilate. Managers are also provided with information about their own responsibility centers. Essentially, this internal information compares actual performance with planned performance with respect to both costs and outputs. Information on actual costs is collected in a double-entry accounting system whose accounts are entirely consistent with those in the budget. If feasible, accounting information is integrated with other information, both environmental and internal, in a single system.

There is an adequate internal audit effort to minimize the possibility of loss and to insure that information is recorded accurately in the accounts. In particular, the practice of making charges to improper accounts is not condoned.

As a nonprofit organization, the organization probably uses fund accounting. It operates with only a few separate funds, however. There is one fund for operations, and others for various asset categories, particularly working capital funds that hold material and services costs in suspense between the time of acquisition and the time of consumption. In a government organization, the system insulates operating managers from the dysfunctional messages that are often signalled by obligation accounting to the extent that it can do so.

Operating managers are expected to adhere reasonably closely to authorized spending amounts, unless there is good reason to depart from these authorizations. If the original authorization has to be increased, this is done either by use of a contingency allowance or by decreasing some other authorization.

Top management is personally involved in the review of actual performance. In particular, top management is aware of the natural tendency to spend 100 percent of the amount authorized, whether needed or not, and attempts to counter this tendency by making appropriate rewards to those who are able to reduce spending and still accomplish the planned outputs.

REPORTING AND ANALYZING PERFORMANCE

Periodic reports of performance compare actual costs with budgeted costs and, if feasible, actual outputs with budgeted outputs. The reports are structured in such a way that the comparison of budgeted and actual amounts is valid, that is, that the actual amount is defined in the same way and relates to the same time period as the budgeted amount. If feasible, variances are isolated by cause: volume, price, efficiency, and/or mix. The interpretation of the variances is governed by the nature of the responsibility center, that is, whether it has a fixed amount of resources, whether it has a fixed job to do, or whether there is a relationship between the level of activity and costs.

In a well managed organization, considerable attention is paid to analysis of output information, as well as to costs. Outputs are, to the extent feasible, related to the organization's objectives. Considerable attention is also paid to information on the quality of performance; if feasible, peer reviews of quality are made, despite professionals' resistance to such reviews.

The organization also engages in operational auditing, recognizing that this type of auditing requires a different skill from compliance auditing, and that unless properly done it can lead to friction and resentment that negate its possible benefits.

SYSTEM DESIGN AND INSTALLATION

Since a well managed organization already has a good management control system, this section does not describe the system design process in such an organization. Rather, it assumes that a new management comes on board in an organization, perceives the need for a good system, and proceeds to meet that need.

The preconditions for a successful effort are top management support, acquiescence from outside agencies, a competent system design team, and the allowance of almost enough time. The new management is assumed to provide the first, to devote time in discussions with outside agencies so as to assure the second, to assemble the necessary staff or hire outside system designers, and to set up a timetable covering one, two, or three years, depending on the complexity of the problem.

Top management spends a fair amount of time on the system development effort. It satisfies itself that the system is consistent with is own management style. It seeks to convince operating managers that the new system will in fact be used and that the former system will be discarded. It holds meetings with immediate subordinates to discuss how information can be used, and expects them to hold similar meetings with their subordinates. It uses information from the new system, and only from that system, as soon as it becomes available, and wipes out the old system, beyond possibility of resurrection, as soon as it is reasonably safe to do so.

In developing the system, the design staff relies primarily on an analysis of what information operating managers *should* need, rather than on what *they say* they need. Existing operating data is used to the maximum extent feasible. Crosswalks, or other techniques that permit information collected in the new system to meet the need of outside agencies are developed. The staff spends a considerable fraction of the available time on education efforts.

If top management decides that it is not feasible to install a complete new system all at once, it approaches the task in stages. The first stage is to have annual budgets prepared by programs and responsibility centers, but without an accounting backup. Next, a formal programming process is instituted. Then the accounting system is revised so that it matches the new structure. Finally, better output measures and accounting refinements are instituted. The task of improving the system, particularly finding better output measures, is a never ending one.

MAIN LINES FOR IMPROVEMENT

In conclusion, and with considerable trepidation, we venture to list below what seem to us to be the principal measures that will lead to improvement in the management control process in nonprofit organizations. The items are listed roughly in the order of their importance:

1. More active interest in the effective and efficient functioning of the organization by its governing board (including legislative committees in the case of government organizations). (This is listed first because, if well done, it can trigger all the other improvements.)

2. More top management involvement in programming, in performance evaluation, and in systems improvement. (Involvement in budgeting is generally adequate already.)

3. Better compensation for senior managers.

4. Better rewards for good management, and refusal to tolerate poor management (including refusal to accept the cliche that Civil Service, by tenure, protects incompetents).

5. Use of accrual accounting; downgrading of obligation accounting. An accounting system that is exactly consistent with the program and responsibility budgets.

6. Zero-base review of ongoing programs on a regular basis. Look for opportunities to privatize. Use performance data from comparable organizations as a benchmark, and support industry-wide efforts to improve such data.

7. More thorough attention to programming in public-oriented organizations. A carefully designed program structure. (The need is not so great in client-oriented and member-oriented organizations.)

8. More use of benefit/cost analysis in appropriate circumstances (but a recognition that such analyses are snow jobs in other circumstances).

9. Creation of revenue centers (i.e., responsibility centers that sell services to others) and a well designed set of transfer prices. Provide no significant amount of "free" material or services to anyone.

10. More attention to the selling prices for services rendered to clients. A unit of pricing that is as narrow as feasible. Recognition of the importance of prices in both the technical and behavioral aspects of the management control process.

11. More emphasis on output measures. More effort devoted to finding better measures. Output measures included in both programs and budgets. Performance measured in terms of outputs as well as costs.

12. Cost accounting.

13. Analysis of variances.

Earl F. Cheit has raised the question: "Can colleges and universities be academic though systematic?"[3] His own answer to that question is equivocal. Our answer is unequivocal: yes! We would give the same answer for other types of nonprofit organizations.

---

[3] *Chronicle of Higher Education* (October 15, 1973), p. 16.

Index

*This book has been set in 10 and 9 point Cale-
donia, leaded 2 points. Chapter numbers are
16 point Helvetica italic and chapter titles are
24 point (small) Helvetica Regular. The size
of the type page is 27 × 46½ picas.*